Representing the Past

Representing

Studies in **THEATRE HISTORY AND CULTURE**

Edited by Thomas Postlewait

the Past

ESSAYS IN PERFORMANCE HISTORIOGRAPHY

Edited by

CHARLOTTE M. CANNING

& THOMAS POSTLEWAIT

UNIVERSITY OF IOWA PRESS

IOWA CITY

University of Iowa Press, Iowa City 52242

Printed in the United States of America

Design by Richard Hendel

www.uiowapress.org

The University of Iowa Press is a member of Green Press Initiative and is committed to preserving natural resources.

Printed on acid-free paper

Library of Congress Cataloging-in-Publication Data
Representing the past: essays in performance historiography / edited by Charlotte M. Canning and Thomas Postlewait.
p. cm.—(Studies in theatre history and culture)
Includes bibliographical references and index.
ISBN-13: 978-1-58729-905-6 (pbk.)
ISBN-10: 1-58729-905-4 (pbk.)
ISBN-13: 978-1-58729-938-4 (e-book)
ISBN-10: 1-58729-938-0 (e-book)
1. Theater—Historiography. I. Canning, Charlotte, 1964–
II. Postlewait, Thomas.
PN2115.R47 2010
792.09—dc22 2010010259

Contents

Acknowledgments

First things first: we extend our gratitude to Holly Carver, director of the University of Iowa Press. Throughout the development of this book, she has been an unwavering supporter. Her editorial leadership, provided with her calm guidance and timely wit, set the tone for our task—even when a few problems threatened to delay, if not derail, the project. Besides Holly, we thank the full staff at the press, an impressive team of bookmakers at the Kuhl House in Iowa City. We also compliment Kathy Burford Lewis for her sharp editorial eye and fine rhetorical judgment. We are pleased to add this book to the Iowa list.

Of special note, *Representing the Past: Essays in Performance Historiography* appears two decades after the publication of *Interpreting the Theatrical Past: Essays in the Historiography of Performance*, edited by Thomas Postlewait and Bruce McConachie and also published by the University of Iowa Press. The initial success of that book served as the catalyst and precursor for a new book series, Studies in Theatre History and Culture, that Postlewait has edited for the press since 1991. *Representing the Past* is the thirty-ninth book on theatre history in the series. One of those books was Charlotte Canning's award-winning *The Most American Thing in America: Circuit Chautauqua as Performance*, published in 2005. The University of Iowa Press has thus proved to be a scholarly home for both of us. We are especially grateful to the press for its continuing support of scholarship in theatre history.

At an early stage of this project, most of the fifteen contributors were able to join the two editors for a symposium to discuss early drafts of their potential essays on theatre historiography. That gathering, held in conjunction with a meeting of the American Society for Theatre Research (ASTR), provided an opportunity to share ideas, suggestions, questions, and challenges—directed at both the individual essays and the overall purpose of the project. A unified book began to emerge from this symposium, held on Thursday and Sunday—just before and after the ASTR conference in Phoenix. We offer our gratitude to the officers, especially the new president, Tracy C. Davis, and members of the executive committee of ASTR for allowing us to piggyback onto the 2007 ASTR conference. We also thank Nancy Erickson, the executive officer for ASTR, for her administrative help in arranging a room and services at the hotel.

Two of the essays in this collection were published previously: Susan Leigh Foster's "Textual Evidances" appeared originally in *Bodies of the Text: Dance as Theory, Literature as Dance*, edited by Ellen W. Goellner and Jacqueline Shea Murphy (New Brunswick, NJ: Rutgers University Press, 1995: 231–246). An earlier version of Claire Sponsler's essay, published under the title "Writing the Unwritten: Morris Dance and the Study of Medieval Theatre," appeared in *Theatre Survey* 38.1 (May 1997): 73–95, edited by Gary Jay Williams. We thank the publishers, editors, and authors for permission to publish the current versions of these essays.

We dedicate this book to our students who have taken seminars with us over the years. Their discussions and papers helped us to identify and define the five organizing concepts in *Representing the Past*. We are also beholden to the many active scholars throughout the world who carry out scholarship in theatre history, theatre and cultural studies, dance history, and performance studies. Their publications, especially the essays and books that touch upon issues and questions in theatre historiography, serve as the foundation for this collection of essays. It is our hope that *Representing the Past*, which features a diversity of scholars and a broad range of topics, serves as a microcosm of the talents and interests of the much larger community of scholars.

Finally, we extend our thanks to our chairs and colleagues at the University of Texas and University of Washington. Most importantly, we offer our abiding gratitude to those closest to us: Fritz and Fritzie for Charlotte, Marilyn for Tom. Yet again, and always.

Representing the Past

Representing the Past An Introduction on Five Themes

> Things in themselves perhaps have their own weights, measures, and states; but inwardly, when they enter into us, the mind cuts them to its own conceptions. — Michel de Montaigne, "Of Democritus and Heraclitus," Book One, *Essays*, 1580

> There are concepts we think about, concepts we use in thinking, and concepts (usually called *a priori*) we think with. . . . A concept may move (not without change) from one function to another: hence there are no unique examples of each class. But allowing for this we may say that in many contexts the concepts of energy, man, social class, and alienation are concepts we think about; the concepts of quantity, function, value, and change are concepts we use in thinking; and the concepts of time, space, identity, and causation are concepts we think with. — Louis O. Mink, *Historical Understanding*, 1987

How do historians represent the past? How do theatre historians represent performance events? As the title of this book, *Representing the Past: Essays in Performance Historiography*, spells out, this basic issue of historical representation provides the organizing principle for this collection of essays. We have conceived and developed this book in order to address some fundamental ideas in historical inquiry. Consequently, this is a book in historiography, not just history. It gathers together fifteen essays by a quite diverse group of scholars in the fields of theatre history, cultural studies, critical theory, dance history, and performance studies. They offer their insights on some of the abiding issues, questions, and challenges that all historians face in the task of representing human events and actions.[1] From the Americas to Africa, from Europe to India and China, the essayists cover a very expansive range of topics, case studies, issues, and problems in the historical study of performance. And because the essayists are interested in historiography—the epistemological conditions and procedures for historical understanding—they also offer their reflections on foundational ideas that guide all historians in their endeavors.

These ideas, as we want to demonstrate, operate in all stages of historical study. Historians, including historians of performance events, must depend upon certain fundamental ideas or categories of thought that allow them to carry out their research, compile their evidence, develop their analyses and explanations, and complete their final reports. In great measure these ideas—a small core of categorical imperatives, as it were—

shape, control, and even determine the archival procedures and assumptions that historians depend upon. They also contribute to the ways that historians identify and characterize the historical agents and events.[2] In turn, these ideas help historians to construct the historical conditions, institutions, attitudes, and values that provide the spatial and temporal coordinates for the historical actions and events. Likewise, these ideas offer the analytical and interpretive procedures that guide the descriptive and narrative modes of historical representation.

What, then, are these fundamental ideas; how many of them can we identify? Although, as Louis O. Mink states in the epigraph, no set number of concepts organize human thought (including the basic concepts that guide historical thinking), we decided to focus on five primary ideas that establish both the topics and the intellectual parameters for this book. Each of the five ideas derives in part from the organizational concept of historical representation. These five primary ideas are *archive, time, space, identity*, and *narrative*. Together they establish the conceptual framework for historical representation.

How and why did these five ideas emerge as the basis for a collection of essays on performance historiography? As is often the case in history, the search for origins takes us down several paths. This book came into being after some lengthy discussions, occasional debates, and false starts. Early in our discussions we agreed that we wanted to develop a book on historiography that would serve students and colleagues in our broadly defined fields of theatre, dance, and performance studies, whatever their areas of study or their critical methodologies. But initially we did not have a clear idea of what kind of book would best meet our aims. Consequently, as our dialogue went forward—by way of e-mail exchanges and face-to-face discussions at several scholarly meetings[3]—we slowly developed our plan.

There are, of course, myriad ways to organize a book on historiography, but before we could make any decision, we had to clarify for ourselves why a book on "performance historiography" was needed. We had to define what we meant by the term and then decide how best to address it. That is, we had to justify the value and purpose of the book. Both of us have taught graduate seminars on theatre historiography, so we had a solid understanding of the available scholarship and the notable gaps. We knew that we were not interested in restaging tired debates based upon false polarities (such as history versus theory, theatre studies versus performance studies). Nor did we see the need for a collection of essays that featured various critical methods and theories in our discipline. Janelle Reinelt and

Joseph Roach had already addressed that need handily in *Critical Theory and Performance* (Ann Arbor: University of Michigan Press, 1992; revised 2007).

Right from the beginning, we recognized that any historiographical book we proposed would be the product of a complex disciplinary genealogy—a genealogy, moreover, that carried special meanings for anyone who had experienced the developments of our discipline firsthand, especially during the last two decades. Genealogy, as Michel Foucault construes it through his engagement with several of Friedrich Nietzsche's works, "operates on a field of entangled and confused parchments, on documents that have been scratched over and recopied many times."[4] We recognized that it would take a genealogist such as Nietzsche or Foucault to unpack the multiple and contradictory precedents of our possible project.

From the beginning we saw the need to clarify the relationship between our new volume and the predecessor, *Interpreting the Theatrical Past: Essays in the Historiography of Performance* (Iowa City: University of Iowa Press, 1989), edited by Thomas Postlewait and Bruce McConachie. How has the historical understanding of our field of study both changed and remained the same since 1989? Of course, as we understood, *Interpreting the Theatrical Past* was a product of its time—a transforming moment in the discipline. Thus any palimpsest that we might produce two decades later was dependent upon how professional events and scholarly texts, beginning in 1989, had generated our own understanding in the subsequent years. The genealogy was part of the task, even though we did not wish to rethink, reformulate, or reconstitute *Interpreting the Theatrical Past*.[5] Despite our apparent echoing of its title by calling our new book *Representing the Past*, we did not conceive of the new collection as a revision or replacement. We were clear on this basic matter: though the new book might be a companion to *Interpreting the Theatrical Past*, it was not to be put forward as a supplement.

Instead, though we were fully prepared to acknowledge (and even honor) certain disciplinary changes in historical methods since 1989 (a genealogy of notable developments in which both of us have participated during the last two decades), we sought to produce a new collection of essays that would investigate some of the fundamental conditions of historical inquiry and understanding. We hoped to focus on aspects of historical research, analysis, and writing that do not change. Paradoxically, the new collection could be timely by taking up timeless (or at least recurring) ideas in historical study. But how should we address these abiding conditions? Without question, we have contributed to and benefited from major new perspectives and methods in the humanities during the last few decades (such as feminist studies, gender studies, postcolonialism, cultural materialism, and new historicism), but what about certain fundamental conditions of historical study? How might we engage the historiographical issues and concerns that are basic to any historical method and therefore apply to any graduate seminar we attempt to present?

Interpreting the Theatrical Past was published in 1989, a year that witnessed several ongoing debates with immense ramifications for the field, as Sue-Ellen Case and Janelle Reinelt insisted in their 1991 collection of scholarly essays, *The Performance of Power: Theatrical Discourse and Politics*: "For us, the ongoing experience in our professional lives of these cross-currents of politics, academics, and theatrics became especially acute during the . . . academic year [1989–1990]."[6] In 1989, as Case and Reinelt pointed out, both the Association for Theatre in Higher Education (ATHE) and the American Society for Theatre Research (ASTR) held conferences that quickly became landmarks for performance scholars. Key papers from those conferences were published in Case and Reinelt's book as well as other essay collections and monographs.

Sue-Ellen Case, Marvin Carlson, and Tom Postlewait were on a panel together at ATHE in August 1989. It was one of two conference sessions on "History/Theory/Revolution: The New Convergence." The participants in the additional session were Joseph Roach, Timothy Murray, Rosemarie Bank, and Elin Diamond.[7] These papers, as Case described the presentations, addressed how the "rise of contemporary critical theory . . . began in response to a historical and social challenge to epistemology and notions of ontology as they had been produced in the academy."[8] In the audience was Charlotte Canning, a doctoral student who had just entered candidacy (with Case on her dissertation committee) and had, the day before, delivered her paper on historical periodization for the debut panel on "theory and criticism." Thus, for both Postlewait and Canning as well as many other participants and observers, the ATHE conference signaled new developments—critical, historical, theoretical, and political—in our discipline.

Three months later ASTR met in Williamsburg, Virginia. This conference, as Simon Williams reported at the time, was "regarded by members who participated in it as representing, for good or ill, a watershed in the history of the Society." Gary Jay Williams, in his recently published history of ASTR, concurred. The 1989 meeting "represented approaches that, explicitly or implicitly, constituted challenges to the positivist methodology and/or the humanist ideology that had been foundational for ASTR."[9] Marvin Carlson, who delivered a "state of the profession" paper at the end of the 1989 ASTR conference, summed up the spirit of many participants. He observed that the "task of today's historian . . . would seem to be to recognize the new multiplicity of the discipline created by the challenge of modern theory and to utilize this freedom for the positive expansion of the discipline."[10]

Without question, the publication of *Interpreting the Theatrical Past* (1989), *The Performance of Power* (1991), and *Critical Theory and Performance* (1992) caught the spirit of the age. Twenty years later we offer *Representing the Past* as direct evidence of "the positive expansion of the discipline," an expansion that no longer needs to demonize positivism. One possible way to acknowledge this genealogy would have been to gather ten to twenty essays on theatre historiography published during the last two decades.[11] Both of us have used many of these publications for class readers when we teach our seminars on theatre historiography. We were tempted by this possibility, which would have been the easiest and quickest way to proceed. But despite the fine quality of many essays of the last two decades, a collection of them would be rather arbitrary. Except for the general topic of historiography, such a collection would have no unifying idea and purpose. Besides, we wanted to do something more substantial than merely preparing an anthology of some notable publications since 1989. That approach (though still needed) fails to do justice to our developing idea of historiography, especially the fundamental idea of historical representation, which had challenged us from the early days of this developing project. We sought something other than Foucault's "documents that have been scratched over and recopied many times," as was the case with any version of a class reader that we might throw together.

Another possibility occurred to us: we could commission new essays that would feature the topics, issues, and problems in historical methodology (such as kinds of evidence, primary and secondary sources, testimony or eyewitness reports, matters of objectivity and subjectivity, methods for cross-examining the evidence, issues of the credibility and reliability of documents, the problems of forgery and plagiarism, anecdotes as evidence, oral history, period concepts, and distinctions between possible and probable evidence). No doubt those of us who do historical scholarship in the arts need to attend to such issues and to train our students in the basics of historical methodology. Sad to say, far too much of the historical scholarship in our discipline fails to do justice to such principles and methods. Very few of our doctoral students get training in the basics of historical scholarship. Consequently, the methodological faults in various publications are glaring (and embarrassing).

But do we actually need a primer in historical methodology? The general field of history already has several worthy textbooks, extending from mid-century classics such as R. G. Collingwood's *The Idea of History* (1946), Marc Bloch's *The Historian's Craft* (1953), and Louis Gottschalk's *Understanding History: A Primer of Historical Method* (1958) to more recent contributions, including Georg G. Iggers's *Historiography in the Twentieth Century: From Scientific Objectivity to Postmodern Challenge* (1997), Peter Burke's *New Perspectives on Historical Writing* (1992), and John Lewis Gaddis's *The Landscape of History: How Historians Map the Past* (2002).[12] Instead of adding yet another book on the general principles and methods of historical research, we wanted to use some of those basic ideas for the study of historical study in performance.[13]

When we launched this project, we considered how other fields in recent years have attempted to provide collections of essays. Looking for possible models, we noticed that some recent books in art history and literary studies tried to offer an ambitious overview of the many aspects of the field by compiling fifteen, twenty, or twenty-five essays on key concepts in the field (each topic covered by a single essay). For example, a collection in literary studies, *Critical Terms for Literary Study*, edited by Frank Lentricchia and Thomas McLaughlin (Chicago: University of Chicago Press, 1990), has twenty-two separate essays by various scholars on topics such as gender, ethnicity, structure, author, canon, culture, unconscious, figurative language, race, ideology, discourse, value/evaluation, rhetoric, literary history, performance, and representation. Likewise, a collection in art history, *Critical Terms for Art History*, edited by Robert S. Nelson and Richard Shiff (2nd ed., Chicago: University of Chicago Press, 2003), also provides twenty-two essays on an equally diverse range of topics, including gender, commodity, gaze, fetish, modes of production, value, modernism, avant-garde, originality, word and image, sign, simulacrum, postmodernism/postcolonialism, context, and, yes, representation.

Although we were impressed by the quality of some (but far from all) of the essays in each collection, we were bothered by two key factors. We did not like the idea of a single essay on each topic, as if each essayist, in the process of trying to summarize a number of issues and ideas, was the anointed expert who had to offer the last (or at least the latest) word on the topic. Also, the twenty-two topics of each collection, instead of demonstrating in a convincing manner that these were the essential and definitive topics in each field of study, produced a kind of scatter-gun effect. Why these topics but not others? What was the principle of selection or exclusion? On this matter, both collections seemed rather arbitrary to us—

topically up-to-date on critical trends and hot themes (hence the repetition of certain topics) but lacking any foundational perspective on the scholarly practice and principles of either literary study or art history. The strategies for selecting topics for the two collections were not only amazingly at odds with one another but also close to inexplicable in terms of each discipline (despite the brilliance of some of the essayists). Each collection offered a hodgepodge of themes, topics, methodologies, and concepts. Accordingly, even though students and professors benefit from knowing these various critical terms and concepts, this knowledge fails not only to define a discipline but also to provide fundamental ideas for historical inquiry in these disciplines.

These two collections consequently lacked an appropriate model for us to adopt or adapt. Yet they turned out to be a valuable catalyst for us to rethink our aim and our approach, even though we rejected the organizational strategies of these two collections. We noted that both collections featured an essay on the topic of representation. Unlike some of the other concepts in each collection, this is clearly a foundational concept in all of the arts.[14] It is also a primary concept in historical thinking, for all historical studies represent past events. Without question, then, we had identified our organizing idea. Accordingly, instead of limiting our project to the specific genealogies and practices of our own discipline—theatre and performance—we decided to develop a collection that had a double or two-part purpose. We wanted the idea of representation, as it applied to the discipline of history, to serve as the unifying topic of the collection. Then we could develop an organizational plan true to our initial idea of providing a study of performance historiography.

With the idea of representation before us, we asked ourselves some basic questions about historical inquiry and historical understanding as they apply to performance studies. At first, as we probed at the idea of representation, we had a list of two dozen potential topics. But as we considered these topics we discovered that they distributed themselves quite nicely into a half-dozen categorical ideas. Finally, we settled on five abiding topics—the five categorical ideas of *archive*, *time*, *space*, *identity*, and *narrative*. All five are necessary components of historical representation and are fundamental to performance historiography. The job of our collection, then, would be to demonstrate this double agenda.

Despite our commitment to these five ideas, we did not want to publish five authoritative essays that might be taken as the definitive word on each idea. We did not want students to assume that we were supplying the final or correct explanation of these five ideas, as if a single essay, no matter how good it might be, could offer a comprehensive model to be applied and reproduced. Unlike concepts such as modernism, commodity, gender, modes of production, unconscious, and ideology, these five ideas have nothing to do with an interpretive strategy, a definitive position, a privileged viewpoint, or model building. Our discipline of theatre and performance is far too various and complex for any such definitive statement. Moreover, historical inquiry itself is amazingly various in its perspectives and methods.

Accordingly, from our perspective the collection had to include more than one essay on each topic. As we developed our plan, we thought about having two essays on each of the five topics, followed by a third essay that featured commentary upon the two essays. But that approach, instead of solving the problem, created two new ones. By featuring two essays, we were in danger of presenting two opposing views—an overly neat version of thesis and antithesis. Then the person who responded to the two essays would become the new authority, who could supposedly mediate the disagreements and summarize the problem, thereby providing the synthesis.

Back to the drawing board. Our solution was to offer three essayists on each of the five ideas. The book, as we have designed and developed it, has no single agenda or critical perspective. No single essayist provides exclusive authority on a topic. Even if we as editors or any of the contributors disagreed with a perspective or argument, it would not matter, because a variety of approaches would be on display. Although we identified the five ideas and selected the fifteen leading scholars to write on them, we have not proscribed or sanctioned any specific methodology or argument. These essays, accordingly, offer a diverse set of learned assays, trials, inquiries, critiques, self-examinations, expositions, demonstrations, arguments, and interpretations of the five concepts. With such a diversity of perspectives, the essays illustrate the contemporary richness of historical thinking and writing in the field of performance history. Yet, because all of them consider how historians represent the past, the collection addresses a shared topic and problem—without any suggestion that a singular comprehension of the idea of representation is possible. By presenting three distinct perspectives on each of the five ideas, the book reveals multiple, even contending, perspectives on and engagements with each of these ideas, while also demonstrating the fundamental nature of the five concepts in historical thinking, research, analysis, and writing.

Once we had figured out what we were doing (and not doing), the project moved forward as planned. We selected the contributors and submitted the proposal to the University of Iowa Press, which accepted it. We distributed a detailed description of the design and purpose of the project to each participant. We spelled out some of the historiographical topics and issues, provided a select bibliography on the historiography of each idea, and established a writing schedule that included a meeting of most of the participants in Phoenix in November 2007 to discuss the early drafts and the overall aims of the book. This means of organization integrated the project. We were able to provide a hands-on response to the essays while they were being written and revised. But we took a hands-off approach in terms of the contributors' areas of study, specific topics, viewpoints, and arguments. Each essay reflects the expertise and independent judgment of its writer. A balance was achieved, we believe, between our historiographical agendas and the individual perspectives of the essayists.

In this way, the book is able to demonstrate that each of the five categorical ideas is quite complex in the ways it contributes to how we think historically and that each idea generates a variety of perspectives on how historians carry out research and represent the past. Despite the complexity of the ideas and the diversity of perspectives, each of the five categories is central and essential to historical inquiry; also, each idea, because of its fundamental nature in human thinking, cannot be reduced to a singular model that historians could or should impose upon their historical thinking, research methods, modes of critical analysis, and writing procedures. The fifteen essays thus are capable of showing that all of us, as we carry out our historical inquiry, *think with*—not just about—each of these five modes of comprehension in our tasks of representing the past.

Our argument, then, is that these five ideas of *archive, time, space, identity*, and *narrative* serve as essential categories of historical research, description, analysis, and writing. In the process of doing their work, historians develop representations of the past by means of these five contingent ideas. These ideas set in place epistemological modes of comprehension that guide historical inquiry and understanding. By means of these ideas, which serve the task of historical representation, historians conceptualize both the general and specific features of the past. No doubt historians depend upon other essential concepts for historical understanding and methods of inquiry (for example, the vital ideas of action, event, change, and causality). We will return to this point presently. Yet we concluded that a study of *archive, time, space, identity*, and *narrative* would be most productive and valuable for the discipline of theatre historiography.

Each of the essayists agreed to write on one of these five categories of thought. But all fifteen writers discovered that it is impossible to stay focused on one primary idea to the exclusion of the others. In one way or another, each of the fifteen essays, despite its singular topic, offers its own application and engagement with aspects of the other four concepts. This result, we are pleased to point out, is a convincing demonstration of the centrality of all five concepts, from initial research procedures to the writing process. Consequently, each of the fifteen essays, though focused on one of the five ideas, could easily be redistributed to additional categories. For instance, Harry J. Elam, Jr., focuses on the idea of historical identity in the plays and experiences of two playwrights, but just as tellingly his essay investigates the category of historical narrative. David Wiles examines the idea of space in theatre iconography, but his essay also has much to say about the problematic nature of the archive for iconography. And Aparna Dharwadker investigates the concepts of time in histories of theatre in India; but she also reflects upon the attributes of identity and narrative in those histories. Similar acts of redistribution might be carried out for the rest of the fifteen essays. Yet despite these border crossings, each essay has its assigned topic, purpose, and home base, and that is where we have placed it. Thus readers who are interested in the idea of archive should begin with the essays by Christopher Balme, Susan Bennett, and Claire Sponsler—but do not stop there. Several additional essays have significant things to say not only about how archives are organized and used but also about how and why the idea of archives shapes historical inquiry.

Because the essays investigate performance practices across the globe and throughout many centuries, the collection provides a valuable diversity of historical perspectives, topics, case studies, and methods. Yet the concept of representation provides a common concern and a unifying topic.[15] All historians, no matter what their approach and subject matter, attempt to represent the past truthfully. This is the fundamental principle of historical inquiry. Of course, the historical task of delineating past events accurately and fully is often difficult to achieve because of the silences and lacunae of the past, especially as we move back through the centuries.

Moreover, besides the gaps in the historical record, a more fundamental problem troubles our historical endeavors. This idea of representation carries two basic yet contradictory meanings: Mimesis I: to mirror accurately, to present a truthful, faithful copy; and Mimesis II: to substitute, to offer an alternative version.[16] When historians discuss the idea of representation they often take sides. Supposedly, one group is committed to facts and objectivity; accurate description of past events is the fundamental task of historians. This group understands representation as Mimesis I.

But another group embraces an alternative perspective, arguing that historical representation is interpretive and subjective; historical writing depends upon the tropes of narrative. This group understands representation as Mimesis II. Are we required to accept this polarity? Does historical representation divide into either Mimesis I or Mimesis II?

A representation, apparently, is simultaneously a facsimile and a simulacrum, a copy and a counterfeit.[17] This polarity seems to be the case with any discourse or code of representation we use (such as languages, drawings, and photographs). The representation makes a show—a deceptive performance—of the original, as if the reality of the thing itself is possessed by a disruptive *Doppelgänger*. The same thing is delivered as another thing. The historical representation seeks to be an objective image of the thing itself, yet it cannot avoid being, in some capacity, a subjective distortion of that thing. Even the most objective code articulates a subjective perspective or formal order. If not similitude, the historian aims for verisimilitude in the representation of the past. Of course the aim may be easy to articulate, but the method of achieving such a representation is difficult. The aim of telling the truth about past events is a necessary first principle of historical inquiry, but whose truth, what truth, which truth? Many truths deserve and require representation. The historian often must negotiate among contending versions of past events, as the archive may allow, seeking the most equivalent representation within the possible temporal and spatial coordinates.[18]

All representations, in the process of describing past events, require temporal and spatial coordinates. All require documentation: access to and use of the historical archive (in its many manifestations, from public records to personal memories and oral reports). In the process of representing the past events, we draw upon narrative methods and assumptions (about the historical subjects and the time and place of their actions). By attempting to explain the nature of representation in terms of concepts such as identity, time, space, archive, and narrative, are we moving in circles? How can the idea of representation be the foundational term for the ideas of time, space, narrative, and identity? Moreover, is this definitional circle actually a hermeneutic circle that yokes the objective "facts" of history to the subjective perceptions of the historian? The mind has its own agenda and coordinates, as Montaigne noted.

Montaigne was hardly alone in this recognition. From the debates between Plato and Aristotle over the purpose and nature of mimesis to Paul Ricoeur's reformulation of a "threefold mimesis" in *Time and Narrative*, the disjunction between the world and our conception and delineation of that world has remained a central problem in the idea—and ideal—of representation.[19] Apparently caught within the double nature of representation—its accurate and distorting signs and codes—historians are suspended in what Ricoeur calls "the entanglement of the circle of the Same and the Other," a necessary condition of the hermeneutics of historical consciousness.[20] When historians reflect upon the nature of this problem (instead of either ignoring or denying it), they enter the domain of historiography.

Do we, as historians, have a way out of these conundrums on the nature and meaning of representation? Can we leave the philosophical struggles to the philosophers and just go about our business of historical research, description, and analysis? Such is the desire and practical attitude of most historians. Uninterested in (or unprepared to take on) the philosophical issues, we just proclaim that to describe is to represent. All historical descriptions, accordingly, are representations. But this equation tells us nothing yet. We still need to define and analyze what we mean by the ideas of both description and representation. What are their definitive traits? How can they be negotiated and explained by our available discourses?

It is true, of course, that the process of historical representation is often seen as a method of description in many discussions. But Frank Ankersmit argues in *Historical Representation* (2001) that the concept of representation is not the same as the concept of description. Representation, he insists, cannot be reduced to description:

> A true description identifies an object in reality by means of its subject-term to which a property is attributed by the predicate-term of the description. This well-known structure, which has painstakingly been analyzed by philosophers of language since Frege, is absent in the case of representation. Though historical representations are built up of true descriptions, a (historical) representation itself cannot be interpreted as one large (true or false) description. I would not hesitate to say that this—and nothing else—is the central problem in all philosophy of history.[21]

Ankersmit takes us into the philosophy of language in order to investigate the nature of the idea of historical representation. He thus argues:

> The three central notions of philosophy of language—reference, meaning, and truth—have to be redefined in order to come to an adequate understanding of the nature of representation. Reference should be replaced by "aboutness": a representation does not refer to what it repre-

> sents, but is about it. Meaning has to be replaced by "intertextuality": the meaning of the text of a historical representation can never be identified if one takes into account only the text itself. Its meaning only reveals itself in a comparison with other texts about (roughly) the same represented. And this necessarily has its consequences for the notion of truth. Representations are not true or false in the proper, technical sense of these words, but only more or less plausible. And their relative plausibility articulates itself in this comparison with these other texts.[22]

In this appeal to plausibility we hear the echo of Aristotle's analysis of possibility and plausibility in his distinction between history and poetry in the *Poetics*. (We will return to this issue below in our discussion of the ways in which historical representations are narratives.) For the moment, though, it would seem, whether or not we wish to confront the philosophical issues that pertain to the idea of representation, its meaning (or meanings, to be more exact) suggests an inescapable hermeneutical entanglement of intertextuality that resides equally in the nature of historical events and the language we must use to describe or recover those events. Even if it teases most historians out of thought, the troubling idea of representation remains an underlying condition of historical thinking.

Historical understanding is further complicated, as most historians acknowledge, not only by the split identity of the concept of representation (which reproduces both the "Same" and the "Other") but also by the disjunctions between past and present. Not one but two double binds confront all historians. Of course the gap between past and present is a familiar condition for historians, even a truism of historical understanding. As we look backward to previous events, we perceive the past through a contemporary lens that necessarily refracts the distant events we seek to represent. We describe and transcribe them simultaneously. Past actions are reenacted in present discourse; they are joined yet still separated in the representation. Indeed, the double identity of representation is caused and compounded by the disjunction between past and present. Accordingly, in their etymologies and tripartite relationship, these three words—present, past, represent (or re-present)—signal some logical contradictions (or at least confusions) that trouble all historians as they negotiate the relationship between past events and present perspective.

As both of these problems demonstrate, language (the dominant semiotic code) intervenes in historical representation. It mediates between the world and our understanding of it. Or, more to the point, it mediates between the past events and each historian's configuration (or reconfiguration) of them. Our descriptions of historical events and conditions depend upon—and are limited by—the available discourses that we have access to (and have facility in). We think and write within discourses that formulate our understanding of the historical topic; they guide our descriptive and analytical choices of terminology. As we attempt to comprehend past events and represent them, language provides the ideas we think with (such as archive, time, space, identity, and narrative).

Likewise, our historical sources, such as written documents and records, are already mediated representations of the historical actions, events, and thoughts that we seek to recover. The "original" documents are not the events themselves; they are representations by the historical agents and eyewitnesses, who themselves must negotiate their own double binds within the codes of representation. Consequently, the documents themselves reproduce the problem of the double identity of all representations. The hermeneutical condition of Same and Other pertains to the archival record, its representation of the events it documents. And the historical agents and eyewitnesses, like us, have their own cultural concepts of archive, time, space, identity, and narrative that they think with (and that historians attempt to decode). Thus yet another double bind operates in historical study, which must negotiate two levels of communicative discourses and codes. Even "primary" documents are "secondary" in their representational codes. Talented historians are skilled at cracking codes. These mediating codes of the communicative systems—and the problems that attend them—are part and parcel of the other two double binds: the double identity of any representation and the split between past and present. Language, always operating metaphorically in the search for a truthful representation, achieves a compromised yoking of past and present.

Unavoidably, then, these double binds set up a temporal as well as a spatial disjunction between the identities of the historical subjects and the identity of the historian. Unavoidably, the concepts of identities, time, and space are part of the definition of the idea of representation. The archive delivers, by means of its own codes, the identities of the historical subjects we study who are located within time and space, a period and place. It also delivers the identities of the eyewitnesses, distributed in the documents, who contribute their representations to the significance of the historical events. No wonder the concept of identity is so important. It is the basic and pervasive idea that we discover and derive from the archive; it is the subject or subjects (both human subjects and events as subject matter) that we attempt to designate and construct (or should we say reconstruct?) as we delve into any historical topic.

In order to carry out this construction, we also draw upon and develop certain temporal and spatial configurations of the historical moment and era that help us to identify the contexts for these identities. The archival sources have identities; the historical subjects we derive from these documents have (or are given) identities; the events we discover or reconstruct have (or are given) identities; the conditions that frame and contribute to these various identities have (or are given) their own identities. All of these identities exist and take their meaning from and within the temporal and spatial conditions of their historical moment. Throughout this whole process, the historian's own identity participates in all stages of the historical research, analysis, description, and argument that generates, piece by piece, the descriptive features and analytical strategies of the historical narrative.[23] Thus the concepts of archive, time, space, and identity are fundamental to historical research and representation. Moreover, as this collection of essays demonstrates at least partially, all representations—those provided by the historical subjects and eyewitnesses and those offered by the historians—are elements of the narrative techniques that historians use for representing human identities and actions within the temporal and spatial conditions of past, present, and future.

Yet despite these various disjunctions, gaps, mediations, and configurations of historical inquiry and understanding, historians attempt to represent the past accurately. The historian, describing the past as accurately and fully as possible, is still committed to the principle of historical truth. Anything less is irresponsible. The aim is admirable; the task is difficult. Yet the achievement is often impressive.[24] The rival principles of objective and subjective comprehension do not nullify one another, creating a stalemate, but instead work together in a counterpoint relationship.[25] As additional historians provide their investigations and narratives, a cumulative process of historical inquiry by the community of scholars delivers the dynamic interchange of statements and counterstatements. Even though documentary evidence is partial and the epistemological problems of historical inquiry are inescapable, it is still possible to discover and understand much about the past. As we learn to carry out historical inquiries and to evaluate historical reports, we also learn that there is a world of difference between good and bad historical representations.[26] In a community endeavor, historians put forward their representations and negotiate their differences; they apply rules of evidence (and challenge and overturn inadequate representations based on flawed constructions of evidence). A community of scholars is not to be confused with an ideal of a collective; community disagreement is the norm. In the process, as in well-constructed cases in the law, solid judgments emerge for representing historical events and their conditions (including the motives of the subjects and the causes of the events).[27] Subjects and events attain their identities.

Necessarily, then, the organizing ideas of *archive, time, space, identity*, and *narrative* exist and function within the epistemological problems and challenges outlined here. Any consideration of how historians *think with* these five ideas must confront the split identity of representation, the gap between past and present, the metaphoric nature of discourse, and the disjunctions between the communicative codes of the historical agents and those of the historians. All historians, whether or not they reflect directly on these matters, must contend with them. Consequently, though the essays in this collection make no attempt to provide a comprehensive analysis or systematic theory of the epistemological conditions and methodologies of historical inquiry, they reveal, from their multiple perspectives, the shaping power and significance of the five concepts. This engagement with the five ideas should provide a valuable contribution to the historiography of performance—for students and teachers alike.

These five formulated ideas of *archive, time, space, identity*, and *narrative* serve as coordinates of the mind, as categories of thought. They deliver the epistemological terms of perception and analysis, the ensemble of ideas needed for historical inquiry and understanding. Even without the need to reflect upon these organizing ideas, historians use and apply these concepts categorically in all phases of historical research, analysis, interpretation, and writing. As productive, busy historians, we may not spend much time thinking about these concepts, but we think with them all the same (and all the time). They help—and, yes, sometimes hinder—us as we mediate the gaps and disjunctions not only between past and present but also between the two contending ideas of representation.

In the words of Louis O. Mink, these categories offer the "concepts we think with," not just topics we think about or use. Mink, who wrote often as a philosopher of history on the problems of historical consciousness, pointed out that there is no set number of such concepts, but he named four key ones: *time, space, identity*, and *causality*. Without question, they are primary ideas in historical understanding. In the process of designing this book, we immediately concurred with him and decided to feature three of them: *time*, *space*, and *identity*. Indeed, their importance in human thinking is obvious. Each concept has generated an extensive bibliography of intellectual commentary—in philosophy, historiography, the social sciences, the study of the arts. For this reason we do not feel the need to justify our privileging of these ideas. A little reflection makes clear how and why these ideas are central to historical research, analysis, and writing. It is impossible to understand the past without the primary ideas of *identity*, *time*, and *space*.

In the case of the idea of identity, for example, modern philosophy ever since René Descartes's "cogito ergo sum" ("Je pense, donc je suis") has made questions of human identity central to procedures of rational inquiry and understanding, not simply in philosophy but also in science, the arts, and history.[28] Likewise, Descartes's methods of doubt, spelled out in the *Discourse on the Method* (1637), are basic to matters of both objective and subjective identity and are now inscribed in training procedures for historical methodology (such as procedures for identifying reliable sources and credible reports). Today even a novice historian, after accepting a source too readily without critical examination, learns some basic methods of doubting—not only others but oneself. Since the seventeenth century, as philosophers from René Descartes, Baruch Spinoza, and John Locke to Immanuel Kant, David Hume, and G. W. F. Hegel took up basic matters of identity in epistemology, the discipline of history likewise learned to question the procedures of identification.[29] Indeed, many of the debates over the objectivity and subjectivity of the historian rested on ideas of identity.

As for Mink's fourth concept, *causality*, we agreed that it is an essential idea in historical study. History is the study of changes, and these changes must have their causes. But for this collection of essays we have replaced the idea of causality with—or actually circumscribed it within—the idea of *narrative* because we wanted to show how and why causal factors, for the historian, are usually located in methods of not only identifying historical agents and their motives but also giving order and meaning to their actions. Likewise, these factors emerge in the ways historians construct the temporal and spatial conditions in which these identified agents are constrained to act (and react).

Narrative understanding for the historian provides formal order and direction—a developmental arc of action, if not always a neat design of beginning, middle, and end. Despite their ambitions, historians must sometimes be narrators—not unlike Samuel Beckett—of an extended middle action, with both the beginning and end of the events under study buried in the deep, dark, and uncertain shadows of history. Causality operates within (and is constricted by) these representations. Yet whatever the design we discover in the representation, we regularly think with the idea of causality—in tandem with the idea of change—by means of the ideas of time, space, identity, and narrative. Mink actually supports this modification, for in several of his essays he has placed "narrative form" at the center of historical thinking about events, their sequences, their relations, and their causes. Narrative form is "a cognitive instrument" for acquiring evidence about past actions and causes. It also provides patterns and plots for representing those actions.[30]

The idea of narrative form should be a familiar one to scholars of drama, for it is what Aristotle called *mythos*, the plotting technique, method, or operation needed for representing human actions in an ordered, connected sequence. As Aristotle insisted in his *Poetics*, *mythos* is the most important element in the mimetic mission of drama. It organizes possible (or, even better, probable) events in time and space, giving human actions their intentions and identities. The actions reveal and express *ethos* (character) and *diaonia* (thought), by which we identify the dramatic agents. For Aristotle, poetry "is a more philosophical and a higher thing" than history because it attains universality by representing human actions in accord with the principles of probability or necessity. "The true difference" between history and poetry, Aristotle argued, "is that one relates what has happened, the other what may happen, . . . for poetry tends to express the universal, history the particular."[31] The universal or typical trait of poetry is achieved by a full demonstration and plotting of causal intelligibility, something that history cannot always provide. Both are closely related, however, because they represent human actions, and those actions attain their meaning for us by means of some kind of narrative plot that links and joins credible actions.[32]

Aristotle recognized that history and drama share many mimetic attributes and aims because they represent the possible and probable structures of action. Indeed, the ideas of possibility and probability are essential for Aristotle in the making of a viable plot. Both the playwright and the historian construct coherent, unified narratives based upon the actions of the agents.[33] Causal explanation derives from a sense of necessity, a retrospective discovery of pattern and purpose that narrative form configures. But historical narratives, dependent upon the partiality of the archival sources, cannot usually offer or deliver the full causal order of necessity and rationality that a poetic tragedy is capable of attaining and representing. Less ambitiously, history provides particular, not universal, order and meaning for the infinite complexity of *res gestae*. In these cases, causal intelligibility may often be lacking or at best partial. Historians attend to matters of possibility—and sometimes probability—but not necessity.[34] Nonetheless, history is capable of providing narrative order and meaning; this it shares with poetry. Both the historian and the playwright, in their task of representation, create plots for human actions.[35] The historian seeks to trace probable, not necessary, lines of action and development in historical events. Causal certainty (or necessity) is usually missing from historical narratives. But both poetry and history still narrate their events. From this perspective, then, the idea of narrative is more comprehensive than the idea of causality in historical inquiry and explanation. Consequently, the idea of narrative, rather than the idea of causality, is one of our five ideas in this collection.

This understanding of narrative order, of the operation of *mythos*, should make sense to theatre historians, especially as they reflect upon the ways that narrative form gives shape and meaning not only to drama but to all kinds of performance events. And if Aristotle saw similarities in the ways the dramatist and the historian make narratives, we should have little trouble in seeing how and why the idea of mimesis or representation provides the foundation for historical inquiry and writing.

Beyond these Aristotelian ideas of mimesis, *mythos*, and human action (as well as the related principles of possibility and probability, which are central to historical analysis), the idea of narrative—like those of time, space, and identity—serves all historical understanding. Narrative is a fundamental idea in historical comprehension. Moreover—and this is an essential principle of epistemology—these organizing ideas serve all human beings as they reflect upon their lives and the world about them. For this reason, we encourage historians of performance events to extend their understanding of these Aristotelian factors in drama to the recognition that narrative organizes both individual and communal identities for human beings, shapes and composes memories and expectations, and orders the phenomenology of time consciousness.

Individually each of us participates in the continuous processes of telling and retelling the stories of our lives. And socially all communities are equally involved in the telling and retelling of their identities, their traditions and conventions, their activities and accomplishments. We narrate our lives, including not only our past actions but also our expectations and our predictive thoughts and plans. These narratives offer records of (that is, versions of) past accomplishments, present endeavors, and future undertakings. Historical inquiry requires an examination of the narrative events and reports (individual and communal, psychological and social) that historical agents and eyewitnesses provide. In turn, the mission of history is to trace human actions within time, to configure the representations—or re-presentations—of these past events into narrative form. The old narratives, as formulated by the historical agents and eyewitnesses, are reformulated as new narratives, as configured by the historians. Separating out the many stories, often in contention with one another, the historian attempts to take the measure of individual and communal versions of identity, to discover the realities of the past.

Equivalences, as David Summers suggests, need to be attended to as we seek the most reliable sources for our representations.[36] The historical actions need to be understood and explained in terms of the identities and narratives of the historical agents and their communities—that is, their personal and cultural memories and expectations within the specific temporal and spatial coordinates. Equally important, these historical actions must be placed within the time consciousness and the retrospective modes of understanding and analysis of historians as they reflect upon and attend to the developmental order (design, plot, *mythos*) of change and causality in the actions of human agents. History and historiography join together in the making of the narratives. Narrative form is thus central to historical understanding, over and beyond the ways in which it also provides many of the formal traits, tropes, genres, and rhetorical voices for historical writing.[37]

For our fifth concept, we have selected the one that is immediately apparent in historical inquiry: the *archive*, the repository of historical information about the many identities and narratives of human beings throughout time and space. The archive establishes the framing network for all methods of investigation. It sanctions not only research procedures but also the historical questions and problems that serve as the catalyst for historical inquiry. Across the centuries the archive has had various identities (yet another reason why the idea of identity is one of our five concepts). From the hearsay reports and eyewitness accounts of Herodotus to the modern repository of the Internet, the archive is always "in process" (especially as Google carries out its grand archival missions).

In recent centuries libraries large and small have collected manuscripts and published works on the history of performance, from the drafts of plays to letters, memoirs, theatre reviews in newspapers and journals, scrapbooks, contracts, business records, governmental records, and various kinds of iconographical sources. Accordingly, historians of performance need to develop many of the same research skills that all other historians learn and apply. Yet the performance archive also encompasses materials not typically storehoused by most libraries, including costume drawings and three-dimensional design sets. Especially in the case of dance, the archive has struggled to document performance records of the body in motion, beyond the familiar written sources. These kinds of special archival materials are not normally what a trained librarian would consider or know how to compile and catalogue. As the essays by Claire Sponsler on archive, Susan Foster on narrative, and Shannon Jackson on space illustrate, in their unique ways, historical scholarship in dance and performance studies requires us to reconceive and reformulate not only the idea of the archive but also the ideas of space, time, identity, and narrative. The task is to find new ways to locate and identify the performers and creators, to describe motion in space as well as time, to join formal analysis of performance to cultural history, to recover the perceptions and responses of the audiences, and to write historical narratives that are true to the explicit and implicit narratives of dance itself. What qualifies as evidence; what qualifies as performance? And, for the dance scholar, what are the descriptive and interpretive possibilities for historical reconstruction?

Concomitantly, as Jacques Derrida points out, our formulated idea of the archive also "determines the structure of archival content even in its very coming into existence and in its relationship to the future."[38] Derrida is hardly alone in recognizing this basic fact. The category of the archive engages two meanings of "source." The first, and more quotidian for the historian, is source as information and data that can serve the historical project, when verified as evidence. The other idea of source is more conceptual; it is understood as a beginning or initiating cause. Though these two meanings are sometimes collapsed together in a confusing manner by some historians (despite the fact that the meanings are not always compatible), we fully agree with Derrida that the source—as document and archival process—"produces as much as it records the event."[39] Accepting this perspective, we recognize that an archive is not merely something we use; it is, as a category of thought, a way of conceiving and reconceiving the identities and meanings of past events. It is a kind of mind game—a hermeneutics of historical consciousness—that puts in play the rules and procedures for historical research, analysis, argument, and reporting.

So, from the perspective of performance history, these five concepts provide the essential order for historical thinking: *archive, time, space, identity*, and *narrative*. They organize—and we hope justify—a collection of fifteen essays on the historiography of performance. In making this claim, we are not arguing that these five categories of thought are the only ones that guide historical inquiry and understanding. Let us be very clear on this matter. Even though we admire the rigor and unity of certain systematic models of analysis (such as Aristotle's model of six definitive elements of tragedy), we are not so ambitious (or perhaps foolish) as to put forward a poetics or system of historical thinking. As we have already noted, it is possible to identify several other key concepts that historians think with, including the ideas of action and causality. And without question the idea of change, though an aspect of both action and causality, is a necessary category of thought for historians. Indeed, as we prepared this project, we considered the possibility of adding the idea of change to our list of five primary categories of historical thought.[40] But instead of offering three additional essays in the category of change, we decided to let the idea emerge within the essays, as it intersects with the other five categories. Readers would then confront it, in various manifestations, within the contending functions of the other five concepts. It cannot be denied that the processes of change are always operating in history: in the making of archives, in the temporal and spatial dynamics of historical events, in the developmental conditions of individuals, communities, and societies, and in the narrative construction of history (the anecdotes, tales, stories, memoirs, biographies, and grand surveys). Despite the obvious significance of the idea of change, we decided to limit our investigation to the five ideas, which seem to be the most relevant and prevalent for the study of historical inquiry in our intersecting fields of study.[41]

Two additional comments (or cautions): first, despite the categorical nature of the five concepts, as historians we must insist that their meanings are not fixed. We resist any effort to contain the five ideas within set definitions, as if we were compiling dictionary entries. From person to person, society to society, country to country, and era to era, they take on different meanings and applications in the thoughts of people, including historical agents as well as historians. Just as the idea of the archive is best understood as a continuum of transformations, so are the ideas of time, space, identity, and narrative. Second, in other fields of inquiry (besides the discipline of history) additional categorical ideas may operate, organizing thought and understanding in primary ways. Also, these other fields may comprehend and apply one or more of the five concepts in special, even unique, ways.

Of course, the field of philosophy has a long tradition of systematic attempts to establish primary categories of thought. Aristotle first established the idea of primary "Categories" in the posthumously titled *Orga-*

non. There he identified ten classes or divisions of conceptual schema: substance, quantity, quality, relation, time, place (or space), position, state, action, and passion. The Aristotelian categories can be understood in two ways: (1) as ontological classes for identifying reality, which the mind is able to represent across the categories; (2) as linguistic classes for making distinctions grammatically, a terminological perspective on how the mind describes by means of language or symbolic terms. This double focus on ontological and linguistic applications also applies, in some similar ways, to narrative form, which can be understood as an essential principle of human thinking. It serves as a cognitive instrument of temporal and spatial consciousness that allows us to discover the patterns of human events (of identity within a temporal-spatial domain). Moreover, narrative form serves as a writing principle for organizing or plotting human action, an idea of mimetic representation for composing a play or a historical report. These classes, if understood as ontological categories for identifying and representing aspects of reality, are quite suggestive, because they require and apply the distinction between "Same" and "Other." Here we seem to return to Ricoeur's basic problem of representation, at the heart of hermeneutics.[42]

Yet despite the centrality of these classes and distinctions in Aristotle's works, and their subsequent influence in Western thought (notably in the medieval and Renaissance eras), it is fair to say that these categorical ideas have had very limited influence on historians, from Herodotus and Thucydides to Edward Gibbon and Voltaire.[43] With the contributions of Immanuel Kant (1724–1804), however, the idea of categories took on a more telling though still indirect influence on historiography, as the field of historical studies developed in the nineteenth and twentieth centuries. Kant's theory of categories spelled out a system of classification for human judgments and modes of reasoning. In *The Critique of Pure Reason* (1781, 1787) Kant made four primary divisions for categorical judgments: *quantity*, *quality*, *relation*, and *modality*.[44] Obviously, these four categories of thought apply directly to modes of comprehension in all human endeavors, including historical inquiry and analysis. All historians, in their descriptions of past events and objects, make distinctions on the basis of quantity, quality, relation, and modality. It would be impossible to write history without the ability to make such distinctions. As categories of understanding, these four provide a logic of "pure principles" which can be used for making judgments about the data of sense perceptions. But these concepts, though definitive, do not generate "concepts we think with" in the same manner as do the ideas of archive, time, space, identity, and narrative (or, indeed, plot, character, thought, diction, song, and spectacle). Kant did, however, generate *a priori* or transcendental ideas which are distinct from sensuous entities of perception.[45] Kantian philosophy thus distinguished things-in-themselves, which we cannot know directly, from the forms of reason—such as the organizing ideas of space, time, causality, and identity—that we impose upon the world we perceive. In Kant's words, "our representation of things, as they are given to us, does not conform to these things as they are in themselves. . . . These objects as appearances conform to our mode of representation."[46] In this way Kant's categories confront the basic problems of representation, the gaps between the world and the mind. They therefore correspond to the kinds of categories that we are putting forward in this collection of essays.

We acknowledge, then, that the heritage of Aristotelian and Kantian philosophy offers some justifications—though not a systematic model—for our historiographical project that features the five categorical ideas. We are not manufacturing them out of thin air. We also derive some insights and guidance from the productive flow of ideas and influences that occurs in the arts and humanities. Our consideration of the principle of representation, for instance, benefits from the commentary in philosophy, history, literary theory, and linguistics.[47] Yet we must insist that our basic purpose is not to announce a categorical system for the philosophy of history.[48] We willingly admit that we have no talent for constructing philosophical models and systems. More to the point, we believe that for historians these five ideas operate pervasively yet not systematically. They have a purchase on historical understanding at the basic level of practice. Every historian, in the practical task of representing the past, needs and applies the ideas of archive, time, space, identity, and narrative. Accordingly, if a type of philosophy needs to be named or a philosophical justification is needed (and we believe it is not), these ideas are justified by pragmatism (loosely defined and applied).

Basically, then, these five ideas are the ones that captured our own understanding, as we reflected on our own experiences as historians. We settled on them because they derive from our professional activities as historians and teachers of theatre historiography. As we carry out our own research, analysis, and writing, these five concepts emerged as fundamental to our thinking. They are the ones that seem to us most directly relevant for historians of performance. They are essential to the procedures of historical understanding, inquiry, and practice that historians depend upon, even though most historians spend little or no time reflecting upon matters of epistemology.

By attending to how the five ideas function in historical understanding, we want to offer some helpful and practical guidance in historiography—at the foundation level of our basic commitment to represent the past as accurately as we are able. If we appreciate the ways in which the five ideas shape historical practices, we should be able to fulfill that commitment more effectively. Yet we also want to point out—another pragmatic consideration—that the essayists in this collection are not writing philosophical treatises on these five ideas; nor are they, for the most part, even attempting to offer theoretical arguments, except in the normal ways that historiography itself requires theoretical reflection and performance theory has a place in scholarship today. The essayists, on occasion, also draw upon the rich heritage of dramatic theory, which is another foundation for theatre history. See, for example, the analysis of space and theatre history in Marvin Carlson's essay or the appeal to current theories of performativity in Tracy Davis's essay. But in the main the significance of these essays depends upon their direct engagement with historical writing and understanding. Instead of offering theoretical treatises, the contributors are primarily investigating and demonstrating how these five ideas function practically in historical research, analysis, and writing.

To this practical end, we invite our readers to follow their own best interests as they delve into the book. We have established one organizational strategy that starts with archive and finishes with narrative, but the sequence has no special justification beyond the obvious one that scholars tend to begin with the archive and finish with the writing of the historical narrative. Even if archive and narrative suggest the standard beginning and end of historical scholarship, time need not come before space and identity could either follow or precede these two ideas. Take your pick, for we insist that the essays can and should be read in whatever order appeals to each reader. Within each of the five categories, the order of the three essays is basically arbitrary.

Although the essays are separated into five topical categories, we remind readers that each takes up not only its declared topic but aspects of the other four ideas. Consequently, the full significance of each of the five ideas extends throughout the fifteen essays. Many paths can be taken through the essays, revealing many perspectives on how to represent the past. Nonetheless—our final point—all of us in our historical understanding and our methods of historical inquiry share a deep and abiding epistemological condition, carved into our minds and imaginations: our consciousness of the past, of all human events, is shaped by our ideas of archive, time, space, identity, and narrative. This is true for the many kinds of historical study, so it must be true for performance history—a truth with a thousand and one sources, identities, temporal and spatial locations, and, of course, narratives. Human kind is one yet infinite.

NOTES

1. The fifteen contributors provide a wide and deep cross-section of scholarship today, for the essays take up issues and methods in theatre history, dance history, performance studies and theory, theatre semiotics, theatre iconography, dramatic theory, cultural studies, reception theory, cultural anthropology, national theatre histories, postcolonial studies, performance and politics, cognitive studies, and feminist, gender, and racial studies. Because of this range of scholarly perspectives and practices, this collection of essays also applies to the related fields of literary history, opera history, musicology, media studies, art history, film history, and of course general history and historiography.

2. As we also want to demonstrate, these processes of identification serve the historical agents as they function within their time and place, working out their acts and aims in terms of the contextual conditions.

3. Besides attending the annual meetings of the American Society for Theatre Research in Durham, North Carolina, Chicago, and Phoenix, we met at conferences of the International Federation for Theatre Research in College Park, Maryland, St. Petersburg, and Helsinki. In accord with this schedule, we can claim that the book has cost us thousands of dollars to develop. No doubt our colleagues in the sciences, who often spend millions of dollars to develop labs for their projects, would be bemused at this version of scholarly expenditures. Still, the travel has been fun—and worthwhile.

4. Michel Foucault, "Nietzsche, Genealogy, History," in *Foucault Reader*, ed. Paul Rabinow, trans. Josué V. Harari (New York: Pantheon Books, 1984), p. 76.

5. We note that in recent years McConachie and Postlewait had mulled over the possibility of publishing a revised edition of *Interpreting the Theatrical Past*. But after considering the matter and discussing options with Holly Carver, director of the University of Iowa Press, they decided that the collection continued to serve its purpose and that any revision would require major rethinking of the nature and purpose of the book. They decided to let it retain its identity as a successful textbook that continues to be in print and to be used in classrooms, thereby serving its basic function.

6. Sue-Ellen Case and Janelle Reinelt, "Introduction," in *The Performance of Power: Theatrical Discourse and Politics*, ed. Sue-Ellen Case and Janelle Reinelt (Iowa City: University of Iowa Press, 1991), p. x. *The Performance of Power* was the first book in the series Studies in Theatre History and Culture at the University of Iowa Press, which Tom Postlewait has edited since 1991.

7. These two panel sessions at the Roosevelt Hotel in New York City (August 1989) were jointly sponsored by the two ATHE forums on theatre history and theory and criticism. Carlson, Postlewait, Roach, and Bank represented the theatre history forum; Case, Murray, and Diamond were leaders of the theory and criticism forum. In 1989 Sue-Ellen

Case and Tim Murray were serving as editors of *Theatre Journal*, pushing the journal in new directions.

8. Sue-Ellen Case, "Theory/History/Revolution," in *Critical Theory and Performance*, ed. Janelle Reinelt and Joseph Roach (Ann Arbor: University of Michigan Press, 1992), p. 419. In the opening of this essay Case noted that it had originated as a paper for "The New Convergence" panels at the 1989 ATHE conference.

9. Simon Williams, "The Challenge to Professional Training and Development," in *The Performance of Power: Theatrical Discourse and Politics*, ed. Sue-Ellen Case and Janelle Reinelt (Iowa City: University of Iowa Press, 1991), p. 242. The essay by Simon Williams was one of several timely essays in the final section of *The Performance of Power* that took up pedagogical issues and sociopolitical developments in the field. Gary Jay Williams, "A Serious Joy: ASTR from 1981–2006," *Theatre Survey* 48.1 (May 2007): 42. For a specific focus on the Williamsburg conference itself, see Gay Gibson Cima's essay "Conferring Power in the Theatre," in *The Performance of Power*, ed. Case and Reinelt, pp. 256–264. The program committee included Gay Gibson Cima (program chair), Alicia Kay Koger, Tom Postlewait, Joseph Roach, Gary Williams, Simon Williams, and Bruce McConachie (local arrangements).

10. Marvin Carlson, "The Theory of History," in *The Performance of Power*, ed. Case and Reinelt, p. 278. This 1991 essay drew upon Carlson's commentary and experience from both his ASTR address and his ATHE paper in 1989. His ironic evocation of positivism in this statement was most fitting at that moment, as Gary Jay Williams's subsequent perspective on the ASTR meeting suggests.

11. If these three collections of essays were perhaps the most visible aspects of the new disciplinary ideas, the field of study featured many essays and books that contributed to the transformation of theatre history, critical theory, and performance studies. The studies on historiography and critical methods published in the 1990s and early 2000s easily fill a substantial bibliography.

12. R. G. Collingwood, *The Idea of History* (Oxford: Clarendon Press, 1946); revised and ed. Jan van der Dussen (Oxford: Oxford University Press, 1993); Marc Bloch, *The Historian's Craft*, trans. Peter Putnam, intro. Joseph R. Strayer, note on manuscript by Lucien Febvre (New York: Random House, 1953); Louis Gottschalk, *Understanding History: A Primer of Historical Methods* (1958), 2nd ed. (New York: Alfred A. Knopf, 1969); Georg G. Iggers, *Historiography in the Twentieth Century: From Scientific Objectivity to Postmodern Challenge* (Hanover, Conn.: Wesleyan University Press, 1997); Peter Burke, ed., *New Perspectives on Historical Writing* (1992), 2nd ed. (University Park: Pennsylvania State University Press, 2001); John Lewis Gaddis, *The Landscape of History: How Historians Map the Past* (Oxford: Oxford University Press, 2002). All of these books are available in paperback and can be assigned in doctoral seminars on historical method without breaking the bank. A number of other guides to historical methodology are also available, including a guide to library and web resources for historians: Jenny L. Presnell, *The Information-Literate Historian* (Oxford: Oxford University Press, 2007; also in paperback).

13. It is noteworthy, however, how many of these basic issues in historical methodology still emerged in this book. Though the fifteen contributors did not develop their

essays in terms of basic issues in historical research, most of these concerns found their way into the studies of archive, time, space, identity, and narrative.

14. All of the arts represent aspects of the world and human life, and part of our pleasure in these arts arises from the representational methods. Thus Aristotle made mimesis his essential idea for a poetics of literary arts. The idea of representation remains essential in the arts, even in modern times, with the disruption and reformulation of the representational codes and traditions in the arts. In turn, scholarship in the arts represents the artists and their works in biographies, critical studies, and histories. Representation (including description, explanation, and evaluation) is not the exclusive task of scholarship, but it remains an abiding purpose of the study of art. Even in music this representational agenda for artists and scholars is apparent, especially in folk music, songs, and opera. Music without lyrics and narrative can still be studied in terms of representational codes of melody, emotional feelings and pleasures, formal order and pattern, and so forth.

15. The fifteen essayists also share a basic question: how do historians represent the past? This question provided the main title for the book and set up our historiographical focus on the five organizing ideas.

16. This understanding of the two contending ideas of representation has a long history in Western philosophy and aesthetics. For a recent perspective in literary studies, see Christopher Prendergast, *The Triangle of Representation* (New York: Columbia University Press, 2000). He investigates two basic meanings of representation, which he summarizes as Mimesis I: making present again; re-presenting; a direct copy; a truthful, faithful, positive image; and Mimesis II: a standing in for; a substitution; a sign or graphic image that is other than the thing being portrayed; alternative versions and languages for a thing; a simulacrum; an illusion. These two versions of representation can stand in for the apparent difference between history and literature in their modes of presenting the world. History aims for a truthful, positive image of past events, while literature seeks the freedom of a substitute, illusionist version of the past. Of course, we are in danger of settling for an overly neat polarity with this two-part formulation, as Prendergast illustrates. A more complex formulation would recognize that historical and fictional representations combine both types of mimesis.

17. This double identity of representation engendered Michel Foucault's clever (though perhaps unhelpful) comment: "The philosophy of representation—of the original, the first time, resemblance, imitation, faithfulness—is dissolving; and the arrow of the simulacrum released by the Epicureans is headed in our direction. It gives birth—rebirth—to a 'phantasmetaphysics'" ("Theatrum Philosophicum," in *Language, Counter-Memory, Practice: Selected Essays and Interviews*, ed. Donald F. Bouchard, trans. Daniel F. Bouchard and Sherry Simon [Ithaca, NY: Cornell University Press, 1977], p. 172).

18. David Summers has also attempted to define and describe the idea of representation. See "Representations," in *Critical Terms for Art History*, 2nd ed., ed. Robert S. Nelson and Richard Shiff (Chicago: University of Chicago Press, 2003). His strategy is to begin with etymology and thus complicate the overly neat formulation of likeness versus substitution. Here are two statements by Summers:

> *Repraesentatio* is a construction around the verb "to be." *Praesens* is a participial form of *praeesse*, "to be before," which it means in two senses: the first is simple spatial, prepositional location; the second involves precedence or command, being higher in rank, more important than. Perhaps then "presence" implies that which is not simply before us but which "stands out" and concerns us, that to which we are in a sense subject. Then by extension the temporal "present" might also be what is at hand, what can and usually does actually occupy our attention, as opposed to the past and the future, which are "out of reach." (p. 6)

> *Repraesentatio* could also mean a payment in cash. The implicit third term that unites the disparate uses of *repraesentatio* might be said to be "fullest equivalent"; a *repraesentatio* is something of equal present force or value. In these terms to make an image means not to make an impossible double, but to fashion a fullest equivalent presence. Words cannot re-create, but they may be fused to memory and feeling and may have an equivalent force in the imagination, much as cash is most immediately equivalent to goods exchanged. ("Representation" is thus at least in part descended from commercial analogy, like the word "interpretation" itself, which is related to "price." To interpret is to negotiate, to have no leisure, to do business, to trade, bargain, haggle, but also to find an equivalent in other terms.) *Equivalence* has definitively replaced substitution or resemblance in our argument. (p. 7)

Summers appeals to spatial and temporal ideas in order to define representation. He also conjures with the two contending meanings: substitution and resemblance, but he begins to suggest that the concept requires a more complex negotiation between (and among) the terms of description and analysis.

19. Paul Ricoeur, *Time and Narrative*, vol. 3, trans. Kathleen Blamey and David Pellauer (Chicago: University of Chicago Press, 1985), p. 263. In the opening sections of volume 1 (Chicago: University of Chicago Press, 1984), Ricoeur elaborates a "dialectic of the threefold present," a distended relation of time and representation that joins expectation, memory, and attention (pp. 9, 20). He develops this distinction into his reformulation of the idea of mimesis, with mimesis-1 defined as prefiguration, mimesis-2 as configuration, and mimesis-3 as refiguration. Mimesis-1 evokes the act of reference, the world that is represented; mimesis-2 offers an act of mediation and evokes the act of creation, as in the poetics of narrative; and mimesis-3 engages the attention of the observer, spectator, or reader, who refigures or reformulates a representation (and for whom the configuration is performed). Joining semiotics and hermeneutics, Ricoeur builds upon his reading of Augustine and Aristotle. "We are following therefore the destiny of a prefigured time that becomes a refigured time through the mediation of a configured time" (vol. 1, p. 54). On the three types of mimesis, see vol. 1, pp. 52–87.

20. Paul Ricoeur, *Time and Narrative*, trans. Kathleen Blamey and David Pellauer (Chicago: University of Chicago Press, 1986), vol. 3, p. 246. Ricoeur's study of the problem of "the Same and the Other" in human understanding has its foundation not only in his analysis of temporal consciousness and the nature of narrative but also in his studies

of metaphor, symbol, language, memory, personal identity, interpretation theory, and hermeneutics. See also *Interpretation Theory: Discourse and the Surplus of Meaning* (Fort Worth: Texas Christian University Press, 1976); *Hermeneutics and the Human Sciences*, ed. and trans. John B. Thompson (Cambridge: Cambridge University Press/Paris: Éditions de la Maison des Sciences de l'Homme, 1981); *Oneself as Another*, trans. Kathleen Blamey (Chicago: University of Chicago Press, 1992); and *The Course of Recognition*, trans. David Pellauer (Cambridge, Mass.: Harvard University Press, 2005).

21. Frank Ankersmit, *Historical Representation* (Stanford: Stanford University Press, 2001), p. 281.

22. Ibid., p. 284. Like David Summers's attempt to replace the ideas of substitution and resemblance with the concept of equivalence (see note 18 above), Ankersmit attempts to move us beyond the polarity of sameness or difference (description or narrative). Like Ricoeur, he negotiates the apparent hermeneutical circle of Same and Other by reformulating an overly neat division into a more complex and ambiguous formulation of multiple perspectives on reference, meaning, and truth.

23. Ankersmit wants to wean us from the assumption that historical representations are descriptions, but of course we will continue to hold to this basic historical task of describing past events and subjects. But perhaps, even if we refuse to abandon the basic mission of describing the past, we can acknowledge that the discourses we use complicate our efforts.

24. These double binds are unavoidable because the whole historical project of representing the past remains separated from the events themselves, which we can never reach. The disjunctive nature of representation could be overcome only if the mind and the world were joined. Yet with great skill and cunning we find ways to reconstitute distant events, even the origins of certain occurrences, even though we cannot transport ourselves into the earlier times and places. Looking back through time and space we locate the origin of the universe; through archaeology we recover lost civilizations; by means of genetic research we trace the heritage of individuals and communities. However imperfect our historical tools, we achieve much.

25. We think best with a counterpoint intellect, honed not only on a feeling for the metaphoric nature of all language (including the seemingly straightforward descriptive terminology we use) but also on a recognition of the paradoxical and ironic nature of human character and events. A sense of self-irony is also helpful.

26. Our sense of the gaps, disjunctions, and polarities in human understanding comes almost too easily to our contemporary minds, disciplined as they are by modernism and postmodernism in the arts, relativity in the sciences, and poststructuralist theories in the academy. We have an ingrained distrust of the principles of objectivity and are leery of most forms of idealism. But perhaps we can separate ourselves sufficiently from our protective formulas of intellectual distrust (formulas that sanction ironic distancing) in order to concentrate on the demands of disciplined historical scholarship.

27. When there is insufficient documentation, of course, our constructions of historical evidence (which we make out of the available documentation) are often, at best, based on the principle of possibility instead of probability. We build arguments based upon par-

tial and circumstantial analysis. Yet even in these cases we can usually eliminate many inadequate and false possibilities; though certainty may be elusive, we are quite capable of identifying the remaining elements and definitive aspects of events, actions, situations, and conditions by a process of elimination as well as construction. In this sense historical inquiry is both an art and a science in the handling of documents and evidence.

28. The development of modern literature also has been tied to this issue of identity, as we see in the novel, with its reliable and unreliable narrators, its experiments with first-person and third-person narrators, and its embrace of multiple narrators in modernism, as in William Faulkner's *The Sound and the Fury*. Often the modern novel, whatever its setting and plot, is concerned primarily with the subjectivity and objectivity of represented subjects and narrators. Henry James's notebooks and prefaces can thus serve as a touchstone on the modern ideas of identity and narrative voice in the novel.

29. For a contemporary reflection on some of these matters of human identity, as they apply explicitly in philosophy and implicitly in historical thinking, see Paul Ricoeur's *Oneself as Another*, trans. Kathleen Blamey (Chicago: University of Chicago Press, 1992), and *The Course of Recognition*, trans. David Pellauer (Cambridge, Mass.: Harvard University Press, 2005). Just as Ricoeur's valuable three volumes on *Time and Narrative* help to clarify the two concepts in his title, so these two later studies offer valuable reflections on the hermeneutics of selfhood, personal identity, and the idea of a universal subject (or transcendental ego). These studies repay the historian's investigation. Among the various rich topics, Ricoeur takes up the ideas of agent, the character of others, the actions of historical agents, and the narrative voice—all central to historical thinking about identity. As always in Ricoeur's studies, the topics of language, memory, the self, the concept of the other, and narrative remain central to his analysis.

30. Louis O. Mink, "Narrative Form as a Cognitive Instrument," in *Historical Understanding*, ed. Brian Fay, Eugene O. Golob, and Richard T. Vann (Ithaca: Cornell University Press, 1987), pp. 182–203. In Mink's words: "Even histories that are synchronic studies of the culture of an epoch inevitably take in account the larger process of development or change in which that epoch was a stage. . . . The most 'analytic' historical monograph, one may say and could show, presupposes the historian's more general understanding, narrative in form, of patterns of change, and is a contribution to the correction or elaboration of that narrative understanding" (p. 184).

31. Aristotle, *Poetics*, ch. 9, from S. H. Butcher, *Aristotle's Theory of Poetry and Fine Art, with a Critical Text and Translation of The Poetics*, 4th ed. (New York: Dover Publications, 1951), p. 37. For a more recent translation of *The Poetics*, see Stephen Halliwell, *The Poetics of Aristotle: Translation and Commentary* (Chapel Hill: University of North Carolina Press, 1987). Also see his extended commentary in *Aristotle's Poetics* (Chapel Hill: University of North Carolina Press, 1986), where he notes: "On the argument of *Poetics* 9, it is not immediately to life that the poet must turn for his material, but to an imagined world (including that of inherited myth) in which the underlying design of causality, so often obscured in the world as we encounter it, will be manifest" (p. 135). This is an important distinction between poetic narrative and historical narrative; causal intelligibility is often unavailable in historical investigations, despite the bits and pieces of evidence on

the motives and intentions of some of the historical subjects. The historian makes conjectures based on possibility—not necessity, understood as causal inevitability.

32. Note that Aristotle's two-part distinction between history and poetry sets up many of the same divisions between Mimesis I and Mimesis II: representation as likeness, representation as substitution. One relates what has happened, the other what may happen. But both forms of representation are delivered as modes of narrative.

33. In Ricoeur's terms, the action provides a synchronic or paradigmatic order; the narrative provides a diachronic or syntagmatic order. See *Time and Narrative*, vol. 1, p. 56.

34. Stephen Halliwell makes an important distinction here, for he insists that the idea of "necessity in the *Poetics* . . . has nothing whatever to do with tragic destiny or inevitability, as is occasionally supposed" (*The Poetics of Aristotle: Translation and Commentary*, pp. 106–107). From this perspective, then, necessity provides a full causal order in poetry, something that is seldom possible in historical understanding, which is always partial.

35. Good playwrights, according to Aristotle, avoid "episodic" plots; but good historians often have no choice; the available information only allows for an episodic plot. And the plot may be partial, not whole. So be it. Good history may still emerge from this kind of narrative.

36. Summers, "Representations." See endnote 18.

37. The basis for these admittedly general statements on history and narrative can be found in Ricoeur's *Time and Narrative* and Mink's *Historical Understanding*, noted above. Also directly relevant are David Carr, *Time, Narrative, and History* (Bloomington: Indiana University Press, 1986); George Kubler, *The Shape of Time: Remarks on the History of Things* (New Haven: Yale University Press, 1962); Reinhart Koselleck, *Futures Past: On the Semantics of Historical Time*, trans. Keith Tribe (Cambridge, Mass.: MIT Press, 1985); Jörn Rüsen, *History: Narration, Interpretation, Orientation* (New York: Berghahn Books, 2005); and Collingwood, *The Idea of History*. See also the works of Hayden White for his arguments on narrative tropes and rhetoric in historical scholarship, including *The Content of the Form: Narrative Discourse and Historical Representation* (Baltimore: Johns Hopkins University Press, 1987) and *Tropics of Discourse: Essays in Cultural Criticism* (Baltimore: Johns Hopkins University Press, 1978). White's ideas on narrative have caused a fair amount of debate in historical studies, but these disputes usually miss the larger picture—the essential place of narrative in human consciousness and in historical understanding. White himself sometimes misses the epistemological basis of narrative understanding, especially when he becomes focused on literary genre and rhetorical tropes in the writing styles of historians. See his *Metahistory: The Historical Imagination in Nineteenth-Century Europe* (Baltimore: Johns Hopkins University Press, 1973). We therefore need to return to Ricoeur for the foundational ideas on narrative and time, which he considers in terms of not only Aristotle's concept of mimesis and model of *mythos* but also the studies of narrative in modern philosophy and historiography.

38. Jacques Derrida, *Archive Fever: A Freudian Impression*, trans. Eric Prenowitz (Chicago: University of Chicago Press, 1995), p. 17.

39. Ibid., p. 17. For a necessary extension of Derrida's point, see the essay by Susan Bennett in this volume.

40. If our publisher had sanctioned an even larger book, we could easily have featured three more essays on the idea of change within the history of performance. Its importance in historical thinking is easy to demonstrate. For example, the idea of change, as an organizing principle, percolates throughout two of Marvin Carlson's books, *Theories of the Theatre* (Ithaca, N.Y.: Cornell University Press, 1984) and *The Haunted Stage* (Ann Arbor: University of Michigan Press, 2001). It is also a key historical topic and problem in Thomas Postlewait, *The Cambridge Introduction to Theatre Historiography* (Cambridge: Cambridge University Press, 2009). Indeed, the idea is ever-present in most historical scholarship, from biography to the history of any developmental topic. Consider, for instance, the changing identity of *A Midsummer Night's Dream* in the 400 years of productions in Gary J. Williams's historical narrative *Our Moonlight Revels: A Midsummer Night's Dream in the Theatre* (Iowa City: University of Iowa Press, 1997). His book is an excellent demonstration of a scholar thinking with not only the idea of change but also the other five concepts of archive, time, space, identity, and narrative. But we want to note that the idea of change is almost always a component of the idea of narrative form.

41. We must acknowledge, though, that the idea of change presents major complications in the ways in which we constitute the identities, meanings, and relations for our five historical categories of thought, especially time and narrative. Both of them depend upon ideas of sequence and causality, as does the idea of change quite often. In some cases, as well, the idea of change throws a wrench into the works when we attempt to apply and use the category of identity. Normally, the category of identity serves to fix a definition and meaning on whatever it is applied to. But this way of thinking ignores how and why identities modify and transform (for example, across time and space). One obvious case is the way we identify periods or eras, as if both identity and time are frozen throughout an age, period, era, or epoch. Period identities, by definition, tend to ignore change (which is left to occur in the gap between periods). But change is also a problem when we attempt to represent the identities of human subjects over time and space, as if their identities are fixed despite many other factors being quite unfixed.

42. These classes and distinctions may also be related to Aristotle's concept of the four causes: efficient, material, formal, and final.

43. The exception, perhaps, to this catalogue of unsystematic historians might be Giambattista Vico (1668–1744), whose *Scienza nuova* (The New Science) offered a distinctly philosophical analysis of history, tied to his theories of language, myth, and change. His awareness of how language shapes understanding points, at least in some ways, to the manner in which Mink describes key ideas we think with. But because Vico was highly critical of any scientific claim for historical knowledge and rejected the Cartesian paradigm for knowledge, he refused to build a system based upon categories of the mind. His sense of change in human history required a rejection of any *a priori* concept of human nature, but he also developed his own idea of cyclical history. Nonetheless, his ideas on historical knowledge influenced certain philosophical, if not always systematic,

ideas of Jules Michelet, Benedetto Croce, and R. G. Collingwood. For helpful surveys of Vico's ideas in terms of historiography, see Collingwood's *The Idea of History* and Isaiah Berlin's "The Philosophical Ideas of Giambattista Vico," in *Vico and Herder: Two Studies in the History of Ideas* (New York: Viking, 1976).

44. In turn, Kant developed twelve ways that the four principles of judgments operate or can be identified logically in human understanding: *quantity* can be distinguished as universal, particular, or singular; *quality* as affirmative, negative, or infinite; *relation* as categorical, hypothetical, or disjunctive; and *modality* as problematic, assertoric, or apodictic. Unlike the biological categories of kind, which are used to describe empirical conditions that can be identified in animals and plants, Kant's categories are rational ideas or judgments that exist formally in the mind rather than in nature itself.

45. We note, in these terms, that Mink's *a priori* concepts to think with share many features with the Kantian categories.

46. Immanuel Kant, *The Critique of Pure Reason*, quoted by Summers, "Representations," p. 12.

47. The topic of representation has received much scholarly attention, of course. We note here only a few commentaries. Besides Ricoeur's works and Prendergast's *The Triangle of Representation*, mentioned above, see M. H. Abrams, *The Mirror and the Lamp* (New York: W. W. Norton, 1962), which offers an analysis of the ideas of representation and imagination from Aristotle to the Romantic poets. See also Ankersmit, *Historical Representation*; Jean Baudrillard, *Simulacra and Simulation*, trans. Sheila Faria Glaser (Ann Arbor: University of Michigan Press, 1994); Roger Chartier, *Cultural History: Between Practices and Representations,* trans. Lydia G. Cochrane (Ithaca, N.Y.: Cornell University Press, 1988); Murray Krieger, ed., *The Aims of Representation: Subject/Text/History* (Stanford: Stanford University Press, 1987); Louis Marin, *On Representation*, trans. Catherine Porter (Stanford: Stanford University Press, 2001); and Allan Megill, ed., *Rethinking Objectivity* (Durham, N.C.: Duke University Press, 1994). Two recent short overviews are noteworthy. From the perspective of art history, see Summers, "Representations." And from the perspective of literary study, see W. J. T. Mitchell, "Representation," in *Critical Terms for Literary Study*, ed. Frank Lentricchia and Thomas McLaughlin (Chicago: University of Chicago Press, 1990).

48. Nor are we attempting to find a niche in the philosophical developments of the nineteenth and twentieth centuries, though we note that some valuable ideas of philosophers have worked their way into the theory and practice of theatre studies by way of semiotics (C. S. Peirce), speech-act theory (J. L. Austin), and the philosophy of history (Hegel, Croce, and Collingwood). Indeed, the ideas of Collingwood have a significant place in the essay by Bruce McConachie in this volume. Speech-act theories contribute to the contributions of both Tracy C. Davis and Shannon Jackson. And semiotics has proved to be a productive source for Marvin Carlson's essay on space as well as his several books on aspects of theatre semiotics, including *Theatre Semiotics: Signs of Life* (Bloomington: Indiana University Press, 1990) and *Places of Performance: The Semiotics of Theatre Architecture* (Ithaca, N.Y.: Cornell University Press, 1989).

1 Archive

Playbills and the Theatrical Public Sphere

> Playbill, *n.* A bill, placard, or poster advertising a play and giving the names of the actors playing the different parts.
> — *Oxford English Dictionary*, 1971

> [B]y the way a Bill he doth espie,
> Which showes there's acted some new Comedie;
> Then thither he is full and wholly bent,
> There's nothing that shall hinder his intent
> — George Wither, *Abuses Stript and Whipt*, 1613

The definition of the playbill provided by the *Oxford English Dictionary* is as symptomatic in its laconism as in its inaccuracy. While playbills eponymously advertise the "play," they did not always give the names of actors throughout their checkered history. At different times over the four centuries of their existence they did much, much more. A witty example of their power can be gleaned from the pejorative reference in George Wither's satirical *Abuses Stript and Whipt* (1613), which demonstrates how a playbill's powerful lures distract a gentleman on the way to a sermon and redirect him to a playhouse. Like the performances they puff, they are ephemeral documents whose exact origins are unclear. Despite their intrinsic ephemerality, playbills have survived in their hundreds of thousands, maybe even millions, and been archived in myriad ways: in hand-pasted theatrical scrapbooks, on eyestrain-inducing microfilms, and most recently in the form of digitally accessible images online. They can be found individually in various archives, among records for particular theatres, and within the collected documents from various performers. Yet, despite their ubiquity, playbills belong to the most neglected category of sources in the theatre historical archive, where they are often literally catalogued under the heading "ephemera," and for this reason alone need to be investigated from a theoretical as well as empirical perspective. Despite a recent upsurge in interest in treating playbills in a more systematic fashion, they remain largely ignored. Jacky Bratton's recent comment that playbills are "a very unimaginatively used resource" remains largely accurate.[1]

As with any source, the playbill—like the theatrical image to which it is sometimes compared—cannot just speak for itself. While scholars, of course, have been extracting information from them ever since the discipline of theatre history began, the question to be explored here is how this particular type of material can be read in a critical and theoretically resonant way. There seem to be two main reasons why playbills have not been subjected to the same kind of methodological interrogation that theatrical images, for example, have received.[2] Because the information playbills provide is largely (but not exclusively, as we shall see) verbal, they do not appear to pose any particular problems in interpreting them. Depending on the period of production, they are replete with names, dates, prices, in fact all kinds of empirical data that warm the cockles of the positivist historian's heart. On a playbill one can, it would seem, call a fact a fact. The second reason for theoretical and methodological neglect is more difficult to prove but perhaps goes to the heart of any theatre historiographical reassessment of playbills. In comparison to theatre iconography—which in superficial readings would seem to offer the promise of access to the theatrical event, a performance on the stage (which of course it seldom does)—the playbill is foreplay but not the act itself. Like most foreplay, the playbill is clearly designed to excite, to stimulate; but for the scholar in search of the real thing, the transcendent experience and enchantment that is the "performance," playbills represent a kind of archival *ludus interruptus*.

One way for theatre historians to reconnect with the playbill is to ask if the event must necessarily be their main focus of attention. While playbills certainly draw attention to and indeed index performance events, they remain by definition before the event. They are never part of it, and theatre historians need to be wary of trying to draw incontrovertible conclusions about an enacted performance event exclusively from a playbill. It is well known that playbills occasionally advertise performances that never actually took place. The theatre does not, however, just consist of a succession of performance events where bodies and spaces are transformed by semiotic processes into signs and perceived by spectators in the here and now. The theatre also consists of a realm outside its architectural and performative coordinates. Every theatre exists in a spatial and temporal realm that is more conditioned by structure than by event. Most theatres are first and foremost institutions that function over a *longue durée* in a public sphere that is located temporally and spatially outside the heightened enchantment of the "event." Theatres are examples of institutional cultures that need to be addressed from perspectives that are culturally and not just aesthetically determined.

How, then, can we begin to study playbills in relation to the theatrical public sphere as a central constitutive factor in such institutional cultures?

Theatres communicate with their publics both before and after and not just during performances: they inform, attract, and provide them with informational and aesthetic stimuli with the ultimate aim of attracting individual spectators who will form a collective audience. These are complex processes sustained sometimes over a short period to attract people to a specific production but also over much longer periods in terms of a theatre's history and audiences. The central idea to be explored here revolves around concepts that modulate the relationship between inside and outside. The endeavor of creating a public and attracting an audience needs to be seen as a process consisting of a series of "articulations"—connections at joints or points—where the internal (the potential performances in the building) and the external (the sphere of communication and exchange outside but focused on the particular institution) meet in reciprocal although sometimes conflictual relationships and cultural practices.

Whereas these relations and processes of articulation can easily be studied in contemporary theatre through the departments of public relations employed by most theatres, the advertising campaigns, and a host of other exchanges (including televised broadcasts of performances), the study of similar kinds of practices in earlier epochs is much more difficult. For almost the entire history of theatre from the invention of printing until the end of the nineteenth century the playbill constituted a central point of articulation between theatres and their public spheres. The following discussion is primarily theoretical and methodological in orientation and proceeds in a series of three interlocking steps. In the first section I draw a fairly obvious but not always clearly made distinction between spectators, audiences, and the public. The focus is squarely on perhaps the most elusive of the three categories, "the public," an entity located sometimes inside, sometimes outside the theatre. In a second step, the concept of the theatrical public sphere is discussed. On the basis of Jürgen Habermas's famous study *The Structural Transformation of the Public Sphere* and its reception in the 1990s, I outline a perspective which can be applied to the analysis of theatrical institutions.[3] In the third and main section I analyze a series of playbills in terms of how they communicate with the public sphere. My intention is not to provide a potted history of the playbill but rather to demonstrate how such documents can be read in relation to institutional questions of theatre history. By "institution" I mean a complex of norms regulating social action; institutions invariably operate on the basis of law and impact collectivities as much as individuals. Theatrical institutions can range in complexity from itinerant troupes to national theatres. This analysis moves between Germany and the United Kingdom, an oscillation motivated first by reason of accessibility to source material and second by virtue of my own scholarly competence.

LOOKING FOR THE PUBLIC

To assert that theatre historians are centrally concerned with reviving, resuscitating, reconstructing, or retelling the theatrical events of the past is a relatively incontrovertible claim. These events are normally understood to be the performances: aesthetically loaded events lost the moment they occur and, once they lie beyond communicative memory, retrievable only through the archive. The idea of theatre history as event-recuperation has a long genealogy. Its theoretical and methodological lineaments were outlined by Max Herrmann, the founder of modern European theatre studies, who declared that the reconstruction of past performances should be the main object of scientific study. In his major work, *The History of German Theatre in the Middle Ages and the Renaissance* (1914), Herrmann described the goal of the theatre historian as "the task of making a theatrical performance of the past live again in such detail that, if the financial means were made available, one could indeed present it to a modern audience without fear of provoking offense."[4]

Whether analyzing performances of the past or present, most theatre scholars agree that the ephemeral performance (as opposed to the relatively fixed written text) is their proper field of inquiry. If we broaden the focus somewhat, we could add that most attention has been focused on what could be termed the aesthetic object in its many dimensions: scenography, acting, costume, actors and their bodies. In general, the signs onstage have been exhaustively analyzed by semiotics. Since the late 1980s theatre studies have also engaged with the theatrical reception from two main perspectives: the spectator and the audience. The spectator is the *individualized* aesthetic subject, the audience the *collectivized* aesthetic subject, "receiving" and making sense of the aesthetic product on the stage or wherever it may happen to occur.[5]

A more difficult and much less researched dimension is the role of the *public*. While "spectators" and "audiences" refer to individual or collective bodies inside the building or actively attending the performance—participants in the *hic et nunc* of theatrical encounter and exchange—the terms "public" and even more broadly "the public sphere" refer to a potential audience or perhaps not even that.[6] The public might include those individuals who regularly attend a particular theatre or indeed theatre in general—the theatregoing public—independent of a particular building. In this sense, the public is a potential audience to be realized rather than an actualized one. Theatres communicate continually with the theatregoing public, by anticipating its aesthetic tastes, estimating its size and moods, or, in the avant-garde tradition, rhetorically denying its importance or offending it. The space where this communication is enacted can be defined as the theatrical public sphere. The existence of such an entity not only characterizes highly mediatized societies, where theatres of whatever size and level of support compete daily for attention and money, but also can be posited for any theatrical institution.

The shift in focus away from the spectator or audience actively engaged in the performance event and its aesthetic codes requires a rearrangement of perspective for theatre historians. Focusing on the public rather than the spectator or audience implies a shift in historiographical attention from the performance to the institution. Theatrical institutions, I argue, have received proportionally less attention than performances, plays, or performers. Generally speaking, theatres as institutions certainly remain under-theorized and, more generally, under-researched.[7] While a body of work has been carried out on theatre buildings and the idea of theatre topographies, an institution is by no means coterminous with the building and vice versa. Although I cannot develop a detailed discussion of the institutional aspects of theatre history here, a perspective that focuses on the continuity (and occasional discontinuity) of the institution remains crucial for understanding the relationship between the playbill and the theatrical public sphere.[8]

Although the question of institutional continuity might seem to be even more ephemeral and intangible than past performance events themselves, it needs to be posed. For centuries playbills regulated the communication between theatres as institutions and their publics. Before the invention of theatre posters and programs they also fulfilled a double function of advertising performances as well as providing information on casts, contents, and prices. Playbills in fact formed a crucial link between the inside and the outside of the institution, between the social world of the public and the socio-aesthetic practices of the theatre.

THE THEATRICAL PUBLIC SPHERE

Any study of the theatregoing public needs to engage with the political and social sphere(s) in which it is situated. The public sphere or *Öffentlich-*

keit, as defined by Jürgen Habermas, emerges in the eighteenth century when, according to Habermas's now intensively critiqued argument, the emerging bourgeois class engaged in processes of self-definition, political emancipation, and aesthetic taste-refinement. In the context of feudal structures in France and Germany, Habermas defines the public sphere as a domain where bourgeois virtues of Enlightenment reason and discourses could be practiced, more or less outside the strictures of absolutist political control. Habermas's concept is primarily a political one, in which he problematizes the notion of political discourse as a precondition of democracy. While the political thrust of Habermas's argument is too general to be applied broadly to theatre (although in specific highly politicized contexts in which theatre and theatrical behavior come to the forefront it can be), its implied spatiality can be usefully expanded as a concept for thinking about theatre's role in civic and political life.

An important variation on the concept of the public sphere is offered by Richard Sennett in *The Fall of Public Man* (1977), a large-scale study of the transformation of Western society from the eighteenth to the twentieth century.[9] The theatre plays a much more central role in Sennett's study than in Habermas's argument. The focus, however, is different. Sennett is primarily concerned with uncovering the factors that have contributed to what he sees as a serious problem of the present: the impoverishment of public life, the enervation of community, and the retreat into the limitations of the conjugal family and the narcissism of the individual psyche. Although rich in theatrical material, Sennett's theory is less useful than Habermas for actually defining the public sphere theoretically and historically because of its somewhat teleological argument predicated on explaining social practices of the present.

In its much discussed and often maligned role as arbiter of taste and aesthetic judgment, the public emerges as a rhetorical entity of adjudication, a central function defined in the late seventeenth century which continues today.[10] The famous statement often attributed to H. L. Mencken—"Nobody ever went broke underestimating the taste of the American public"—offers perhaps the definitive cynical statement on this issue. The public's taste in art and/or entertainment is of course an important question, especially in an ephemeral art form such as theatre. I use the term "art form" in this context to refer to a particular historical development in the relationship between theatre and its public. The context between public taste and purely aesthetic judgment, however, is not a problem that I wish to pursue here.[11] My concern is instead the special combination of social, aesthetic, political, and institutional relations that theatrical *mediality*, by definition, creates and sustains. Like television, the medium of theatre fulfills a number of functions, the main one being the purveying of entertainment in different genres and degrees of complexity.

Since its original definition by Habermas the semantic field of the term "public sphere" has been extended considerably, especially in the wake of the English translation of Habermas's book in 1989. These extensions can be divided into three main areas: the public sphere as (1) a space or location, (2) a substantialized concept, and (3) a relational object.

1. In its English translation as "public sphere," the German term *Öffentlichkeit*, which could be rendered more precisely as "publicness," has a clear spatial orientation.[12] The spatiality of the term, however, is not just a chance residue of translation. In Habermas's definition of the concept and particularly in the context of its historical emergence, it can be thought of concretely in terms of a particular space. Central to the concept is the distinction between public and private spheres. As bourgeois society placed ever more emphasis and value on privacy and the private realm, particularly on the conjugal family in contrast to the theatrical openness of aristocratic intercourse (from the *levée* to the court festivals), so too did it define and emphasize the importance of public discourse. This took place either through media such as journals, newspapers, or books or, as Habermas famously argues, in new socially sanctioned spaces of communication such as salons and coffee houses. Here meanings were made, opinions formed and debated, and the seeds of democratic processes sown.
2. Beyond its spatial connotations, the public sphere has become a substantialized concept *sui generis*. The public sphere does not just reside somewhere, a specific place of communication; it is also a conceptual entity with a history and discrete semantic dimensions. This identifiable something changes over time; it has a diachronic dimension, which we can trace developmentally, yet it is also subject to social differentiation on the synchronic plane. An important part of Habermas's argument focuses on the multiple semantic dimensions of the term "public." It must be seen not just in contradistinction to the idea of the "private" but also in the terms and sense of public service—that is, the emergence of bureaucratic institutions developed as a counterbalance to the "representative" publicness of feudal rule.[13] While the diachronic dimension lies at the heart of Habermas's argument—the structural transformation

and ultimately degeneration of the public sphere—its social and functional differentiation is less apparent in the original formulation. A focus on differentiation, however, is one of the major contributions of recent studies on the idea of the public sphere.[14]

3. For a theatre-historical perspective it is important to understand the public sphere as a *relational object*. Certainly the public, and perhaps also the public sphere in its spatial sense, came to be regarded as something that can be acted on, appealed to, influenced, and even manipulated. This conception of a somewhat passive entity ultimately provides the precondition for the emergence of the practices of publicity and public relations. All institutions highly dependent on public participation (such as museums, concert houses, or theatres) expend considerable energy in assessing the nature of the public and the public sphere. What are their spatial and quantitative limits? How can the public be reached, exploited, or nurtured?

In summary we can say that the theatrical public sphere must be understood as the interaction of these three mutually dependent categories. The spatial concept of a realm of theatrical interaction primarily outside the building merges into a conceptual entity that ultimately becomes so palpable that it functions as an extension of the institution.

On an operational level it is possible to differentiate the theatrical public sphere into at least two distinct realms. The first realm can be understood in terms of institutional communication strategies, using playbills but also later advertisements, articles in newspapers, and broadsheets. The second realm of the theatrical public sphere refers to the debates surrounding particular productions, usually issuing from professional criticism but not coterminous with it. Occasionally this exchange of opinions can transform into scandals when aesthetic and/or social transgressions within the context of theatre are debated. When institutional communication (realm 1) cites reviews (realm 2) for publicity purposes, then the two realms are intertextually combined. In this case, the theatre review—the familiar document of theatrical reception research traditionally used by scholars to reconstruct aesthetic response to a production—begins to circulate outside the inner realm of theatrical space and enters the theatrical public sphere.

The concept of a theatrical public sphere poses additional questions of semantic spatiality that Habermas already anticipates in his study. The rise of a theatregoing "public" in the context of courtly theatre culture throws into sharp relief a distinction between the audience (*Publikum*) and the public sphere (*Öffentlichkeit*). A simple distinction between the collectivized group of individuals inside the building and the larger sociological entity of those outside—or from the point of view of the marketing department (to use a deliberate anachronism) those who have bought a ticket and those who have not—is somewhat facile when it comes to theorizing the social and political place of theatre in a public sphere. The important differentiation between inside and outside, or in Habermas's terms between the private and the public, is a tricky one in reference to theatre. From the point of view of political and juridical control—in the eighteenth and nineteenth centuries—a theatre is a public gathering place with a high potential for unrest. From the point of view of contemporary theatre and performance studies with an emphasis on gauging the aesthetic response to a performance or discussions of performances on the arts pages of newspapers, the theatre is largely separated from the outside world. In European theatrical culture at least, the status of the theatregoing public as part of the outside public changes perceptibly between the nineteenth and twentieth centuries, an alteration that can be measured by two yardsticks. These changes are revealed, on the one hand, by the gradual disappearance of censorship (at different times in different countries) and, on the other, by the famous darkening of the auditorium with its concomitant exclusive focus on the artistic event onstage and the near invisibility of the other spectators. By the beginning of the twentieth century we can observe the lineaments of fragmented theatrical public spheres, at least in the larger metropolitan centers, as particular institutions develop strategies to cultivate "their" public, the emergence of a pluralized public sphere.[15] Indeed, a central feature of late nineteenth-century theatres in large cities is their cultivation of particular audiences and by definition the public spheres in which they act and communicate. In London theatre, the famous actor-managers such as Herbert Beerbohm Tree at Her/His Majesty's, Henry Irving at the Lyceum, the Bancrofts at the Haymarket, and George Alexander at St. James's expended considerable time and energy on reading and catering to the diversified theatregoing public.

As these comments suggest, the theatrical public sphere has many dimensions and involves a number of unresolved theoretical and conceptual questions. Although theatre scholars have continually engaged with questions of the audience from a variety of perspectives, few attempts have been made to theorize and establish a conceptual entity known as the "theatrical public sphere." Some recent research is beginning to rectify this lacuna, but even studies that work explicitly with the concept still have a tendency to conflate audience and public or to read the public sphere in aesthetic terms.[16]

One conclusion can be drawn from these critiques: although we may not be able to define it, and we may know it when we see it, the crucial factor lacking is a more precise way to investigate the theatrical public sphere. The playbill, a key element in maintaining dialogue between institutions and their publics, provides a valuable resource.

THE PLAYBILL AND THE THEATRICAL PUBLIC SPHERE

The playbill belongs to a special group of theatre-historical documents that—while extensively used—remain under-researched as a discrete category of archival source material. As Marvin Carlson notes in an essay on the theatre program, the program or playbill, although "a privileged primary document" of theatre historians, has only received the scarcest treatment from a methodological and historical perspective. This may reflect an earlier disinterest among theatre historians in metatheoretical research or interrogation of their sources, with the result that even basic terminological distinctions are unclear. Carlson points out that in the nineteenth century even a clear-cut distinction between playbill and theatre program is not possible:

> One sometimes finds in modern historical writing on the theatre a distinction attempted between a playbill, taken to mean the long and narrow theatrical announcements almost universally employed in England and America in the eighteenth and early nineteenth centuries, and a program, containing perhaps identical information but composed of one or more folded sheets printed on both sides. Connected with this distinction is the assumption that the function of playbills is for public posting, and that of programs for distribution or sale within the theatre.[17]

Carlson goes on to argue that playbills, as well as being publicly posted, were also sold or distributed inside theatres and therefore fulfilled the same function as programs. While he focuses on material "designed to be available to the audience member during the actual production,"[18] the playbill can be more expansively examined in terms of its use for "public posting" and by looking at the articulations between inside and outside, between the public and private spheres as they changed over time. Playbills provide a plethora of detailed and largely neglected information on these articulations and points of contact.

As Carlson indicates, systematic research into playbills (especially in the English and American theatre) is hard to come by. Scholars traditionally located the origins of the English playbill in the late seventeenth century, its heyday roughly in the eighteenth and nineteenth centuries, and the medium's disappearance toward the end of the nineteenth century (as it became superseded by the theatre program on the one hand and the poster on the other, when its double function was effectively divided between two specialist media). This chronology is based on the archival record. The earliest surviving playbill in the English-speaking theatre dates from the Restoration period, from the year 1670 or 1692, depending on which lexicon is consulted.[19] German scholars have located examples as early as the fifteenth and sixteenth century; by the middle of the seventeenth centuries playbills were in widespread use, especially among the strolling English players and their German spin-offs.[20] Recent research demonstrates incontrovertibly that playbills were in use in the early modern period for any kind of performed entertainment on offer when a printing press was available to produce them. In a 2006 essay Tiffany Stern sifts the written evidence and produces a wealth of references that demonstrate the ubiquity of playbills throughout the Elizabethan period. Her earliest example dates from 1567 and records, significantly perhaps, the story of a swindler who advertises a performance of an "antyke play" by means of playbills, collects money from the spectators, and then absconds, leaving the audience wondering when the performance will begin. It is such examples, of course, that give playbills a bad name. In this case, our earliest evidence for playbills is for a performance that never took place.[21]

Stern's research makes clear that London houses and "posts" were regularly pasted with playbills and other kinds of printed advertisements. It was not unusual to send out a servant around nine o'clock in the morning to collect the newest bills of the day for the master's or mistress's perusal. The ubiquity of bills reached such a level that, much like the theatre itself, they came to be seen as an evil among the antitheatrical fraternity (whose diatribes, significantly, provide some of our most reliable documents). Stern notes the example of the "inconstant" gentleman diverted from church to the playhouse by means of a playbill portrayed in George Wither's *Abuses Stript and Whipt* (1613): "Through the medium of bills the theater has corrupted the pedestrians in the streets of London."[22]

The sparse research on playbills can be divided into roughly two groups. The first, which could be termed the "hunter and gatherer" approach, is primarily concerned with collecting, collating, and commenting on these sources. This approach goes back to the nineteenth century, when the first collections began to be compiled. Some of them, such as the holdings in the Victoria and Albert Museum, run into the hundreds of thousands. At its best, the hunter and gatherer approach has provided us with a history of the medium itself from its debatable origins in the late sixteenth century to its disappearance and replacement in the early twentieth.[23]

Attempts to theorize the medium itself or at least to harness it for more complex readings of theatre history—the second approach—are much less widespread. Jacky Bratton, however, has proposed within the framework of what she terms "intertheatricality" a new way to analyze playbills. In Bratton's understanding an intertheatrical reading—in analogy to intertextuality—goes beyond a focus on a particular text or event and seeks to reconstruct, as far as possible, "the mesh of connections between all kinds of theatre texts, and between texts and their users." She emphasizes the interdependence of performances within a given theatrical tradition, the importance of memory on the part of audiences and performers, and the dynamics of transmission, even across generations. A key source to gaining access to this complex web of memory and meaning is the playbill, which, she argues, needs to be read in more complex ways in order to gain an understanding of "those most difficult and evanescent aspects of theatre history—the expectations and disposition of the audience."[24]

Playbills can be read in a variety of ways, as Bratton's approach makes clear. Most recent approaches attempt to mine the bills for information relating to a particular performance, set of plays or authors, or even mobility on the part of actors. Some scholars are also drawing on playbills to assemble biographical records on various performers—the range of roles, the types of plays, the theatre performed at—as part of the chronological record of a career. Alas, they are seldom studied in terms of their internal textuality, interreferentiality, and communication structures.[25]

Playbills can also be analyzed in order to understand the role of the theatre in the public sphere. This means harnessing a number of the previously discussed approaches and expanding on these to examine not the putative performance but the public itself and how specific theatres relate to it. By definition playbills are part of the public space of any community. As media whose primary function is to advertise and communicate by a variety of mainly verbal means (ranging from precise information on times, places, and processes to emotive appeals to the public's attention), they are part of an ongoing "broadcast culture" that begins in the early modern period, when they vied for attention with other documents of the public domain, such as official pronouncements, legal bills, broadsides and broadsheets, and even libels. As Tiffany Stern demonstrates for the early modern period, these different documents were posted in the same visual field and were therefore decoded in relation to one another: "Space itself was 'read'; playbills were not only hung with siquises [*sic*] and libels, but also in apposition to the formal, sanctioned authorized space of the printed legal bill."[26] The question of legality is crucial, because the theatres were continually being constrained by permissions, legal requirements, and even interdictions.

By the mid-seventeenth century playbills took on a fixed form, consisting of around half a dozen different informational and communication units. Utilizing a variety of typographical formats, a late seventeenth-century German playbill was usually structured as follows:

Authorization (civic or courtly)
Name and privileges of the troupe
Title of plays
Contents of main play (usually in highly ornate language)
Title of comical afterpiece
Prices
Place and time of performance
(sometimes located after the authorization)

During the eighteenth century this basic formula began to be expanded to include additional information, the most important being the names of characters, performers, and authors. Because troupes in German-speaking Europe were almost invariably itinerant until the mid-eighteenth century, and the permission to perform by no means guaranteed, the formulaic pronouncements of authorization ("By permission of his most esteemed . . .") constituted the first and most expressly political point of articulation between the troupe and the public sphere. Without the perlocutionary force of such declarations of assent, often iconographically underscored by the largest and most ornate typeface on the bill, the performances could not take place. The public was provided with a kind of aristocratic seal of approval and sanction. As the eye travels down the bill, the information becomes more prosaic and pragmatic, culminating in the mundane practicalities of prices, times, and places.

The most important addition to the playbills in German-speaking countries after the mid-eighteenth century is the naming of actors and authors. While the names of characters and their interrelationships ("son of"; "servant to") are frequently found on playbills, often in the context of plot summaries, available evidence suggests that actors only entered the public gaze on the bill after 1750 as part of a concerted effort to increase their social status.[27] The deliberate and, initially at least, ostentatious identification of actors and actresses marks a crucial reorganization of the relationship between theatres and the public sphere. Theatres begin to use the charismatic (and sometimes erotic) appeal of their performers to establish a more permanent point of articulation between the institution and the public. The promise of propinquity with performers is clearly a crucial appeal of theatrical performance, and all the more so when the objects of attraction enjoy a somewhat questionable social and moral status. The often less than prominent positioning of authors (if they feature at all) can also be attributed to such communication strategies that privilege the present live performer over the (normally) absent author.

As the troupes became settled, they were granted access to longer-term leases of playhouses or at least buildings convertible to that purpose. Therefore the necessity for courtly or civic patronage became less crucial for the functioning of theatre. This probably explains why the first line of playbills proclaiming political authorization begins to disappear or becomes integrated into the institutional frame of the theatre. Often such patronage retains little more than the incorporation of the term "Royal" or its various continental cognates. In London it would indicate the possession of a patent; in Germany or France it might index a more substantial financial contribution or the granting of a license on the part of the court. This shift in status is reflected iconographically in the playbills, which retain such information, although it no longer carries the performative force of actual permission being granted. Whatever the actual legal status of such political references, they retain (albeit in a much reduced form) a direct acknowledgment of the institution's dependence on political and legal forces. They indicate an important point of articulation between the artistic and institutional functions of the theatre or troupe.

Such changes of articulation can be observed in the frequently reproduced playbill announcing the première of Wolfgang Amadeus Mozart's *The Magic Flute* in Vienna on September 30, 1791, at the Theater auf der Wieden (fig. 1). Although essentially a commercial popular theatre located in what was then a suburban part of Vienna, it still required a license to operate: hence the ornate banderole "K.K. [kaiserlich-königlich: imperial-royal, the official designation of the Austrian throne] priviligiertes Wiedner Theater" playfully interwoven with the imperial double eagle and capering cherubs. The title takes iconographical pride of place, followed

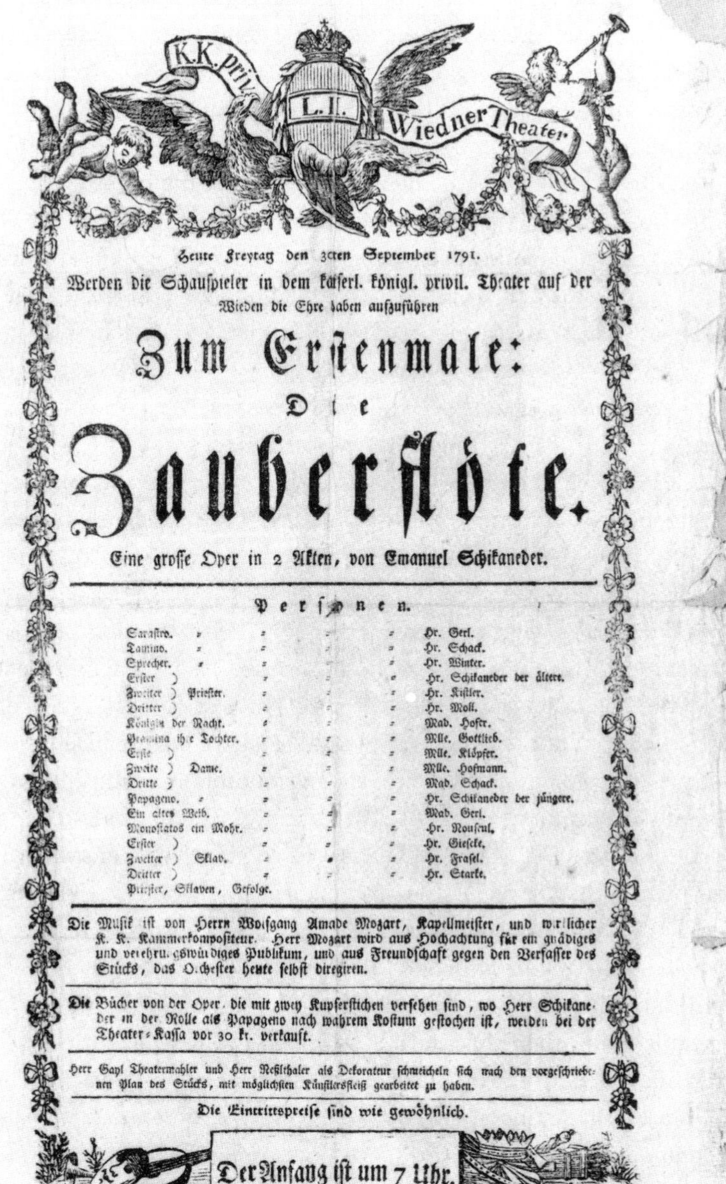
K.K. priv. L.I. Wiedner Theater

Heute Freytag den 30ten September 1791.

Werden die Schauspieler in dem kaiserl. königl. privil. Theater auf der Wieden die Ehre haben aufzuführen

Zum Erstenmale:

Die

Zauberflöte.

Eine grosse Oper in 2 Akten, von Emanuel Schikaneder.

Personen.

Sarastro.	Hr. Gerl.
Tamino.	Hr. Schack.
Sprecher.	Hr. Winter.
Erster)	Hr. Schikaneder der ältere.
Zweiter) Priester.	Hr. Kistler.
Dritter)	Hr. Moll.
Königin der Nacht.	Mad. Hofer.
Pamina ihre Tochter.	Mlle. Gottlieb.
Erste)	Mlle. Klöpfer.
Zweite) Dame.	Mlle. Hofmann.
Dritte)	Mad. Schack.
Papageno.	Hr. Schikaneder der jüngere.
Ein altes Weib.	Mad. Gerl.
Monostatos ein Mohr.	Hr. Nouseul.
Erster)	Hr. Giesecke.
Zweiter) Sklav.	Hr. Frasel.
Dritter)	Hr. Starke.
Priester, Sklaven, Gefolge.	

Die Musik ist von Herrn Wolfgang Amade Mozart, Kapellmeister, und wirklicher K. K. Kammerkompositeur. Herr Mozart wird aus Hochachtung für ein gnädiges und verehrungswürdiges Publikum, und aus Freundschaft gegen den Verfasser des Stücks, das Orchester heute selbst diregiren.

Die Bücher von der Oper, die mit zwey Kupferstichen versehen sind, wo Herr Schikaneder in der Rolle als Papageno nach wahrem Kostum gestochen ist, werden bei der Theater-Kassa vor 30 kr. verkauft.

Herr Gayl Theatermahler und Herr Neßlthaler als Dekorateur schmeicheln sich nach dem vorgeschriebenen Plan des Stücks, mit möglichsten Künstlersfleiß gearbeitet zu haben.

Die Eintrittspreise sind wie gewöhnlich.

Der Anfang ist um 7 Uhr.

1. Playbill for the première of *Die Zauberflöte* at the Theater auf der Wieden, September 30, 1791. Folio format. Private collection.

by the name of librettist, manager, and first Papageno, Emanuel Schikaneder. Characters and performers are all named. A separate section of the bill in a smaller typeface mentions the composer, a "Mister Wolfgang Amade Mozart," the "conductor and court composer," who "out of respect for a gracious and esteemed public and friendship toward the author of the play will conduct the orchestra himself." Beneath the section on the composer, the playbill alerts the public to the sale of the libretti: "The books of the opera, which are provided with two engravings, where Mr. Schikaneder is depicted in the role of Papageno in the true costume, are on sale at the box office for 30 crowns." The final section of the bill makes reference to the scene painters, Mr. Sayl and Mr. Kesslthaler, who "flatter themselves to have worked from the prescribed plan of the play and with the greatest possible artistic diligence." The bill concludes with the reference to prices, here "as usual," and the time of the performance: 7 P.M.

These playbills combine basic information (times, prices, and so forth) with appeals to the public's aesthetic sensibilities. Evidently the promise of an engraving of Schikaneder in "the true costume" of Papageno (presumably referring to the costume actually worn onstage rather than being a product of the engraver's creative imagination) served to promote the sale of the libretti. The reference to the artistically diligent scene painters evokes Schikaneder's reputation for spectacular scenery and stage effects. The delegation of the composer to a subsidiary typographical position is not just symptomatic of the status of composers in eighteenth-century operatic theatre in general but also indicative of the standard pattern of communication between the theatre and its public. The drawing card on this popular stage was the theatre's manager and principal actor Schikaneder, not the court composer and conductor Mozart. The reference to the "gracious and esteemed public" is particularly important. Half a century earlier such appellations would have been reserved for the local prince or mayor, but now the public itself has entered the playbill.

While this information may be very specific to a particular theatre and its impresario, its inclusion in a playbill serves to demonstrate that the medium itself is the main transporter of communication between the institution and the public. It is not so much the specificity of particular snippets of information but the actual medium of the playbill that is crucial. Compared to the basic form developed in the mid-sixteenth century and developed further during the seventeenth century, by the end of the eighteenth century the playbill had become a medium in its own right and probably the most important point of articulation between the institution and its public. All institutions, and particularly complex ones such as theatres, are reliant on additional media to communicate and sustain contact with the public sphere.

As we move into the nineteenth century, we can see a spectacular expansion of this communicative function. Most theatres in Europe were privately run commercial operations, so the need to provide the public with information over and above the performance-related data clearly gained in importance. An early nineteenth-century playbill (fig. 2) documents how theatres needed to locate themselves in the civic life of the towns and cities that supported them (although usually not by direct subsidy). The playbill from the New Theatre Royal in Glasgow in 1840 demonstrates that a typical theatrical evening in the first half of the nineteenth century consisted of four or five different items and performative genres: a tragedy, a song, an interlude (short play), a highland fling, and a farce. Playbills of this period, as this example indicates, usually included metacommentary in the form of self-laudatory critical responses: "received last night with loud laughter and applause." Apart from performance-related data, playbills were often used by theatre managers for a variety of communicative functions, ranging from self-promotion to audience regulation. In this case the playbill announces in detail the reopening of the theatre by its proprietor, John Henry Alexander, and includes a form of promotional advertising for the local tradesmen involved in the building. The playbill also advertises for doormen, contains information of a regulatory nature ("Children in arms not Admitted" and "no Smoking allowed in the Galleries"), and describes in the "Notice to the Frequenters of the Boxes" an innovation to provide better circulation of air. Playbills invariably include information on pricing; in this case, we learn that it was common practice to be admitted later in the evening at a reduced price for the remaining performances.[28]

Playbills have become "complex texts," at least in the sense that they cannot be scanned quickly but need to be carefully scrutinized. This very act of intense reading, it could be argued, produces an engagement with the institution, almost a state of absorption, as the public is informed of all manner of activities related to the theatre. We gain the impression of an authorial voice speaking to a readership. In this case the voice is unmistakably that of Alexander, the embattled manager of the New Theatre Royal, who engages in a conversation with his "public."

One of the striking aspects of this bill is the explicit and repeated mention of the public itself. As Habermas argues in *The Structural Transfor-*

W. 2. N. 12.

New Theatre Royal, Dunlop Street.

Continued Success! Crowded Houses—and roars of laughter and applause!!!

THE PUBLIC is respectfully informed that this THEATRE, being COMPLETED, has now

Opened for the Season.

In announcing the Completion of this important and hazardous undertaking, the Proprietor wishes as much as possible to abstain from the too hacknied custom of "puffing," or lavishing on his exertions that praise which the magnitude of this speculation might warrant, the Public alone will judge of the efforts which have been made for their Accommodation, it may not, however, be too much to say, that this Edifice has been erected with a splendour and magnificence (regardless of cost), and will bear comparison, it is presumed, with any thing of a Theatrical nature in this country. The Manager has, on many occasions, found his exertions responded to by the Citizens of Glasgow, and has not thought it too much, at least, a third time, to peril his capital and "hazard the die," in the service of that Public who have so frequently honoured his exertions with patronage and support.

THE BUILDING,

From Designs by Mr. W SPENCE, Architect, is Erected by Mr. W. BROOM. The JOINER WORK, by ARCHIBALD EDMISTON, Esq. The PLUMBER DEPARTMENT, by Mr. ARCHD. FERGUSON. The SLATER WORK, by Mr. S. WILSON. The PILLARS and other CASTINGS, from the Foundry of Mr. W. GRAY. The PLASTER and ORNAMENTAL STUCCO WORK, by Mr. J. CAIRD. The GAS FITTINGS, by Messrs. ANDREW LIDDELL & Co. The CHANDELIERS, by Mr. ALEXANDER BROWNE. The ROYAL ARMS, over the Stage, and ORNAMENTAL CARVING, by Mr. MURRAY. The STAINED GLASS WINDOW, in Front of the Building, by Mr W. CAIRNEY. The DECORATIVE PAINTING, by Messrs. MICHAEL BOGLE & Co. The whole of the Scenery, by Mr. DUDGEON, of that Firm. The IMITATION MARBLE, PILASTERS, and COLUMNS, by Monsieur VICTOR BOURGEOT, Decorative Painter from Paris. The MACHINERY of the STAGE, upon the improved Principles of the Theatres Royal, Drury Lane, Covent Garden, and Liverpool, by Mr. W. HARVEY, and numerous Assistants. The whole under the entire direction of Mr. ALEXANDER.

THE COMPANY,

So far as the superintendence of this important undertaking would permit, has been selected with the utmost care, from the principal Theatres in the United Kingdom, but as this is a portion of the undertaking negociated for at a distance, the Manager does not warrant with the same freedom as that contracted for on the spot, and which has been submitted to his judgment, he can only say, that in point of numbers it is Efficient, and complete in many Departments, and whatever is found dissatisfactory will be changed or improved, according to trial and the opinion of the true unprejudiced patrons of the Drama in this City.

This Evening, Saturday, March 28, 1840,

Will be presented, the favourite Tragedy of,

Jane Shore:

Or, The Unfortunate Favourite.

Lord Hastings, Mr. CHARLES PITT—Duke of Glo'ster, Mr. ALEXANDER—Dumont, Mr. J. W. BENSON—Belmour, Mr. HOLMES.
Sir William Catesby, Mr. CLIFTON—Sir Richard Ratcliffe, Mr. BECKETT—Lord Derby, Mr. CHAPMAN—Lord Lenox, Mr. BELFOUR.
Earl of Pembroke, Mr. COVENEY—Porter, Mr. J. NEWTON—Officer, Mr. ARMSTRONG.
Jane Shore, Mrs. FISHER—Alicia, Mrs. J. NEWTON.

END OF THE PLAY,
A FAVOURITE SONG, BY MISS J. COVENEY.

After which, for the third time this season, the very popular Interlude, in one Act, entitled

STATE SECRETS:

OR, THE TAILOR OF TAMWORTH.

Received on Tuesday evening, with shouts of laughter and applause.
Gregory Thimblewell, the Tailor of Tamworth, Mr. ALEXANDER.
Master Hugh Neville, (an officer serving in the army of the Parliament, commanded by General, Fairfax,) Mr. HOLMES.
Calverton Hal, a Cavalier belonging to the army of Prince Rupert, Mr. BELLAIR.
Humphrey Hedgehog, a wealthy Miller, and Landlord of the Black Bull Inn, Tamworth, Mr J. NEWTON.
Robert, Son of Gregory Thimblewell, Mr. BECKETT—Soldiers, Peasants, &c.
Maude Thimblewell, (the Tailor's Wife), Mrs. CLIFTON—Letty, Daughter of Hedgehog, Mrs. J. NEWTON.

IN THE COURSE OF THE EVENING,
THE HIGHLAND FLING, BY MISS H. COVENEY.

To conclude with, for the second time this season, the laughable Farce of,

ENGLISH,
Irish, and Scotch.

Received last night with loud laughter and applause.
Patrick O'Shocknessy, Mr. J. DALY—Donald, Mr. ALEXANDER—Timothy Clod, Mr. J. NEWTON—Captain Charleton, Mr. J. W. BENSON.
Charles Fairfield, Mr. HOLMES—Old Drossly, Mr. FISHER—Young Drossly, Mr. BECKETT.
Dick, Mr. CHAPMAN—John, Mr. BELFOUR—Gardner, Mr. COVENEY—Servant, Mr. ARMSTRONG.
Maria Wilburton, Mrs. J. NEWTON—Louisa, Drossly, with a Song, Miss J. COVENEY—Peggy, Mrs. ARMSTRONG.

On MONDAY, Massinger's admired Play of **A New Way to Pay Old Debts,** after which **Mr and Mrs White.** To Conclude with, **False and True;** Or, **The Irishman in Naples.**

☞ In preparation, a New Farce entitled **THE HAPPY MAN,** which will shortly be produced, with various other Novelties.

WANTED,
Two active, steady, respectable Persons, as CHECKERS at the Doors. Apply to the MANAGER.

Tickets and Places for the Boxes may be had of Mr MUIR, at the Box Office of the Theatre, from 11 till 3 o'clock.

Pass-out Checks not Transferable—Children in arms not Admitted to any part of the Theatre—and no Smoking allowed in the Galleries on any account.

PRICES:—
FIRST PRICE.—Lower Boxes, **4s. 0d.**—Upper Do., **3s. 6d.**—Pitt, **2s. 6d.**—First Gallery, **1s. 6d.**—Second Do., **1s. 0d.**
SECOND DO.—Lower Boxes, **2s. 6d.**—Upper Do., **2s. 0d.**—Pitt, **1s. 6d.**—First Gallery, **1s. 0d.**—Second Do., **0s. 6d.**
SECOND PRICE AT A QUARTER BEFORE NINE O'CLOCK.

☞ NOTICE TO THE FREQUENTERS OF THE BOXES.

This part of the Theatre has been constructed on a novel and it is hoped improved principle, the backs have sliding pannels, which on a night when the Theatre is crowded the Manager has reserved to himself the power of opening, for the purpose of allowing the heated air to escape, and of giving accommodation to any persons wishing to occupy the lobbies. This intimation is considered necessary in order that no complaint may be made against such privilege, at the same time it is respectfully submitted to public approval and hoped will be found an improvement rather than an inconvenience to any person frequenting that part of the Theatre.

☞ The following Certificate from the Lord DEAN OF GUILD, is respectfully submitted to the Public:—
Having again considered this Petition, with the Report of Mr. Robert Taylor, Mason and Builder, and John Scott, Wright and Builder, Find it established by the said Report, that the NEW THEATRE, in DUNLOP STREET, lately erected by the Petitioner, has been Constructed in a Sufficient Manner; and that it may be Opened for the Reception of the Public, with complete Safety to the Lieges, and particularly to the persons frequenting the same; and declare and decern accordingly.

(Signed) JAS. BROWNE, D. G.

P. MACKENZIE & Co., PRINTERS

2. Playbill from the New Theatre Royal, Dunlop Street, Glasgow, Saturday, March 28, 1840. By permission of the Special Collections Department, Glasgow University Library.

mation of the Public Sphere, the term "public" undergoes a crucial transformation in the second half of the eighteenth century, which begins in the realm of literature, theatre, and the arts.[29] The opening paragraph of this bill bears out Habermas's thesis in striking fashion. "The Public" is the direct object of appellation in a variety of guises. "The PUBLIC is respectfully informed" that it will be the sole judge of the proprietor's efforts in rebuilding the New Theatre Royal and that his efforts in running the theatre have been "in the service of that Public who have so frequently honoured his exertions with patronage and support." Commercial business is clothed here in the language of "public service." The abstract "public" alternates significantly with "Citizens of Glasgow," so we gain a clear perception that the envisaged public sphere potentially encompasses the whole city. Direct exhortations to the public return at the bottom of the bill, where a certificate of safety from the lord dean of the Guild of Builders is cited to inform the said public of the building's conformity with safety regulations.

Of particular interest is the second to last section of the bill, signposted by a pointed finger: "NOTICE TO THE FREQUENTERS OF THE BOXES." The public is informed of an innovation whereby the boxes have been fitted with sliding panels, which can be removed at the manager's discretion to release "heated air." Alexander evidently considered the notice necessary because the intimate private space of the boxes could be opened up to public scrutiny from the adjacent lobbies. I am less interested in the specific architectural innovation being documented here than in the politics of communication it indexes. This novelty too is "respectfully submitted to public approval." This statement demonstrates the existence (at least in the proprietor's mind) of an entity that needs to be informed and prepared before being transformed into a paying audience.

Alexander's concern to communicate between the "inner-life" of his building and the outside world demonstrates a central function of the playbill in the nineteenth century. While the removal of the back panels of the boxes is an architectural measure with potentially intimate consequences for the "frequenters," it remains in the realm of the material building. German playbills of the mid- to late nineteenth century go a few steps further by regularly reporting on the conditions, locations, and status of performers, sometimes even exposing the most intimate details of the performers' bodies to the public gaze. Playbills issued by Munich's court theatres in the mid-nineteenth century informed the public about the absences of performers on a daily basis. For example, a bill issued on March 26, 1874 (fig. 3) alerts the reader near the bottom of the sheet:

München. Donnerstag den 26. März 1874. № 84.

Anzeiger für die Königlichen Theater.

Der von der Kgl. Hofbuchdruckerei Dr. C. Wolf & Sohn herausgegebene „Anzeiger für die Königlichen Theater" tritt an Stelle der bisher veröffentlichten Theaterzettel mit Ausnahme der für die Straßenecken bestimmten Anschlagzettel. Der „Anzeiger" bringt außer den vollständigen Theaterzetteln für das Kgl. Hof- und Nationaltheater, das Kgl. Residenztheater und das Kgl. Theater am Gärtnerplatz in zwangloser Folge officielle Mittheilungen über die Kgl. Theater in München, Nachrichten über auswärtige Schauspiel- und Opern-Aufführungen u. s. w., sowie die Wochen-Repertoires der hervorragensten Bühnen Deutschlands.

Abonnementspreis jährlich 3 fl. Einzelne Nummern 3 kr. Expedition: Kgl. Hofbuchdruckerei von Dr. C. Wolf & Sohn

Königliches Residenz-Theater.

Außer Abonnement.

Zum ersten Male:

Ehre um Ehre.

Schauspiel in fünf Aufzügen von Paul Heyse.

In Scene gesetzt vom K. Ober-Regisseur Herrn Possart.

Personen:

König Ludwig XV. . . . . Herr Richter.
Marquis von Chavigny . . . . Herr Herz.
Marquise von Chavigny . . . . Frau Dahn-Hausmann.
Blanche von Villarçon, ihre Nichte . . . . . Fräulein Johanna Meyer.
Herzog von Bienville . . . . Herr Possart.
Robert von Boissy, Gardecapitaine . . . . . . Herr Rüthling.
Patelin, Haushofmeister des Marquis . . . . . Herr Christen.
Charles, Robert von Boissy's Bedienter . . . . Herr Häusser.
Manon, Blanche's Kammerjungfer . . . . . . Fräulein Marie Meyer.
Der Wirth zu den „beiden Schwertern" . . . . . Herr Davideit.
Ein Offizier . . . . Herr Lewinger.
Erster } Lakai . . . . Herr Thoms.
Zweiter } Lakai . . . . Herr Nachreiner.
Herren und Damen vom Hofe. Lakaien.

as Stück spielt im Jahre 1746, die beiden ersten Aufzüge in einer kleinen Stadt, eine halbe Tagereise rdlich von Paris, der dritte Aufzug im Parke von Berneuil, der vierte in Paris, der fünfte wieder in Berneuil.

Kleine Preise:

Ein Parketsitz	1 fl. 12 kr.	Ein Platz im III. Rang	— fl. 36 kr.
Ein Platz in einer Parterreloge	1 fl. 12 kr.	Parterre	— fl. 24 kr.
Ein Platz im I. Rang	1 fl. 24 kr.	Amphitheater	— fl. 15 kr.
Ein Platz im II. Rang	— fl. 48 kr.		

Die Kasse wird um sechs Uhr geöffnet.

Anfang um 7 Uhr, Ende nach halb zehn Uhr.

Freier Eintritt ist Niemand gestattet.

Freitag den 27. März: (Im K. Hof- und Nationaltheater) (39.) **Julius Cäsar,** Trauerspiel von Shakespeare. (Marcus Antonius — Herr Barnay, vom Stadttheater in Frankfurt a. M., als letzte Gastrolle.) (Kleine Preise.)

Krank vom Opernpersonal: Herr **Weixlstorfer.**
Unpäßlich vom Schauspielpersonal: Fräulein **Ziegler.**
Beurlaubt vom Schauspielpersonal: Herr **Lang.**

Die Besucher des K. Theaters werden zur Vermeidung von Störungen um pünktliches Erscheinen ersucht.

Der einzelne Anzeiger kostet 3 kr. Kgl. Hofbuchdruckerei von Dr. C. Wolf & Sohn.

3. Playbill from the Königliches Residenz-Theater, Munich, Thursday, March 26, 1874. Source: *Münchner Theaterzettel 1807–1982: Altes Residenztheater, Nationaltheater, Prinzregenten-Theater, Odeon*, ed. Klaus Schulz (Munich/New York: Saur 1982).

SICK: Mr. Weixlstorfer of the opera personnel
INDISPOSED: Miss Ziegler of the acting personnel
ON VACATION: Mr. Lang of the acting personnel.[30]

The mention of Mr. Weixlstorfer's illness and Miss Ziegler's "indisposition" demonstrates that the health of performers is a subject deemed fit for public knowledge. Such notices are a regular feature of German playbills of the period and highlight that performers' private lives had an intrinsic public dimension as well, if only because their state of health impacted their function as performers. The reference to Ziegler's indisposition has an additional dimension: it can be, and probably was, read as a public announcement that Clara Ziegler, Munich's acclaimed acting diva, was menstruating. Like the English term "indisposed," the German word *unpäßlich* is euphemistic; but in the nineteenth century it was somewhat less ambiguous in reference to women.[31] Even with due regard to a nineteenth-century proclivity for euphemism, the distinction between "sick" and "indisposed" on a public playbill clearly needed to be made. Such an announcement raises a number of issues. The first is that the state of health or presence of actors at the court theatre was monitored and communicated daily. This was no doubt due to the public's expectation of seeing "their" performers and being given an explanation if this was not the case.

The second issue is obviously a gender one. The announcement of intimate physical details, albeit euphemistically camouflaged, highlights in almost explicit terms the function of performers as the most important point of articulation in late nineteenth-century European theatre. Since the inclusion of names of actors on playbills in the mid-eighteenth century, their social status had increased to the point where the public took an almost voyeuristic interest in their well-being. By 1874 Clara Ziegler was one of the leading actresses in the German-speaking world, specializing in tragic heroines. After a short-lived marriage to a mentor thirty years her senior, she never remarried; questions were raised — on the level of gossip — regarding her proclivities. Of course, gossip about performers and their personal lives had always circulated in various social networks and media across the centuries (such as coffee houses and newspaper caricatures in the eighteenth century). The important distinction here is that some of this information was now being officially promulgated via playbills.

The third point refers to the form of the playbill itself. It is entitled "Anzeiger für die Königlichen Theater" (Gazette for the Royal Theatres) and, as explained in a separate section of the bill, constitutes a new form of playbill, an addition to those of the individual Royal Theatres.[32] The announcement, placed directly under the main title, reads: "The Gazette for the Royal Theatres replaces the previously published playbills with the exception of the bills posted on street corners. Except for the full playbills for the Hof- und Nationaltheater, the Residenztheater, and the Royal Gärtnerplatz Theatre the 'gazette' provides official announcements pertaining to the Royal Theatres in Munich, news about other opera and drama performances, etc., as well as the weekly repertoires of Germany's outstanding stages." The gazette was a commercial operation—it could be purchased for a small sum or subscribed to—produced by the official court printer, Wolff & Son. After the unification of Germany and the expansion of rail transport, theatre was clearly becoming something of interest outside the local space. Troupes and actors traveled (Clara Ziegler would later make her living entirely from touring), but some spectators traveled too, it would seem. Whether traveling or not, the theatregoing public had a keen interest in the offerings outside the precincts of the city. We see here the emergence of a translocal theatrical public sphere, predicated on an imagined community of the new nation.

The decline of the playbill in the form discussed here is well known. As already mentioned, its informational functions were separated into two other media: the iconographic poster and the theatre program. Both emerged in the nineteenth century and coexisted with the playbill. In the same period we also see a proliferation of other print media (specialist magazines and periodicals, arts pages in newspapers) that began to expand and occupy the theatrical public sphere.

CONCLUSION

Playbills are an insufficiently studied and theorized category of sources in the theatre-historical archive. They are exceptionally varied in their form and content, ranging from laconic advices on time, place, and cost of a performance to extended treatises on the inner workings of an institution. The playbill is very clearly an institutional means to occupy the theatrical public sphere. It is largely univocal and does not easily accommodate feedback or a two-way conversation—it is the mouthpiece of the institution, not its blog. Nevertheless, these documents can be read in terms of their "implied" public. From the very earliest examples they speak to a reader and potential audience member. They inform but also cajole, appeal, solicit, even implore. By defining the public sphere, as opposed to the spectator or audience, as an object of theatre-historical research and by building on Habermas's concept and its later critiques, we can study the theatre public independent of the performance event. Theatre is thus much more than the sum of the individual performances; it consists of a complex set of institutional as much as artistic practices that need to be brought into historiographical focus. By extracting the playbill from the archive we can begin to gain access to these institutional cultures and practices.

NOTES

This essay benefited from discussions with Peter Marx (Bern), Meike Wagner (Munich), and the editors of this volume.

1. Jacky Bratton, *New Readings in Theatre History* (Cambridge: Cambridge University Press, 2003), p. 39.

2. For a discussion of theatre iconography, see Christopher Balme, "Interpreting the Pictorial Record: Theatre Iconography and the Referential Dilemma," *Theatre Research International* 22 (1997): 190–201; and Thomas Postlewait, "Eyewitness to History: Visual Evidence for Theatre in Early Modern England," in *The Oxford Handbook of Early Modern Theatre*, ed. Richard Dutton (Oxford: Oxford University Press, 2009), pp. 575–606. See also the essay "Seeing Is Believing: The Historian's Use of Images" by David Wiles (this volume).

3. Jürgen Habermas, *The Structural Transformation of the Public Sphere: An Inquiry into a Category of Bourgeois Society*, trans. Thomas Burger and Frederick Lawrence (Cambridge, Mass.: MIT Press, 1989; original German text published in 1962).

4. Max Herrmann, *Forschungen zur deutschen Theatergeschichte des Mittelalters und der Renaissance* (Berlin: Weidmann, 1914), p. 13 (my translation of the title and text).

5. For a more detailed discussion of the different approaches to studying "spectators" and "audiences," see Christopher Balme, *Cambridge Introduction to Theatre Studies* (Cambridge: Cambridge University Press, 2008), chapter 2. A considerable body of scholarship on both "spectators" and "audiences" exists. The link between space and audiences is investigated in Marvin Carlson, *Places of Performance: The Semiotics of Theatre Architecture* (Ithaca: Cornell University Press, 1989); and David Wiles, *A Short History of Western Performance Space* (Cambridge: Cambridge University Press, 2003). The broader question of "perception" and "performance" is explored in distinct ways in Susan Bennett, *Theatre Audiences*, rev. ed. (New York: Routledge, 1997); Marvin Carlson, "Theatre Audiences and the Reading of Performance," in *Interpreting the Theatrical Past: Essays in the Historiography of Performance*, ed. Thomas Postlewait and Bruce McConachie (Iowa City: University of Iowa Press, 1989), pp. 82–98; Willmar Sauter, *The Theatrical Event: Dynamics of Performance and Perception* (Iowa City: University of Iowa Press, 2000); and John Tulloch, *Shakespeare and Chekhov in Production: Theatrical Events and Their Audiences* (Iowa City: University of Iowa Press, 2005).

6. Historical theatre audiences have been the subject of study throughout the second half of the twentieth century. Alfred Harbage's *Shakespeare's Audience* (New York: Columbia University Press, 1941) ushered in a new sociological perspective on Elizabethan theatre and remains an important point of reference even though some of the factual details have been superseded by more recent studies such as Andrew Gurr's *Playgoing in Shakespeare's London*, 3rd ed. (Cambridge: Cambridge University Press, 2004). John Lough's *Paris Theatre Audiences in the Seventeenth and Eighteenth Centuries* (London: Oxford University Press 1957; revised 1972) provides a similar approach to the theatre of seventeenth- and eighteenth-century France.

7. Notable exceptions include work on the national theatre idea, which bridges the gap between a history of ideas and specific institutional histories. For the former, see Loren Kruger, *The National Stage: Theatre and Cultural Legitimation in England, France, and America* (Chicago: University of Chicago Press 1992); for a combination of the two, see Steve Wilmer, ed., *Writing and Rewriting National Theatre Histories* (Iowa City: University of Iowa Press, 2004).

8. Although not strictly a theoretical or historical treatment of institutions, Tracy Davis's major study *The Economics of the British Stage: 1800–1914* (Cambridge: Cambridge University Press, 2000) does in fact cover many institutional aspects.

9. Richard Sennett, *The Fall of Public Man* (New York: Norton, 1977; reissued in 1992). Sennett only acknowledges Habermas in passing.

10. Although the exact etymology is difficult to reconstruct, the concept of a public as an adjudicator of taste is found in the context of the French *doctrine classique* in the late seventeenth century and in England around the same time; see *Oxford English Dictionary*, online edition (http://www.oed.com), s.v. "public." A similar usage in German, "Publikum," emerges in the mid eighteenth century; see Peter Uwe Hohendahl, ed., *Öffentlichkeit: Geschichte eines kritischen Begriffs* (Stuttgart: Metzler, 2000), pp. 5–6.

11. A radicalized version of this debate emerges in modernism. With reference to both Habermas and Sennett, Martin Puchner has suggested that the affinity between the theatre (with its inherent collaborative production and collective reception) and the public sphere was a "key factor in the formation of specifically modernist anti-theatricalism" (*Stage Fright: Modernism, Anti-Theatricality, and Drama* [Baltimore: Johns Hopkins University Press, 2002], p. 11).

12. In the German original Habermas refers continually to *Öffentlichkeit* as a *Sphäre*, so that the English rendering of the term as "public sphere," while emphasizing spatiality more than the German does, is very close to Habermas's elaboration.

13. Habermas's historical argument hinges on two transformations: from a feudal "representative" public sphere to a bourgeois rational-critical one during the eighteenth century and then to the degeneration of the latter in the late nineteenth and twentieth centuries under the influence of mass media and the commodification of culture.

14. The reception of Habermas's book in the English-speaking world only really begins in the 1990s in the wake of its translation in 1989. The first critical stocktaking can be found in Craig Calhoun, ed., *Habermas and the Public Sphere* (Cambridge, Mass.: MIT Press, 1992); see especially his "Introduction." A review of post-1992 research and criti-

cism of the concept within historical studies is provided by Andreas Gestrich, "The Public Sphere and the Habermas Debate," *German History* 24.3 (2006): 413–430.

15. A central argument of Habermas's later (and some early) critics has been that his conception is too monolithic and not permissive of "counterspheres" responsive to class or, in the later versions, gender and ethnic difference. On this point, see Calhoun's caution about simply pluralizing the concept: "Introduction," p. 37.

16. For an example of the latter, see Lynn Voskuil, "Sensation Theater, Commodity Culture, and the Victorian Public Sphere," *Victorian Studies* 44.2 (2002): 245–274. Voskuil's argument focuses on reconstructing the "bodily sensations" generated by the genre of sensation drama and in this sense is interested more in the individual and collectivized spectator (audience) than in the public in the sense I have defined here.

17. Marvin Carlson, "The Development of the Theatre Program," in *The American Stage: Social and Economic Issues from the Colonial Period to the Present*, ed. Ron Engle and Tice L. Miller (New York: Cambridge University Press, 1993), pp. 101–114 (quotation on p. 102).

18. Ibid., p. 102.

19. For these dates, see the two articles in *Oxford Encyclopedia of Theatre and Performance*, ed. Dennis Kennedy (Oxford: Oxford University Press, 2003), vol. 2, p. 1043; and *Oxford Companion to the Theatre*, ed. Phyliss Hartnoll (Oxford: Oxford University Press, 1952), p. 619.

20. The earliest extant playbill in German is a 1466 handwritten bill from Hamburg advertising a passion play. The earliest printed playbill is from 1520 in Rostock and announces an allegorical play on the "seven ages of man" and the suffering of Jesus Christ, "weather permitting." On these dates, see Eike Pies, *Einem hocherfreuten Publikum wird heute präsentiert eine kleine Chronik des Theaterzettels* (Hamburg: Claassen, 1973), p. 7. The scholarly discussion of handbills, as opposed to just antiquarian collecting, begins with Carl Hagemann's doctoral dissertation, "Geschichte des Theaters: Ein Beitrag zur Technik des deutschen Dramas" (University of Heidelberg, 1901). Hagemann explains the function of the late medieval and early Renaissance German playbills within the framework of a teleological history of drama. He argues that the information conveyed by early playbills resulted from the low level of education of spectators, on the one hand, and dramaturgical incompetence of authors, on the other. A doctoral dissertation by Johann-Richard Hänsel, "Die Geschichte des Theaterzettels und seine Wirkung in der Öffentlichkeit" (Berlin: Free University, 1962), focuses on the seventeenth and eighteenth centuries and devotes only a few pages to the whole of the nineteenth century.

21. Tiffany Stern, "'On Each Wall and Corner Poast': Playbills, Title-pages, and Advertising in Early Modern London," *English Literary Renaissance* 36.1 (2006): 57–89 (quotation on p. 60).

22. Ibid., p. 70.

23. The definitive history to date for the United Kingdom is provided in David Robert Gowen, "Studies in the History and Function of the British Theatre Playbill and Programme, 1564–1914" (Ph.D. dissertation, Oxford, 1998). Unfortunately it remains unpublished and hence fairly inaccessible.

24. Bratton, *New Readings in Theatre History*, p. 39.

25. See Mariana Net, "Semiotics and Interfictionality in a Postmodern Age: The Case of the Playbill," *Semiotica* 97.3–4 (1993): pp. 315–323. This article, despite its title, is in fact a study of theatre programs in recent Rumanian theatre. See also the article by James Harbeck, "A Case Study in the Pragmatics of American Theatrical Programs," *Semiotica* 118.3–4 (1998): 215–238. These kinds of approaches could, however, be usefully applied to playbills in the narrower sense of the term.

26. Stern, "'On Each Wall and Corner Poast,'" p. 77. *Siquis* (from Latin *si quis*, meaning "if anyone") refers to a general kind of bill that advertises goods or services.

27. Exceptions to this date no doubt exist, but the bulk of information available to me would suggest a significant change after 1750.

28. The New Theatre Royal in Dunlop Street was involved in a long-standing dispute between Alexander and a rival manager, Frank Seymour. See http://www.arthurlloyd.co.uk/Glasgow/TRDunlop.htm.

29. Habermas, *The Structural Transformation of the Public Sphere*, pp. 38–39.

30. Ruth Eder, *Theaterzettel* (Dortmund: Harenberg, 1980), reproduces a number of these playbills, pp. 149–159.

31. It should be noted, however, that the term *unpäßlich* can be found on playbills in connection with male performers as well, particularly opera singers, but more rarely than for women.

32. In 1874 the Royal Theatres, as today, were the Court and National Theatre focusing on opera, the Residenz-Theater for drama, and the Gärtnerplatz Theatre for more popular offerings such as operetta and opera in the vernacular.

The Making of Theatre History

> The history of the archive, on the one hand a history of conservation, is, on the other hand, a history of loss. — Paul J. Voss and Marta L. Werner, "Towards a Poetics of the Archive," 1999

How have scholars in the last twenty years or so challenged assumptions in the making of theatre history? The statement that theatre historiography has been under challenge probably provokes little debate, since theatre historians (in common with scholars across the full range of the arts disciplines) have been vigorously engaged in rethinking and revising the traditional narratives that construed a particular discipline. What interests me here, however, is a kind of critical stocktaking that allows a better understanding of how these various challenges to the making of theatre history have been staged and how revisionist historiographies have produced new narratives (often counternarratives) for thinking about a more diverse and inclusive history of theatre and performance practices. In other words, at the beginning of the twenty-first century theatre scholars look to an archive that is radically different from that of even a few years ago. I argue here that recent critical excavations of how archives work, what Ann Laura Stoler describes as "enquiry into the grids of intelligibility,"[1] might usefully be deployed to demonstrate the remarkable tenacity of certain principles in the making of theatre history that we otherwise imagine have been effectively superseded by the revisionist turn. My goal is to review assumptions and practices as they shape theatre history and to point to continuing gaps in our discipline's archive. This is an argument, then, about the interplay of conservation and loss.

In many ways, the making of theatre history over the last two decades has been concerned primarily with acts of revision and often staged as a correction to old-style history that relied, as Helen Freshwater has trenchantly summarized, on "the recalcitrant, but dependable, 'thing': archival evidence."[2] Certainly, revisionist theatre history has embraced the necessity of "complex negotiation of the space between thing and theory," in Freshwater's terms, which has brought about a concerted focus on expanding critical histories to include both people and practices that had heretofore been ignored. Such progressive historiography has quickly allowed for a much different vista of what constituted theatre across the centuries and has enabled the study of individuals, institutions, and performances that encompass both Western and Eastern geographies as well as a dazzling variety of production and reception contexts. Let me be clear on this point: cumulatively, revisionist scholarship has insisted upon an extraordinarily expanded archive for the making of theatre history, relying on new evidence and innovative critical analysis that has significantly benefited the discipline at large. But it is timely, I think, to annotate some omissions in this otherwise productive trajectory and to speculate on limitations of the historiographical turn we call revisionist history.

Two spheres of activity at the heart of this revision of theatre history both declare the importance of the archive. The first, as noted above, is a commitment to inclusion, publishing narratives of conservation that record the contributions of a much wider range of peoples—a strand of inquiry driven in the 1990s by the prevalence of identity-based theorizing. The second, certainly related to the first, concerns the recovery of what has been previously "lost." But in order to calibrate the kinds of revision that this activity has in fact produced, it is crucial to understand what Michel de Certeau has called the "*laws* of the milieu."[3] In *The Writing of History* de Certeau asks:

> What is a "valued work" in history? It is a work recognized as such by peers, a work that can be situated within an operative set, a work that represents some progress in respect to the current status of historical "objects" and methods. . . . Akin to a car produced by a factory, the historical study is bound to the complex of a specific and collective fabrication more than it is the effect merely of a personal philosophy or the resurgence of a past "reality." It is the *product of a place*.[4]

Thus, beyond the "thing" of archival evidence (old history) and the more expansive vision of revisionist narratives (new history), all renditions of history necessarily appear "within an operative set," as de Certeau suggests. The publication of Errol Hill and James Hatch's *A History of African American Theatre* (2003), described on the cover as "the first definitive history of African American theatre," introduced valued (and welcome) work that perhaps epitomizes contemporary revisionist theatre history.[5] It chronicles a group whose contributions had been woefully underrepresented across American theatre history and also provides a new archive of evidence concerning those contributions to which future scholarship must certainly refer. Yet, in the first paragraph of his preface to this important volume, Hatch offers an instructive example of earlier archival research in this same field: "Fannin Saffore Belcher Jr. wrote a . . . comprehensive history entitled *The Place of the Negro in the Evolution of the American Theatre, 1767 to 1940*, his 1945 dissertation at Yale University. It was never published."[6] That Hatch takes this earlier, "lost" history as an opening gambit for his own and Errol Hill's project actively marks a historical shift in what is recognized as valuable by the field as a whole.

From this perspective—to think about the *laws* of theatre history and what accounts for value in its archive—I want to examine the contours of revisionist scholarship in respect to the contributions of women. In contrast to the Hill/Hatch volume on African American theatre, no definitive theatre history for women in the United States yet exists. We also lack a comprehensive history for women dramatists in Canada and the British Isles (as well as any attempt at a possible transnational history of women dramatists who wrote in English and/or French in these countries). Moreover, theatre histories produced within the operative set of revisionist history making seem to have had little more than a passing interest in women's contributions and have generally provided only a very short list of names, accommodated chiefly under categories overburdened by gender (see the discussion below). Arguably, today's theatre history knows no more than—or perhaps just the same things as—it knew about this topic of women before the appraisals of new historiographic methodologies and taxonomies.

In "Questions for a Feminist Methodology in Theatre History" (1989), Tracy C. Davis suggests that "most of the published work on women and theatre fits comfortably in one of two categories": on the one hand, scholarship of recovery and revision "which highlights women's activities in contrast or opposition to dominant traditions" and, on the other hand, "feminist literary criticism complementing historians' work by reclaiming 'lost' plays and uncanonized playwrights, providing an alternate reading of texts, and reprinting and publishing modern plays by women."[7] This work, organized in these distinct but related fields, has continued and (as I have already suggested) is a commonplace strategy within revisionist historiography broadly cast. In terms of scholarship on women's dramatic writing, essays, collections, and monographs are now available that range over historical periods, performance genres, and national literatures. In this way we can acknowledge—and celebrate—the production of a great deal of new knowledge through the conservation and recovery of evidence. Irrespective of the actual quantity of this work, it remains collectively marginal, still in the shadow of theatre history's customary archives. If this body of new critical work about women and theatre has had little impact not only on the scope of theatre history but also on the practices of theatre historiography, then it is timely indeed to question the revisionist turn. To initiate an interrogation of revisionist practices, I take as axiomatic Jacques Derrida's assertion that "archivization produces as much as it records an event."[8] Derrida observes that archives acquire, hold, and classify documents "by virtue of a privileged *topology*."[9]

If the proposition of conservation and loss is at the heart of the archive and if the archive is at the heart of the making of theatre history, then it is important to engage critical rethinking about what constitutes an archive. I hope to suggest, echoing Ann Laura Stoler, what critical histories of women in theatre and performance "have to gain by turning further toward a politics of knowledge that reckons with archival genres, cultures of documentation, fictions of access, and archival conventions."[10] As Davis insisted in 1989, "everything bearing on the operation of gender difference and sexuality in the theatre is appropriate to the endeavor."[11] With such a motive in mind, we might acknowledge, in Pierre Nora's terms, that the critical formation of an archive is made up "of moments of history torn away from the movement of history, then returned."[12] The archive, Nora contends, functions as a particularly privileged site of memory; at the same time memory must instate what Joseph Roach calls "a rigorous and highly specialized process of forgetting."[13]

Carolyn Steedman has provided a useful working definition of the archive: "a name for the many places in which the past (which does not now exist, but which once did actually happen; which cannot be retrieved, but which may be represented) has deposited some traces and fragments."[14] Scholarly studies, however, have put emphasis on two more elaborate trajectories. The first of these demonstrates that "the archive is a key source of the nation, the basis for the construction of the national tradition";[15] the second explores the archive as a "centre of interpretation."[16] This description usefully suggests an active role for both archivists and historians—in relation to the archive's institutional ambit. The archive only preserves a minute sample of the past's traces and fragments; nonetheless, in history—as de Certeau would have it—"everything begins with the gesture of *setting aside*, of putting together, of transforming certain classified objects into 'documents.'"[17] The historian, then, takes up evidence "which had its own definite status and role" and, through writing, turns it "into *something else* which functions differently."[18] Or, to echo a term Roach has elaborated in a rather different context, the archive is a sublime act of surrogation.[19]

As well as self-consciously interrogating the archive's implication in knowledge production, scholars have paid extended attention to its broad institutional weight. Where this is understood as a key memory function that contributes to the formation and maintenance of national identity—the role of national archives in much of the Western world—the contours of its arrangement and dissemination predominate. As Antoinette Burton suggests, "all archives come into being in and as history as a result of specific political, cultural, and socioeconomic pressures—pressures which leave traces and which render archives themselves artifacts of history."[20] And, of course, for Michel Foucault the archive is foundational, its compass the structures of the linguistic system—the archaeology of knowledge. Indeed, Foucault goes to some lengths to avoid and counter more prosaic definitions: he insists that the archive is not "the sum of all the texts that a culture has kept upon its person as documents attesting to its own past, or as evidence of a continuing identity; nor do I mean the institutions, which, in a given society, make it possible to record and preserve those discourses that one wishes to remember and keep in circulation."[21] Instead, "the archive is first the law of what can be said, the system that governs the appearance of statements as unique events. . . . It is *the general system of the formation and transformation of statements*."[22] In other words, the archive's crucial function is to represent statements as things, "the yield of the discursive practice of the epistème."[23]

If Foucault's analysis of the archive seeks to lay bare underlying structures of the linguistic system, then Derrida is more direct in *Archive Fever*: "There is no political power without control of the archive, if not of memory."[24] This understanding emphatically illustrates the force of conservation, and such a blunt statement aligns productively with historian Bonnie Smith's observation that "women's archives had a diasporic relationship to the official archival enterprise of the nineteenth century."[25] In Smith's words, "Papers about women survived in various places—the attics of suffragists, flea markets, dank basements, local libraries, crumbling châteaus, government repositories—with very little concern for their preservation, in contrast to the attention given to highly prized, primary documents about men."[26] This diaspora, both geographic and figurative, created "a category bursting its bounds and swamped in various impulses and movements" that Smith persuasively argues "provided the basis for changes in professional history," including, for women, increased entry into the discipline.[27]

Even when women's writing has been archived in mainstream institutional settings, this endeavor has not necessarily meant increased accessibility. Sometimes women's texts have endured loss even in the act of conservation. In a telling description at the beginning of an essay concerned with research about women in the early modern period, Georgianna Ziegler writes:

> Joyse Jeffreys, Sarah King, Eliza St. George, and Dorothy Wylde—not household names, perhaps, but these women have several things in common. They lived in seventeenth-century England, they each owned at least one important book in which they wrote their names, and all these books made their way to the Folger Library. . . . The names have been there for a very long time for anyone to see, but only recently have they been noted. None of the names appears in the Folger's Provenance File of former owners, nor do they appear on the catalog cards for these volumes. These women have effectively been silent for three hundred years.[28]

As Ziegler curtly summarizes, "Even if you look in the places where you would expect to find traces of them [women], they have often remained invisible through omission."[29] In other words, "loss" does not occur only outside the archive but can happen equally (and equally effectively) through the custodial system of conservation and especially in the selection processes used by archivists and researchers. If we interrogate what constitutes an archive as well as how it creates and disseminates the possibilities for history, however, we are faced with a number of important considerations in thinking through the (in)visibility of women in revisionist theatre history. To describe this fraught relationship between conservation and loss, I want to look at two particular constructions of theatre history and their representation of women.

My first example works within a framework of twentieth-century British theatre history and illustrates specific contours for a revisionist practice that accommodates women's theatre and performance in certain but hardly comprehensive contexts. In general, the beginning of the twenty-first century has predictably led to a review of the immediately previous century and the production of histories that archive its full range of activity. In this context, it is interesting to look at the inclusion of women at a historical moment when scholarly practice assumes a responsibility to represent. In histories of twentieth-century British theatre (which, as such, offer a kind of national archive), it is conventional, and for good reason, to understand the 1950s as the century's watershed decade. But I want to suggest its significance in a context other than the usual emphasis on a new postwar drama.

I came to an interest in the 1950s by accident—a commission to write an essay for a volume on British women playwrights in the twentieth century from its editors, Elaine Aston and Janelle Reinelt.[30] They asked me to account for the presence of women alongside the better-known group of "angry young men." I was not sure what I might say that had not already been said about Shelagh Delaney's *A Taste of Honey*. This is the one play by a woman from the 1950s that generally makes the cut in any critical discussion or theatre history of the decade, either for the purpose of including a single representative woman among the "angry young men" or (now more commonly) because Delaney's drama can be categorized as a failed but worthy protofeminist text. Even in my undergraduate days I knew that the Royal Court Theatre had emerged in this decade as the most important venue for the production of new plays that drew in younger audiences through its commitment to a progressive, left-leaning social agenda. But what, I began to wonder, was available on the commercial stages of the West End at the same time? Was the West End really dominated by the residual genre of the "well-made" play, sounding a death knell for theatre in the face of a livelier, more relevant, and more vital experience in the cinema? It was a surprise to discover after some preliminary research that in the 1950s commercial theatre was in fact thriving and that many of the longest-running plays had been written by women, few of whose names I recognized.

Many of these women also worked in other literary genres, such as the novel (where they were sometimes much better known); several saw their work produced as often on the New York stage as in London theatres (and were the recipients of awards there); some of their plays were adapted for film very quickly after their success in theatrical versions. Yet almost none of the women ever appear in theatre history or dramatic criticism today. This discovery has become, it would seem, an archival project, although not in the simple sense of recovering so-called lost plays. As I reflect upon these women's careers, my primary or immediate impulse is not to fill in the gaps in the historical descriptions of this period in a particular place (though that in itself is an outcome with genuine merit). Rather, I see this project as a historiographical test case from which I might explore "the laws of the milieu" (de Certeau's term again) as well as interrogate ideas of "value" within revisionist theatre history.

First, however, let us consider some facts about plays by women in this decade. Between 1950 and 1960 more than 200 of the plays, either single- or co-authored, appeared on the London stage. Of these plays, 12 ran for more than a year apiece, including the usual lone representative for women's writing in the period, *A Taste of Honey* (close to 400 performances between May 1958 and December 1959). Enid Bagnold's *The Chalk*

Garden (658 performances between April 1956 and November 1957) was lauded by many contemporary drama critics as the Best Play of 1956—an accolade later transferred to John Osborne's *Look Back in Anger* by theatre historians. Bagnold's play is still regularly produced, including a staging in London's West End in 2008.[31] And, of course, Agatha Christie's *The Mousetrap*, which opened in November 1952, continues its record-breaking run, having racked up more than 23,000 performances by 2009 (a record for the London theatre that is not likely to be broken). Notwithstanding the achievements of women playwrights in the 1950s, the very well-regarded critic Michael Billington tells us in his recently published theatre history of British drama in the twentieth century (2007) that the decade was "a time when women's voices were virtually unheard in the British theatre."[32] Christopher Innes paints an equally dire picture in the 2002 version of the standard work *Modern British Drama: The Twentieth Century*: "Apart from some minor exceptions, such as Elizabeth Robins' *Votes for Women* (1906), female playwrights have been conspicuous by their absence from British theatre up until the late 1950s. Even then, Anne [*sic*] Jellicoe found the commercial stage inappropriate to her feminist aims, while Shelagh Delaney's only success was a compromise with popular taste."[33] These brief synopses of women dramatists' contributions to the first half of the twentieth century are just not accurate. Yet almost every critic and historian of the last century's drama repeats, in one way or another, the assumption that women did not have any role in writing for the stage except in the few examples from first-wave feminism (particularly in the context of the suffrage movement) and then not again until the emergence of second-wave feminism in the 1960s.

As I observed recently, historical reference to feminist theatre in contemporary scholarship "has not meant any widespread revision to account more inclusively for women's contributions to the theatre"; even when these contributions are given critical and historical attention, "women's work often tends to be ghettoized in a single chapter devoted to this period-inscribed phenomenon of feminist theatre (predominantly 1970s and 1980s), something that seems to assure the continued absence of women elsewhere."[34] A commitment to and desire for the inclusion of women in British theatre histories has in fact produced two distinctive and now uncontroversial appearances for women. The earlier record comes from citation of plays that are valued for their aesthetic treatment of the political actions leading toward suffrage. The second appearance is tied to the radical social shifts of the late 1960s and includes the development of an explicitly feminist drama through the following decades, often formally anchored to an emergent critical interest in identity-based theorizing. Even then, as Billington has to admit in his own summary of the 1960s, "Looking back, it is astonishing how thinly the experience of both women and ethnic minorities was represented: to all intents and purposes, British theatre was still a white, male-dominated club."[35] This is undoubtedly true in the context of an "angry young men" theatre history trajectory, less so if the evidence is drawn from the full performance archive of the period.

The third volume of *The Cambridge History of British Theatre* (2004), edited by Baz Kershaw, has a much more obviously progressive agenda—shown both by the range and approaches of the authors and by the topics they discuss. In his introduction to part 3 of the volume ("British Theatre, 1940–2002"), Kershaw describes his project as "an attempt at identifying the main interacting energies of theatrical change in the sixty-year period,"[36] an initiative that significantly extends the more traditional vista of twentieth-century British theatre in earlier surveys. Dramatic writing by women more regularly appears in the chapters concerned with particular periods or geographies. Yet this survey, too, gives short shrift to the women of the commercial stage. Derek Paget makes the case for "a new political theatre" by way of a chapter-long study of Joan Littlewood's production of *Oh What a Lovely War* by the Theatre Workshop in 1963,[37] while John Bull (in his chapter on "The Establishment of Mainstream Theatre, 1946–1979") mentions Littlewood's production as a transfer to the West End that "did much to alter the terms of reference of mainstream theatre."[38] Yet this account otherwise describes only plays authored by men.

What has registered so emphatically in revisionist theatre histories is the inclusion of women whose appearance is based on their contribution to a political drama, defined explicitly by gender—a designation which encompasses their identity as writers and also provides the definitive topic of their work. Traditional histories of modern British drama may have excluded women entirely, but revisionist histories appear to include them only in the context of that predominant organizational category of the political: their gender is the criterion for the relevance of their writing. This problematic strategy has had a number of effects, including the provision of a predetermined discourse for the discussion of women's plays, along with a reinscription of the post-Osborne impulse toward seeing British drama (if not all late twentieth-century drama) as per se political. Here I think of Tamsen Wolff's timely comment: "To make silence in theatre history voice our own political sensibilities severely limits the scope and possibilities of the field."[39] Do we ignore the work of women who wrote for the commercial mainstream stages of the 1950s because, after all, their work does not comply with a prescriptive focus on an emergent radical theatre practice where a particular kind of cultural and social change was imagined and disseminated? Apparently, both these writers and the women they wrote about in their plays have disappeared from the historical record because they simply do not fit within the political perspectives of the new liberal, university-educated middle class who both authored and attended the new postwar drama that revisionist histories have conserved and celebrated.

Whatever the reasons for the scholarly compartmentalization of women's dramatic writing during the twentieth century, the readership for such studies (especially the undergraduate student readership) is left with the impression that, among all women, only feminists of the first or second wave write for the theatre. This revisionist perspective—which only allows women visibility as exceptions, under pressing political claims—is premised on a narrow amendment to the usual standards for constructing and disseminating the archive of texts available for study. To cite de Certeau again, "intelligibility is established through a relation with the other; it moves (or 'progresses') by changing what it makes of its 'other.'"[40] Marking women's plays by their definitional relation to the issue of gender assures that their writing receives our attention. But the plays and careers are limited to and only located in this overdetermined category of political theatre, which sustains a claim for theatre practice that is fraught with questionable assumptions, as Tamsen Wolff suggests: "No matter how tempting, the urge to read theatre history as chock-full of thrilling, crafty efforts to overthrow the status quo needs serious scrutiny."[41] Jill Dolan reflects, perhaps even more sharply than Wolff, on the effects of a political imperative: "I now find tedious the somewhat facile pose of scholars always looking for the next new outlaw or the most outré performance examples to boast as aesthetically radical and politically subversive. While the work they uncover is often effective and important, in the rush to innovation, already-noted artists are too often dismissed."[42]

Both Wolff's and Dolan's arguments, as well as the archival evidence from the 1950s, suggest that scholarship continues to highlight women's contributions "in contrast or opposition to dominant traditions,"[43] rather than in any comprehensive articulation of historical complexities. Significant historiographical labor has done little, it seems, to shift either the theatre histories themselves or the practices by which we imagine "valued works." Where the density of feminist performance criticism might appear to be a conservation project (one that is, *pace* Dolan's concerns, effective and important), it has at the same time rendered other work by women as hopelessly lost as the work of women in theatres in far more remote historical periods. This is an outcome that Paul Voss and Marta Werner suggest is inherent to the making of archives (and thus histories): "Founded in order to preserve the official records of successive cultures but comprised of material 'citations' often wrenched out of context, the archive is necessarily established in proximity to a loss — of *other* citations, citations of *otherness*."[44]

If, as Voss and Werner claim, what we bring into the archive and thus to theatre histories depends on "proximity to a loss," then I also want to look at that other node of revisionist activity: the process of recovery. In *New Readings in Theatre History*, Jacky Bratton notes that "[i]t was in the 1830s that the field [of theatre history] became defined and its procedures set up so as to mark limits to what theatre is, and to establish it in a system of difference — text and context, high and low, the written drama and the materiality of the stage."[45] In other words, this was a time when a normative archive came into play in the formation of the discipline. It became the basis on which the discipline would be practiced and disseminated. In looking at an example of how revisionist historiography has understood the recovery of what was previously "lost," I want to take a short historical step back from Bratton's foundational disciplinary horizon of the 1830s to review the extraordinary contribution of Elizabeth Inchbald to the making of British theatre. Inchbald's work immediately precedes what Bratton identifies as the sedimentation of theatre historiographical practices in service of the field. Understanding Inchbald's work as a critic and anthologist is thus particularly significant, if only to recognize principles of organization and appraisal that antedate those practices that would coalesce over the rest of the nineteenth century and emerge to establish the profession of theatre historian. Bratton astutely observes that "it was a necessary condition of successful hegemonic control of the theatre that women's work within the public space should be disguised, discounted, or appropriated to male control; and therefore entertainment, embodied as female, became the Other of the 'National drama' of male genius."[46] In this context, it is particularly instructive to look at Inchbald's labor in the development of a "national drama."

Traditionally, Elizabeth Inchbald (1753–1821) was considered a minor figure in eighteenth-century British theatre, described as "an actress, beautiful and hard-working but of moderate talent."[47] More recently, a wealth of scholarship has drawn attention to Inchbald's prolific work in the theatre, especially as a dramatist, as well as her signal contributions to the development of the English novel through her two books, *A Simple Story* and

Nature and Art.[48] My example here, however, is a little-discussed aspect of Inchbald's career: her work as a critic and anthologist, where she played a vital role in the cultural imagination of a history of British theatre. Sometime in 1805 Inchbald was approached by her publisher Longmans to write a series of remarks for a multivolume collection of plays that it intended to bring out under the title *The British Theatre*. Longmans had recently bought a list from another publisher, Bell, which had published a successful series of Shakespeare plays followed by *Bell's British Theatre*, from 1775 until the sale to Longmans. As Annibel Jenkins points out, "When the Longmans came to Inchbald, they had already selected the plays to be included, and they had already set the procedure."[49] Nonetheless, this was a substantial commission requiring the authorship of 125 prefaces to support play-by-play publication (which, as Jenkins notes, had "no pattern of publication by date or genre."[50] It culminated in a collected edition of 25 volumes (5 plays per volume) that appeared in 1808. Inchbald's contract with Longmans was signed early in 1806, and her pocket-books for 1807 and 1808 often reveal that this demanding and exhausting task occupied much of her time.[51] Inchbald appears to have received plays regularly, read them, then wrote up a preface, checked, and copyedited. The plays were ones that had been staged at the Covent Garden, Haymarket, and Drury Lane theatres, and the Inchbald/Longmans collaboration was intended to meet an increasing demand for inexpensive editions. The project was an unreserved commercial triumph.

The reach and the success of *The British Theatre* clearly made Inchbald the foremost drama critic of the period, and she certainly contributed to the making of early nineteenth-century theatre history.[52] While she had no influence on the selection of the plays, the way in which she shaped each preface created an implicit hierarchy among the many texts. Her commentaries were not without their critics, some notoriously so: the bitter response of George Colman the younger (1762–1836) to Inchbald's preface on his father's play *A Jealous Wife* has been frequently cited. He wrote her an angry letter, asking: "Is it grateful from an ingenious lady, who was originally encouraged, and brought forward, as an authoress, by that very man on whose tomb she idly plants this poisonous weed of remark, to choke the laurels which justly grace his memory?"[53] Inchbald provided a measured response to this vitriol, however: "Let it be understood that my obligation to your father amounted to no more than those usual attentions which every manager of a theater is supposed to confer, when he selects a novice in dramatic writing as worthy of being introduced on his stage to the public."[54] I have suggested elsewhere that "[t]here is a genealogy of women critics that needs to be as familiar to theatre history and contemporary historians as the trajectory of male critics we have studied for their views on the theaters of their times,"[55] to promote a collective project that might work beyond the (re)capture of individual achievement and genius—though I would claim precisely that much for Inchbald.

Burgeoning knowledge of Inchbald as a critic, through some recent analyses of the 125 prefaces she authored for the individual and multivolume publication of the *Remarks for the British Theatre*, is important in order to recognize not simply the economic success that attached to her labor but the impact of a new archive. The collected version of *Remarks for the British Theatre* was published in 1808, the same year Colman the younger sent his infuriated response to the author. Had Colman's remarks been typical or even influential, it is hard to imagine that Inchbald would so soon have found herself with other major commissions. First she was asked to edit *A Collection of Farces and Other Afterpieces* (published in 1809 in seven volumes), choosing the plays from a list supplied to her by Longmans. Further, she was commissioned to produce an edition in ten volumes titled *The Modern Theatre*—as the subtitle puts it: "[a] collection of successful modern plays, as acted at The Theatres Royal, London. Printed from the prompt books under the authority of the Managers. Selected by Mrs. Inchbald."[56] All ten volumes of *The Modern Theatre* were published in 1811.

It is particularly interesting that in the subsequent ventures Inchbald herself chose the plays to be anthologized. She had been denied this option in the *Remarks for the British Theatre*, but maybe only because Longmans was anxious to reposition a preexisting list (Bell's) in the commercial marketplace. No doubt the two subsequent anthology projects allowed Longmans to produce collections of plays that it acquired aside from the Bell's list. Equally interesting is the absence of prefaces to introduce the plays selected in these later ventures. Jenkins notes that the pocket-books show Inchbald to have been suffering from depression, often the result of the exhausting and continuous work of preparing the prefaces and/or the negative critiques they received.[57] Did Inchbald refuse to continue preparation of dramatic criticism that she had found so demanding and difficult? Or did Longmans simply want her as an anthologist rather than a drama critic—was her name alone, by this date, sufficient imprimatur? In any event, Longmans obviously held Inchbald's work in high regard and believed that it would translate into robust sales. It was not alone in this opinion, apparently. Jenkins concludes: "Everyone agreed that she [Inchbald] was the leading authority on drama in the last years of the eighteenth century and the first decade of the nineteenth."[58]

The index to Inchbald's collection *The Modern Theatre* raises some interesting questions for thinking about archival practices and canon formation within theatre studies. An analysis of the volume's table of contents offers three immediate conclusions beyond the observation that her selections for *The Modern Theatre* are in general plays that are little, if at all, known today. First, the commanding presence of Frederick Reynolds (twelve plays included) and Richard Cumberland (six plays included) makes no sense to the twentieth-century reader, especially in light of only one selection for Richard Brinsley Sheridan, *A Trip to Scarborough*. Second, the proportion of plays by women (six of fifty or 12 percent) equals or betters the representation of women in most period or general drama anthologies published today, sensitive though they may be to the expectations of revisionist historiography. Finally, despite the fallout from her prefaces in *The British Theatre*, Inchbald appears to have chosen plays that she thought represented *The Modern Theatre*, including a play by George Colman the elder and another by Colman the younger as well as three of her own. Inchbald played a very significant role in the construction of a record of English theatre at the very beginning of the nineteenth century, since these collections and her analyses were influential and widely circulated. If, as Bratton suggests, this is a historical moment *before* the limits for theatre history took their grip, a more thorough account of Inchbald's practices and principles as critic and anthologist is surely useful for the imagination of different and more fully inclusive trajectories of theatre history.

Specifically, what might be abstracted for a revisionist theatre historiography to rethink divisions constructed from gendered appraisal? Certainly, the range, diversity, and ambition of Inchbald's career (actress, playwright, novelist, translator, investor, critic, anthologist) models the kind of complexity required for a full and inclusive production of history. It challenges, too, the definitions of "career" composed from the histories of men of the theatre. It is more than relevant to draw from the breadth of Inchbald's corpus: in our own historical moment, few research projects have had the scope and impact that hers achieved in her own time. Evidently, Inchbald herself deserves a much more emphatic place in theatre history. Yet the field still barely knows Inchbald at all: although recent years have produced more critical attention, modern editions, and two biographies, it would be stretching the imagination to consider her a well-known eighteenth-century playwright.[59] She does not appear in anthologies of drama, generally even those of her period.[60] In Bonnie Smith's terms, Inchbald's work remains diasporic in relationship to the archive of theatre history.

With this assessment in mind, it is useful to review one recent summary of Inchbald in Dennis Kennedy's impressively edited, progressive, and responsible *Oxford Encyclopedia of Theatre and Performance*—a volume heralded on its back cover as "the first authority on theatre in the twenty-first century."[61] Here Inchbald does garner an entry of 165 words, authored by Matthew Kinservik. In this succinct appraisal of her career, Kinservik covers her best-known acting roles as well as briefly noting her plays, translations, and editing work. Unfortunately, however, he repeats the traditional explanation of why Inchbald made the transition from actress to playwright: "She was tall, beautiful, and (although self-taught) highly intelligent. Realizing that she could not achieve great fame on the London stage, she left off acting at the age of 37 and devoted herself to writing."[62] Rather than suggesting that Inchbald was the preeminent authority on the drama of her time, Kinservik relies on a conventional emphasis on physical attributes that should, apparently, explain her career. It is as if none of the "recovery-based" critical publications on Inchbald have registered on the field at large and she can only be archived in the context of the acting profession, where women, in effect, "belong." Moreover, it is Inchbald's gender that here interprets (indeed, overdetermines) the measure of her success in that specific performance field.

Feminist theatre historians, not surprisingly, have understood the progression of Inchbald's work differently, as "a diverse career pattern."[63] This scholarship relies instead on financial evidence for Inchbald's migration from acting to writing professions, a topic on which a young widow might reasonably be expected to base her decisions. As Ellen Donkin describes Inchbald's professional development, "She straddled two careers for well over a decade, watching plays from the wings, both as the actress waiting to make an entrance, and also as the playwright, sizing up the moment-to-moment impact of her own work and other people's."[64] In economic terms, as an actress, Inchbald would have earned less than £1 a week; for her first play, a farcical afterpiece entitled *The Mogul Tale*, she was paid 100 guineas (£105). The archive against which Inchbald's career traditionally has been measured, like feminist theatre in the twentieth century, is constructed out of gender categories. A shift to another category of appraisal—economics—suggests a rather different evaluation of her work.

Financial matters are a marked category in the account of Inchbald in the feminist-inflected digital archive of the ORLANDO Project.[65] Information provided there notes that when Joseph Inchbald died in 1779 he left his wife "£252 in investments plus £128 in money. . . . At the time of her retirement . . . she had an investment income of £58 a week." When Inchbald died in 1821 (forty-two years after her husband's death) she had an estate worth between £,5000 and £,6000, an extraordinary accomplishment that more than proves how much she achieved.

Whether it is the career of Elizabeth Inchbald or the extensive repertoire of women writing for the London stage in the 1950s, revisionist theatre historiography has not yet accommodated their work in any comprehensive form. This suggests, time and again, that conservation continues to involve loss for women. How, then, do we ensure that the making of theatre history provides a more thorough and more accurately explained account of women's many contributions? Generally, of course, historians warn against the impulse toward the encyclopedic, a concern that I share, although I think this defensive agenda often works to obscure "the laws of the milieu." Peter Thomson, in his general preface to *The Cambridge History of British Theatre* (three volumes, 2004–2005), also attempts to address this issue: "The aim has been to provide a comprehensive 'history' that makes no vain pretence to all-inclusiveness."[66] This first major theatre history of the twenty-first century starts by reminding its readers of the distinction drawn between "comprehensive" and "all-inclusive," a strategy that is not only credible but indeed commonsensical in historiographic terms, yet which turns out, once again, virtually to exclude women from its view. Given the volume and diversity of scholarship on women's dramatic writing—supported in general by a political commitment to represent the historical conditions of women's lives and careers—it does not seem unrealistic to expect "comprehensive" to work rather differently.

With such a project in mind, let me return to de Certeau's perspective on historiography: "The issue is not only one of bringing these 'immense dormant sectors of documentation' to life, of giving a voice to silence, or of lending currency to a possibility. It means changing something which had its own definite status and role into *something else* which functions differently."[67] Among the "somethings" that might be contested and even changed in such a historical context would be the representation and analysis of women's plays. But the transformation to "something else" requires, at the very least, not only the recognition of the dominant epistemic tropes that operate in theatre histories but also the explicit articulation of the ways these tropes organize and often control theatre histories.

At that point, other definitional "somethings" (say, the concepts of the political or masculinity) are equally available for scrutiny.

But the recuperation of data about women's drama in the 1950s and the limited recovery of Inchbald's extensive contributions (more importantly for me) allow this examination of the dynamic of conservation and loss. It perhaps requires flagrant examples of forgetting to demonstrate the terms and conditions of how we remember. The task at hand, then, is a thick description, as Ann Laura Stoler has characterized it, of "the legitimating social coordinates of epistemologies: how people imagine they know what they know and what institutions validate that knowledge, and how they do so."[68] Certainly, Foucault's methods for identifying accidents, fissures, and the like have enabled the kinds of politically motivated work that have long dominated discourses of theatre history and criticism, but it is now time to review more carefully the omissions of revisionist practice and gain a better understanding of the precepts of traditional history that continue to extend their grasp on what we otherwise imagine as new, progressive narratives. To that end, the historiographic endeavor requires us to traverse the contours of both received and revisionist histories, not merely to "display confident knowledge and know-how," as Stoler cautions, but to question historiographic assumptions and agendas.[69] Otherwise we are at risk of trading one authoritative stance for another, caught yet again by the impeditive binaries that Jacky Bratton has appropriately critiqued. Rather, we must approach the archive in "disquieted and expectant modes" (Stoler's phrase) so that we recognize and acknowledge, always, the stakes at play in the making of theatre history.[70]

NOTES

1. Ann Laura Stoler, "Colonial Archives and the Arts of Governance," *Archival Science* 2 (2002): 91. I am indebted to Stoler's move from archive-as-source to archive-as-subject and appreciate her understanding of the significance of archival form as well as its content. This double perspective provides a useful way to construct an argument for the making of theatre history.

2. Helen Freshwater, "The Allure of the Archive," *Poetics Today* 24.4 (Winter 2003): 731.

3. Michel de Certeau, *The Writing of History*, trans. Tom Conley (New York: Columbia University Press, 1988), p. 63 (emphasis in original).

4. Ibid., 64 (emphasis in original).

5. Errol G. Hill and James V. Hatch, *A History of African American Theatre* (Cambridge: Cambridge University Press, 2003).

6. Ibid., p. xiv.

7. Tracy C. Davis, "Questions for a Feminist Methodology in Theatre History," in *Inter-*

preting the Theatrical Past, ed. Thomas Postlewait and Bruce A. McConachie (Iowa City: University of Iowa Press, 1989), p. 63.

8. Jacques Derrida, *Archive Fever*, trans. Eric Prenowitz (Chicago: University of Chicago Press, 1995), p. 17.

9. Ibid., p. 3 (emphasis in original).

10. Stoler, "Colonial Archives," p. 88.

11. Davis, "Questions for a Feminist Methodology," p. 77.

12. Pierre Nora, "Between Memory and History: Les Lieux de Mémoire," *Representations* 26 (Spring 1989): 12.

13. Joseph Roach, *Cities of the Dead: Circum-Atlantic Performance* (New York: Columbia University Press, 1996), p. 12.

14. Carolyn Steedman, "The Space of Memory: In an Archive," in *History of the Human Sciences* (London: Routledge, 1998), p. 67.

15. Mike Featherstone, "Archive," *Theory, Culture and Society* 23.2–3 (2006): 591–596 (quotation on 592).

16. Thomas Osborne, "The Ordinariness of the Archive," in *History of the Human Sciences* (London: Routledge, 1999), p. 53.

17. de Certeau, *The Writing of History*, p. 72 (emphasis in original).

18. Ibid., p. 74 (emphasis in original).

19. See Roach's *Cities of the Dead* for his elaboration of the idea of surrogation.

20. Antoinette Burton, *Archive Stories: Fact, Fiction and the Writing of History* (Durham, N.C.: Duke University Press, 2005), p. 6.

21. Michel Foucault, *The Archaeology of Knowledge*, trans. A. M. Sheridan Smith (New York: Pantheon Books, 1972), pp. 128–129.

22. Ibid., pp. 129, 130 (emphasis in original).

23. Alun Munslow, *Deconstructing History* (London: Routledge, 1997), p. 136.

24. Derrida, *Archive Fever*, p. 4.

25. Bonnie G. Smith, *The Gender of History: Men, Women, and Historical Practice* (Cambridge, Mass.: Harvard University Press, 2000), p. 182.

26. Ibid.

27. Ibid., p. 183.

28. Georgianna Ziegler, "Lost in the Archives? Searching for Records of Early Modern Women," in *Teaching Tudor and Stuart Women Writers*, ed. Susanne Woods and Margaret P. Hannay (New York: Modern Language Association of America, 2000), pp. 315–316.

29. Ibid., p. 316.

30. This essay, "New Plays and Women's Voices in the 1950s," was published in *The Cambridge Companion to Modern British Women Playwrights*, ed. Elaine Aston and Janelle Reinelt (Cambridge: Cambridge University Press, 2000).

31. A preliminary version of this part of my argument, concerned in detail with the example of Bagnold's play, appears in "A Commercial Success: Women Playwrights in the 1950s," in *A Companion to Modern British and Irish Drama 1880–2005*, ed. Mary Luckhurst (Oxford: Blackwell Publishing, 2006), pp. 175–187.

32. Michael Billington, *State of the Nation: British Theatre since 1945* (London: Faber and Faber, 2007), p. 111.

33. C. D. Innes, *Modern British Drama: The Twentieth Century*, 2nd ed., revised and updated (Cambridge: Cambridge University Press, 2002), p. 233. The first edition was published in 1992.

34. Susan Bennett, ed., *Feminist Theatre and Performance: Critical Perspectives on Canadian Theatre in English* (Toronto: Playwrights Canada Press, 2006), p. viii.

35. Billington, *State of the Nation*, p. 204.

36. Baz Kershaw, ed., *The Cambridge History of British Theatre, Vol. 3: Since 1895* (Cambridge: Cambridge University Press, 2004), p. 293.

37. Ibid., p. 399.

38. Ibid., p. 336.

39. Tamsen Wolff, "Problems with Theatre Historiography," *Theatre Survey* 47.1 (May 2006): 10.

40. de Certeau, *The Writing of History*, p. 3.

41. Wolff, "Problems with Theatre Historiography," p. 10.

42. Jill Dolan, "Feminist Performance Criticism and the Popular: Reviewing Wendy Wasserstein," *Theatre Journal* 60.4 (2008): 435.

43. Davis, "Questions for a Feminist Methodology," p. 63.

44. Paul J. Voss and Marta L. Werner, "Towards a Poetics of the Archive," *Studies in the Literary Imagination* 32.1 (Spring 1999): ii (emphasis in original).

45. Jacky Bratton, *New Readings in Theatre History* (Cambridge: Cambridge University Press, 2003), pp. 10–11. See especially pp. 5–16 for an introduction to her revisionist project, which recognizes, importantly, that "underlying the organization of the field of theatre history is, unsurprisingly, a series of binary assumptions" (p. 5).

46. Ibid., p. 16.

47. Website of the Chawton House Library, a home for early English women's writing: http://www.chawtonhouse.org/library/biographies/inchbald.html (accessed October 12, 2008). Elma Scott, the author of the Inchbald biography, goes on to establish her subject as a popular dramatist and author of two novels, but I quote her first sentence because it was for a long time what theatre history "knew" of Inchbald.

48. Perhaps because women writers have always been recognized as crucial to the history of the English novel, Inchbald's two books are readily available in modern editions. The same is not true for her drama.

49. Annibel Jenkins, *I'll Tell You What: The Life of Elizabeth Inchbald* (Lexington: University Press of Kentucky, 2003), p. 465.

50. Ibid., p. 452.

51. See ibid., pp. 451ff. I am indebted to Jenkins's painstaking and engaging scholarship on Inchbald for my own account here.

52. Interestingly, in the context of my argument, Inchbald's *The British Theatre* was republished in December 2008 by BiblioLife. Full details of the BiblioLife consortium can be found on its website (http://bibliolife.com/about-bln/, accessed January 15, 2009); this

consortium is committed to on-demand printing of otherwise "lost" books through on-line distribution partners and e-book platforms as a "renewal community business."

53. Quoted in Ellen Donkin's ground-breaking monograph on eighteenth-century women playwrights, *Getting into the Act: Women Playwrights in London, 1776–1829* (London: Routledge, 1993), p. 128.

54. Ibid., pp. 128–130.

55. Susan Bennett, "Decomposing History (Why Are There So Few Women in Theatre History?)," in *Theorizing Practice: Redefining Theatre History*, ed. Peter Holland and W. B. Worthen (Basingstoke: Palgrave Macmillan, 2003), p. 84.

56. Elizabeth Inchbald, *The Modern Theatre* (reissued in 1969 in 5 volumes; New York: Benjamin Blom, Inc.). For the Library of Congress record, see http://lccn.loc.gov/31028965 (accessed July 7, 2008).

57. Jenkins, *I'll Tell You What*, p. 474.

58. Ibid., p. 11.

59. *A Simple Story* was published in the Oxford World Classics series in 2009 (edited by J. M. S. Tompkins and Jane Spencer). Other recent work includes a scholarly edition of *Nature and Art* (Broadview Press, 2004) and the Jenkins biography mentioned above (2003). See also Roger Manvell, *Elizabeth Inchbald: England's Principal Woman Dramatist and Independent Woman of Letters in 18th-Century London: A Biographical Study* (Lanham, Md.: University Press of America, 1988). *British Women Writers of the Romantic Period: An Anthology of Their Literary Criticism*, ed. Mary A. Waters (Basingstoke: Palgrave Macmillan, 2009), is a critical study of Inchbald as well as thirteen other women writers, including Charlotte Smith, Mary Robinson, Mary Wollstonecraft, Joanna Baillie, Ann Radcliffe, and Harriet Martineau. Amy Garnai's *Revolutionary Imaginings in the 1790s* is forthcoming from Palgrave Macmillan.

60. An exception, now out of print, is Roger Manvell's edition of *Selected Comedies* by Inchbald (Lanham, Md.: University Press of America, 1987), including *I'll Tell You What, Such Things Are, Everyone Has His Fault, The Wedding Day*, and *Wives as They Were and Maids as They Are*.

61. *The Oxford Encyclopedia of Theatre and Performance*, ed. Dennis Kennedy (Oxford: Oxford University Press, 2003).

62. Ibid., p. 618.

63. Susan Bennett, "Decomposing History," in *Theorizing Practice: Redefining Theatre History*, ed. Peter Holland and W. B. Worthen (Basingstoke: Palgrave Macmillan, 2003), p. 81.

64. Donkin, *Getting into the Act*, p. 114.

65. ORLANDO is an electronic database of women's writing in the British Isles from the beginnings to the present. The project's website (http://www.ualberta.ca/ORLANDO/, accessed July 7, 2008) provides detailed information about the database. Access is by subscription with Cambridge University Press.

66. Peter Thomson, ed., *The Cambridge History of British Theatre*, vol. 1 (Cambridge: Cambridge University Press, 2004), p. xvi. Thomson's preface is published in each of the

three volumes of the *Cambridge History*, which features chapters by more than five dozen scholars.

67. de Certeau, *The Writing of History*, p. 64 (emphasis in original).

68. Stoler, "Colonial Archives," p. 95.

69. Ibid., p. 109.

70. Ibid.

Writing the Unwritten Morris Dance and Theatre History

During the course of her summer's progress in 1575, Elizabeth I spent nineteen days at Kenilworth, the Earl of Leicester's castle in Warwickshire. She was presented with various entertainments—including plays, fireworks, bear-baitings, water-pageants, acrobatic performances, and dancing—at a cost of over a thousand pounds a day, part of what has been called "unquestionably sixteenth-century England's grandest and most extravagant party."[1] Robert Langham, a minor court functionary who wrote an eyewitness account of the party, describes a "lyvely morisdauns" that was featured in this festive show of fealty to the queen. According to Langham, the morris performed for Elizabeth was danced "acording to the auncient manner" and featured "six daunserz, Mawdmarion, and the fool."[2] The dance was part of a "bride-ale" procession made up of "lusty lads and bolld bachelarz of the parish" arranged two by two in "marciall order," who preceded sixteen horsemen and the bridegroom; after the horsemen came the morris dance, followed by three "prety puzels" carrying spicecakes and leading the bride ("ill smellyng" and "ugly fooul ill favord"), who was accompanied by "too auncient parishionerz, honest toounsmen" and a dozen bridesmaids. The procession marched to the castle in the great court, in which a quintain had been set up for feats of arms; when these games were concluded, a performance of the traditional Hock Tuesday play from nearby Coventry was enacted. Though these festivities were staged outside her window, apparently the queen did not see much of them because, Langham tells us, "her highnes beholldin in the chamber delectabl dauncing indeed: and heerwith the great throng and unruliness of the peopl, waz cauz that this solemnitee of Brydeale and dauncing had not the full muster waz hoped for" (ll. 722–726). Elizabeth asked that the Hocktide play be performed again for her on the following Tuesday; Langham does not mention whether the morris dance was also repeated for the queen's pleasure.

I begin with this anecdote because it marks an early, and loaded, moment in the complex history of the cultural performance known as morris dance. Langham's account makes it clear that morris dance was understood by him, and presumably by the other spectators at Kenilworth, to be a traditional country dance of the lower classes, a rustic entertainment linked with somewhat coarse and buffoonish parish rituals and games. Its social and cultural nexus, then, is in Langham's eyes the world of the "folk" and of "tradition," concepts that by the late sixteenth century were already accruing considerable ideological weight. At the same time, the Kenilworth morris dance was taken to be entertainment fit for a queen and, moreover, suitable for proclaiming an aristocratic subject's loyalty to her. Tellingly, although Langham's attitude is that of a would-be urban sophisticate observing country customs, he does not explicitly question the appropriateness of these rustic performances for the occasion, although he treats them with some condescension. As a calculated gesture of homage, the Kenilworth morris dance might well have been designed to conjure up a shared national identity rooted in an "auncient" folk culture linking commoners and royals alike.[3] That the queen preferred the "delectabl dauncing" in her chamber to the rustic festivities outside her window suggests something about her personal tastes; that she requested the reenactment of the rustic entertainments on another day seems to imply that she nonetheless recognized their importance as symbolic gesture.[4]

The Kenilworth morris dance can be seen in part as a careful staging of reciprocal power relations, a theatrical gift designed to reaffirm a network of patron-client relations connecting sovereign to lord to commoners through what was presumed to be a mutual interest in traditional "English" pastimes.[5] But when inscribed within Langham's account—which, though self-styled a letter "untoo hiz freend a Citizen, and Merchaunt of London," was published in the form of an octavo black-letter pamphlet—the Kenilworth morris dance entered into a broader set of social relations, and its meanings became less determinate and more complicated. What R. J. P. Kuin has called the pamphlet's "racily colloquial description of especially the more popular entertainments" suggests that the pamphlet was geared to a broad spectrum of readers and was perhaps deliberately designed to feed the growing appetite for accounts of both popular performances and extravagant spectacles.[6] In Langham's pamphlet the morris dance of Leicester's gesture of fealty has become a marketable commodity projected out into wider circuits of consumption, a rustic performance stamped with the mark of "English tradition" and offered up for the enjoyment of urban readers.

To put it more broadly, in Langham's letter we can see in some detail the epistemological conditions and procedures that shape historical understanding. Today Langham's pamphlet counts as an important source for information about medieval and early modern morris dance: it offers a rare description of a morris dance and its performers, costumes, and context. Yet it is hardly a neutral document. The obviously slanted nature of Langham's account of the Kenilworth morris dance serves as a reminder of a fundamental aspect of archival documents, which are not transparent windows onto past events but representations shaped by those who recorded them. Even if in extreme form, Langham's record of the morris dance performed for Elizabeth I points to the situatedness and interestedness of all documentary evidence—whether eyewitness accounts, legal records, costume and property lists, records of payments, or personal memories—by means of which we may seek to understand past performances.

As Langham's pamphlet reveals, it is hard to find a better example than the morris dance for exploring the complexities of both medieval performance practices and subsequent appropriations of those practices. I should perhaps note here that, although the examples of medieval morris dancing that I discuss date from the sixteenth century, this does not disqualify them from consideration as medieval performances. Indeed the issue of periodization is vexed, particularly as it relates to medieval and early modern drama. Historians of medieval theatre stress that only at the end of the sixteenth century did the cultural conditions that had given shape to the dramatic performances so central to medieval community life change irrevocably under the joined impulses of a growing centralization of power in London, the removal of performance from public areas to playhouses, and the increasing dominance of religious reform movements that regulated and repressed popular culture.[7] Given the problematic nature of period concepts and the messiness of historical events and practices, with their disconcerting tendency to spill beyond the ends of centuries and across the boundaries of eras and ages, a flexible approach to the historical contexts of early morris dance seems warranted for any attempt to understand its historical representation.

Because it is a dance-based performance, morris dancing brings to the foreground problems of historical recovery and interpretation that are shared by many, if not most, medieval performances, even those for which scripts exist. The act of dancing is by its very nature difficult to record or preserve, often surviving in unwritten forms such as personal memory and passed-down or reconstructed performances; hence historic dance of necessity exists largely outside of representation.[8] Moreover, like the many medieval performances that never existed in the form of a written script (such as bear-baiting, processions, king games, mummings, and other ceremonials and festive rituals), whenever dance enters into systems of signification, it does so in haphazard, partial, and inevitably distorted ways. Much of what we know about medieval morris dancing, for example, comes obliquely from records of payment for costumes and performers or from prohibitions and complaints. While these records point to a number of occasions on which morris dancing took place, they do not reveal much about what those performances consisted of, why they occurred, who performed, or who watched. Nor is it at all clear how representative the extant records are and therefore how much we can generalize from them.

As Michael Heaney points out, only one brief record of the hiring out of its "morice gere" in 1530 reveals that there were morris dancers at Guildford, Surrey, who had presumably been performing for a number of years, because their costumes were in storage at the Church of the Holy Trinity.[9] Without this one record, what Heaney believes to have been a lengthy history of morris dancing at Guildford would be unknown. In addition to the patchiness of the records, early documents come disproportionately from the wealthy, literate classes in cities, towns, large households, and at court, which also distorts the history of early morris dancing. Additionally, because for dance the memory of performers is a key part of the archive that allows us access to the past and because memory is so vulnerable to loss, the archive for early morris dancing necessarily contains a large gap. As a result, questions about morris dancing's venues in the premodern period, the auspices under which it occurred, what it consisted of, and what people thought of it resist easy answers.

What should interest performance historians is that these difficulties are by no means unique to morris dancing but rather are an inescapable feature of the historical study of medieval performances. The archive offers a rich resource but also to some degree a problematic one, particularly in its incompleteness and elusiveness, for investigating the cultural work of early and indeed many later performances. Even in the case of those performances for which a script is extant, performance practices and cultural uses can be hard to discover. In fact, recent archival projects such as the Records of Early English Drama (commonly known as REED) have shown—paradoxically, given their aim of retrieving as much information about early performances as possible—just how much remains unknown and unknowable, no matter how many records are located and published. Part of this unknowability results from the very methods used for retrieval and dissemination. With their practice of extracting records from archival depositories, for instance, such archival projects inadvertently erase the intricate connections linking a specific performance to surrounding events and practices. At the same time, by systematizing the information they retrieve—sorting it into categories determined by chronology or topic—archival projects sometimes destroy traces of the representational practices within which early performances were embedded. As a result, the situational density of the performance and its representational modes can be obliterated.[10] Morris dancing deserves notice precisely because it provides such an illuminating example of the gap that is thus opened up between medieval practices and modern historiography.

In the past several decades the study of medieval drama has been virtually transformed by a return to the archive, with effects that deserve scrutiny. When, after centuries of nearly total neglect, medieval plays began to receive serious scholarly attention in the late nineteenth and early twentieth centuries, the archival work of editors and critics such as Edmund Chambers and Karl Young or collections of records published by the Malone Society was at best haphazard and impressionistic. That state of affairs continued for much of the twentieth century, changing only recently with the introduction of large-scale archival projects aimed at a systematic sifting of extant records for evidence of performances.

The best-known attempt is the REED project, which seeks to find and publish all extant references to early drama in England. Founded in 1975 and operating under the auspices of the University of Toronto and with financial support from the Canadian government, REED is a long-term attempt by a team of more than fifty scholars to find, transcribe, and publish all surviving records pertaining to medieval drama in Britain. Fifty volumes are projected, each devoted to a specific geographic region of England. Typical entries record information such as accounts of payments, items of costume, names of actors, prohibitions, and disputes. The focus of the REED project is not dramatic texts but rather records that reveal details about the circumstances surrounding the original performance. As Theresa Coletti has noted, the assumption behind the REED project is that unearthing every detail related to performance will lead to "a true and full history of English drama."[11] This dream of wholeness may be a flaw more specific to the REED project than to other returns to the archive, but nearly all reliance on the archive runs the risk of removing evidentiary material from the contexts within which its meanings arise, as Peter Holland has noted about REED.[12] The critique of REED mounted by Coletti and Holland, among others, calls attention to the limitations of uncritical reliance on the archive. While the specificity of archival work such as the REED project promises to provide local habitations and homes to dramatic activity, it can do so only if archival information is recontextualized within the social, economic, and political conditions and contexts of performance.

Morris dance has remained a living performance practice in at least some locations since the sixteenth century and, more importantly, has been appropriated by various political and cultural agendas at specific moments. It thus usefully focuses attention on how the act of appropriation can color historical analysis. Because it was performed by village groups up through the nineteenth century, a tradition that Keith Chandler has chronicled,[13] medieval morris dancing is both accessible through those performances and inaccessible, given that continuity and change have to be factored into any act of historical retrieval based on living examples. The late nineteenth- and early twentieth-century revival of morris dancing by folk dance enthusiasts also has had an inevitably distorting effect on our ability to come to terms with earlier performances. Roy Judge has noted, for instance, that the revivalist version of the morris dance espoused by Cecil Sharp in the early twentieth century came to dominate performance studies so completely that "it is difficult to have a clear perspective of what was there before him."[14] Attempts to trace the early history of morris dancing have been strongly marked by revivalism (whose onset can already be seen in the Kenilworth morris dance), which aimed not just to revive but also to reshape existing village performances in ways consistent with assumptions about the nature of medieval morris dancing. Given those revivalist interventions, it is all but impossible to study morris dancing without being continually reminded of how past practices are mediated by subsequent appropriations that both reveal and conceal them.[15]

Among those appropriations, of course, is the archive, that body of documentary evidence that is at once our best source of information about past performance practices and, by virtue of its mediatory nature, an obstacle to full recovery of those practices (if full recovery was ever possible). As with the jig (another neglected form of early performance), scholars have been slow to gather the archival traces of morris dance, most of which have remained buried in the historical record until quite recently.[16] With the return to the archive, morris dance has become more visible as a performance practice, even if it has yet to be fully considered within the context of other early performances, especially plays for which scripts survive. Reliance on the archive has in great measure rescued early morris dance from oblivion, if at the risk of obscuring its relations to other forms of early performance, particularly plays for which scripts survive.

Morris dance overlapped with other cultural activities in complex ways, intersecting with civic pageants, parish festivities, and courtly entertainments as well as quasi-criminal acts such as ritual trespass, robbery, and riot. My first task, then, is to outline the cultural spaces occupied by late medieval morris dancing; in so doing, I draw on, but to some degree read against the grain of, recent archival work—especially the valuable research of the *Annals of Early Morris* and the REED project—as I try to reposition the documentary records within a specifiable network of cultural practices and read them as representational arts. My second task is to trace the complex patterns of appropriation, recuperation, and revival that intervene between, but also connect, the present historiographer and the past performance. Starting in the seventeenth century, when Robert Dover revived the defunct Whitsun revels as the Cotswold Games and when James I's *Declaration of Sports* (popularly known as "the Morris Book") sought to promote traditional games and performances, and continuing through the medieval revival of the nineteenth and twentieth centuries, morris dance has been subjected to the shifting desires of successive waves of enthusiasts. The effects of these revivals are by now so pervasive that investigation of medieval morris dancing can scarcely be separated from its received history.

One obvious legacy of the received history of morris dancing, whose modern phase tellingly overlaps with growing interest in nationalism and folk cultures, has been a preoccupation with the question of origins. Many modern revivalists, including Cecil Sharp, Mary Dean, and D'Arcy Ferris, viewed morris dancing as a survival of primitive pan-European religious fertility ceremonies, and folklorists still argue for the dance's origins in folk ritual.[17] This interest in ritual exhibited by scholars of the morris dance echoed the work of the Cambridge anthropologists, whose turn-of-the-century writings on ritual were widely influential, particularly for the study of Greek drama.[18] As Chandler notes, one problem with claims for the ritual beginnings of morris dance is that they are highly conjectural.[19] Despite that limitation, the preoccupation with origins certainly says something about the desire to see morris dance as a folk performance originating in the distant past, a desire that is already visible in Langham's description of the Kenilworth morris dance as having been performed according to "the auncient manner."

But, in fact, the recorded history of morris dancing in England is far from ancient. The two earliest references to English morris dance are found in wills of 1458 that mention objects with representations of what might be morris dancing on them; one of the objects was a silver cup bearing a "sculpt. de moreys dauns," bequeathed by Alice Wetenhalle of Bury St. Edmunds and London to her son.[20] References to actual dancing first appear in 1466 in Cornwall, where a "moruske" is mentioned, and in 1477 in London, for a dance called the "morisse." The 1466 reference is in a household account book from the estate of the Arundell family in Cornwall, recording Christmas festivities; Sir John Arundell had served as a general for Henry VI in the war with France, which is perhaps significant for theories arguing for the continental origin of morris dancing.[21] The 1477 allusion appears in the records of the Company of Drapers in a reference to the London Midsummer Watch procession of that year, which featured a morris dance sponsored by the Drapers.[22] It should be stressed that all of these early mentions are in objects or texts associated not with "the folk" but with the wealthier classes.

In the sixteenth century references to morris dance multiply along with problems of interpretation. At Plymouth, for instance, was the dancing mentioned in 1498–1499 to raise money for Saint Andrews parish the same as the morris dancing frequently mentioned in later Plymouth records or was it some other kind of dance?[23] At Chester in 1583–1584 the Cordwainers and Shoemakers paid "the morris dauncers" for performing in the Midsummer show; does their earlier payment in 1562–1563 to the "cheldren that dansed the hobbe horses" refer to a morris dance as well? And, since the Chester Midsummer show is said to have begun in 1499, did it include morris dancing at that time too?[24] When the Newcastle Merchant Adventurers' Book of Orders in 1603 forbids apprentices "to daunce, dice, carde, Mum, or vse anye musick," are the apprentices being forbidden to dance the morris?[25] When the household accounts of Edward Stafford, Duke of Buckingham, record payment in 1516–1517 for "moresbelles" and for red and black buckram for "Tunicis pro le moresdaunce," presumably they refer to performers who danced for the duke, but who were those performers?[26] And when the Saint Mary's churchwardens' accounts from Shropshire in 1584–1585 ask "whether there haue bene any Lordes of mysrule, or sommer hordes, or ladies or any Disguised persons, as morice dauncers, maskers, or mummers or such lyke within ye parishe ether in ye natiuititide or in sommer, or at any other tyme, and what Ix their names?" are morris dancers being understood as lords of misrule or as disguisers or both?[27]

Perhaps the most surprising thing about these accounts is that they pay so little attention to the actual performance. They provide no description of what the dancing was like and only the slightest of hints as to who the dancers and spectators were, with just a bit more information about costumes. Certainly this omission has a great deal to do with the nature of the early accounts, which are usually just that: accounts concerned with payments for costumes or performers. But even eyewitness reports such as those in Henry Machyn's diary or in Langham's letter provide few details of the actual performance. Although John Forrest and Michael Heaney argue with some justification that "it is unreasonable to expect a sixteenth-century ambassador to England watching a Midsummer guild procession to record the features of the morris dance therein with the exquisite precision expected of a twentieth-century fieldworker,"[28] the lack of descriptive detail might also suggest that both the recorders and audiences were quite familiar with the conventions of the performance. Elaboration of descriptive detail is therefore unnecessary. It seems at least possible that the terse and prosaic nature of these accounts reveals the ordinariness and, quite literally, the unremarkableness of the dance. Such terseness might also hint at a value judgment on the part of early recorders: morris dancing neither required nor warranted detailed description. Only by the time of Langham, when the entertainment and commercial possibilities of "folk" performances were becoming visible, do lengthier accounts of morris dancing begin to appear.

Philip Stubbes's *Anatomie of Abuses* (1583), which follows Langham's account by half a dozen years, gives the fullest description of early morris dancers that we have:

> thie tye about either legge twentie, or fourtie belles, with riche hande kercheefes in their handes, and somtymes laied a crosse ouer their shoulders and neckes. . . . Thus all thynges sette in order, then haue thei their Hobbie horses, Dragons and other Antiques, together with their baudie Pipers, and thundderyng Drommers, to strike vp the Deuilles Daunce withall, then marche these Heathen companie towardes the Churche and Church yarde, their Pipers pipyng, their Drommers thonderyng, their stumppes Dauncyng, their belles iynglyng, their handerchefes swyngyng about their heades like madmen, their Hobbie horses, and other monsters skirmishyng amongest the throng.[29]

Stubbes goes on to complain that the dancers would enter the church, disturb the sermon, and then go into the churchyard, where they would dance away the day and the night. It seems probable that the fullness of Stubbes's account has as much to do with a desire to anatomize (and hence demonize) the target of his attack in all its outrageousness as with the need to remind readers of the features of the performance. Most certainly he does not valorize the performance in any way. Stubbes's description is aimed at detailing the offending accouterments of morris dancers. As his adjectives richly reveal, everything from bells and pipers to hobby-horses and monsters shocked the reformer's sensibilities. Records earlier than these suggest that morris dancing was viewed as a familiar and fairly common activity that merited no special attention and attracted no unusual interest from the account-keeping classes. However often it was performed, morris dancing up to the 1570s and 1580s seems to have existed largely outside of official recognition, at the fringes of the written record.

A striking aspect of these early records is that they point to the tangle of cultural performances in which early morris dance is embedded. In early accounts, morris dancing is usually mentioned along with other kinds of performances and spectacles to which it contributed, such as Midsummer watches, May games, church ales, processions, court masques, and plays. Although morris dancing could occur alone, most famously in the solo morris dance from London to Norwich performed by Will Kemp in 1600, it was more often just one element of entertainment at organized seasonal festivities that usually included drama, dancing, music, feasting, drinking, athletic contests, rough humor, disguising, and role reversals.[30] The considerable overlap between morris dancing and other kinds of performances within which it occurred can be seen in the way that characters from those performances (for example, Robin Hood, Maid Marian, the fool, the hobbyhorse, and the friar from the May games) gradually were folded into the morris dance, especially after the May games died out. Overlap also can be seen in the confusion of terms in sixteenth-century references to dances, suggesting a lack of clear distinctions among different kinds of song-dance performances: the terms "jig," "hornpipe," "morris," "sword-dance," and even "ballad" are often used interchangeably.[31] Early records thus imply that morris dancing was not understood as a discrete, autonomous performance but rather as a performative activity contiguous with, and integral to, other forms of festivity and ceremonial spectacle.

One outcome of this lack of detailed description of morris dance, combined with its inextricability from other performances, is to reveal a disparity between modern historiography and medieval practice. Our tendency as scholars is to seek to pinpoint morris dance as a single entity, to delineate its constituent parts, and to isolate it from other events and performances. But no amount of archival searching will ever fully satisfy these desires when the representational practices encoding medieval morris dance refuse to pinpoint, delineate, and isolate in our categorical manner. Although morris dance's lack of visibility and its entanglement with other performances may prove frustrating to modern scholars, that entanglement nonetheless points beneficially to the ways in which our attempts to organize, define, and understand are often at odds with early performance and representational practices.[32] One has to wonder, for instance, how often medieval morris dances are implied in references to various kinds of festivity but (because not designated by the term "morris dance") never show up in modern taxonomies that require an act of naming before the existence of a performance practice can be recognized.[33]

By the end of the sixteenth century, however, dance treatises began to appear, starting the process of defining and stabilizing morris dance as a discrete cultural performance. This stabilization took place even though village morris dancing continued to be performed and, by being performed, continued to change, as does any living performance. The most important of the early dance treatises was the *Orchesographie* of Thoinot Arbeau (1588), which describes various traditional and new dances, including a solo morris, and John Davies's *Orchestra* (1594), which gives a history of dance in England and outlines the features of specific dances. In 1651 John Playford's *The Dancing Master* ambitiously took on the task of classifying various folk dances (including sword, morris, and country-dance), establishing labels and categories still in use today.[34] Unfortunately, these attempts at categorization do not really offer a satisfactory way of understanding medieval morris dancing. To take one vivid example, what can they say about the fact that, as Heaney points out, some of the best evidence of medieval morris dance comes not from any mention of the dance itself but rather from records of the trade in bells (with accounts from the port of London, for instance, showing that in 1567–1568 ten thousand morris bells were imported, most from Antwerp)?[35]

As these bells suggest, morris dancing in late medieval England had an economic valence and involved monetary transactions, whether for the purchase of costumes and accessories such as bells or for payment of the dancers. Moreover, morris dance was usually associated with specific kinds of performance occasions: all of the documented morris dances occurred on festive occasions during which a mix of music, dance, mimetic representation, spectacle, impersonation or disguising, and athletic feats came together, usually as part of irreverent holiday revelry with militaristic or antidisciplinary overtones. Thus morris dance was situated within a particular kind of performance in which the dancing added to the atmosphere of licensed misrule and inversions that informed these festivities. These contexts suggest that medieval morris dancing often contributed to the communal rituals of social exchange and negotiation.

Medieval morris dancing, however, apparently was not restricted to one particular social group or even to one locale. Instead it was relatively fluid in terms of its geographic and social venues, appearing at court, in rural parishes, and in urban settings.[36] The ease with which morris dance could cross social and geographic borders is part of what makes any search for the dance's origins nearly impossible. Is it, for instance, an aristocratic dance imitated by commoners or the other way around? Answering that question is difficult, given the social fluidity of morris dance. It is true that morris dancers themselves usually came from social groups lower than those who hired or sponsored them, as was the case at the Kenilworth entertainments as well as in guild and parish performances.[37] While the serially inferior position of the dancers does not necessarily point to the dance's origins in the "folk," it does suggest why later observers and appropriators of morris dancing could so readily turn it into a privileged sign of a native folk culture. It also suggests something about the kinds of cultural work, including the work of softening social antagonisms, that medieval morris dancing might have performed.

Before the 1570s morris dancing took place in a number of different locales. One of these was parish summer entertainments such as the Whitsun festivities at Kingston upon Thames, where the churchwardens' accounts provide an unusually full record of morris dancing. The dancing at Kingston was associated with the Whitsun Robin Hood and King games starting in 1507, the year morris dancing was first mentioned as part of the entertainments, and continuing until 1538, the final year of the account book and the year in which the inventory of goods in the wardens' keeping included "a fryeres Cote of Russett & a Kyrtell of wostedde weltyd wt Redd cloth a mowrens Cote of Bvckrame & iiij morres Dawnseres Cotes of whitte fustyan spangelyd & ij gryne saten Cotes and a Dysarddes [fool's] Cote of Cotten and vj payre of garderes wt Belles."[38]

Records from other parishes also mention morris dancing as part of summer festivities. On August 10, 1513, Reading held a celebration on the church's dedication day that included 3d paid for "a hope for the joyaunt and for ale to the Moreys dawncers."[39] In 1525 the churchwardens' accounts from Saint John's Bow in Exeter, which staged a Robin Hood play, record the mending of morris dancers' bells, although morris dancing itself is never mentioned in the accounts.[40] In Leicester in 1558–1559 there was a "mawrys daunce of chyldren." In Northill, Bedfordshire, in 1562 and again in 1565 accounts show that a fool and a morris dance with six dancers were part of a May game with a summer lord. The village of Winterslow in Wiltshire held a series of king ales featuring morris dancers from 1564 to 1574 and hired "morris gere" in 1564.[41]

London parishes similarly put on shows that included morris dancing. St. Olave's parish, Southwark, hired morris dancers to perform on the parish church's feast day, July 29, ca. 1559.[42] In 1571 the parish of St. Giles Cripplegate recorded payment "for the settinge forth of a gyaunt Morres Daunce. With vj. calyvers and iij boies on Horsbak, to go in the watche befoore the Lorde Maiore uppon midsummer even."[43] Machyn describes several instances of morris dancing, including a maypole, a giant, and a castle that came into Fanchurch parish on May 26, 1552. Machyn recounts a May game at Westminster on June 3, 1555 (Whitmonday), which included giants, "mores-pykes," guns and drums, devils and three "mores-dansses," bagpipes and viols, with many people disguised, a lord and lady of the May, and minstrels. He also makes note of a May game in the London parish of St. John Zachary at Midsummer, June 24, 1559, that featured a giant, guns, morris dancers, and pageants with the Nine Worthies, St. George and the Dragon, and Robin Hood.[44] In parish entertainments such as these, morris dancing took its place alongside rituals of festive misrule that often included displays of physical and at times even militaristic might. The antic leaps and bounds of morris dancing (commented upon by later observers) make sense within this quasi-military setting, where grotesque display, extravagant spectacle, and exhibits of physical prowess came together.[45]

Morris dancing was also a feature of street pageants such as the mock entry of Edward VI's lord of misrule, George Ferrers, into London on January 4, 1552.[46] According to Machyn, young knights and gentlemen on horseback landed at the Tower wharf and rode through the streets accompanied by guns, trumpets, bagpipes, flutes, a company of men dressed in yellow and green, and "then the mores danse dansyng with a tabret"; the lord of misrule wore "a gowne of gold furyd with fur of the goodlyest collers" and was followed by a company of men in red and white and a cart carrying instruments of punishment, including a gibbet and stocks. When the procession arrived at the scaffold that was set up at the cross in Chepe, a proclamation was made; afterward everyone drank, and the lord of misrule rode to the mayor's house for dinner, later sailing back to Greenwich.[47] On March 17, 1553, the sheriff of London processed through town with a standard and drums, giants, hobbyhorses, men on horseback, a "mores dansse," minstrels, a devil, a sultan, and Jake-of-Lent.[48] On January 31, 1557, the Marquis of Winchester's lord of misrule visited the lord mayor of London; and on New Year's Day in 1558 an unspecified lord of misrule came "from Westmynster" to the City of London.

Midsummer watches in London and other cities included morris dances, which are first mentioned in London in 1477, again in 1512, and then in 1521, 1522, and 1525, all years when a Draper was mayor, as Heaney notes.[49] In 1521 the Drapers agreed to "renew all the old pageants for the house," including "the *gyant*, Lord *Moryspyks*, and a morys dance" as well as costumes for a King of the Moors.[50] The 1522 procession was canceled and replaced by a reception for Charles VI on June 6, and payment was made by the Drapers "to William Burnet for a morysdaunce of viij &ij minstrelles riding in our apprelles. ij hattes &. xviij s." In 1529 Walter Fount supplied a morris dance on two nights for the fee of 13s 4d plus breakfast for the dancers; a giant and hobbyhorse were also featured that year. In 1541, the last year in which the Livery Companies' records mention morris dancing, the Drapers prepared for Midsummer processions with morris dancers but complained about the expense of hiring performers, particularly the outlay of 23s 4d paid to John Lymyr, a bowstring maker who lived in St. John's street, for the services of his company of seven morris dancers and their minstrel for two nights.[51]

At Chester the Painters supplied a dragon, six naked boys to beat the dragon, morris dancers, and music for the Midsummer show.[52] Although this record is undated, Chester's Midsummer show may have begun in the late fifteenth century or perhaps earlier and remained a more or less annual feature of the city's festivities until 1641. In 1562–1563 payment was made to the "cheldren that dansed the hobbe horses" and in 1583–1584 to "the morris dauncers."[53] David Mills argues that Chester's show was regarded as a celebration of the city and its government, a sort of Lord Mayor's Show that tried to emulate London's Midsummer show, which perhaps explains both the extravagance of the Chester show and its use of morris dancers.[54]

Christmas revels provided another venue for morris dancing. In 1511 Epiphany was celebrated by a revel in the banquet hall at Richmond: from a pageant car shaped like a hill came a "morryke dancyd by the kynges yong gentyllmen as hynsmen and ther to a lady."[55] According to Edward Hall's *Chronicle*, masques and morris dances were part of the staging of a Christmas play produced at Gray's Inn in 1526; the play showed how "lord gouernance" was ruled by dissipation and negligence, resulting in a great uprising that restored "Publik welth again to her estate."[56] The court revels of Edward VI probably included a morris dance among the entertainments in 1552–1553 that featured a drum-and-fife duo appareled like Turks, a "disard," jugglers, tumblers, fools, friars, "and suche other," along with mock hobbyhorse fights.[57]

These accounts offer ample evidence of the frequency of morris dancing in the ceremonial and festive culture of fifteenth- and sixteenth-century England. What they do not offer is a ready-made narrative that might explain the cultural functions and meanings of morris dance, and of course no archive can. A crucial factor in historical research has been the search for, and critique of, controlling narratives that promise to explain what it is that archival sources have to say. The history of performance scholarship is in some ways a history of the trying-on of various narratives that aim to make sense of evidence from the archive. In the case of morris dancing, documents from the fifteenth and sixteenth centuries point in several directions and open up a number of possible interpretive narratives.

One of the most obvious is a narrative of misrule, subversion, and symbolic exchange. As documents show, morris dancing was often associated with civic or household holidays, whether Christmas and Shrovetide revels or summer ceremonies. A consistent trait of these dances, no matter which community performed or watched them, was their connection with festive misrule. Like the Robin Hood, lords of misrule, and king games, with which it was associated, morris dancing was part of a world of entertainments that offered staged resistance to authority. Morris dancing was often linked to grotesque, antic, exotic, militaristic, and sexual display—hence the giants, hobbyhorses, naked boys, guns, drums, and maypoles that frequently accompanied it. The bells too—so often associated with morris dancing—can be seen as a kind of "rough music" that was often featured in other performances of raucous inversions.[58]

As performance historians and theorists have argued, the theatrical roles allow for displays of resistance within the space of festive performance. The costumes can be tried on; the rebellious acts can be tried out. In medieval culture the boundaries separating rebellion and its theatrical enactment were fluid; as Sandra Billington has said, "the customs of festive kings were embedded in outlawry and rebellion, and festivity was itself influenced by the exploits of outlaws and rebels."[59] The work of Mikhail Bakhtin offers a way of theorizing the relation between festivity and outlawry, between "performed" and "real" misrule (to use an obviously imprecise opposition), as recent scholarship has demonstrated. Yet we might also turn more profitably elsewhere: for instance, to Pierre Bourdieu's description of the relations between orthodoxy and heterodoxy and, more subtly, the workings of symbolic capital.[60] According to Bourdieu, both orthodoxy and heterodoxy inhabit what he calls opinion or "the universe of discourse." In other words, the discourses invite or allow everything that is discussible or able to be represented. The field of opinion is in turn contained within *doxa*, the universe of unquestioned assumptions. Certain strategies are available to dominant and subordinate groups in their relations with orthodoxy and heterodoxy. The most important of these for early morris dancing has to do with the way in which heterodoxy or misrule could be used to negotiate and contest orthodoxy and, more strongly, interrogate the boundaries between *doxa* and opinion, thus questioning the terrain on which orthodoxy and heterodoxy alike are constructed. What Bourdieu suggests is that attempts to impose definitions of reality (the thinkable and sayable) are always part of power struggles; and to the extent that misrule can assert an alternate reality, however temporarily, a certain realignment of *doxa* and opinion has taken place.

From the perspective of the interpretive narrative of misrule, morris dancing can be viewed as part of the symbolic labor of feasts, ceremonies, gift exchanges, visits, and other rituals of reciprocal relations. In this way morris dancing and other activities of performative and social exchange worked toward reproducing established relations as much as toward overthrowing them, no matter how much the activities may have contested orthodoxy. For this reason, medieval festivities of misrule were, perhaps not surprisingly, rarely genuinely subversive and were in fact most often deeply conservative, not only because they were usually sponsored by a local authority—whether king, mayor, guild, lord of a household, or parish church—but also because, as Michael Bristol argues, they were specifically designed to "restrain and limit all radicalization" whether from above or below.[61] Especially within the context of civic processions, court revels, and parish games, festive disorder in large part reaffirmed authority, offering reassurances about authority's ability to contain disorder and resolving it in a final image of unity and concord.

Moreover, even though such festivities of misrule also represented the invasion of space by outsiders who did not belong or by those who had no rights to that territory, the reciprocal gift giving on such occasions, as Peter Greenfield observes, "transforms this apparently discordant intrusion into a representation of social harmony."[62] Greenfield notes that various sorts of lords of misrule who intruded into the court or invaded the streets of the town did so by at least tacit invitation. Consequently, even if their symbolic invasion might have included overtones of usurpation—acts of defiance and challenge that would have been intensified by the mock-king theme associated with lords of misrule—that usurpation was neutralized by the ceremonial or festive context. This framed the usurpation as temporary and fictive and ultimately resolved it into an entertaining gift offered to those it initially seemed to threaten. As the archival evidence suggests, morris dance seems to have enacted ritual as well as actual trespass and staged something that looked like rebellion, but it did so within a carefully framed and controlled situation in which misrule was reassuringly only temporary.[63]

Although the narrative of subversion and misrule fits neatly with much of the documentary record, it is too singular and reductive to be fully satisfactory as an explanatory account. The extant records show morris dance to have been part of a cash nexus that encompassed the growing commercialization of leisure. Although it is often overlooked, especially by those who view medieval performances as the product of communal needs or as responding to social tensions, medieval ceremonial culture was by no means divorced from commercial interests, whether connected indirectly (for example, the York plays and the economic interests of the town's oligarchy) or directly (such as the use of Robin Hood games for parish fund-raisers). The records of medieval morris dancing are full of financial concerns about payment for performers or costumes and, in the case of parishes, about revenues raised from performances. At Exeter, for instance, the churchwardens' accounts from St. John's Bow in 1524–1525 state that, disappointingly, nothing was received that year from the "Campanarum pro le Morys danse."[64] In pointing explicitly to the financial interests underlying parish morris dance, Michael Heaney argues that the increase in the mention of morris dancing and church ales during the reign of Mary Tudor and the early years of Elizabeth I might reflect the parishes' need to raise money to reequip churches that had been stripped of their accouterments in earlier years.[65] Other records reveal contractual business arrangements between guilds and entertainers. In 1525, for example, payment was made by the London Drapers to "Walter ffount & his company that is to say viij persones with there mynstrell for a morisdance bothe nyghtes for the Mair' all goyng on fote bifore the constables sma xv s." The mayor that year, Sir William Bailey, provided "for a Reward to the moresdawncers iiij d And for Ale to the mynstrelles & moresdancers ij d sma vj d."[66]

A lengthy record from Salisbury in 1564 clearly shows the commercialization of morris dance and its marketing as an entertainment:

> and yt ys agreyd that Gregory Clerke shall have the keypynge of the ffyve morrys-cots, with xxti dosyn of Myllan-bellis, for the space of xii yeres, yf he so longe lyve, payeng yerely to the ocupacon iii s iv d and also the said Gregory do stand bound to the occupacon in the some of ffive pounds of lawful money of England, to delywer the same ffyve morys cots and xx doysen of Mylla-bells, at the end of said xii yeres, or at the oure of death of the said Gregory if he diye before, in as good case as he receuved it, and further the said Gregory byndyth hymself

> by these presents to delyver the said Cotts and bells at all tymes to the said occupation yf they wyll haue them to the use of the occupacion, and yt ys agreyd that the said Gregory shalbe bound to the Wardens of the occupacion, by wrytyng, obligatory in the some of ffyve poundes.[67]

As this suggests and as Heaney has argued, whereas the earlier history of morris dance showed sponsorship by a community (or lord of the manor) and payment to performers within that context, later morris dances were performed chiefly by self-sponsored traveling troupes that hired themselves out. The household accounts of the Duchess of Suffolk at Grimsthorpe, Lincolnshire, in 1562, for instance, note the payment of 2s to a solo morris dancer from the nearby village of Little Bytham, who came on his own initiative just as any other traveling player would. Corroborating this trend, evidence indicates that touring companies of morris dancers solicited money from the gentry during the early years of Elizabeth's reign.[68]

Although commercial and economic matters do not nullify the social factors, the archival evidence for a cash nexus surrounding morris dancing reveals the limitations of an interpretive narrative too narrowly focused on issues of class and rebellion. In short, the documents of early morris dancing are full enough to open up a number of possible interpretive narratives, yet too scanty to eliminate any of them. This is the situation for many performances from the past. As scholars, we seek historical interpretations that are probable or even certain. But much of the time we can go no further than to suggest what is possible. We must realize that the meaning of archival evidence depends to a large extent upon not only where and how we look at the records but also which narratives we bring to bear on the task of interpretation.

The later history of appropriations and revivals of morris dancing is remarkable for its reworking of medieval morris dance. Surprisingly, the process starts early, in the latter half of the sixteenth century, when morris dance enters the political and religious spheres as a loaded code, trope, or sign system deployable by various interested parties. Puritans used it as a mark of the licentiousness and misbehavior associated with their opponents; royalists and defenders of traditional religion treated it as a sign of a festive past shared by elites and commoners alike. Jane Garry argues that by the late 1500s mention of the morris dance had become "something of a literary conceit" used to invoke the festivity and merrymaking with which the dance was associated. Seasonal festivities, though easy targets for reformers, survived well into the Reformation. For instance, churchwardens' records of the Elizabethan period continue to include payments for maypoles and morris dancers, although mention of such payments becomes increasingly rare after the 1570s. Like maypoles, which were often seen as a source of community pride and a sign of harmless pleasure while at the same time being attacked as scandalous, morris dance became the focus of competing cultural traditions in the century after the Reformation.[69] In 1541 the Protestant Miles Coverdale complained about the "apish people, a nombre of desertes and scornefull mockers," who scorn the man who tries to "do as he is warned by Gods worde" because he "will not daunc in the devels morrys with them, ner kepe theyr companye in the bondage of synne and vyce."[70] Archbishop Edmund Grindal's visitation articles for York in 1571 echo Coverdale's sentiments, with their inquiry for the first time about morris dancing in churches and churchyards and their attempt to prohibit it. When the churchwarden of the parish of Didcot in Berkshire was cited in ecclesiastical court in 1580 for having made off with the Communion linen, he defended himself by protesting that the linen had been taken "owte of his howse by the morrice Dancers in his absence."[71] In a similar complaint, an observer in 1598 at Oxford described how men dressed in women's clothing brought a garlanded woman into town on Rogation Day and declared her queen of May and also introduced "morris dances and other disordered and unseemly sports."[72] It is perhaps not irrelevant that Rogation was a time of often rowdy perambulations and processions, being known in some parts as "roguing" week or "gang days."

In the following century morris dance continued to be treated with ambivalence. The churchwardens of Saint Cuthbert's parish in 1607 received permission from the dean to hold an ale to raise money for building repairs and improvements; the climax of the festivities was a procession that included the Lord of the May, the Pindar of Wakefield, Robin Hood, St. George and the Dragon, Noah's Ark, and the Sultan of Egypt, along with morris dancers and giants.[73] In Stafford in 1612 the maypole was converted into fire-fighting ladders; but morris dancing was still allowed, and the churchwardens allocated money for a new "fool's coat" to be worn at "The Hobby Horse."[74] Although a puritan-dominated House of Commons in 1614 passed an act prohibiting morris dancing and bear-baiting, the royal orders of 1617 (James I) and 1633 (reissued by Charles I) authorized May games, Whitsun ales, morris dances, and maypoles as long as they did not interfere with divine service.[75] These orders seem to have inspired Robert Dover's Cotswold games circa 1618, which attempted to revive the old pastimes. Yet attacks against morris dancing continued. In Shrewsbury in 1618–1619, for instance, Ralph Woode, a "lord of misrule," was brought to town court with his troupe of morris dancers because of their absence from evening prayer as well as assaults and disorder.[76] In 1628 Henry Burton, rector of St. Matthew Friday Street, London, in a wave of more stringent puritanism, attacked John Cosin for allowing "all kind of festivity and jollity and joviality, such as he terms necessary recreations; for example, rush-bearings, Whitsun ales, Morris dances, setting up of Maypoles, hearing of a play or seeing of a masque, or dicing and carding, or bowling or boozing."[77]

The Civil War of 1642–1653 curtailed entertainments, but supporters of the Royalist cause tried to maintain traditional games and pastimes. The Witney Wakes attended by Cavaliers in May 1646 included a morris dance of "some 6. or 7. Country fellowes with Napkins, and Scarfes, and Ribons tyed about them, and bells at their knees, according to the manner of that sport, and with them a *Mayd Marian*, and two fooles, who fell a dansing and capering."[78] In 1652, at Woodborough in Wiltshire, a "lewd company" with drummer and fiddler "very disorderely danced the morris-dance . . . drinking and tippling in the inn and alehouse till many of them were drunk."[79] With the Restoration in 1660, maypoles and morris dancing came back. On May 29, 1660, Charles II rode on horseback to the plain at Blackheath, where he watched "a kind of rural triumph, expressed by the country swains, in a morrice dance with the old music of taber and pipe."[80]

By the late nineteenth century, despite a continuous history of performance in villages in the intervening centuries, morris dancing was widely assumed to be an extinct activity of "ancient England" and hence evocative of supposed folk customs usually associated with that idealized past. When morris dancing was revived, it was often via antiquarians' accounts of early morris; D'Arcy Ferris, for instance, pasted his readings of antiquarian accounts onto the existing village morris of Bidford-on-Avon and used the resulting reconstruction as the basis for the morris shows he presented in London in the 1880s.[81] An advertisement for the 1886 show aptly catches contemporary attitudes toward morris dancing: "The Old English Morris Dance (not seen in London for 40 years) by villagers from Shakespeare's country, with Robin Hood, Friar Tuck, Little John and the Hobby Horse, and others."[82] Morris dancing had also become popular as a tool for teaching the lower classes, as evidenced by Maude Stanley's remarks in 1890 in *Clubs for Working Girls*: "The dances the girls like in our clubs are Valses, Polkas, Schottisches, Quadrilles, lancers, and the Morris dance."[83] At the same time, the nineteenth-century medieval revival was in full swing, and the most famous of the attempts to revive medieval performances had begun. The Elizabethan Stage Society was founded in 1894 by William Poel with the goal of performing Elizabethan plays as authentically as possible. In 1898 a morris dance was included in Poel's revivalist performance of *The Sad Shepherd*.[84]

The most influential modern revivalist of morris dance was Cecil Sharp, who in 1907 published the first volume of *The Morris Book* and two years later persuaded the Board of Education to use morris dancing in physical education programs. In 1911 Sharp helped found the English Folk Dance Society, which would become a center for the study and promulgation of morris dance. Sharp had first seen a morris dance at Christmas time in Headington, England, in 1899 but only became involved in its revival when the Esperance Working Girls' Club asked him to teach the dance to its members. In 1916 Olive Dame Campbell persuaded Sharp to come to the mountains of North Carolina, where he joined her and other settlement-school workers in introducing morris dance to their students, usually as a deliberate replacement of rowdier and hence less desirable activities. The introduction of morris dance into settlement-school curricula in America was part of a process of cultural reshaping that culminated in the 1939 White Top Festival in Virginia, the crowning event of the decades-long American folk revival movement. That year Richard Chase, who has been described as "one of the more audacious folk-revival entrepreneurs," coached a morris-dance team to perform at the festival. Although morris dancing had never been indigenous to Appalachia, Chase believed that he was reinstituting the superior cultural traditions of the Anglo-Saxon forebears of the Appalachian settlers, which in his view had been forgotten or had devolved into coarse and riotous local customs. In an article that must have met with his approval, a Richmond newspaper claimed that children trained by Chase would show "how the children of 'Merrie England' some 500 years ago played and danced on the village green."[85]

In the White Top Festival's uncanny echoing of Dover's Cotswold Games, it is possible to see the persistence of cultural appropriations of morris dance that continue to bear upon the retrieval and study of medieval morris dances. As the historical survey of morris dancing suggests, later appropriations of the dance are fundamentally at odds with medieval morris—despite the claims of scholarly authenticity by many of the revivalists. Forgotten by the time of White Top are the dense entanglements of medieval morris dancing with other performances; its associations with misrule; its involvement in contesting definitions of reality and the establishment of social relations through the enactment of misrule; and, finally, its intersection with the commercialization of leisure. It is in fact probably not inaccurate to say that the history of appropriations of morris dancing from the late sixteenth century on has been to a large extent a history of erasure of many constituent features of morris dancing in the late Middle Ages. As morris dancing was transformed into a sign of cultural superiority, innocent vitality, and "racial purity," medieval morris dancing receded ever further into unrecognizable form. At the same time, of course, revivalist interest in morris dance undoubtedly has been responsible for directing scholarly attention in recent decades (including my own) toward medieval morris dancing. This is yet another ironic transaction in historical study and research methods, a transaction between understanding and misunderstanding.

Representing the past inevitably involves a reliance on the archive. As morris dance reveals, this asks us to reflect on the limits of the documentary evidence for performance history. Historians have traditionally shown a preference for events over records, tending to sift through historical documents to find traces of what happened in the past. This form of historiography tends to ignore textuality—that is, it tends literally to look through historical documents as if they were transparent or neutral—in the search for an empirical reality that is imagined to lie somewhere beyond the documents that record it innocently and without motive. This historical perspective, which has operated widely in theatrical and literary history, has guided and justified the gathering and publication of many collections of medieval and Renaissance documents over the last century (such as the Malone Society Collections). But aspects of these historical methods and assumptions have been called into question by scholars who have come to recognize, in Hayden White's words, "the historically conditioned character" of historical understanding.[86] Such a perspective acknowledges that the past is always mediated, which is not to challenge archival research as a scholarly practice but to recognize that both the scholar and the archive are historically situated.

If archival documents do not mirror events but instead are themselves representations shaped by those who remembered and recorded the events, then the circumstances and media of those acts of recording or remembering deserve special consideration. Most records of early morris dance were written down under specific institutional auspices (as urban histories, household accounts, guild records, or court documents) that had a powerful effect on what events entered the written record and how they were described. In other words, accounts of early morris are usually motivated (rather than random) acts of appropriation by means of which events and practices entered the written record. A second round of appropriation occurred when documents in manuscript were selectively extracted and published in printed volumes, starting in the nineteenth century and continuing in archival-retrieval projects such as REED. Those analogue sources in manuscript or print are now undergoing a conversion into electronic format, a further appropriation with effects that are not yet clear. Recollected and reconstructed performances, such as morris dance revivals, constitute yet another medium for the representation of early performances and present their own challenges for anyone seeking to use them as resources for understanding past performances.

The archive, as this collection argues, is a key foundational idea that guides all historians—including those whose central concern is performance. It provides the most basic of the conceptual frameworks for historical representation. Reflecting on the importance of the archive for scholars of medieval drama, Alexandra Johnston, one of the prime movers of the REED project, once asked: "What if no texts survived?" Although her question assumes an overly neat opposition between "texts" (scripts of plays—a scarce commodity before the sixteenth century) and "external evidence" (archival documents), she still made an explicit point that served to demonstrate the importance of the archive for the study of early performance (as well as an implicit defense of the archive's supposed neutrality and thus reliability).[87] If we turned her question around to ask "What if no archive survived?" we would quickly recognize that the historical study of premodern performance would be nearly impossible.

Charlotte Canning and Tom Postlewait correctly argue in the introduction to this collection that every discipline has its own genealogy of perspectives and developments. In step with the humanities as a whole, the field of performance studies in recent years has been influenced by gender studies, postcolonialism, and new materialism, among others. With their challenges to the humanistic and positivist approaches that had earlier dominated the field of performance studies, these developments ushered in a rethinking of the aims and methods of performance historiography. For archival research, this rethinking brought new attention to the nature of documentary evidence, to questions about objectivity, and to the cultural contexts of documentary sources. At heart, all of that rethinking has been about mediation, particularly about the ways in which language mediates between the world and our understanding of it, which is to say, between us and the past. My discussion of the history of morris dance also has called attention to the mediating effects of successive waves of appropriation, which need to be considered a formative feature of the performance archive.

Although morris dance presents an extreme case, its situation is not unlike that of other medieval performances that are similarly available for scrutiny only through successive layers of appropriation that condition, often distort, but also help construct the interplay between past performance and subsequent historiographic reproductions of it. In this sense, morris dance provides a useful example for reflecting on the historiography of performances (and not just medieval performance). At a time when recent scholarship on medieval drama has increasingly turned to an exploration of medieval performances less as literary representations than as cultural practices or events, such reflection would seem to be especially warranted. As Clifford Flanigan has pointed out, during the formative years of the disciplines of literary and theatrical study, medieval drama was "everywhere regarded as a curiosity."[88] The subsequent history of medieval drama studies has been in large part a series of attempts to find ways of categorizing and accessing those dramatic curiosities. As Flanigan notes, the study of medieval drama has never fit well within literary studies; it also has generally been excluded from the larger field of theatre history. Instead, it has flourished at the margins of scholarly inquiry, where popular entertainment meets historiography. Morris dancing, too, has flourished at the same margins, from the moment when Langham recognized its mass-market appeal through present-day morris teams dancing with their bells and handkerchiefs at folk festivals and Renaissance fairs.[89] The history of morris dancing throws into relief some of the most vexing issues involved in studying medieval performances. Not least, it reminds us of how past practices, if they capture our attention at all, are legible only through the powerful lens of the present.

NOTES

1. R. J. P. Kuin, "Introduction," in Robert Langham, *A Letter*, introduction, notes, and commentary by R. J. P. Kuin (Leiden: Brill, 1983), p. 16.

2. Langham, *Letter*, ll. 498–564.

3. See Michael Heaney, "From Kingston to Kenilworth: Early Plebeian Morris," *Folklore* 100 (1989): 102, for a similar reading of the Kenilworth morris dance.

4. This was not the first morris dance Elizabeth had watched. Henry Machyn describes a May game in the London parish of St. John Zachary at Midsummer, June 24, 1559, which included a giant, guns, morris dancers, pageants of the Nine Worthies, St. George and the dragon, and Robin Hood. The May game was later played for Elizabeth at Greenwich. See *The Diary of Henry Machyn*, ed. John G. Nichols, Camden Society 42 (London: J. B. Nichols, 1848), p. 201.

5. Peter H. Greenfield's discussion of Christmas entertainments performed in aristocratic households as mechanisms for cementing relations between locals and lords is also relevant to the social dynamics of the festivities at Kenilworth; see his "Festive Drama at

Christmas in Aristocratic Households," in *Festive Drama*, ed. Meg Twycross (Cambridge: D. S. Brewer, 1996), pp. 34–53.

6. Langham, *A Letter*, line 7; and Kuin, "Introduction," p. 11. Two other pamphlets describing the Kenilworth festivities were also published: *The Pastime of the Progresse*, now lost, and George Gascoigne's *The Princely Pleasures at the Courte at Kenelwoorth* (1576). Gascoigne's pamphlet, apparently written for a "gentle" audience, dismisses the popular entertainments, including the "countrie shewe" and "the merry marriage" as "so plaine as needeth no further explication"; see J. W. Cunliffe, ed., *The Complete Works of George Gascoigne*, 2 vols. (Cambridge: Cambridge University Press, 1910), vol. 2, p. 106.

7. For a succinct discussion of these developments and their consequences for the study of medieval drama, see Kathleen M. Ashley, "Cultural Approaches to Medieval Drama," in *Approaches to Teaching Medieval English Drama*, ed. Richard Emmerson (New York: MLA, 1990), pp. 64–65. Glynne Wickham sees 1576 as a "watershed year" for medieval theater, because it marks the establishment of permanent playhouses as well as the start of the central government's suppression of religious drama; see his *Early English Stages, 1300 to 1660*, 4 vols. (London: Routledge and Kegan Paul, 1981), vol. 3, p. xix.

8. For a useful discussion of the difficulties of studying dance as well as an argument in favor of making dance research part of the project of cultural studies, see Jane C. Desmond, "Embodying Difference: Issues in Dance and Cultural Studies," *Cultural Critique* 26 (1993–1994): 33–63. See also the collection she edited, *Meaning in Motion: New Cultural Studies in Dance* (Durham, N.C.: Duke University Press, 1997).

9. Heaney, "From Kingston to Kenilworth," p. 96. For the 1530 record, see P. Palmer, *The Church of the Holy Trinity, Guildford* (Guildford: Frank Lasham, 1886), p. 8.

10. Skillful and creative use of the findings of archival projects can restore some of this situational density, but that does not lessen the degree of erasure of context that has taken place in the process of gathering archival information.

11. Theresa M. Coletti, "Reading REED: History and the Records of Early English Drama," in *Literary Practice and Social Change in Britain, 1380–1530*, ed. Lee Patterson (Berkeley: University of California Press, 1990), pp. 248–284 (quotation on p. 249).

12. Peter Holland, "Theatre without Drama: Reading *REED*," in *From Script to Stage in Early Modern England*, ed. Peter Holland and Stephen Orgel (New York: Palgrave Macmillan, 2004), pp. 43–67 (see p. 51).

13. Keith Chandler, *"Ribbons, Bells and Squeaking Fiddles": The Social History of Morris Dancing in the English South Midlands, 1660–1900* (London: Folklore Society, 1993).

14. Roy Judge, "Merrie England and the Morris, 1881–1910," *Folklore* 104 (1993): 124.

15. For instance, the dancers on the famous Betley window (ca. 1500–1520) are usually assumed to be morris dancers, but this assumption is chiefly based on later understandings of what morris dancers looked like; see Clifford Davidson, *Illustrations of the Stage and Acting in England to 1580* (Kalamazoo, Mich.: Medieval Institute Publications, 1991), pp. 94–98. Nonetheless, the new costumes made for the Abbots Bromley Horn Dancers in the late nineteenth century were based on the window, which was taken to represent what morris dancers were supposed to look like rather than on morris costumes in use by the village dancers; see Judge, "Merrie England," pp. 132–133.

16. In "Theatre without Drama," pp. 58–59, Holland briefly considers the limited investigation of the jig.

17. The most thorough argument for the pan-European folk origins of morris dancing is Violet Alford's *Sword Dance and Drama* (London: Merlin Press, 1962).

18. J. G. Frazer's *The Golden Bough* (1911–1915) is the best-known of these studies of ritual, but the writings of Gilbert Murray, Jane Ellen Harrison, and Francis M. Cornford were also influential. For a bibliography of the ritual scholars, see Shelley Arlen, *The Cambridge Ritualists: An Annotated Bibliography* (Metuchen, N.J.: Scarecrow Press, 1990).

19. Chandler, "*Ribbons*," p. 11.

20. John Forrest and Michael Heaney, "Charting Early Morris," *Folk Music Journal* 6 (1991): 169. It is possible that these objects were made on the continent, as Chandler notes ("*Ribbons*," p. 42). Figures that might be morris dancers also appear on the mid-fifteenth-century roof bosses at the Guildhall in York; see Davidson, *Illustrations of the Stage*, p. 162*n*75.

21. H. L. Douch, "Household Account at Lanherne," *Journal of the Royal Institution of Cornwall*, n.s. 2.1 (1953): 27–29; cited in Chandler, "*Ribbons*," p. 42.

22. A. H. Johnson, *The History of the Worshipful Company of the Drapers of London*, 2 vols. (Oxford: Clarendon Press, 1915), vol. 2, p. 273.

23. This question is raised by John Wasson in the introduction to *Records of Early English Drama: Devon*, ed. John Wasson (Toronto: University of Toronto Press, 1986), pp. xix–xx.

24. *Records of Early English Drama: Chester*, ed. Lawrence M. Clopper (Toronto: University of Toronto Press, 1979), pp. 137, 69, lii–liii.

25. *Records of Early English Drama: Newcastle*, ed. J. J. Anderson (Toronto: University of Toronto Press, 1982), p. 139.

26. *Records of Early English Drama: Cumberland, Westmorland, Gloucestershire*, ed. Audrey Douglas and Peter Greenfield (Toronto: University of Toronto Press, 1986), p. 359.

27. *Records of Early English Drama: Shropshire*, ed. Alan B. Somerset, 2 vols. (Toronto: University of Toronto Press, 1994), vol. 1, p. 239.

28. Forrest and Heaney, "Charting Early Morris," p. 170.

29. Philip Stubbes, *Anatomie of Abuses* (London: Richard Jones, 1583), fols. 92v–93r.

30. For a discussion of Kemp's dance, see Max Thomas, "*Kemps Nine Daies Wonder*: Dancing Carnival into Market," *PMLA* 107 (1992): 511–523.

31. See Charles Read Baskervill, *The Elizabethan Jig and Related Song Drama* (Chicago: University of Chicago Press, 1929).

32. Theresa Coletti's critique of the REED project is relevant here; see her "Reading REED: History and the Records of Early English Drama," in *Literary Practice and Social Change in Britain, 1380–1530*, ed. Lee Patterson (Berkeley: University of California Press, 1990), pp. 248–284.

33. For mentions of morris dancing in masques, interludes, and other entertainments, see John Forrest and Michael Heaney, *Annals of Early Morris*, based on the Early Morris Project (Sheffield: Centre for English Cultural Tradition and Language, University of

Sheffield, 1991). But they do not consider morris in plays or take up the general prohibitions against dancing. For additional information, see Forrest and Heaney, "Charting Early Morris," p. 174; and for a full account of the dance's history, see John Forrest, *The History of Morris Dancing, 1458–1750*, vol. 5 in the series Studies in Early English Drama (Toronto: University of Toronto Press, 1999).

34. See the discussion of these works in Baskervill, *The Elizabethan Jig*, p. 365.

35. Heaney, "From Kingston to Kenilworth," pp. 99–100.

36. See the charts of social/geographic distribution in Forrest and Heaney, "Charting Early Morris," pp. 179–185.

37. Thomas Pettitt, "English Folk Drama in the Eighteenth Century: A Defense of the *Revesby Sword Play*," *Comparative Drama* 15 (1981): 6, has argued that most folk performances involve performers who are of a lower status than their audience as part of "the relationship between such socially adjacent and interdependent groups."

38. Heaney, "From Kingston to Kenilworth," p. 92. Note that numbers are recorded as "ij" (2), "iiij" (4), and "vj" (6).

39. C. Kerry, *A History of the Municipal Church of St Lawrence, Reading* (Reading: published by the author, 1883), p. 227.

40. *Records of Early English Drama: Devon*, ed. Wasson, pp. 108, 118, 122–123.

41. T. North, *The Accounts of the Churchwardens of St Martin's, Leicester* (Leicester: S. Clarke, 1884), p. 80; J. E. Farmiloe and Rosita Nixseaman, *Elizabethan Churchwardens' Accounts*, Bedfordshire Historical Record Society 33 (Bedford: The Society, 1953), pp. 6–7; and Winterslow churchwardens' account, MS 45; all cited in Heaney, "From Kingston to Kenilworth," p. 100.

42. L. Blair, "Dramatic Activity of the Church as Seen in English Churchwardens' Accounts and Other Archival Sources of the Fourteenth, Fifteenth and Sixteenth Centuries" (Ph.D. dissertation, Yale University, 1933), p. 358; cited in Heaney, "From Kingston to Kenilworth," p. 99.

43. British Library Add. MS 12222, f. 5; cited in Heaney, "From Kingston to Kenilworth," p. 99.

44. Machyn, *Diary*, pp. 20, 89, 201.

45. Morris dancing in the sixteenth century apparently featured abrupt movement. In act 4 of *John a Kent and John a Cumber*, the leader of the morris dance says, "Let us jerk it over the greene." Quoted in Baskervill, *The Elizabethan Jig*, p. 353.

46. For a discussion of the political/ceremonial uses of street pageants, see David M. Bergeron, "Pageants, Politics, and Patrons," *Medieval and Renaissance Drama in England* 6 (1993): 139–152.

47. Machyn, *Diary*, pp. 13–14. Sydney Anglo, *Spectacle, Pageantry, and Early Tudor Policy* (Oxford: Clarendon Press, 1969), p. 308, notes that it was probably no coincidence that the next public entertainment at Tower Hill was the beheading of Somerset.

48. Machyn, *Diary*, p. 33.

49. Heaney, "From Kingston to Kenilworth," p. 94.

50. William Herbert, *The History of the Twelve Great Livery Companies of London*, 2 vols. (London, 1831 and 1834; reprint, New York: Augustus M. Kelley, 1968), vol. 1, p. 455.

51. J. Robertson and D. J. Gordon, *A Calendar of the Dramatic Records in the Books of the Livery Companies of London, 1485–1640*, Malone Society Collections, vol. 3 (London: Oxford University Press, 1954), pp. 11, 12, 17, 19, 20, 32.

52. British Library MS Harley 2150; discussed in David Mills, "Chester's Midsummer Show: Creation and Adaptation," in *Festive Drama*, ed. Meg Twycross (Cambridge: D. S. Brewer, 1996), p. 134.

53. *Records of Early English Drama: Chester*, ed. Clopper, pp. 69, 137.

54. Mills, "Chester's Midsummer Show," esp. pp. 135, 137.

55. Public Record Office, E 36/217, fols., 33–40; cited in Anglo, *Spectacle*, p. 118. Although earlier dances at courtly disguisings are not specifically designated as morris dancing, that is what they might have been, not least because they resemble this one in so many ways, once again suggesting the difficulties that modern scholars face in identifying what was and what was not a morris dance.

56. The play was largely the work of John Rowe, sergeant at law; Wolsey believed that it was about him and had Rowe sent to Fleet Prison along with one of the actors. Edward Hall, *Chronicle*, ed. Henry Ellis (London: n.p., 1809), p. 719, discussed in Anglo, *Spectacle*, pp. 238–239.

57. *Documents Relating to the Revels at Court in the Time of Edward VI and Queen Mary (The Losely Manuscripts)*, ed. Albert Feuillerat (Louvain: A. Uystpruyst, 1914), pp. 89–90.

58. See David Cressy, *Bonfires and Bells: National Memory and the Protestant Calendar in Elizabethan and Stuart England* (London: Weidenfeld and Nicolson, 1989), pp. 67–80, on bell ringing as a crucial part of festive celebrations that carried political overtones.

59. Sandra Billington, *Mock Kings in Medieval Society and Renaissance Drama* (Oxford: Clarendon Press, 1991), pp. 27–28.

60. See Pierre Bourdieu, *Outline of a Theory of Practice*, trans. Richard Nice (Cambridge: Cambridge University Press, 1977), pp. 158–183.

61. Michael D. Bristol, *Carnival and Theatre: Plebeian Culture and the Structure of Authority in Renaissance England* (London: Methuen, 1985), p. 52.

62. Greenfield, "Festive Drama at Christmas," p. 37.

63. Baskervill, *The Elizabethan Jig*, p. 362, observes that "morris" often seems to have referred to any "folk dance serving as a kind of antimasque": that is, morris suggested a form of ritual disorder, like the antimasque that was enveloped within the more orderly masque.

64. *Records of Early English Drama: Devon*, ed. Wasson, p. 126.

65. Heaney, "From Kingston to Kenilworth," p. 98. When Mary Tudor came to power in 1553, she ordered the restoration of altars, images, and festive performances as a real and symbolic reinstitution of the old faith abolished under the Protestant reform of the 1540s and early 1550s. The response from St. Lawrence's in Reading describes how morris costumes had been lost or sold; see C. Kerry, *A History of the Municipal Church of St Lawrence, Reading* (Reading: published by the author, 1883), p. 227.

66. Robertson and Gordon, *A Calendar of the Dramatic Records*, p. 17.

67. C. Haskins, *The Ancient Trade Guilds and Companies of Salisbury* (Salisbury: Bennett Brothers, 1912), pp. 171–172; cited in Heaney, "From Kingston to Kenilworth," p. 100.

68. Both examples are cited in Heaney, "From Kingston to Kenilworth," pp. 100–101.

69. Jane Garry, "The Literary History of the English Morris Dance," *Folklore* 94 (1983): 219–228 (quotation on 220). London's great maypole was in Cornhill until it was cut down in 1644; Cressy, *Bonfires*, p. 22.

70. Miles Coverdale, *The Olde Faythe* (Antwerp: M. Crom?, 1541), sig. *ij verso; quoted in Heaney, "From Kingston to Kenilworth," p. 96.

71. Berkshire Record Once, D/A2/C.16, fol. 89; cited in Alexandra F. Johnston, "'All the World Was a Stage': Records of Early English Drama," in *The Theatre of Medieval Europe: New Research in Early Drama*, ed. Eckehard Simon (Cambridge: Cambridge University Press, 1991), pp. 121–122.

72. Historical Manuscripts Commission, *Calendar of the Manuscripts of the Most Honourable the Marquis of Salisbury Preserved at Hatfield House, Hertfordshire*, 24 vols. (London: Her Majesty's Stationery Office, 1883–1976), 8:201; cited in Cressy, *Bonfires*, p. 23.

73. See David Underdown, *Revel, Riot, and Rebellion: Popular Politics and Culture in England, 1603–1660* (Oxford: Oxford University Press, 1985), p. 55.

74. Frederick W. Hackwood, *Staffordshire Customs, Superstitions and Folklore* (Lichfield: n.p., 1924), pp. 16–17.

75. Cited in Maija Jansson, *Proceedings in Parliament 1614* (House of Commons) (Philadelphia: American Philosophical Society, 1982), p. 316.

76. *Records of Early English Drama: Shropshire*, ed. Somerset, vol. 1, pp. 310–312.

77. Henry Burton, *Tryall of Private Devotions* (London, 1628), sig. F2.

78. Anthony Wood, *The Life and Times of Anthony Wood, Antiquary, of Oxford, 1632–1695*, ed. Andrew Clark, 5 vols. (Oxford: Clarendon Press, 1891–1900), vol. 1, p. 299 (emphasis in original).

79. *Records of Wiltshire*, pp. 221–222; cited in David Underdown, *Revel, Riot, and Rebellion: Popular Politics and Culture in England, 1603–1660* (Oxford: Oxford University Press, 1985), p. 264.

80. *England's Joy, or, A Relation of the Most Remarkable Passages, from His Majesty's Arrival at Dover, to His Entrance at Whitehall*, in C. H. Frith, ed., *An English Garner: Stuart Tracts 1603–1693* (Westminster: Constable, 1903), p. 428.

81. See Roy Judge, "D'Arcy Ferris and the Bidford Morris," *Folk Music Journal* 4 (1984): 443–480.

82. *City Press*, May 8, 1886, p. 1; quoted in Judge, "Merrie England," p. 126.

83. Quoted in Judge, "Merrie England," p. 131.

84. See Robert Speaight, *William Poel and the Elizabethan Revival* (London: Heinemann, 1954).

85. The information in this paragraph comes from David E. Whisnant, *All That Is Native and Fine* (Chapel Hill: University of North Carolina Press, 1983), pp. 79, 49–50, 209–230 (the newspaper article is quoted on p. 202).

86. Hayden White, *Tropics of Discourse: Essays in Cultural Criticism* (Baltimore: Johns Hopkins University Press, 1978), p. 20.

87. Alexandra F. Johnston, "What If No Texts Survived?: External Evidence for Early

English Drama," in *Contexts for Early English Drama*, ed. Marianne G. Briscoe and John C. Coldewey (Bloomington: Indiana University Press, 1989), pp. 1–19.

88. C. Clifford Flanigan, "Comparative Literature and the Study of Medieval Drama," *Yearbook of Comparative and General Literature* 35 (1986): 58.

89. For an account of recent American morris teams, see David M. Schwartz, "Morris Dancers Are Coming and So It Must Be May," *Smithsonian* 12 (May 1981): 118–125. I wish to thank Tami Kaplan for sharing her collection of material on modern morris dancing teams.

2 Time

Cyclic Perseverance and Linear Mobility of Theatrical Events

During the debate preceding the première of *The Marriage of Figaro* by Pierre-Augustine Caron de Beaumarchais in 1784, the French king Louis XVI is said to have declared: "The production of the play would be a dangerous inconsequence, unless one would first tear down the Bastille."[1] *Figaro* did première in 1784 at the Comédie Française, as we know, and five years later the Bastille was stormed by the people of Paris. Perhaps the French monarch would not have expressed himself in this way had he known that the fall of the Bastille and the fall of his own head were so close in time.

Because historians know what happened in France in the 1780s, they tend to use the French Revolution as a reference point for understanding *Figaro*. This coupling of the two events produces a historical problem, however, because a retrospective meaning is imposed upon the initial event, as if the future event and its consequences already existed in embryo within the earlier event. Is it possible to create an adequate picture of a historical event by mentally eliminating the events that followed it? Is it appropriate? Do events lose part of their meaning if they are dealt with separately, apart from what came after? Because historians always look backward, they usually see events as part of a sequence and often assume that a causal linkage joins the events and gives them their identities and meanings. Such a perspective is common because of the traditional concept of time as a progressive movement. Time is thus conceived in terms of the organizing idea of a developmental progress. Yet for the participants within an event the present experience lacks a future result. Even when agents are attempting to produce an event or action that will influence or bring about a future event or action, they rarely know what will actually happen in the future. The future is still open, full of potential but no certainties. Instead participants within events are much more aware of how and why an event derives from or is related to previous events. Its identity is retrospective. At the initiating moment of an event, the agents and participants often derive their understanding from references to—and patterns of—past experiences. Therefore, in order to make sense of an experience, participants usually seek to understand their present actions by means of similarities with previous actions.

FIGARO AS EVENT

To understand the furor around the première of *Le Marriage de Figaro*, I suggest a closer look at what happened at the Comédie Française on April 27, 1784. Luckily there are some useful documents. In his *Mémoires*, the French comedian Abraham-Josef Bénard Fleury describes the actors who appeared onstage:

> Dazingcourt was full of spirit and intelligence; Preville rendered Bridoison a masterly character; Mademoiselle Sainval, in the Countess, evinced a degree of talent which she was not previously supposed to possess; Molé increased his already high reputation, by his personation of the Count Almaviva; Mademoiselle Olivier threw the most enchanting archness and roguishness into the character of the Page. But the gem of the whole performance was Mademoiselle Contat's personation of Suzanne. That actress had heretofore played only the fine ladies of comedy; but it was a happy thought of Beaumarchais to offer her the role of the soubrette. He anticipated successfully the versatility of her talent.[2]

Monsieur Fleury not only commented upon his fellow comedians but also remembered the crowd that entered the theatre. Long before the première "persons of the highest rank, even princes of blood," had besieged Beaumarchais for tickets.[3] Noblewomen not only sent their valets but joined the excited mass that violently tried to force the doors of the theatre open. Fleury continues:

> But whilst all this was happening outside, the disorder which prevailed within the theatre was, if possible, still greater. No less than three hundred persons who had procured tickets at an early period, dined in the boxes. Our theatre seemed transformed into a tavern, and nothing was heard but the clattering of plates and the drawing of corks. Then, when the audience was assembled, what a brilliant picture presented itself. The *élite* of the rank and talent of Paris was congregated there. What a radiant line of beauty was exhibited by the first tier of boxes![4]

As these statements suggest, a lively interaction involving the actors, the play, and the audience had occurred from the very beginning of the performance. But when did the performance actually start? Conventionally, the rising of the curtain would indicate the proper beginning of a performance. But the audience members—or many of them—were in the theatre long before that. Can their dining and drinking be considered part of the performance? If so, then the turmoil outside the theatre, the fighting for tickets, and the curious bystanders observing the crowd would also be included. Some distinctions seem to be needed.

As long as we limit the theatre event to the actual interaction between the actors playing onstage and the spectators participating in the auditorium, I call this interaction *Theatrical Playing*. This kind of playing includes not only the players onstage but also the spectators engaging actively in the playing, both physically through their bodily attention and mentally through their willingness to imagine the characters and the plot presented on the other side of the footlights. And only at the end of the performance do the spectators achieve a retrospective perspective that allows them to reflect upon the entire play. They perceive the arc of the performance and narrative in order to make sense of what they have seen and heard.

Theatrical Playing is a complex process that is completed when the curtain goes down, but only in a preliminary way. As the première of *Figaro* so clearly demonstrates, *Theatrical Playing* does not take place in a vacuum. The context of a theatrical event, however, is not something that exists outside or apart from the event itself; it is fully present in the Theatrical Event. In a model that has been developed over the last decade or so,[5] four components are spelled out that together constitute the Theatrical Event. In addition to *Theatrical Playing* these components are *Playing Culture, Cultural Context*, and *Contextual Theatricality*. To avoid any temptation to establish a hierarchical order among these components, they are best represented as part of a circle, which in its entirety represents a Theatrical Event (fig. 1).

This model has proved to be quite useful for demonstrating the interplay of circumstances and contexts that are activated during a performance.[6] Nothing is denoted as mere "background" for something else; all components are simultaneously present, which allows more precision in terms of the various aspects of historical time and place.

Although it is possible to identify the exact time of the *Theatrical Playing* (the beginning and the end of the performance per se), the *Contextual Theatricality* and the *Playing Culture* set a different, more expansive time frame. Thus, while an observer is watching a performance, the action progresses, moment by moment, along a *linear* time axis. But afterward, when that observer reflects upon the action, understanding of the staged action

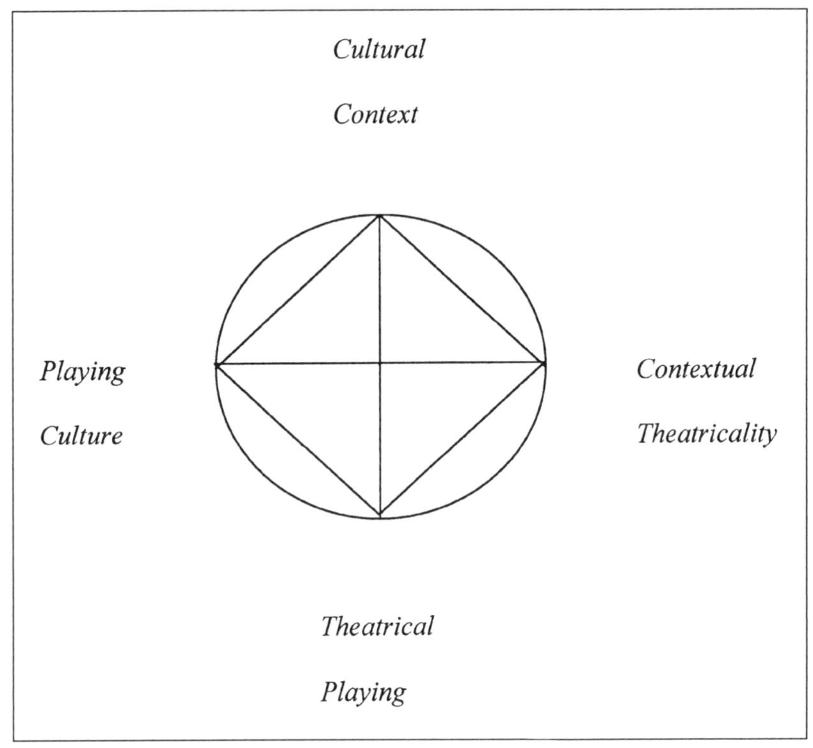

1. Components of the Theatrical Event.

depends upon a mental repetition, a retrospective act of recognition of the already known that can be described as *cyclic* time. In other words, two time concepts exist parallel to each other and complement one another's functions.

The already-known constitutes a considerable condition of theatrical experiences. The spectators as well as the actors need to have a broad competence in order to create and perceive the significations of *Theatrical Playing*, which draws upon and represents human behavior. This competence relates to conventions—everyday life conventions as much as aesthetic conventions—which consist of recognizable patterns that can and will be repeated.

Marvin Carlson has pointed to some additional factors of the cyclic perseverance in theatrical events: the stage history that deeply influences both those who create the events and those who visit them.[7] Theatrical conventions include not only general issues of style and taste but also the stage history of each classical play that nobody can escape, not even those who have never seen an earlier production. In that sense, the stage is really "haunted" by preceding events. The Belgian sociologist Roger Deldime arrived at similar conclusions when he investigated what spectators actually remember from performances that they have seen many years earlier. Spectators tend to remember single characters and isolated or striking visual traits of the stage rather than the stories of the play.[8]

Repetition and recognition are cyclic experiences that run contrary to the progression and innovation of linear time. If cyclic time, in this sense, confronts us with familiar experiences (as well as familiar representations and memories), then linear time, by introducing the new and unexpected, usually confronts us with unfamiliar experiences. Cyclic time is an experience of mediation; linear time offers an immediate experience. Their combined relationship defines our experience of performance events.

DIFFERENCE IN TIME

Cyclic and linear time concepts can easily be misunderstood as oppositions. Typically they are seen as dichotomous or alternative experiences and ideas, one excluding the other. Linear time is thus developmental and perhaps innovative; cyclic time is retrospective and perhaps traditional. Linear and cyclic time can also be related to each other as dialectical opposites, as thesis and antithesis, which sooner or later will produce a synthesis in the form of a superior entity, usually representing some type of evolution. In both the dichotomous and the dialectic conceptions, one type of time will usually be privileged over the other: development is supposedly more desirable than contraction, evolution and innovation are supposedly superior to stability and stagnation.

An alternative view of differences is offered by Jacques Derrida. His neologism *différance* captures another kind of relationship between two utterances or events. A word, for instance, can only be understood because it is repeated (it already existed before it was spoken), but it can never be understood in exactly the same way as it has been used before, because the circumstances of its utterance are necessarily different. In other words: *différance* always includes both ways—the necessary repetition and the unavoidable difference. Derrida writes: "Essentially and lawfully, every concept is inscribed in a chain or in a system within which it refers to the other, to other concepts, by means of the systematic play of differences. Such a play, *différance,* is thus no longer simply a concept, but rather the possibility of conceptuality, of a conceptual process and a system in general."[9] In the same text Derrida provides a few more indications of how this concept can be understood in a way that could prove useful for my discussion of time. Referring to Ferdinand de Saussure, Derrida explains that "we will designate as *différance* the movement according to which language, or any code, any system of referral in general, is constituted 'historically' as a weave of differences."[10] This means that "[i]n any event, it will be understood, by means of the circle, in which we appear to be engaged, that as it is written here, *différance* is no more static than it is genetic, no more structural than historical."[11]

Because of this historical aspect, Derrida must necessarily consider the nature of presence within the weave of differences:

> It is because the movement of signification is possible only if each so-called present element, each element appearing on the scene of presence, is related to something other than itself, thereby keeping within itself the mark of the past element, and already letting itself be vitiated by the mark of its relation to the future element, this trace being related no less to what is called the future than to what is called the past, and constituting what is called the present by means of this very relation to what it is not: what it absolutely is not, not even a past or a future as a modified present. An interval must separate the present from what it is not in order for the present to be itself.[12]

Consequently, Derrida concludes, "this interval is what might be called *spacing*, the becoming-space of time or the becoming-time of space (*temporarization*)."[13] The concept of *différance*—which includes both spatial and temporal aspects—thus provides a useful tool to relate linear and cyclic aspects of time to each other. If we imagine linear and cyclic time as two entities of the same time concept, certain relations can be recognized. Linear time assumes that whatever is being observed or studied has a beginning whereas cyclic time is comparable to Derrida's iteration (something repeatable). This perception suggests that something is always present—available in either the event or one's perception of the event—before each beginning. Linear time constructs the present as a process of development, mostly experienced as progression through innovation; cyclic time reconstructs the present as a process of repetition and imitation, mostly experienced as recall through recognition. Linear time provides a kind of teleological direction, a process of creating or developing autonomous time entities that attain separate identities from earlier ones. Cyclic time provides a process of self-contained integration and fulfillment.

As indicated above, these differences are not dichotomies but two possible aspects of historical events. In other words, when something is described as an innovative, progressive step forward in history, it can at the same time be investigated and understood according to the ways it repeats, imitates, or carries forward already existing forms. For the historian such a double view is gratifying, because unexpected ties and connections may be discovered that usually lie outside the conventional ideology of history as a forward-moving development. A closer look at the *Contextual Theatricality* of *Figaro* might be helpful in illustrating this argument.

FIGARO IN PARIS

The concept of *Contextual Theatricality* evokes two aspects of theatrical events: their conventional traits and their modes of organization. For instance, it had been a convention at the Comédie Française since the days of Jean Racine that the playwrights personally chose and instructed the actors. Typically, actors were selected to play the conventional types of roles they had previously played. But in the case of *Figaro*, as Fleury notes, Beaumarchais was unconventional—and successful—when he asked Louise Contat to impersonate Suzanne in the play. Of course, conventions—along with occasional innovations—contribute to all aspects of dramatic and performance styles in any age. The dramatic heritage always participates in the making and meaning of a theatrical event. This heritage, in all of its complexity, makes up the *Contextual Theatricality* for any performance situation. Thus in the case of *Figaro* the strong tradition of classical comedy in the French theatre, strongly influenced not only by the plays of Molière and Pierre de Marivaux but also by the heritage of the *commedia dell'arte*, was important for Beaumarchais and his audiences. Likewise, the playwright and his spectators carried the heritage of baroque and rococo period styles into the playhouse.

Style is only understandable as repetition—without repetition no style can be established. At the same time, style is an important competence for both actors and spectators. Thomas Postlewait's three-part definition of style is helpful here: period styles, movement styles, and individual styles.[14] We could also add here those cases of a national style which seems to be larger than a movement style (such as expressionism) yet not quite as comprehensive as a period style (such as the baroque). The rules of baroque and rococo drama as well as the organization of the Comédie Française with its *sociétaires* (who held equal shares within the company) guaranteed stability but also enhanced conservative traditions.

The *Cultural Context* implies the connectedness of theatrical enterprises with the public sphere in which they take place. The struggle between

Beaumarchais and the censor is the obvious example. The play was ready for the theatre for more than three years, but the censorship forced him to cut and rewrite the text repeatedly. Despite the revisions, the play still expressed criticism of the aristocracy and its economic and military advantages in eighteenth century France. But was the censor's repression of the play really a question of political ideology?

Here the historians' knowledge of the "future"—the French Revolution that soon would overthrow the political structure of the country—easily misleads the interpretations of the situation in 1784. We have to keep in mind that this play of Beaumarchais was already very popular with the aristocracy before it reached the boards of the Comédie Française. Actually the play had been performed by members of the royal court and nobility before its public première. In the castle of Vaudreuil no less than Queen Marie Antoinette acted the role of the Countess to an amused audience composed of the higher nobility of France.[15] Obviously these nobles did not feel threatened by the tendencies of the play. The broad interest in the public performances among Paris nobles also indicates that no real ideological conflict was at hand. Rather the censor's obstructions of a production at the national theatre can be understood as a power struggle. Who was entitled to decide the suitability of the repertoire—the actors of a theatre, the dramatist, or the state authority? For three years the censor could maintain his verdict. Waiting is another aspect of time. Not only activities measure hours; passive waiting is also time-consuming.

As historians, we need to understand that this waiting for the right to perform *Figaro* had obvious public reverberations. Although the public media suffered from far-reaching restrictions during *l'ancien régime*, other means of spreading the news of the controversial play existed. Long before its première, *Figaro* was the talk of the town, but the political consequences were negligible. No riots were reported, not even a disturbance of a *Cultural Context*. The people who stormed the Bastille five years later probably did not include any of those who could afford tickets for *Figaro* in the theatre.

PLAYING ROCOCO

Playing Culture constitutes one more component of the Theatrical Event. Since theatrical events always involve a kind of playing, they are closely related to other forms of playing. This aspect can be discussed in philosophical terms;[16] but in the case of *Figaro*, this perspective is limited to two examples here. Performers of the Parisian Théâtre de la Foire, which had entertained the common people as well as incognito aristocrats in the marketplaces throughout the eighteenth century, continuously encountered restrictions from the authorities. But when they were not allowed to sing onstage, they interfoliated their performances with songs that the audiences were supposed to sing with the aid of posters on the stage that displayed the song texts. Formal restrictions were always circumvented by playful new alternatives that the authorities could not handle.

A story of the grim sexual games with which the French aristocrats entertained themselves was published just two years before the première of *Figaro*: the novel *Les liaisons dangereuses* by Pierre-Ambroise-François Choderlos de Laclos (1782). This novel consists of letters between the Vincomte de Valmont and the Marquise de Merteuil as the main protagonists, displaying erotic practices as a field of playing (performances of personal identities and social actions within a matrix of power and cunning) reminiscent of the plot of *Figaro*. The disguise of motives—and even identities—operated within the role-playing society. No wonder Paris audiences were keen to see a performance of the Beaumarchais play about sexual games and disguised motives.

Playing in the theatre and outside of it is often governed by rules that serve and maintain existing patterns and codes of behavior. Playfulness, however, makes these rules negotiable and thus allows for innovative changes. Stylistically the tight patterns of the baroque, felt as a kind of heaviness, were broken as an airy and quick (de)lightfulness—an ironic self-image—emerged in not only poetry and painting but also court entertainments of the late eighteenth century. Besides its commitment to maintaining set rules and patterns, *Playing Culture* has the potential to turn subversive, even uncontrollable. Its characteristics, which illustrate Derrida's idea of *différance*, thus join aspects of cyclic time to those of linear time. Past and future meet in present moments of change.

Looking at *The Marriage of Figaro* as a theatrical event, it seems obvious that all components contain elements of linear *and* cyclic time. During the performance of *Figaro* each night, as the story progressed onstage (as the process of *Theatrical Playing* took place), the audience members attempted to understand the complex intrigue by following not only the linear development of the play's dramatic action but also the "recycling" of their own previous experiences of other plays, performances, and life events. All of the seventy-five performances that followed the première and added considerably to the cash flow of the theatre, according to Fleury, constituted good examples of Derrida's idea of iteration: in principle these performances were repetitions of the first night, but of course no evening was identical to any other evening. The ensemble made use of their collective experiences with the ever-changing audiences of each night. These iterable performances of this first run never abandoned the Comédie Française's standard acting style and staging conventions, which served as the *Contextual Theatricality*. As indicated above, the *Playing Culture* of the theatrical event also expressed a dualistic time concept: on the one hand, most human desires and behaviors can be observed in every society; on the other hand, these demands can be satisfied in endless new ways. The human act of playing—on and off the stage—is both repetitive and innovative, always similar but never the same. The *Cultural Context* of 1784 remains complicated. Very few scholars that I have consulted have refrained from mentioning the French Revolution—with or without a capital letter. The temptation to see Figaro as a piece in a progressive puzzle is obvious: the Beaumarchais play is referred to as a "storm-petrel of the French Revolution,"[17] as the embodiment of "the Revolution it predicted,"[18] or as taking place "on the very brink of the French Revolution."[19] Few scholars are able to oppose the progressive narrative, but occasionally we get an alternative perspective: "no startling innovations had been made [in French theatre] before the Revolution inaugurated a new era in France."[20] Of course, we are left to wonder what qualifies as a "startling innovation" in the theatre.

FIGARO OVER TIME

While the French Revolution was five years away, it took less than two years before Figaro had changed genre and appeared as the singing title character in *Le nozze di Figaro*, Mozart and Lorenzo da Ponte's opera. Da Ponte had just arrived in Vienna, where he was appointed as a poet at Emperor Josef II's Court Opera in 1783. In this capacity he was secretly asked to transform the Beaumarchais play into an opera libretto for Wolfgang Amadeus Mozart. The French play was considered politically dangerous in Vienna, at least among some parties, so da Ponte cut out everything that could be perceived as controversial. But he still followed the plot as closely as possible.

It is quite remarkable to compare the first scene of the play and the opera. They contain the same words—"Cinq, dix, vingt, trente"—and also the same actions: Figaro measuring the size of the room for his bridal bed. A visitor who had seen the Paris performance would immediately have recognized the scene in Vienna, although there the text was sung. This change of genre is a good example of gradual changes in the history of theatre. Not all the components of the Theatrical Event change immediately and at once. In 1786 *Figaro* became an opera, and it is certainly remembered mostly as Mozart's opera. We might even say that Mozart kept the Beaumarchais play alive for posterity.

While both Mozart and Beauchmarchais were still alive, the French Revolution changed the entire *Cultural Context* of the play. After July 14, 1789, anybody could shout accusations against the nobility freely in the streets and forums of Paris, so the play at the Comédie Française of course no longer had the same attraction. In addition, since 1791 anybody could start theatrical enterprises, which devalued La Comédie and its repertoire. During this revolutionary decade the *Cultural Context* had an immediate influence upon *Theatrical Playing.* When Napoleon Bonaparte restored the position of the Comédie Française, the aristocracy of *l'ancien régime* had lost its power and its privilege to make the topic of erotics, both sexual and political, into a (public) game. So even the *Playing Culture* changed quickly, thereby changing the perspective on the play for theatre people, spectators, and political figures.

A decade after its first successful run *Le Mariage de Figaro* had become a different matter: it was less political; the erotic intrigue was more pronounced but less recognizable; it was not scandalous but rather frivolous. The Comédie Française continued to perform *Figaro* in the nineteenth and twentieth centuries. The company has given more than a thousand performances. But what are these modern productions expressing? The latest version of the play that I saw there in 2007 suffered from indeterminate politics and a lack of eroticism. In my view, it took no critical stance against class division, neither in the society of King Louis XVI nor in that of President Nicolas Sarkozy. Thus both the past *Cultural Context* and the present *Cultural Context* were confusingly or poorly represented. In the same year I saw a production of *Figaro* in Stockholm. It was best characterized by one of the actresses, who expressed her view in the program notes: "*The Marriage of Figaro* is the story of six horny people in a castle."[21]

Figaro has passed through different genres, social revolutions, erotic restrictions, and gender struggles, but it has also moved from the conventions of classical comedy to being performed as farce. Styles change — even for the same text. The challenge for theatre historians is to take the measure of similarities and differences, as historical time is negotiated. A reminder of Jacques Derrida's observation might be in place here: anything appearing in a present moment (that is, in or on the scene of presence) gains its identity not only from itself but also from its relation to something other than itself—namely, past and future elements. Those elements are distributed throughout the four conditions of *Theatre Playing*, *Playing Culture*, *Cultural Context*, and *Contextual Theatricality*. Historians need not only to keep in mind the tension between past and future elements but also to try to balance them; otherwise *Figaro* stumbles into the French Revolution—with or without Mozart's music. From the perspective of cyclic perseverance, Figaro summarizes a past epoch: the rococo. According to a linear time concept, the play and the opera, instead of deriving their meanings from the French Revolution, were almost completely devalued by it. Beaumarchais barely escaped the guillotine and lived as a refugee in European monarchies, while Mozart died in the shadow of the Viennese court during the early years of the Revolution in France. The story of Figaro survived through the conventions of musical theatre, which in time contributed to the revival of the spoken drama—one of many ironies about the Beaumarchais play. Changes in theatre history do not necessarily point toward progression; development is instead a roller coaster of historical circumstances.

IMITATIONS OF INNOVATIONS

On the first days of March 1964 every household of the Old Town of Stockholm received the following card:

> Georg Suttner exhibits the Old City—
> a drop-in and drive-by exhibition of polyrealistic character.
> Since this exhibition would not be complete without your participation, I want to
> thank you and wish you welcome to the opening on
> Tuesday, March 3, 1964, at 7 P.M. at Stortorget.
> The exhibition is open until March 31.
> Georg Suttner, Tavastgatan 6, Stockholm, Sweden[22]

Full of curiosity, a lot of people turned up at the central square in the Old Town, where they gathered around a historical public urinal. The media and even the police were in attendance, suspecting some act of sabotage. The head of the local police department asked the organizers what all this was about. From Suttner's brother he got the answer: "This is an artistic manifestation!" Soon afterward the same policeman was asked the same question by a television reporter. He answered straightforwardly: "This is an artistic manifestation!" According to the artist, this was the correct answer. He had declared the Old Town, including its inhabitants, a work of art and put his signature as an artist on the urinal. Georg Suttner said he was inspired by Greek vase paintings and African masks but wanted to go further in eliminating the border between art and life.[23]

Of course, this "manifestation" caused a public debate about the meaning of art, the limits of artistic endeavors, the "suicide of the artist,"[24] the futility of interpretation, and so on. But neither the type of artistic manifestation nor the debate was particularly new—not even in 1964 in Stockholm. Already in 1961 the Museum of Modern Art in Stockholm had arranged an exhibition entitled Movement in Art. Movement was considered to be the link between the timeless stability of traditional art and the dynamics of reality. In this sense, Georg Suttner's term "polyrealistic" hits right at the heart of the matter.

In the 1960s a broad and various move toward artistic expression clearly manifested itself, a move (and series of movements) located at the crossroad of various artistic genres, such as painting, sculpture, dance, poetry reading, performance, and music. Suttner's exhibition of an entire part of the city can be compared to Merce Cunningham and John Cage's *Untitled Event* at Black Mountain College in the 1950s, Oskar Schlemmer's experiments at the Bauhaus School of the 1920s, or the Dada cabarets in Zürich in the 1910s—not to mention the reminiscences of Marcel Duchamp's *The Fountain*, the urinal that he exhibited in 1917 in New York. Theatre historians provide a variety of answers to the question of the origin of the avant-garde. Christopher Innes refers this movement to the rediscovery of so-called primitive art that was first visible in paintings from the turn of the century, in 1900.[25] Erika Fischer-Lichte sets her focus on the refiguration of the human body—its new modes of representation onstage—as the important turning point that happened at the same time proposed by Innes. The materiality of the human body became more important than the language of literature and drama.[26] RoseLee Goldberg seeks the roots of the early avant-garde in the history of theatrical revolts, including the dissolution of forms such as in Alfred Jarry's *King Ubu*.[27] Scholars seem to have reached a certain agreement about the time when this innovative move of linear development took place, although they lay out the reasons differently.

Georg Suttner's exhibition of Stockholm's Old Town can also be interpreted from a different perspective. What he attempted and most probably achieved was a halt in time. When the policeman repeated that this event was an "artistic manifestation," he confirmed that the flow of time—the ordinary business in the Old Town—was suspended and made visible as "pure" presence. Instead of living their lives, people around the urinal could observe their lives as a piece of art. Place had replaced or displaced time. This reminds us of Derrida's claim that "this interval is what might be called *spacing*, the becoming-space of time," when time becomes a visible moment of frozen space. The Old Town was not converted into a painting, not even into an architectural place, but into a living space of presence.

How have historians attempted to explain such historical moments that are an abstraction of an artistic movement? In her book *Performance: Live Art since the 60s*, RoseLee Goldberg chooses a particular way of representing this movement.[28] Under various headings she writes short introductions to the chapters, which mainly consist of photographs with extensive captions. Page after page we see marvelous pictures and read texts about the artists who created these events, when, and where, but without any plots or narratives. A similar book in German by Elisabeth Jappe called *Performance, Ritual, Prozeß* uses the very adequate term "Protokolle."[29] Through documentary texts and photographs, thirty-two of the major creators of Performance Art are (re)presented. Both Goldberg and Jappe retreat to a form of presentation that tries to document rather than to explain or interpret the decisive moments of a movement. The reader of these books is invited to relate to these moments of historical presence as the visitors of the galleries in which these events took place did. This historical methodology is certainly not very far from the notes that Monsieur Fleury wrote about the première of *Figaro*. Identification rather than explanation provides the basic historical mission in these cases. As historians we are set to locate these representations in their historical context—the main task of which is giving them a name, an identity.

Naming means including and excluding. The "Untitled Events" became "Happenings" that were part of the Fluxus movement, which was paralleled by action paintings and other manifestations that perhaps could be called Minimalist art. Over the years the term "Performance Art" was applied to these kinds of events, as we see in RoseLee Goldberg's *Performance Art* and Marvin Carlson's *Performance*. This label now sticks quite tightly to artistic presentations that fill the space between performance and art.[30] In other words: Performance Art has become a type of behavior (with some defining traits and styles) that often attempts to collapse or merge the traditional distance between performer and observer.

As pointed out in connection with *Figaro*, a style becomes a style through imitation or patterns of repetition.[31] Only when certain features of an expressive mode are repeated—one could say: repeated sufficiently often—are they recognizable as a style (for the works of an individual artist, a movement, and even a period). But an element of innovation is needed at some point to distinguish a new style from already existing styles. Again Derrida's idea of *différance* might be a useful tool in understanding this process. To communicate at all, expressions need to be iterable, repetitive, referring to something already known, but without being identical to previous iterations. When the *différance* between the past and the present use of expressive means widens, the basis of understanding narrows: it excludes those who are not prepared to follow, to seek new meanings, to invite alternative interpretations. This exclusive phase has characterized the avant-garde as long as it can be considered an avant-garde. Indeed, our definition of avant-garde art requires *différance*. Once the general public catches up and familiarizes itself with new ways of expression, the avant-garde becomes part of the mainstream. Even Performance Art is slowly moving out of art galleries and entering the arenas of conventional theatres and institutional art museums.

Georg Suttner was only representing his artistic self, so the presentation of the performance act remained cyclic and self-referential; no fictional plot was developed. *Theatrical Playing* as a communicative process became fragmented and complex. But this does not mean that Performance Art is beyond interpretation—on the contrary.

For many commentators, it is obvious that numerous performance artists have strong political causes. Marina Abramović, Joseph Beuys, Laurie Anderson, Hermann Nitsch, and Carolee Schneemann represent just a few performance artists who have appeared as and remained political radicals, attacking totalitarian oppression, gender politics, racism, and other kinds of false authority. Although their stylistic means might appear to be quite sophisticated, complex, and ambiguous, their political statements are usually clear and direct. Georg Suttner's incorporation of Stockholm's Old Town strongly questioned the primacy of pretense in art, which can be interpreted as a political act of questioning the cultural segregation of art from life.

A CYCLIC PLAY OF DREAMS

These narratives about *Figaro* by Beaumarchais and the exhibition by Georg Suttner in Stockholm's Old Town have been used to illustrate how the two time concepts are constantly intermingling in historiography (including the construction of historical narratives). I have tried to show how repetition and imitation interact with progression and innovation at all points in time. I would like to add the example of August Strindberg's *A Dream Play*, a fascinating drama from my own country, in which time as such is thematized in the play itself.

In *A Dream Play* Indra's Daughter, the goddess who descends to earth, discovers why humankind suffers. During her wanderings on earth, she passes several so-called stations and meets a variety of persons. In the first half of the play she encounters environments such as the Growing Castle, the Opera Corridor, the Lawyer's Office, and the Cathedral. During this series of experiences, the play moves in a seemingly familiar manner of linear direction. By the middle of the play, when Indra's Daughter has obviously seen how humans suffer and complain, the dramatic action shifts to a cyclic movement, passing in reverse order through the Cathedral, the Lawyer's Office, the Opera Corridor, and the Growing Castle. In the second half of the play we begin to recognize that the events are not presented in a developmental, causal manner of plot structure. Instead, the events and the "progress" of Indra's Daughter through the world become circular, a repetition that shifts her (and us) from a linear sense of time to a cyclic temporality. Strindberg created a new dramatic expression that breaks away from the idea of linear progression, an idea which had prevailed in dramatic techniques from Aristotle to epic drama. Paradoxically, the "progress" through the play—for the spectators as well as the main character—became a regress. In this sense, this cyclic dramaturgy was completely new in 1900 when the play was written. The play's content suggests the cyclic time of a dream. But who is the dreamer?

Jai-Ung Hong studied this question by investigating three major Swedish productions of Strindberg's *A Dream Play* in the twentieth century.[32] In Olof Molander's staging from 1935, it was obvious that Strindberg himself was dreaming. Not only did the set represent the milieu from the writer's own life, but the character of Strindberg appeared on the stage in the mask of the poet. When Ingmar Bergman produced the play in 1970, no such personal references to Strindberg were visible. Instead the poet of the play became the director's alter ego, sitting at a desk onstage and projecting the director's own dream into the worldly journey of Indra's Daughter. In 1998 Robert Wilson contributed to Stockholm's honor as Cultural Capital of Europe that year by staging *A Dream Play* from his own visual point of view. According to Jai-Ung Hong, Wilson managed to maneuver the audience so skillfully from station to station, which were modeled as much from Wilson's fantasies as from Strindberg's dialogues, that he gave the spectators the feeling they were dreaming *A Dream Play* themselves.

Are these dreamers just varieties of interpretations or are they in some way linked historically?

Many other Stockholm productions of this play could be noted, including those of Max Reinhardt with a revolving stage (1921) and Robert Lepage with a vertically revolving stage (1994), but my point is that every production of *A Dream Play* in Sweden, and in Stockholm in particular, simultaneously stretches over several time concepts. Besides the interchange of linear progression and cyclic repetition of time in the play, the various productions reveal the continuous and innovative creativity of directors, who always repeat and yet reconceive the story that Strindberg wrote more than a hundred years ago. Molander's religiously inspired interpretation was conceptualized in opposition to Reinhardt's expressionist rendition of the play. Ingmar Bergman has reported that as a twenty-year-old student he saw Molander's production numerous times. This influenced him profoundly; he staged Strindberg's play no less than four times, always trying to break away from Molander's concept, which at the same time deeply fascinated him. In his visions the dreamer became visible as a director/actor who remained onstage, a version of himself being observed by a double of Indra's Daughter. This chain of directorial references established a *Contextual Theatricality*, in which Strindberg's play was stabilized and at the same time mobilized anew with every attempt to bring it onstage. While every Swedish director had to relate to the national legacy of Strindberg, Lepage and Wilson (both from North America) seemed not to be haunted by the ghosts of Swedish traditions. Their productions opened new entries into the *Theatrical Playing* of Strindberg. Yet for large parts of the audiences, who had seen Bergman's and other productions, the condition of *Contextual Theatricality* was still at play. Thus the history of productions of *A Dream Play* has created not only the doubling of linear and cyclic time but also the doubling of present and past in dialectical exchange between *Theatrical Playing* and *Contextual Theatricality*. Each production negotiates the relationships between innovation and heritage or linear and cyclic time; the historian likewise needs to negotiate these relationships.

Many mature theatregoers in Stockholm have most likely seen several productions of *A Dream Play* and carry earlier versions with them to the next occasion. I have myself seen about a dozen productions of *A Dream Play* since my first encounter with this dramatic poem (in Bergman's 1970 version) that made a lasting impression on me. I remember visual details and the faces of actors, and Bergman's view of the dream as enacted in front of the dreamer has marked the metatheatrical qualities of the play. Later Lepage's vertically revolving stage, where the actors hardly ever stepped down on the stage floor, turned my perception of time literally upside-down. The continuous motion of the three-sided box and the crawling performers, appearing and disappearing through slots in the "walls," completely dissolved the sense of successive narrative. It created its own *Playing Culture,* suggesting the motion of a carousel or other Tivoli attractions, although at a reduced, dreamlike speed. I then carried this remarkable experience—an innovative concept to express repetition—along to Wilson's production. Wilson's actors performed the entire *Dream Play* but used only one-third of Strindberg's text. I easily accepted the disappearance of the text, because Wilson's production of more than three hours was just as complete as any other due to his expansive imagery, the unexpected turns that equaled Strindberg's play, with an internalized text that no longer needed to be spoken. Again my own range of *Dreams* was widened, adding to my earlier references. As a historian I need to see myself as part of a tradition of a seemingly endless chain of variations, none of which is necessarily superior to any other. At the same time, my description adds to the establishment of a canon that risks emphasizing a chronological order, a linear development formulated as the production history of *A Dream Play* since 1970. My historical narrative, honoring linear time, fails to do justice to cyclical time. My experiences over the years, however, were rather accumulative and destabilizing, cyclically oscillating among various points in time. For me, every performance added new dimensions of temporal experiences that I try to convey to my students, who never have seen Strindberg's *A Dream Play* onstage. For them, the next productions might become the opening chapter of a theatrical experience equal to Bergman's own visit to Molander's *Dream* in 1935.

CONCLUDING REMARKS

Cyclic repetitions and linear jumps happen continuously—in the theatre, in history—without ever reaching a progressive and conclusive truth or final meaning. Because the idea of evolution and progression is still so deeply rooted in the perception of time, other ways of looking at history have been either slighted or ignored. A look into theatre history books used in academic programs reveals an explicit or implicit scheme of linear development for theatre—from early prehistoric traces (considered mere precursors of theatre) through certain highpoints such as Greek antiquity, Shakespeare, and the French classics and then modern theatre with its shining electric lights, revolving stages, and psychological realism. We highlight the peaks, above the clouds that hide other activities (including recurring forms of popular entertainment). Typically the twentieth-century theatre culminates our histories, which feature the stages of avant-garde works and movements up to contemporary performance art. Our historical narratives catalogue (and celebrate) these developments. One would think that the major critique of Cultural Darwinism that O. B. Hardison, Jr., made in 1965 against the idea that medieval theatre evolved into Renaissance theatre had liberated us from the dictate of linear progress.[33] But one of the latest and best contributions in this field, *Theatre Histories: An Introduction*, though committed to offering an alternative to the chronological narratives of most histories of theatre, still depends upon organizing ideas of linear progression. The book makes the techniques of reproducing dramatic texts the basis of historical progression: from oral tradition to written dramas in manuscript forms to printed dramas to digitalized recordings.[34] Time is once again represented basically as a straightforward development, a linear process of succession and progress. The cyclical conditions and practices of theatre, including those that I have attempted to identify in the productions of *A Dream Play*, are slighted (and sometimes ignored).[35]

I have tried to demonstrate how a theatrical event can be concretized through four particular aspects or components. Each of these components can in turn be viewed from a linear and a cyclic time perspective. For the theatre historian this means that a number of questions need to be asked; the differentiation between linear, swift, and frequent changes, on the one hand, and cyclic, slow, and repetitive movements, on the other hand, provides a tool to balance these complementary aspects of time.

Theatrical Playing typically has both time aspects tightly interwoven. Central to the operation of this component is the interaction between performers and spectators. The architectural frame for this interaction has changed very slowly—or rather one could say that a few prototypes are used again and again. What kind of relationship do the various theatre architectures allow for? The ways in which spectators watch a performance are also limited to a few behavioral alternatives, from complete silence in the dark to active participation in daylight. The same question can be asked concerning acting: to what degree has the actor's identification with or distancing from the role—basic concerns already expressed in antiquity—been expanded during theatre history? Which preferences are given priority during which period or according to which writers? Keeping these questions in mind, we can also consider various theatrical aspects that are objects of major changes.

The stage space or podium, on which performers address their audiences, has always been a place of technical experimentation. Besides the performers, what else might occupy the space, the location? From the Greek painted panels to the flat wings of the baroque stage to the electric light—every novelty was tried out in the theatre. The most recent addition would be digital devices in performance. Or consider the themes that are presented onstage. How quickly have they changed or remained the same? Alongside the classics and the classical topics, performances have been able to reflect upon and respond to the most urging societal questions. In this sense, I would be willing to speak of social and political development and progress. For instance, though plays since the classical age have dealt with the place of women in society, this theme has been transformed in the modern world. The aesthetics of theatre operate at both slow and high speed.

Playing Culture has heavy anthropological aspects as well as more fashionable traits. In anthropology human playing can be interpreted either as an eternal human behavior that never changes or as one that develops new desires. What might appear as cyclic stability is easily turned into a conservative ideology. Although the basic human needs and desires may remain the same in principle, their ways of being satisfied change continuously. The historian must ask whether these changes only concern the technical surface or if they affect human behavior on a deeper level. The rules of playing are negotiated again and again, as new activities are introduced. What is fashionable at one point is outdated a few years later. What impact do these fashions have on the objects that the historian is investigating? The most recent games on computers, for example, are such an innovation that they severely challenge the ontology of *Theatrical Playing*. Spectators are given the chance to behave like actors in a virtual reality. This is only a recent illustration of the urgent need to elaborate new theories and new understandings that stretch over the wide and various conditions of human playing.

Cultural Context, with its ties to the public spheres of authority and control beyond the theatre event and its playing space, is usually a matter of power and money, often in the same hands—but not always. It is certainly true that the production of theatrical events costs money (even for the wandering minstrel who begs a few pennies). While the question of costs is a recurring fact, the question of "who paid for it?" is answered in shifting ways. What modes of payment existed at any point in time? Who paid for what and why? The answers do not simply provide an economic history of theatre; they are of major significance for all the other components of the theatrical event, including the sociopolitical conditions, biological factors of human behavior, ecological factors, and much more. Economic systems are not operating merely as the backdrop of aesthetic production but can be felt even by the spectators in the auditorium.

The power structure that connects public institutions with the organizational bodies of theatrical enterprises is a complex but underdeveloped field of investigation. Who represents a theatrical company or enterprise to the political public sphere? In modern times this representative may be the managing director, the members of the board, the chair of the board (who has been selected by the political authorities themselves), or the funding agency (be it a public institution or a governmental agency). How did these matters operate before the capitalist model established itself? What were the cultural politics of a region or nation, even in times when theatrical activities occurred apart from political decisions?

Another power factor is located in the media. Which media were available at any specific historical time? Who was in control of newspapers, pamphlets, and schools? Who had access to them? The *Cultural Context* represents a complex entanglement of economy, politics, laws, publicity, social status, and communal organizations—and all of these aspects are subject both to sudden changes in terms of linear progression and to long-lasting, repetitive cycles. The temporal factors never disappear for the historian, yet all too often they are diminished or even ignored because of a reductive model for identifying the context for theatre.[36]

Contextual Theatricality designates the theatrical field as a specific area of cultural activities, encompassing the rich heritage of artistic practices, codes, rules, and styles. It represents aesthetic values that are maintained over long periods, during which stable conventions unite the activities onstage with the taste of the audiences. Are there conventions that go beyond questions of style? How are these conventions organized in a manner that preserves established values? How are they open to innovations and progression? How open is this theatrical field to influences from other art forms, other kinds of playing, or new philosophical and aesthetic perspectives? How does the theatrical world relate to other sectors in society? Publicity is an important aspect of entertainment today; can it be compared to the pro-agon of Greek classical times or to the parades of a *commedia dell'arte* troupe upon arriving in a new town?

Theatre historians usually write about innovations, whereas audiences have often preferred continuity and unbroken traditions. Part of the appeal of art depends upon familiar codes and rules (such as the sonnet form in poetry; genre conventions in the novel, from the *Bildungsroman* to mystery novels). Opera is perhaps the theatrical genre in which established conventions are most sacred to audiences. Interpretations of classical operas are usually limited to the visual aspects, whereas the score—the basis of the audible parts of the productions—remains utterly conservative. New conventions bring about new organizations, but these are rarely synchronized in theatre history. The changes in the period styles for playwriting, scenic design, costuming, acting methods, and theatre architecture are rarely synchronized. Or consider the long organizational homelessness of dance as an independent genre or art form; across the centuries, for instance, Western dance was often tied to developments in other art forms, such as theatre and opera. How should we investigate its history, its temporal coordinates, in relation to the four aspects in my scheme? The establishment and history of genres is both dependent upon and free from organizational restraints. In our historical representations, we need to take the measure of the artistic expressions and the developing organizations as they operate within the processes of cyclic perseverance and linear renewal.

The double-sided view of the past and the future of each moment brings us once more back to Jacques Derrida's idea of iteration. Theatre historians can learn from Derrida, among other things, that theatrical events never can be repeated; nor can they be entirely new. The multiple dimensions of presence in history—the components of the theatrical event—are comparable to the "pluri-dimensionality" that Derrida comments upon in *Of Grammatology*: "This pluri-dimensionality does not paralyze history within simultaneity; it corresponds to another level of historical experience, and one may just as well consider, conversely, linear thought as a reduction of history. It is true that another word ought perhaps to be used; the word history has no doubt always been associated with a linear scheme of the unfolding of presence, when the line relates the final presence to the originary presence according to the straight line or the circle."[37]

I would not go as far as Derrida and suggest that we ought to substitute a new word for the familiar concept of history. My emphasis on a cyclical time concept is meant as a complementary view that allows for imitations, deviations, and variations of existing expressive modes as constitutive elements of a particular culture. Although I do not deny the driving force of invention and innovation in aesthetics, I question their dominance as values in our historical narratives (which often lack a balanced understanding of temporal processes). The storytelling traditions of southern Africa, maintained by women who retell the adventures they have heard from their grandmothers, are not inferior to digitalized recordings of avant-garde performance artists. We need not impose a developmental process or narrative on history that fails to see the value of both the grandmother and the performance artist, irrespective of the techniques that govern their artistic devices. Nor do we gain any advantage in historical understanding when we place these events in only a linear development. A dialogic relationship between linear and cyclic time schemes, I hope, will bring the historian closer to past moments of Theatrical Events.

NOTES

1. Statement attributed to Louis XVI from *Kindlers Literatur Lexikon* (Munich: Deutscher Taschenbuch Verlag, 1974), vol. 14, p. 6028 (my translation).

2. Quoted in Alois M. Nagler, *A Source Book in Theatrical History* (New York: Dover Publications, 1959), p. 339.

3. Ibid., p. 338.

4. Ibid., p. 339.

5. See Willmar Sauter, *The Theatrical Event: Dynamics of Production and Perception* (Iowa City: University of Iowa Press, 2000), and *Eventness: A Concept of the Theatrical Event* (Stockholm: STUTS, 2006 [2008]). See also Vicki Ann Cremona et al., eds., *Theatrical Events: Borders, Dynamics, Frames* (Amsterdam and New York: Rodopi, 2004).

6. Thomas Postlewait set up a similar scheme in his "Introduction" to *The Cambridge Introduction to Theatre Historiography* (Cambridge: Cambridge University Press, 2009), pp. 9–20. Beginning with the familiar formula of event and context, which he rejects as too reductive, he reformulates the model by showing how any performance event needs to be understood in terms of four contributing factors: the Agents/Agency, the Surrounding World/Historical Context, the Artistic Heritage/Traditions, and the Audience/Reception. He then sets up four triangulated relationships with the event: (1) Agents/Agency—Surrounding World/Historical Context—Event; (2) Agents/Agency—Artistic Heritage/Traditions—Event; (3) Audience—Surrounding World/Historical Context—Event; and (4) Audience—Artistic Heritage/Traditions—Event. The possible meanings of a performance event depend upon these four dynamic factors. See the illustrations in his introductory chapter.

7. Marvin Carlson, *The Haunted Stage: The Theatre as Memory Machine* (Ann Arbor: University of Michigan Press, 2001).

8. Roger Deldime, *Le théâtre et le temps qui passe: Mémoires singulières* (Carnières-Morlanweltz: Edition Lansman, 1995).

9. Peggy Kamuf, ed., *A Derrida Reader: Between the Binds* (New York: Columbia University Press 1991), p. 63. This statement and subsequent statements in English by Derrida originally appeared in *Margins of Philosophy*, trans. Alan Bass (Chicago: University of Chicago Press, 1982).

10. Ibid., p. 65.

11. Ibid.

12. Ibid.

13. Ibid., p. 66 (emphasis in original).

14. Thomas Postlewait, "The Concept of 'Period Style' in Cultural History: Problems in Definition and Classification," in *Nordic Theatre Studies*, Special International Issue (Copenhagen: Munksgaard 1990), pp. 52–55.

15. *Kindlers Literaturlexikon*, 18 vols. (Stuttgart: Metzler, 2009), vol. 17.

16. See, for example, Hans-Georg Gadamer, *Wahrheit und Methode: Grundzüge einer philosophischen Hermeneutik* (Tübingen: J. C. B. Mohr [Paul Siebeck], 1960 [1974]), pp. 70ff.

17. Folke H. Törnblom, *Operans historia* (Stockholm: Bonniers, 1965 [1984]), p. 179 (my translation).

18. Phyllis Hartnoll, *A Concise History of the Theatre* (London: Thames and Hudson, 1968), p. 161.

19. Kenneth Macgowan and William Melnitz, *The Living Stage: A History of the World Theatre* (Englewood Cliffs, N.J.: Prentice-Hall, 1955), p. 277.

20. Oscar G. Brockett with Franklin Hildy, *History of the Theatre*, 9th ed. (Boston: Allyn and Bacon, 2003), p. 252.

21. *Figaros bröllop*, Stockholms Stadsteatern, season 2007/2008, p. 10.

22. Letter in the personal archive of Georg Suttner.

23. Interview with Georg Suttner on May 4, 2007.

24. *Dagens Nyheter*, March 6, 1964.

25. Christopher Innes, *Avant Garde Theatre 1892–1992* (London and New York: Routledge, 1993).

26. Erika Fischer-Lichte, "Einleitung: Wahrnehmung—Körper—Sprache: Kultureller Wandel und Theateravantgarde," in *Theateravantgarde* (Tübingen and Basel: Francke, 1995), pp. 1–14. Also see her essay "Theatre and the Civilizing Process: An Approach to the History of Acting," in *Interpreting the Theatrical Past: Essays in the Historiography of Performance*, ed. Thomas Postlewait and Bruce McConachie (Iowa City: University of Iowa Press, 1989): pp. 19–36.

27. RoseLee Goldberg, *Performance Art: From Futurism to the Present* (London: Thames and Hudson, 1979). But see chapter 2 of Thomas Postlewait's *The Cambridge Introduction to Theatre Historiography* (Cambridge: Cambridge University Press, 2009) for a critique of the misleading narratives about Jarry's 1896 production of *Ubu Roi*.

28. RoseLee Goldberg, *Performance: Live Art since the 60s* (London: Thames and Hudson, 1998).

29. Elisabeth Jappe, *Performance, Ritual, Prozeß: Handbuch der Aktionskunst in Europa* (Munich/New York: Prestel-Verlag, 1993).

30. Goldberg, *Performance Art*; Marvin Carlson, *Performance: A Critical Introduction* (London and New York: Routledge, 1996). For an analysis of this kind of space in performance art, see Shannon Jackson's essay in this collection.

31. This pattern of repetition allows for a certain amount of difference, of course, as

in the case of the works of an individual artist (such as August Strindberg, Henrik Ibsen, and Anton Chekhov). Although the recurring traits that define an artist's style undergo modifications from work to work, a definitive style can usually be traced in these works.

32. Jai-Ung Hong, *Creating Theatrical Dreams: A Taoist Approach to Molander's, Bergman's and Wilson's Productions of Strindberg's "A Dream Play"* (Stockholm: STUTS, 2003).

33. O. B. Hardison, Jr., *Christian Rite and Christian Drama in the Middle Ages: Essays in the Origin and Early History of Modern Drama* (Baltimore: Johns Hopkins University Press, 1963).

34. Phillip B. Zarrilli, Bruce McConachie, Gary Jay Williams, and Carol Sorgenfrei, *Theatre Histories: An Introduction* (New York/London: Routledge, 2006).

35. For an analysis of various cyclical and recurring patterns in theatre, see Marvin Carlson's *The Haunted Stage: The Theatre as Memory Machine* (Ann Arbor: University of Michigan Press, 2001). His concept of "ghosting" is directly relevant to some of the issues I have raised in this essay, especially the cyclical nature of the heritage in the making of theatre.

36. It should be clear, I hope, that the *Cultural Context*, though given a singular identity in my scheme, needs to be understood as a plural condition, for various factors operate in the making of any context for a theatre event.

37. Kamuf, *A Derrida Reader*, p. 49.

Performative Time

Lady Macbeth cautions her husband not to dwell upon the past: "Things without all remedy / Should be without regard: what's done, is done." But Macbeth cannot stop thinking about the future: "We have scotch'd the snake, not kill'd it; / She'll close, and be herself."[1] Like the Macbeths instantiated before us onstage, we live in the present, and the extent to which we dwell upon the past may be encouraged to a greater or lesser degree, considered more or less healthy, and made a part of the present to varying degrees depending upon our personalities, values, and perceived advantage. As such, the past's relationship to the present is not just a historiographic issue of how the past is narrated but also an ideological and strategic one of how the past is experienced as present. Yet as creatures of the present, what does it mean for us, like Macbeth, to anticipate the future? In some cultures and situations this is a normal preoccupation, whereas in others it is considered futile. Here history is clearer in staking out territory: the future cannot be told either as fact or as memory, so it belongs to other narrative genres, such as theology, science fiction, and meteorology.

In drama, however, the present brokers past and future: this generates tension and excites interest or foreboding because choice, consequence, and destiny are conventions of our cosmology. Temporal concerns which manifest in *Macbeth*, and possibly all drama, as the opposition of past and future held tenuously at odds in the present moment become, in performance, not only a reminder of human beings' temporal ontology but also an experience of it. Drama reconciles these conventions of reminiscence, forecasting, and cross-temporal reflection, while performance holds spectators in their temporal moment even when their imaginations are buffeted from one tense to another by what is depicted before them. Drama, as a discursive practice, foregrounds the multiplicity of temporality, while performance, as an epistemology, demonstrates the incommensurability of past and future to be experienced in the present, even as it requires playgoers to forget this condition. History, as a narrative convention, obeys strictures of temporal differentiation and succession. It may find the present in the past, or vice versa, but holds the future apart as something that may be effected through our better knowledge of the past, not as something impinging upon us now.

As something lived *through* by a witness, an event (of which performance is one example) has a horizon of "presentness" in experience but then elapses. By the same principle, as a reader experiences this text, cognition of one sentence is an event succeeded, in turn, by reading the next sentence. As each instance of presentness elapses, an event is added to the past, possibly as memory or as memory rendered into documentation that may eventually become fodder for grazing, trawling, or echolocating historians. Theatre historians collect and utilize as the evidence of performance the traces of what was, to other people in another time, an event: something experienced rather than something tangible. This commonplace of historiographic succession is famously addressed in Walter Benjamin's "Theses on History." Benjamin explains that the past disappears irretrievably unless images of it—understood merely as fragmentary pictures, not as an entirety—are seized upon as relevant to the present. The conditionality of *historismus*, an organic sequence of events, therefore is a recognition (or an assertion) of relevance between the two temporalities of present and past. The past "does not recognize itself as meant" in the present, but that is where the historian comes in, making the post hoc interpellations, construals, and avowals that are inherent to historical claims.[2]

According to Benjamin, by focusing on remembrance historians record contact of our own time with the past, but time does not stop: we have no way objectively to halt the process of more time unfurling (*Stillstellung*). What we experience as the present is merely a caesura, unmarked upon time but existing, for us, like a rhetorical effect artificially dividing a metrical foot with two contrary ideas (present and future). Becoming conscious of presentness generates tension between the present and the anticipated, immanent future. Thus:

> To *be*, or [. . .] *not* to be: that is the question.

The caesura hovers within the metrical foot, reinforcing the line's meaning that life could be expunged or, more generally, that life is ridden with choices, that choices predicate events, and that events bring changes that contrast with our present condition. Benjamin describes this effect as the present "shot through" with splinters of "messianic time."[3] Though soothsayers contemplate the future—something heterogeneous and full of potential—Benjamin provides an adage whereby the future is not the historians' province: they should focus on the past and so keep the narrowest possible threshold open to a future with no preordination except the continued emergence of time.[4]

Though commonsensical, these ideas are not universally accepted. Just as time can be manifest in various ways (cosmological, genealogical, ecological, social, agricultural, or industrial), variant experiences and their narration contradict the monolithic view of three serial temporalities of past, present, and future. Postmodernist perceptions, in particular, differentiate between atemporal sequences and "a *relation* of temporality" in which past events have "an open relation to a certain *futurity* within the structure of the present."[5] This kind of perception poses a challenge to theatre historians: what recourse do we have to explain the temporal permissiveness of drama to range across imagined pasts and foretold futures and spectators' doubled experience of a depicted time (sped up or slowed down like a relativistic clock) or an assigned temporality (a decision within narrative, like an assigned calendar page) alongside time as experienced as they occupy their seats? Just as spectators differentiate sincerity from the pretense of sincerity in order to recognize the condition of performing, in all aspects of life we recognize how previous performances are reiterated—more or less faithfully—as citations of past performances.[6] We forge the present, and ourselves, out of the past, but the future is subject to the same practice of citation. Judith Butler accounts for this as performativity, the forcible reiteration of norms, which links us to the past yet also enables inauthenticity, masquerade, and parody. Citationality is the mechanism for the Derridean temporal paradox of seeming to come after yet originating before. To render citationality progressive, Butler describes how performance with a difference (essentially a queered performativity) is potentially transformative and inherently future-oriented.[7]

Relations of temporality are also at issue for cultures not benefiting from the insights of postmodernism. Benjamin's "messianic time" anticipates this after a fashion, but so do many other cultures distant in sensibility from today's reigning philosophers. Cataloguing these variants is beyond the scope of this essay, and three contrasting sketches must suffice to depict this challenge to *historismus*, or sequencing, in historical writing. All three of the enumerated cases are concerned with history, but one is written as ethnography and another is a site. Nevertheless, they demonstrate the contentiousness of how, as Benjamin explains, "[t]he historical materialist cannot do without the concept of a present which is not a transition, in which time originates and has come to a standstill. For this concept defines precisely *the* present in which he writes history for his person. Historicism depicts the 'eternal' picture of the past; the historical materialist, an experience with it, which stands alone."[8] This concept of the historical materialist *experience* of the past is key, however postmodernism augments this idea, allowing for experience in any temporality. In three case studies, with different realms of application and different ways of addressing cultural heritage, I explicate this as the challenge of citationality for theatre's depictions of temporality and what is elucidated as theatrical time. Performative time emerges in distinction to theatrical time as an alternate model in which the caesuric present is not just backward-looking toward the past and speculative about the future but engages all three temporalities experientially. Both theatrical time and performative time demonstrate ways which theatre and performance undergird narration, practices of heritage preservation, and thus philosophies of history.

PLENTY-COUPS: THEATRICAL TIME

My initial example, drawn from First Nations oral history collected in an ethnography, exemplifies how narrative can invoke an idea of succession yet escape fateful determination by the seriality of past, present, and future. In the 1860s, the future Crow chief Plenty-Coups (fig. 1) had prophetic visions in which he saw alliance with the United States as the way to preserve his people's claim upon tribal lands in the state of Montana.[9] This was instrumental to the Crow people's decision to sign the Fort Laramie Treaty. The 1868 treaty solidified the alliance between the Crow and the U.S. government, but the tribe's lifestyle was not protected: the political compromise was soon followed by ecological carnage, which brought about extreme loss of folkways. The rapid culling of bison herds from the Crow people's territories in the 1870s, and the bison's near-extinction by the end of the 1880s, forced the Crow to adopt an agrarian lifestyle, overturning patterns of sociability and cultural stability within one generation. In 1928 Plenty-Coups told his life story to Frank Bird Linderman; though the highlight for the ethnographer was the Battle of the Little Big Horn, Plenty-Coups clearly relished the details of many war parties and horse-stealing expeditions in his youth against the Lakota, Peigan, and Arapaho. The book chronicles changes brought about by the incursion of French traders then American soldiers and settlers in the northwest plains and the conflict this wrought as other tribes pushed westward. Plenty-Coups acknowledges the difficulty of telling events in their chronological order not as a failing of memory but as a characteristic of human recall and discourse. Most significantly, however, he *refuses* to tell stories of life after the great change. He states: "I can think back and tell you much more of war and horse stealing. But when the buffalo went away the hearts of my

1. Chief Plenty-Coups. Courtesy of the National Anthropological Archives, Smithsonian Institution.

people fell to the ground, and they could not lift them up again. After this nothing happened. There was little singing anywhere."[10]

The succinctness of this remarkable statement—a summation of history, including a succession of past events that culminate in no further events materializing—makes the content all the more startling. Plenty-Coups' statement shares a pretext with the way that time is treated in theatre. As Alice Rayner points out, "the measure of punctuality, set by a clock . . . gives time a space in which the now has a kind of duration within which the [performance] encounter may be experienced," but this "initial openness" of a performance's commencement culminates at a juncture mutually recognized by actors and audience when "tonight at 8.00" closes as an episode.[11] Yet, as Anne Ubersfeld explains, with the commencement of a performance, "We are not at the Sun King's court, even if that is what they are telling and showing us"; and at its conclusion, "it is not a spring morning, but rather a winter's night that awaits us when we leave the theatre."[12] In the recognition of a play's commencement, duration, and end we do not so much suspend ordinary rules of elapsing clock-based time but augment them with another set of principles: I call this theatrical time, which weathers shifts in our awareness of true durational and represented time. Rayner is interested in precisely this bidimensionality—both being ephemeral—of the unfolding play and phenomenon of performance.

Theatre scholars recognize the ephemerality or fleetingness of performance predicated on its unreproducibility. Ephemerality accounts for attending the theatre as a nondurable serial event in a spectator's life: when the play ceases to unfurl, no more "events" are added to it, and we resume our serial, unichronic relationship to time.[13] The concept of theatrical time describes the bidimensional and often dual-chronic experience of play attendance, rather than the ontology of performance alone. In theatrical time, playgoers experience real time passing in tandem with the play's demands upon their imagination—the represented time—contoured by the representational conventions of the story. Thus theatrical time is bidimensional and usually dual-chronic. By remaining in the theatre, an audience submits "to be present to what happens *while it is happening*"[14]; likewise, when the play is over the audience recognizes the resumption of the ordinary—and singular—rules of temporality. When a play has no more events, the performance ends and its audience disperses: particularities can be recalled, the afterlives of characters can be contemplated, the story may endure, but the audience cannot add to the performance per se. A theatre historian, by contrast, may extend temporal seriality to episodes before and after the instantiation of a performance. That is our prerogative in determining what is relevant, yet we still recognize the "before" and "after" as distinct from the "during" of performance.

Plenty-Coups' history of the Crow does not so much reorder serial time as differently prioritize it. He utilizes an idea very much like theatrical time, with the emphasis not on ephemerality but rather on emphatically insisting on a punctum. "After this nothing happened," like "the end," denies the status of event to further activity, even though time continues to unfurl. Earlier in the ethnography Plenty-Coups states that when he learned his brother was killed by the Sioux his "heart fell to the ground and stayed there"; when his friend Big-Horn died of a wound inflicted in battle with the Flatheads, "my heart was on the ground beside him"; the first time he heard white women mourning their dead, his heart also "fell to the ground" at the sound.[15] In all these cases, and in all other instances of profound loss, his mourning eventually lifted and "singing" could resume: seriality as well as narrative-generating recommenced. Yet "after the buffalo went away" all the Crow people's hearts "fell to the ground"; they "could not lift them up again," which instigated not a new epoch with contrasting events but a consolidation of their subjecthood in which "nothing happened." They had nothing more to sing. This is mythos expressed as history; meaning takes form through narrative, though it is not a Benjaminian narrative.

"Nothing happened" is logically contradicted by the Crow people's turn to farming and ranching, interaction with federal authorities, transformation of tribal government, development of educational facilities and a judiciary, and tenfold growth of tribal membership over a century.[16] Plenty-Coups urged his people to get formal schooling, built himself a log house, and became the proprietor of a general store yet bemoaned his people's idle bodies and minds. His ethnographer also notes signs of change on the reservation: a young Crow listening to Plenty-Coups' stories sports the traditional tuft of hair wound in buckskin over his forehead yet also wears suede Oxfords and smokes Turkish cigarettes, while another young warrior passes Plenty-Coups' ethnographer on the road not on his war horse but in a Ford devoid of fenders.[17]

Linderman includes such anecdotes to register his sense of modernity encroaching on the reservation, so what is Plenty-Coups' claim that after the bison were eradicated "nothing happened"? It is an end-point to cultural continuity, and yet cultural continuity is evident long after the event or episode of the bison's eradication: the ethnographer also narrates how Plenty-Coups is still accompanied by golden eagles (one of his totemic spirits), his wife dries strips of meat in the sun, the old man Bear-Below drums in the ancient way, and young boys spend a summer morning frolicking in a watering hole left by a recent flood.[18] Though durational time still unfurls and some traditional activities are evident, with the epistemic marker delineating the end of the bison no further events *accrue* for the Crow. Only the *past* is ongoing in tribal members' citationality of their migratory hunting-based history. The past was not added to by events even though Plenty-Coups' life went on (with what Western historiography considers considerable eventfulness).[19] In Plenty-Coups' sense, history "lives on" as heritage, which is internal: the citationality of the Crow is unchanged: they still are the Crow, originating as a people according to a mythic history, and ongoing as a nation.

Plenty-Coups' characterization of the Crow is not concerned with Western history's typical telos to vanquish or redeem the actions of any group; nor is it based upon ineradicable forward motion. In his storytelling he instead invokes a caesuric present as a radical form of suspension. The past is "everything," perpetually deferring further events until, in death, he can return to a land with perpetual buffalo.[20] Thus there are no more events per se, only identity. In J. L. Austin's terms, "after this nothing happened" is a powerful enunciation which characterizes the subjecthood of the Crow, in perpetuity. Notably, however, Plenty-Coups' grammar occludes questions of agency as well as causality: is it the loss of the bison, his people's fallen hearts, or their inability to lift up their hearts again that precipitated "nothing" happening? He presents this as fact, plain and simple, evaluatively descriptive. It is not metaphor or other rhetoric: mourning the buffalo's demise is an illocutionary act that performs the Crow's status.

PERFORMATIVE TIME

While the doubled asymmetricality of temporalities and the punctum of "after this nothing happened" resemble theatrical time's conventions of narrative finitude, Plenty-Coups invokes another relationship to temporality which I call performative time. Performative time, crucially dependent upon citationality, is what enables the Crow to inhere as a people: Plenty-Coups expresses this inherence as abiding identity, mutually constituted, extant yet not derivative, referential yet not determinist.

Performative time is a distinct way to account for people's location in history. It allows for nonlinearity, or nonseriality, as a factor in perception as well as the teleology of time's asynchronicity, polychronicity, and achronism, overturning a straightforward concept of temporal succession.[21] If, in theatre, eventhood is multidimensional,[22] performative time participates promiscuously in the past yet is ongoing: it has a fulcrum in the present yet receives appreciable force from both past and future. Seriality depends upon not only succession but also causality, even when the causal attribution is opaque. In contrast, Derridean and Butlerian citationality tracks the production of perceptible consequences without necessarily warranting an attribution as strong as causality. Neither Derrida nor Butler presents a historical position per se, but citationality becomes historical when it tracks the grip of Foucauldian epistemes over entire societies or marks the relationship between artistic expressions and the culturally produced psychic identity of individuals and their affiliated groups. Thus Benedict Anderson's oft-cited "imagined community" and Eric Hobsbawm's "invented tradition" are historical yet not exclusively serial.[23]

Plenty-Coups presents his people's history as paradox: "after this" implies the conventional view that time elapsed between the demise of the bison and the date of his utterance in 1928, and perhaps beyond, yet he specifically denies the occurrence of further events. He conspicuously occludes the future, except in seamless continuity with the past and in the spiritual reconstitution which awaits him. Performative time typically participates in such relationally constituted, co-emergent temporalities. As Daniel Rosenberg and Susan Harding put it in their book *Histories of the Future*, "today our futures feel increasingly citational—each is haunted by the 'semiotic ghosts' of futures past. . . . Our futures are junkyards of memories we have not yet had. They are not merely geometrical extensions of time. They haunt our presents."[24] This "future-nostalgia," they argue, is specifically an aspect of today's highly technologized and globalized culture. But we may also recognize this as *Hedda Gabler*'s complaint, contained within Ibsen's joke that Ejlert Lövborg's new book "deals with the future" and "social forces" that impinge on it, which Hedda—resolutely referential of the past, not her loathed future—is compelled to destroy.[25] Plenty-Coups, too, tells a history of the future in the face of tremendous odds against the Crow's survival, citationally linked to the past rather than unfolding from it in successive time or memory. This represents an important feature of performative time yet not all its facets.

Based on the Derridean "promise of a memory," our habit of Lövborgian prophecy, which saturates politics, capitalism, and mass media, is predicated upon data of dubious credentials, drawn from the future, not the past, spawning distrust and loathing along with dependency and longing.[26] "Futures past" are accrued conditionalities that may or may not have come to pass yet are collective memory, fragments not from the dung heap of history but from the scrap heap of accumulated augury. Two succinct examples illustrate the concept. First, the "Y2K" scare was predicated upon certainty that electric grids *would* go dark, banking systems *would* collapse, and planes *would* fall out of the sky when computers failed to make the transition to January 1, 2000. Second is the pretext given for the 2003 invasion of Iraq, namely, that weapons of mass destruction *would* be found. Thus economics and wars are based on citationality: the consequences can be grave. "The future," Rosenberg and Harding write, "is a placeholder, a placebo, a no-place, but it is also a commonplace that we need to investigate in all its cultural and historical density."[27] Invoking "memories of our futures" is a burden that comes with understanding citational processes and effects *and* giving them credence. This is the soothsayer that Benjamin warned historians about: an optics of augury rather than dialectics revealed in a snapshot. History, for Benjamin, is a post hoc attribution, for "no state of affairs is, as a cause, already a historical one. It becomes this, posthumously."[28] Unbound by theatrical time's conventions of pretense held in common for a designated duration when, as Samuel Taylor Coleridge suggested, "willing suspension of disbelief" would incur, performative time explains the capability not just to show or describe a speculated-upon future as the real world but also to bring that future into the present, or the past, as a claimed observable effect. The future is citable and thus becomes an imperative. The present must account for it.

HERITAGE TOURISM: HOW THE FUTURE (REALLY) IS OURS

Performative time is evident in a form of First World participatory consumer-based history. Heritage tourism accounts for a multibillion-dollar industry worldwide. It provides compelling ways to spend a vacation, weekend afternoon, or school outing and as such has significant implications for the economy, education, and regional identity formation. It is experienced in historic theme parks; stately or humble homes; garden, industrial, or battle sites; and a plethora of museums. The way that many heritage sites infuse artificiality amid authenticity—a presentational exigency borrowed from theatre, making veracity relative—gives professional historians pause yet is precisely what enhances many visitors' enjoyment. Heritage sites have historical pedigrees and chronologies *but serve as citations of historicity itself*: like a homonym of history, they utilize the past in an iteration of collective identity, enabling visitors to connect a site's or artefact's provenance to their own genealogies yet imbuing this with a combination of aspirational cultural capital, glamour, and projected belonging.[29] This is Bourdieu's *habitus*, in which an accrual of history regulates the matrix of improvisation in our future.[30] The capacity for choosing affiliations of possible identities is part of the pleasure of visiting, as is the experience of co-presence with markers of a collectively figured historical authenticity. By trading on the continuity of artefactual history, family history, and national history, these markers project a future in the process of celebrating the connection between past and present. Indeed, they cite this historicity as existing into the future, just as they lay claim to a version of the future being present in the here-and-now of visitors' experience.

Woburn Abbey is one such site, deeded to the Russell family by Edward VI in 1547. By 1945 the estate was in shambles, succumbing to dry rot and the ruinous effects of death taxes. John (Ian) Russell, thirteenth Duke of Bedford, decided to keep the property in the family and preserve the house by making it into a tourist destination, opening it to the public in 1955. The thirteenth duke was masterful in ensuring the venture's commercial viability, adding a safari park; visitors can now "walk offsite with the elephants" in the zoological grounds.[31] Rather like these elephants, the thirteenth duke was an attraction at Woburn, for he made himself conspicuous by strolling through his own home precisely when and where he could be recognized by tourists.[32] As such, he was the living embodiment of continuity between the Tudor golden age and the new Elizabethan age of postwar Britain. In 1973 he arranged for the long-running ITV soap opera *Coronation Street* to film episodes at Woburn, in which he was seen greeting the characters and selling one a tea towel.[33] In these appearances—in person and on television—the Duke was "himself" citationally bearing the lineage that authenticates Woburn, its inhabitants, its contents, and even its future heirs. He gave visitors to the estate and spectators on television an "encounter" with living British heritage, personally embodying the load of a long and demonstrable lineage on one end of the historical lever of time and exerting the effort of projecting versions of Woburn's future (enabled by the visitors' generous support) on the lever's other end. In effect, gaping onlookers (and the *Coronation Street* dramatis personae) reify the validity of the Russell family's historicism, and their witnessing *makes* the Duke a duke (and his heir the next duke, and so on), just as the Duke makes the visitors complicit in England's heritage. The Dukes of Bedford, *Coronation Street*'s beloved characters, and the estate's visitors are unified within the British *habitus*.

This is the citationality of performative time. Though it is referential of linear events, it is crucially dependent upon nonlinear conceptions of existence over time, and in time, stretching into a relationship with times-to-come.

As Hayden White has demonstrated, historians often craft narratives in terms of dramatic logic and conventions.[34] When historians invoke tragedy's structural and rhetorical devices or "acts in a play" as dividers of significant historical episodes, they borrow from dramatic genres to economize exposition.[35] When history utilizes performative time, however, additional processes are involved. Temporal multiplicity and transitivity are inherent in citational practices. Performative time recognizes the simultaneity, difference, separation, overlap, and pretenses of citation through, as, and across temporalities to build upon and multiply the experience of theatrical time's doubling of represented and durational time. But whereas theatrical time has definitive markers—the performance begins, transpires, has convention-bound interruptions, resumes, and ends—performative time may reverberate indefinitely. Theatre historians identify performance as subject to duration, whatever the represented time; performative time, by contrast, is nondurational, temporal order is nonbinding, and it does not necessarily end in the present or at any other marker. Recognizing the distinctions between theatrical conventions and performative time enriches a taxonomy that explains the multiple effects, contingencies, instabilities, indeterminacies, and instantiations asserted about history and experienced in reception.

PERFORMATIVE TIME IN PERFORMANCE HISTORIOGRAPHY

Whereas Richard Schechner's concept of restored behavior is serial, with repetition predicated upon a temporal order of the behaved *then* the twice-behaved behavior,[36] performative time is significantly more ontologically complex. It differentiates Macbeth's "tomorrow and tomorrow and tomorrow" from Jacques Rancière's regimes of historicity and Alain Badiou's concept of excess, the "representative reduplication of the structure (or count-as-one) of presentation."[37] How does this—eclipsed into what I posit as performative time—apply to performance historiography? For Derrida, events are "interminable": through their deferral and substitution they become other events, and for Badiou this leads to a void where signification would otherwise exist. Signs are derivative yet effaced, substitutes that cite originals through a resemblance of naming or pointing yet existing as a void relative to the original.[38] This is often the case in performative time too. The last part of this essay examines in some depth Joseph Roach's reliance on performative time, in both *Cities of the Dead* and his more recent book *It*, to illustrate the concept's application in theatre historiography.

In *It*, Roach claims that theatre-making is part of the service economy, a product that is expended as it is consumed yet can endure in other forms. He writes: "Theater historians need to complicate that definition because they know that the experience of attending a performance is not a thing;

it is a service of a very dynamic and labile kind."[39] This service exists not as *goods*, but essentially as *time spent* in pursuit of something internal (aesthetic delight, emotional purgation, distraction from one's woes, and so forth). I made a similar point in *The Economics of the British Stage: 1800–1914*, expanding upon the ontology of what theatre artists make as distinct from what playgoers consume. The critical issues remain time and durability:

> First and foremost, the theatre organizes people and information. While the organization is intact, any such arrangement of information, materials, and personnel as "a show" may be revitalized daily for another performance. In between these performances, however, the show exists only in potential. In other words, except as "potential," theatre cannot be warehoused for later use, for it is expunged as it is performed. . . . It needs to be re-made for each performance, and fully exists only in the presence of consumers in the same space and time as the performers and operatives whose services are being expended. The show unfolds in this exchange and then is gone unless the exchange is repeated.[40]

This observation about value is expressed as a problem of units and resolved with an explanation of temporal markers (beginning and ending a performance of a given show), yet it leaves open the question of when the production (as a historic episode) expires in relation to each performance (distinct events contributing to a longer episode). It remains a question of value but also of citationality, for a future is implicated in the "potential" of instantiation. How contingent are expressions of citationality in collective applications when it is not one individual or even an identity-based group in question but a collection of workers with distinct specialties manipulating all the tools of their professions (promptbooks, lighting boards, props, costumes, and so on) who collaborate to make a production? How long can these individuals' work be stored as memory and then called upon and still count as the show, not a revival of it? In other words, does citationality have a shelf life, and how is this a historiographic problem? Furthermore, how is the historiographic problem complicated when it is not one production, or a series of showings of a production, at issue but a relationship between two or more different productions?

Peggy Phelan's contention in *Unmarked* that performance is ephemeral, though quickly taken up as a truism, has been challenged in recent work by Marvin Carlson and others interested in how memory haunts performance.[41] The phenomenological recurrence of memory, laminated by spectators onto subsequent performances, bridges productions of a play, interpreters of a character, and events at a site. Though the demonstrable record of performance may be ephemeral, performative ghosting (or haunting) splits the difference between ephemerality as perishable and ephemerality as transitive. "Ghosting" across performances is a citational act, but this begs the question of what gets to count as citational and for how long. Does citationality—or citability—expire?

Roach's book *It* offers an answer to this problem by invoking Michel Serres and Bruno Latour's maxim: "Time doesn't flow; it percolates."[42] In contrast to Rosenberg and Harding's assertion that "future-nostalgia" is "a product of highly technologized and globalized culture," Roach argues that Restoration and eighteenth-century celebrities, including actors, instance how "reenchantment has doctrinally orthodox beginnings but no end in sight."[43] Celebrities' high profile yet remoteness generates "enchanted memories of those imagining themselves in communication with the special, spectral other," generating "an *effigy*, [which] will very likely have only a coincidental relationship to the identity of the actual human person whose peculiar attraction triggered the hunger for the experience in the first place."[44] This is the "It-Effect," which gives celebrities "two bodies, the body natural, which decays and dies, and the body cinematic, which does neither. But the immortal body of their image, even though it is preserved on celluloid, on digitalized files, or in the memory of the theatergoing public as an afterimage, always bears the nagging reminder of the former. ([As in] 'She looks great. Isn't she dead by now?')."[45] This is a succinct rewriting of a section in *Cities of the Dead* ("Echoes in the Bone") in which Roach stipulates his debts to Emile Durkheim, James Frazer, Victor Turner, and Peter Stallybrass and Allon White for his understanding of effigies' power to embody liminal categories, reversing the polarities of center and margin and making even "its most alarmist defenders panic before the specter of its permeability."[46] Surrogation enables the dead to be omnipresent in New Orleans—a sticky black hole for all things European and African and Caribbean and pan-American, where the dead haunt ongoing performances of tangible and intangible memory. Through surrogation, the effects of circum-Atlantic migration are as evident in rhythm and blues (American yet African) as in Elvis Presley (Tennessean yet Deep South). Elvis is from Memphis, 400 miles upriver from New Orleans, but like British stage adaptations of *Uncle Tom's Cabin* in which Eliza forged the Ohio River into Canada or trekked north from Kentucky toward Louisiana,[47] place-names are imaginative placeholders. Thus, for Roach, Elvis is as relevant to the delta as any Cajun. Living and breathing among us, not just until 1977, Elvis is chimeric: white and black, western Tennessee and the Gulf of Mexico, rock 'n roll and gospel testifyin', modernity and the rock of ages. He is not so much reminiscent (a concept requiring serial time) of traditions as co-extant among them, and it is in performance that this surrogation is most evident.

In theatre practice, Anne Ubersfeld describes classic drama's "non-time" or Jean Genet and Samuel Beckett's "zero degree of history" as projecting the final reckoning onto here-and-now. In nontime, "the absence of a past historical referent signifies the present."[48] This is similar to what Elin Diamond terms the "drift" of invoking history in unanchored representation:[49] when ahistorical time, circularity, ceremonialism, and eternity are filtered, presentism is what remains. It is what we colloquially call "timelessness," meaning enduring and reverberating relevance. This presentism becomes seeable and experiential through the contract of theatrical time, but it is recognizable because of the citationality of performative time. As Adrian Kear puts it, theatre rescues, recovers, and makes present through redemption "the future's performativity" in a memory of a forgotten past that is yet to come.[50]

Historiographically, Roach highlights the citational function within history and invokes drift as a condition of surrogated performance. This wreaks havoc with *historismus*. In Paul Klee's *Angelus Novus* (fig. 2), a watercolor that Benjamin bought in 1921 and that inspired a section of his Theses on History,[51] the angel is manifested by painterly technique to appear permanently visible because she—like us—is stuck in our present. Like this angel of the new, or now, theatrical time tames the drift between past and future and makes any representational temporality narratively our own. Andrew Sofer names this phenomenon "temporal perspectivism," the sense that there are planes behind what is depicted—visually on a canvas or narratively in a play—and thus "the dramatist, by making his plot depend on events in the relatively distant past, gives the impression of a temporal continuum extending beyond the limits of what is performed."[52] For Sofer, stage props, as material objects, "move in unidirectional stage time" and propel plots with the force of *kairos*, not *chronos*, toward characters' approaching fate.[53] Roach's effigies differ from this concept of theatrical punctuality. Surrogation is unruly, unpredictable, unpunctual.

Theatre does not have the constraints of history, documentary, or even reenactment to try to cite faithfully. If an episode from the past washes up in a play, it may be related to presentist concerns, but no narrative regimes insist that it be accurately anchored in the past: the order of events can be changed with impunity or historical agents abandoned or eclipsed, and

2. Paul Klee, *Angelus Novus* (1920). Courtesy of the Artists Rights Society.

no one minds. Historians might quibble, but they would have to concede that theatre operates by different principles than history, judged by its uniqueness as art not its salience—or efficiency—as instruction. Indeed, theatre cannot truly show or reenact the past: it reminds us of the past by pointing, citationally, to markers associated as the past and may do so powerfully and persuasively. Fate and chance each play a part in signaling theatre's inherent relationship to futurity. As a time-based art form, theatre accomplishes what the beaux arts generally cannot. In Klee's *Angelus*

Novus, the angel of history is hurtled into the future as time "unceasingly piles rubble on top of rubble and hurls it before his feet." And yet because the angel is a figure rendered in two dimensions, an artistic convention accomplishes what ontology cannot do: it shows the angel in suspension so that we can see its dilemma. Hurtled backward, its wings spread wide by the storm winds from Paradise, eyes diverted sideways yet unable to see the future, the angel can prepare neither the living nor the dead for exactly what is to come. We, the viewers, are positioned out of frame, though this must be where Benjamin places "the rubble-heap" of catastrophe arrayed before the catapulted angel that "grows sky-high."[54]

For Benjamin, this is a wake-up call for dialectical history but more particularly for philosophy in the age of fascism. ("The Theses on History" are his last writings before he attempted to flee Europe and, tragically, took his own life in despair.) The implicit contract between theatre artists and spectators allows for untruth and crafty deception, but even though theatre bends, folds, and mutilates evidence and real-world referentiality under censorship regimes Benjamin saw all such ruses fail by 1940. Those who failed to notice had, in theatrical terms, been guilty of willful or neglectful inattention rather than subject to miscuing or misconstrual. Infelicity in citation does not necessitate that the signification is imprecise. Thus image and metaphor are relationships not facts. And so it is with surrogation too.

Any telling of the future must be fictional, though (as with depictions of the present) resemblance and recognizability may be desirable for an ulterior purpose. Unlike soothsaying, drama set in the future is not necessarily prognostic. The future, like the present and the past, is a convention in theatre, fabricated with its own logic and signified by a tacit "just because we say it is so" that is *true enough* for represented time. Whether it is true enough for absorbed spectatorship is another matter. It is *not* true enough for history.

For Roach, surrogation enables historical insight to bubble up through genealogies of performance and, for example, into Mardi Gras krewes. The borrowing need not entail any consciousness, as with "the ritualized adornment of 'Bead Whores,'" collectors of trinkets along the parade route, whom Roach describes as "a stunning condensation of the circum-Atlantic tradition . . . the creation of an auction community motivated by the transformation of gifts into commodities."[55] In surrogation there is no seriality, only lineage: there is neither causality nor repetition per se, yet associational relevance in what—with hindsight—is foreseeable. This paradox of misordered temporality is instrumental to the concept. As in citation, agency is moot: we may cite but not know that we do it, what is cited, or why. Our performances may include surrogation, but we do not necessarily set out to do this, know we do it, or care that we do it. Surrogation, therefore, is tautologically in the eye of the beholder, whose insight is to see not repetition or mimesis but emulation and prediction.

Roach writes in the epilogue to *Cities of the Dead* that the legacy of circum-Atlantic trade and migration is the hybridity born of diaspora: "One of the purposes of this book has been to show how specifically that destiny was foreseeable and duly foreseen. In the epic vision of Horace Walpole's prognostication of Mesoamerican sightseers taking in the ruins of St. Paul's Cathedral or in Alexander Pope's prediction of 'Feather'd Peoples' sailing up the Thames, rich allusions to the Mediterranean past point the way to the Caribbeanized future. The English, however, often imagine the future in and through ruins." Time and travel have overlaid the Caribbean onto the Mediterranean: both are performed in the great capital of London. History intertwines fallen and falling empires. "In such an evocation of the *lieux de mémoire*, sites lined up along the grand tour, the usurping presence of the speaker as emulator (hence performer) of the past induces his fatalistic prediction of surrogation in the future. . . . That surrogation is viewed as debasement gives emphasis to the pressure the future exerts on the process of imagining the past."[56] Roach's practice of ranging across examples divorced by time and culture and corralling them into "the parade of circum-Atlantic identities" is time as carnival and carnival as time, synchronic, polychronic, and achronic in turns.

Two ideas that compelled readers of *Cities of the Dead* more than a decade ago—namely, that performance makes these historicist forces perceptible and that performance ethnography in the present is performance ethnography of the past—reoriented many in the profession of theatre studies away from theatre as the focus of research to extratheatrical performance and helped to open up a methodology for inquiring into, and behind, performative phenomena in the present day. Work by Roach and Paul Gilroy buoyed research by ethnographers, musicologists, dance scholars, and historians into the many cultural contributions to vernacular performance. The facts of the trans-Atlantic slave trade and other patterns of human migration suggest means to transfer embodied knowledge from one person to another, one culture to a multicultural context, and one period to the next, but the kinds of documentation that exist are not strictly "historical": they are performative or, in Roach's terms, surrogated within political economy.[57] We have largely citational evidence: we see the legacy of transfer—and, in transmission, citational ghosting—but we cannot ascribe a chain of knowing to successive individuals. To demonstrate lineage, continuity, and evolutionary linkage—affirmative versions of relatedness—the scholarship is not only performative in focus: its arguments rely upon performative time.

It does not so much pedal away from some of the grandiosity of *Cities of the Dead* as reiterate surrogation on a more theatre-oriented canvas: Macheath and his gang (traced from *The Beggar's Opera* through three centuries), *Peter Pan*, Bertolt Brecht, a Disney attraction, Wole Soyinka, and Johnny Depp, captured in wax as Captain Jack Sparrow, who "sails through time, masked and disguised but always in one way or another as himself." For Roach, all this is explained by "the It-Effect, the mass desire inspired by glamorous and menacing people—the living, the dead, or the invented." (This is an uncharacteristic admission on Roach's part that invention occurs but hardly serves to limit his historical claims across a 450-year span.) John Gay, it seems, was a deconstructionist too, for he "exploited the paradox he found in his source material" on Jack Shepherd, Jonathan Wild, and "the unbiddable" Sir Robert Walpole.[58] Pirate ships and slave ships get folded together for good measure, linking Macheath, Captain Hook, *Pirates of the Caribbean*, and August Wilson's *Gem of the Ocean*, all giving up their dead like the sea.[59]

PERFORMATIVE TIME'S METHODOLOGY

In legend Clio, the Greek muse of history (born of Zeus's mating with Memory, along with her sisters Thalia, Melpomene, and Terpsichore), holds the tablet upon which history is written. She inspires, but the historian is the trustee preserving memory for the future. For Benjamin, the *Angelus Novus* represents the tensions between temporalities and what might be termed the historian's dilemma to select among and record the rapidly accumulating past while being hurtled—backward in *perpetuum mobile*—toward the future. Construing history with performative time changes the historian's relationship to temporality. This is the crux of my argument: not a judgment on but a recognition of how, among Three Wise Men—a true prophet, a peer of the realm, and a Dilley Professor at Yale—and among three kinds of historical understanding—Crow spirituality, market capitalism, and postmodernism—performative time has explanatory power, albeit with subtle distinction. For Plenty-Coups, seriality comes to an end and the present is at a constant distance, as it were, from this ending. For the Russell family, seriality is their badge of authenticity, and endings are forestalled in the invocation of a collective responsibility for participation in heritage. For Roach, seriality is pretty much irrelevant, for past and future are not so much at relative distances from each other as coextant in proximity.

Relying upon surrogation as an explanatory mechanism is tantamount to "the whirligig of time" that "brings in his revenges":[60] it is not a matter of defining how lengthy the long eighteenth century was but seeing it stretch indefinitely in all directions. Performative time calls attention to the question of who has agency to convey history, as well as how evidence for history is generated, and gives a rationale of what, by other criteria, is vulnerable to accusations of missampling. The rhetorical orthodoxy of data triangulation, a mainstay of historical argumentation, falls by the wayside. In my three case studies, this methodological feature arises from a medley of respectful homage, venerable tradition, and performative conviction. The white ethnographer on whom Plenty-Coups bestowed his story wrote down what was said but could only honor the Crow's experience, not share in it, recording and organizing the data but not analyzing it. The Russells and all the paying visitors to Woburn Abbey collaborate to assert historical forces, the site of their mutual experience being instrumental in the process. For Roach, any cultural informant is potentially a historical agent as well as generative of further evidence. This, depending upon one's point of view, is radically democratized history, appallingly irresponsible history, insightful postcolonialism, or false consciousness run amok.

What unifies the examples is citationality utilized as a historical methodology. Theatre and performance scholars have worried over Judith Butler's evolving explanation of performativity, but it is the underlying concept—citationality, the reiteration of a norm—that makes this impact on performance historiography. Embracing the potentials for citation through the concept of performative time, we not only facilitate a greater range of historical claims but also explore the alternatives to more conventionally understood linearity and causality.

Spectators at the theatre are optically positioned like viewers of Klee's *Angelus Novus*: outside, looking at an unfolding process in which they are implicated, though physically as well as ontologically rooted in the present.[61] Klee's art makes this visible, both as concept and as process. Unlike the angel, theatrical spectators may look straight into a depiction of a future, as it unfolds, or a version of the past, as it is retold. Depicting these "ifs" of future or past is the prerogative of art, while depicting them *unfold* is the prerogative of theatre, which is a temporally based art.[62] In performance, temporalities are reference points subsumed into the here-

and-now. As Brian Walsh puts it: "Performance, in its physical presence, reinforces the absence of the past by calling attention to the real, present, removed-from-history bodies onstage." History is mediated, and "to perform history is to make this evident."[63] The past is always changed by what is told about it, but if the past is predicated on the future the historian no longer just watches the angel stare at the past while it is being propelled backward into the future but looks around the angel to see the future beyond its back. The historian occupies the same kind of position as the theatergoer—conscious of bidimensional temporalities, being in the present but aware of the past—yet also decides what prequels and sequels should accompany the narration of an event. It is another step, still, to invoking performative time's endowment of speaking on behalf of evidence or on behalf of the past, present, or future even in the absence of evidence.

According to François Furet, when historians leave aside concern with facts and instead seek to explain a problem that is not reliant upon human memory, the facts become more secure. Quantitative history is facilitated by aggregating such facts (for example, demographic data, judicial decisions, or climatalogical evidence), identified by their similarity and comparability, and networking them into meaning.[64] As with performative time, this breaks history's thrall to past "events" and suggests that history need not end in the present: such analyses can be prognostic in connection with their historicism. Though Roach loosely moors his analyses in commodity relations, relying upon deconstructive techniques rather than quantitative analysis, he too looks squarely at the fragmented past and describes the future. Like the tourist enthusiast who visits Woburn Abbey and sees her own heritage implicated in the "below stairs" lives of servants or recognizes England's continuity in the Russell family's portraits, Roach describes himself as "fascinated" by Uma Thurman's image on the cover of *GQ* in May 2004, negligée, exuding "it" in a "thin but bright" strand connecting "the Stuart Restoration and the theater it launched . . . to Hollywood."[65] Performance is not the through line: this is not a case of a tradition passed successively from master to student. Roach's analytic criteria are similarity in referentiality, pattern not causality, surrogation not agency. The referent is mutable as well as mute. Citationality is the indexical mechanism, and performative time accounts for the experience of recognition distilled indefinitely into and from future occurrences.

NOTES

I am grateful for several opportunities to engage with interlocutors about drafts of this essay. In addition to Tom Postlewait and Charlotte Canning, who weighed in several times, and other contributors to this volume, I would like to single out Susan Bennett, Shannon Jackson, Ric Knowles, Jon Mackenzie, Heather Nathans, Janelle Reinelt, and Kim Solga.

1. *Macbeth*, act III, scene 2, ll. 11–14.

2. Walter Benjamin, "On the Concept of History," originally published in *Gesammelten Schriften*, 12 vols. (Frankfurt am Main: Suhrkamp Verlag, 1974), vol. 1. p. 2, trans. Dennis Redmond, http://www.efn.org/~dredmond/Theses_on_History.PDF (see especially theses V, VI, and IX).

3. For Benjamin, messianic time refers both to Judaic theology of the messiah's arrival (foretold but not yet come to pass) and to a historiographic recognition of the indebtedness, referentiality, and pull of the past on the present (Thesis II). Thus a conviction about the future is reified by phenomenological experience about the past.

4. Benjamin contrasts historians to soothsayers and then characterizes a historical outlook in kind with the Jewish people: "It is well-known that the Jews were forbidden to look into the future. The Torah and the prayers instructed them, by contrast, in remembrance. This disenchanted those who fell prey to the future, who sought advice from the soothsayers. For that reason the future did not, however, turn into a homogenous and empty time for the Jews. For in it every second was the narrow gate, through which the Messiah could enter" (Addendum B).

5. Louis Armand, *Event States: Discourse, Time, Mediality* (Prague: Litteraria Pragensai, 2007), pp. 43, 9 (emphasis in original).

6. J. L. Austin, *How to do Things with Words* (Cambridge, Mass.: Harvard University Press, 1962); Judith Butler, *Undoing Gender* (London: Routledge, 2004); and Judith Butler, *Bodies That Matter: On the Discursive Limits of "Sex"* (London: Routledge, 1993).

7. Butler, *Undoing Gender*, pp. 2, 23. For elaboration on this concept, see Elizabeth Freeman, "Packing History, Count(er)ing Generations," *New Literary History* 31.4 (2000): 723; Samuel Allen Chambers and Terrell Carver, *Judith Butler and Political Theory: Troubling Politics*, revised ed. (London: Routledge, 2008), pp. 34–50; and Moya Lloyd, *Judith Butler: From Norms to Politics* (Cambridge: Policy, 2007), pp. 61–62.

8. Benjamin, "On the Concept of History," Thesis XVI.

9. The Crow (Apasáalooke or Absarokees) chief Plenty-Coups (Aleek-shea-ahoosh, also called Chíilaphuchissaaleesh) lived from 1848 to 1932.

10. Frank Linderman, *Plenty-Coups: Chief of the Crows* (Lincoln: University of Nebraska Press, 2002), p. 169; originally published as *American: The Life Story of a Great Indian, Plenty-coups, Chief of the Crows* (1930).

11. Alice Rayner, *Ghosts: Death's Double and the Phenomena of Theatre* (Minneapolis: University of Minnesota Press, 2006), pp. xxx, 25.

12. Anne Ubersfeld, *Reading Theatre*, trans. Frank Collins (Toronto: University of Toronto Press, 1999), p. 134.

13. For elaboration, see Marvin Carlson, *The Haunted Stage: The Theatre as Memory Machine* (Ann Arbor: University of Michigan Press, 2001); and Rayner, *Ghosts*.

14. Rayner, *Ghosts*, p. 31 (emphasis in original).

15. Linderman, *Plenty-Coups*, pp. 20, 53, 129–130; see also p. 117.

16. See http://www.crowtribe.com/index.htm.

17. Linderman, *Plenty-Coups*, pp. 112, 124.

18. Ibid., pp. 178, 42, 146, 133.

19. Plenty-Coups' status as a chief is barely established when his narrative ends; he went on to become chief of all the Crow, made several diplomatic missions to Washington, D.C., was visited by heads of state, and represented all First Nations peoples in a wreath-laying ceremony at Arlington National Cemetery in 1920. Deeply moved by the way George Washington was esteemed by Americans and impressed by his visit to Mount Vernon, he bequeathed his home and land as a state park.

20. Plenty-Coups situates the deferral in a "past," whereas Derrida regards the sign of recurrence as "perpetually suspended in the commencement of that which is always and only ever *to come*" in substitution for events and signifiers (Armand, *Event States*, p. 16; emphasis in original).

21. This is not a result of a more lax sense of time, vague perception of time, or any other pejoratively attributed characteristic of a "primitive" attitude. Compare Joseph K. Adjaye, ed., *Time in the Black Experience* (Westport: Greenwood, 1994).

22. See Hans van Maanen, "How Contexts Frame Theatrical Events," in *Theatrical Events: Borders, Dynamics, Frames*, ed. Vicky Ann Cremona, Peters Eversmann, Hans van Maanen, Willmar Sauter, and John Tulloch (Amsterdam: Rodolpi, 2004), pp. 243–277; and Roger Bechtel, *Past Performance: American Theatre and the Historical Imagination* (Lewisburg: Bucknell University Press, 2007).

23. Benedict Anderson, *Imagined Communities: Reflections on the Origin and Spread of Nationalism* (London: Verso, 1983); and Eric Hobsbawm and Terence Ranger, eds., *The Invention of Tradition* (Cambridge: Cambridge University Press, 1992).

24. Daniel Rosenberg and Susan Harding, "Introduction: Histories of the Future," in *Histories of the Future*, ed. Daniel Rosenberg and Susan Harding (Durham: Duke University Press, 2005), p. 4.

25. Henrik Ibsen, *Hedda Gabler*, trans. Jens Arup, in *The Oxford Ibsen*, vol. 7, ed. James McFarlane (Oxford: Oxford University Press, 1966), p. 216.

26. Jacques Derrida, *Of Spirit: Heidegger and the Question*, trans. G. Bennington and R. Bowlby (Chicago: University of Chicago Press, 1989), p. 113.

27. Rosenberg and Harding, "Introduction," p. 9.

28. Benjamin, "On the Concept of History," Addendum A. See also Vanessa Schwartz, "Walter Benjamin for Historians," *American Historical Review* 106.5 (2001): 1739–1741.

29. Laurajane Smith, *Uses of Heritage* (London: Routledge, 2006), p. 122.

30. Pierre Bourdieu, *The Logic of Practice*, trans. Richard Nice (Stanford: Stanford University Press, 1990), pp. 52–65.

31. Woburn Abbey website: http://www.woburnsafari.co.uk/woburn_experiences/elephant.php.

32. Smith, *Uses of Heritage*, pp. 151–152.

33. *Coronation Street*, season 14, episode 42 (series episode 1289, aired May 23, 1973), http://www.tv.com/coronation-street/wed-23-may-1973/episode/486075/summary.html (accessed February 22, 2009).

34. For example, Hayden White, *The Content of the Form: Narrative Discourse and Historical Representation* (Baltimore: Johns Hopkins University Press, 1987).

35. See Tracy C. Davis, "Annie Oakley and Her Ideal Husband of No Importance," in *Critical Theory and Performance*, ed. Joseph Roach and Janelle Reinelt (Ann Arbor: University of Michigan Press, 1992), pp. 299–312.

36. Richard Schechner, *Between Theater and Anthropology* (Philadelphia: University of Pennsylvania, 1985).

37. Jacques Rancière, *The Politics of Aesthetics*, trans. G. Rockhill (London: Continuum, 2004), p. 24; and Alain Badiou, *Being and Event*, trans. Oliver Feltham (London: Continuum, 2005), p. 173. For discussions of each concept, see Adrian Kear, "The Memory of Promise: Theatre and the Ethic of the Future"; and Rustom Bharucha, "Towards Tomorrow? Processing the Limits of Performance into the Real of Time." Both essays are in *A Performance Cosmology: Testimony from the Future, Evidence of the Past*, ed. Judie Christie, Richard Gough, and Daniel Watt (London: Routledge, 2006), pp. 148–151, and 216–228.

38. Armand, *Event States*, pp. 14–16.

39. Joseph Roach, *It* (Ann Arbor: University of Michigan Press, 2007), pp. 28–29.

40. Tracy C. Davis, *The Economics of the British Stage: 1800–1914* (Cambridge: Cambridge University Press, 2000), p. 334.

41. Peggy Phelan, *Unmarked: The Politics of Performance* (London: Routledge, 1993); Carlson, *The Haunted Stage*; Rayner, *Ghosts*; Geraldine Cousin, *Playing for Time: Stories of Lost Children, Ghosts and the Endangered Present in Contemporary Theatre* (Manchester: Manchester University Press, 2007); and Rebecca Schneider, *Reenactment: Essays on Performance Remains in Visual Culture* (forthcoming, Routledge).

42. Roach, *It*, p. 13.

43. Ibid., p. 16.

44. Ibid., p. 17.

45. Ibid., p. 36.

46. Joseph Roach, *Cities of the Dead: Circum-Atlantic Performance* (New York: Columbia University Press, 1996), p. 39. Another debt, to Derridean iteration, is evident but unacknowledged by Roach. For Derrida, iterability passes "between the *re-* of the repeated and the *re-* of repeating, traversing, and transforming reception" to constitute communication's failure to control meaning while inscribing preexisting alterity; quoted in Ann Wordsworth, "Household Words: Alterity, the Unconscious and the Text," in *Jacques Derrida: Critical Thought*, ed. Ian MacLachlan (Aldershot: Ashgate, 2004), p. 30. For a more general discussion, see James Loxley, *Performativity* (London: Routledge, 2007), pp. 74–75.

47. Sarah Meer, *Uncle Tom Mania: Slavery, Minstrelsy and Transatlantic Culture in the 1850s* (Athens: University of Georgia Press, 2005), p. 143.

48. Ubersfeld, *Reading Theatre*, pp. 132, 140. David Barnett describes a similar effect, the dream convention, whereby the flow of time is suspended: "When Is a Play not a Drama? Two Examples of Postdramatic Theatre Texts," *New Theatre Quarterly* 24.1 (2008): 15. Some postmodernist drama invokes a mythic time, not clearly any period or temporality. Sarah Ruhl's *Eurydice* and Caryl Churchill's *Far Away* are indicative of this conven-

tion, never definitively in one period or another, costumed eclectically, and—like late-medieval morality plays—reliant on ongoing relevance to the human condition to quiet temporal sticklers. Some drama posits a subjective time, with recognizable markers of the real loosely indicating the degree of deviation from clock-based time, as in Sarah Kane's *4:48 Psychosis* and Marie Clements's *The Unnatural and Accidental Women*, wherein cinematic devices may be adopted, simulated, or signified in order to depict the narrative convention of psychological anarchy or anguish, manifested as temporal elasticity and mutability.

49. Elin Diamond, "Introduction," in *Performance and Cultural Politics*, ed. Elin Diamond (London: Routledge, 1996), p. 1.

50. Kear, "The Memory of Promise," p. 149.

51. Benjamin, "On the Concept of History," Thesis IX; Paul Klee, *Catalogue Raisonné: Vol. 3, 1919–1922* (London: Thames and Hudson, 1999), pp. 163, 172 [item 2377].

52. Andrew Sofer, *The Stage Life of Props* (Ann Arbor: University of Michigan Press, 2003), p. 183. Sofer cites Benjamin K. Bennett, "Strindberg and Ibsen: Toward a Cubism of Time in Drama," *Modern Drama* 26 (1983): p. 263.

53. Sofer, *The Stage Life of Props*, p. 189.

54. Benjamin, "On the Concept of History," Thesis IX.

55. Roach, *It*, p. 256.

56. Ibid., pp. 284–285.

57. Paul Gilroy, *The Black Atlantic: Modernity and Double Consciousness* (Cambridge, Mass.: Harvard University Press, 1993). See also Eric Lott, *Love and Theft: Blackface Minstrelsy and the American Working Class* (New York: Oxford University Press, 1993); Susan Manning, *Modern Dance, Negro Dance: Race in Motion* (Minneapolis: University of Minnesota Press, 2004); Lynn Abbott, *Ragged But Right: Black Traveling Shows, "Coon Songs," and the Dark Pathway to Blues and Jazz* (Jackson: University of Mississippi Press, 2007); Louis Onuorah Chude-Sokei, *The Last "Darky": Bert Williams, Black-on-Black Minstrelsy, and the African Diaspora* (Durham: Duke University Press, 2006); W. T. Lhamon, *Jump Jim Crow: Lost Plays, Lyrics, and Street Prose of the First Atlantic Popular Culture* (Cambridge, Mass.: Harvard University Press, 2003); and Judith Halberstam, *In a Queer Time and Place: Transgender Bodies, Subcultural Lives* (New York: New York University Press, 2005), p. 8.

58. Roach, *It*, p. 214.

59. Ibid., p. 226.

60. *Twelfth Night*, act V, scene 1, l. 376.

61. Klee begins his "Schöpferische Konfession" (Creative Credo): "Art does not reproduce the visible but makes visible." Later he elaborates: "the beholder's eye, which moves about like an animal grazing, follows paths prepared for it in the picture. . . . The pictorial work was born of movement, is itself recorded movement, and is assimilated through movement (eye muscles)." Paul Klee, "Schöpferische Konfession" (trans. N. Guterman), in *Theories of Modern Art: A Source Book by Artists and Critics*, ed. H. B. Chipp (Berkeley: University of California Press, 1973), pp. 182–186. See also K. Porter Aichele, *Paul Klee's Pictorial Writing* (Cambridge: Cambridge University Press, 2002), p. 7.

62. A case could be made for including performers in this analysis. Yet in character-

based performance, actors' double consciousness sometimes (but not always) relies on the pretense that the characters do not become conscious of the audience, however much the actor might gear actions and reactions to audience presence and response. Perhaps Stanley Cavell's observation that spectators are not in the characters' presence yet they acknowledge their presence is another form of double consciousness. Toril Moi restates Cavell's point: "'The usual joke is about the Southern yokel who rushes to the stage to save Desdemona from the black man. What is the joke? That he doesn't know how to behave in a theater?' The yokel's problem, rather is that he has not understood that *the characters are in our presence, but we are not in theirs.*" Stanley Cavell, *Must We Mean What We Say?* (New York: Scribner, 1969), pp. 327, 332; quoted in Toril Moi, *Henrik Ibsen and the Birth of Modernism: Art, Theater, Philosophy* (Oxford: Oxford University Press, 2006), p. 206 (emphasis in original).

63. Brian Walsh, "Theatrical Temporality and Historical Consciousness in *the Famous Victories of Henry V*," *Theatre Journal* 59.1 (2007): 72.

64. François Furet, "From Narrative History to Problem-Oriented History," in *In the Workshop of History* (Chicago: University of Chicago Press, 1978), pp. 40–74.

65. Roach, *It*, pp. 2–3.

Representing India's Pasts Time, Culture, and the Problems of Performance Historiography

The discipline of theatre historiography in India is an inherently embattled field because, like other forms of modern history writing in India, it seeks to reconstruct methods of historical inquiry in a culture where "history," "historicity," "historical experience," "historical consciousness," and "the historical sense" have been and continue to be deeply contested concepts. Any metacritical reflection on method in Indian theatre history therefore has to begin at an unusual level of generality, by considering the theoretical, conceptual, and historicopolitical reasons for the crisis of representation that pervades the genres of historiography. To a large extent the crisis is a product of cultural difference: it registers the conflicts between intrinsic Indian and extrinsic Western ideas of time and history that were inevitable under the asymmetrical power relations of colonialism between the late eighteenth and the early twentieth centuries.

Indian concepts of time are various, yet prevalent models invoke monumental and repetitive cycles that seem disconnected from individual consciousness or a concrete temporal existence. These kinds of indigenous ideas of history do not sufficiently differentiate documented fact, poetic figuration, and mythic narrative, thus making the historicity of human agents indeterminable. Nineteenth-century European philosophers and historians used these "irrational" concepts, and the differences between Western and Indian social-political formations, to claim that India "had no history"—either as the human experience of existing in time or as the textualized record of that experience.[1] Supposedly, neither individuals nor societies understood or experienced historical processes, including historical change. At the same time, the "discovery" and celebration of Sanskrit by European philologists forged an essentialist identification of "Sanskrit" and "Hinduism" with "India," giving the period of classical antiquity (recognized especially for its literature and theatre) an ahistorical priority over all subsequent eras. Sanskrit thus attained a godlike essence as the origin and abiding condition of Indian identity.

In the postcolonial period a sophisticated rethinking of Western and Indian models of historiography has thoroughly professionalized the academic discipline of history, and revisionist historians (notably the Subaltern Studies collective) have undertaken an "Indian historiography of India" that systematically critiques and displaces colonialist historiography. The study of theatre history, however, remains a largely amateur field fragmented by region and language. Even the more ambitious historians tend to recirculate Orientalist or revivalist positions as they grapple with the challenges of constructing a "national theatre history" for a multilingual, multifaceted performance culture spanning more than two millennia. The activity of *representing* the past in Indian theatre historiography is therefore inseparable from the problem *of* the past: how to approach, define, and order the vast performance archive of an ancient culture that allegedly lacks a sense of history and is deeply invested in tradition even as it negotiates the ruptures of colonial and postcolonial modernity. By the same token, questions of method in theatre historiography are inseparable from the peculiarities of theatre history as a discourse and a discipline in India. In this essay I approach the subject of time as an ordering principle in theatre history by way of the polarized philosophical-cultural arguments that problematize the ideas of time and history and underscore the necessity of creating desiderata for Indian theatre historiography outside both indigenist and Orientalist frameworks.

ANCIENT CONCEPTS: TIME AND HISTORY IN EARLY INDIA

Indigenous Indian concepts of time and history establish a structure of traditional thought on these subjects that can create a broad and informed context for approaching the modern historiography of cultural forms. This juxtaposition of antiquity and modernity is especially helpful, because it accentuates the difference between older ideas and the new modalities introduced by colonialism. From the viewpoint of the present, however, the "unmediated" meaning of these ideas is less important than the history of opposed interpretations they have accumulated over time. Two centuries of Orientalist denigration characterized these ideas as the very antithesis of rational historical thinking, while more recent Indian discussions have offered carefully nuanced, historically contextualized views—and both perspectives have a bearing on how the ideas actually relate to history-as-record. For instance, the "cyclical" nature of time in Hindu cosmology supposedly denotes an uncontainable logic opposed to "linear" Western conceptions of time. The four *yugas* (eons or epochs)—*krita*, *treta*, *dvapar*, and *kali*—follow each other in succession and constitute a *mahayuga* consisting of 4,320,000 human years; at the end of a *mahayuga*, which represents the moral nadir of human existence, the cycle begins again. In *The Philosophy of History* (1831), Hegel refers contemptuously to the "large numbers," often astronomical in scale, attributed to the life-span of Indian gods and kings and concludes that "it would be ridiculous to regard passages of this kind as anything historical."[2]

Romila Thapar has recently argued, however, that the Western preoccupation with cyclicity and magnitude is traceable to an "intellectual fashion," articulated for instance by the historian of religion Mircea Eliade, which involves the following "fundamental assumptions" about time in early India: "[T]here is an eternal cyclic repetition of time, so huge in concept that human activities become minuscule and insignificant in comparison. Cyclic time is continuous, without a beginning or an end. The cycle returns with unchanging regularity and in unchanging form. This amounts to a refusal of history, for no event can be particular or unique and all events are liable to be repeated in the next cycle. Such a sense of time, based on what has been called an orgy of figures, can only support the philosophic notion of the world being illusory."[3] Thapar points out, though, that in Indian thought "cyclic time" does not actually "preclude other categories of time, some more apposite to historical chronology and taking on the functions of linear time." He also notes that cosmological time gradually gives way to "a more realistic kind of time reckoning," including the use of eras and dating by regal years, both linear concepts.[4] But the practice of "ascribing cyclic time alone to non-monotheistic religions and ignoring the evidence for other categories of time in the history of their societies" persisted because of "the more subtle argument . . . that such societies live in another time, and this was a device to define the otherness of those societies."[5]

The linear/cyclic binary becomes entrenched in Western thinking because it supports a series of other binaries: monotheism/polytheism, Christian/pagan, historical/ahistorical, scientific/mythic, rational/prerational, modern/traditional, dynamic/static, and political/apolitical. G. N. Devy's observation that "'cyclical' and 'linear' are in fact only historiographical notions and not attributes either of time or of the perceiving human consciousness" only underscores the resolute nature of the East-West contrast enforced by European discourses.[6] The point here is not that Western and indigenous Indian notions of time are in fact similar but that binaristic thinking fails to *explain* the differences and relate them to a culture's modes of preserving its past.

What kind of historical consciousness, then, accompanies nonlinear concepts of time, and what forms of historiography does it generate? Again, these questions become distorted if they are discussed only with reference to modern Western models of rationalist historiography or even to classical cultures that may seem comparable to India, such as Greece and China. In the early Indian context Thapar proposes a distinction between "*embedded history*—forms in which historical consciousness has to be prised out—and its opposite, *externalized history*—which tends to bring embedded consciousness into the open, as it were, and to be more aware of its deliberate use of the past."[7] Myth, epic, and genealogy are the principal forms of embedded historical consciousness in India; chronicles of families, institutions, and regions and biographies of persons in authority are the principal externalized forms. Because of the legitimating and memorializing functions of the past, the two forms overlap in such a way that a strict distinction between "myth" and "history" is impossible to maintain: prevalent myths contain residues of historical experience, while chronicles incorporate mythical beginnings and lineages connect with epic heroes. Yet the difference between the two is not arbitrary, because embedded forms appear earlier within lineage-based societies, while externalized forms develop later, in conjunction with state systems.

MODERN MEDIATIONS: FROM HISTORY TO HISTORIOGRAPHY

The Western impatience with Indian forms of historiography arises in part from the desire to separate mythic time from historical time and to establish an equivalence between "history" and the Sanskrit term *itihasa*, which literally means "thus it was" or "the way things were" (*iti-hi-asa*). The principal Sanskrit compilation of narratives about the past is the *itihasa-purana*, a continuum of myth/history which belonged to a genre that was "initially transitional from embedded to externalized history" insofar as it was concerned with historical events at all.[8] In the Indian poetic and narrative context, however, *itihasa* does not mean "thus it was" in a verifiable historical sense or in relation to an objective external referent but "thus it was" within the subjective imaginative domain of a given narrative genre. The *purana* is a recognized literary-poetic form that transmits some historical information because of its concern with the past but that cannot be synonymous with history. Ranajit Guha has commented on "the complicity of Orientalism in hitching *itihasa* to World-history. It was as if an imperial imagination had been looking for a name by which to designate history as a graft in the Indian soil and found it in *itihasa*." On the other side of the cultural divide, as Guha notes, "The rendering of 'history' as *itihasa* was construed by a section of the Hindu conservative intelligentsia as evidence that India, too, had a historiography of the world-historical kind as old as the Mahabharata and the Ramayana, and the West had at last come to acknowledge this as a fact."[9] In part, therefore, colonial India responded to the challenge of European historiography with unconvincing claims about the sameness of the two historiographic traditions rather than reasoned arguments about difference.

Guha's critique of ideological attempts to recast Hindu mythology as history during the colonial period reinforces the point that Western conceptions of "history" as the known (and knowable) past and historiography as its temporally ordered textual embodiment do not have credible parallels in precolonial India. Mythic time cannot be separated neatly from historical time, and *itihasa* cannot become synonymous with "history." The modes of historical consciousness that do relate to cultural forms in "traditional" India privilege synchrony over diachrony, and the literary over the performative, even within the genres of performance. Sheldon Pollock invokes the popular Sanskrit genre of *kaviprashansa* (a poem in praise of earlier poets) as evidence that "to see oneself connected to a cultural practice with a great past, and to know something of the temporal structure of that past, were important values for Sanskrit writers."[10] But this version of the past appeared as an ideal order of poets who existed simultaneously in time, not in the differentiated milieux of their individual times: it had a prodigious concern with *chronology*, but "no narrative to tell of decline or progress, or to suggest the strangeness or difference of the past."[11] "Such coevality," Pollock argues, "generated and enforced a model of language, form, and, often, content that was meant to be largely abstracted, isolated, and insulated from the world of historical change—this despite the ever-deeper historicity that historical change was to bring about. . . . However scholars might wish to periodize Sanskrit literary culture, it is crucial to bear in mind such local procedures, by which, as part of its fundamental self-understanding, the culture sought to resist all periodization."[12] The ahistoricity of Sanskrit literary culture is a sign of the conspicuous success of its self-regulation—the poetic strategies designed to transcend the passage of time actually succeeded in circumventing temporality.

The assimilation of performativity to literariness is no less thorough in the Sanskrit discourses on drama and theatre, and the absence of the historical specifics of performance is even starker. It is not the *culture* of performance that is in question — throughout the active period of Sanskrit drama (from the third to the twelfth centuries) playwrights complimented their precursors, invoked earlier plays within the action of their own work, manipulated the audience's familiarity with the dramatic canon, and occasionally created a metatheatrical play-with-the-play structure to highlight the nature of drama as a convention-bound performance art. But no work of "theatre history" in Sanskrit places authors and performances in time or retrieves the historical specificity of an actual theatre event in relation to its vital constituents: author, work, date, performance space, performer, and audience. Indeed, Rakesh Solomon points to the "bewildering paradox" that "the ancient world's most comprehensive and minutely detailed compendium of theatrical information, Bharata's *Natyasastra* or the *Natya Veda*, offers the historian copious data about every conceivable theoretical and practical aspect of theatre. . . . [but] no dates or chronology, no trajectory of the development of the art and craft of theatre, and no verifiable names of playwrights, company leaders, producers, or actors. . . . In short, the *Natyasastra* furnishes little of the kinds of concrete details imperative for historians to practice their craft of providing verifiable evidence and constructing credible contexts."[13] Even the canonical critical tradition is thus concerned primarily with synchronic analysis and description — with the theoretical and poetic aspects of theatre-as-aesthetic-performance rather than with the historicity of authors, texts, and productions.

The pervasive effects of ahistoricism in theatre are fully manifest in the case of Kalidasa, the Sanskrit poet-playwright who has been an iconic figure in world literature since the nineteenth century. Numerous modern Indian studies of Kalidasa begin by acknowledging that "we have absolutely no trustworthy information regarding the personal history of Kalidasa, by universal consent the greatest of Indian poets."[14] Most Indian scholars place him among the "nine gems" at the court of King Vikramaditya in Ujjayini (ca. 57 BCE), while most Western scholars prefer to link him with the court of Chandragupta II in the same city (ca. 375–415 CE). Based on internal and external evidence, his possible dates range over three-quarters of a millennium, from 150 BCE to 600 CE. In the absence of biographical facts, the persistent legend about his origins casts him as an illiterate cowherd who accidentally married a princess and then acquired his poetic gifts by becoming a devotee of the goddess Kali (hence his name, which means "servant of Kali"). Of the forty-one works attributed to Kalidasa, only six (three plays and three poems) are accepted as definitely belonging to him. While these uncertainties stand in radical contrast to Kalidasa's acknowledged canonicity within the Sanskrit world, the dominant premodern *critical* tradition centered on his work consists in commentaries that are fully interlinear with his own text and make no functional distinction between plays and poems.

As a mode of textual criticism and interpretation, the Sanskrit commentary is a dense secondary discourse that begins at the level of the individual word and "covers" the primary work in its entirety, focusing on issues in grammar, prosody, meter, diction, style, characterization, and poetic meaning. In a manuscript culture the authorial text reproduced in a major commentary also "fixes" a particular recension of that text, and the succession of commentaries thus embodies the textual history of a given work. Since the 1930s Indian Sanskritists (notably M. R. Kale) have systematically produced printed editions of the major commentaries on Kalidasa's plays by Raghavabhatta, Mallinatha, Katavayema, Ghanashyam, Abhirama, and others, in the original or in English or Hindi translation. The elaborate editorial apparatus in a typical volume of this kind consists of a conjectural biography of Kalidasa; a discussion of the Sanskrit *nataka* (full-length play) in relation to the taxonomy of classical dramatic genres; a discussion of sources and historical background; an analysis of plot and characterization; an index of verses; a list of *subhasitas* (literally, "well-spoken words"); and extensive textual and explanatory notes. The substantive "history" attached to Kalidasa's plays—as to Sanskrit plays in general—during the period of Sanskrit hegemony is therefore a more or less static structure consisting of textual analysis, explication, and interpretation, not a dynamic mapping of enactment.

The entire culture of theatre as an elite urban form sustained by court patronage came to an end with the Islamic conquest of India, which began in the eleventh century and prepared the way for seven centuries of Muslim rule. The violence of conquest by central Asian invaders who brought in a different language and religion, the consequent decline of classical culture and Sanskrit, and the emergence of the modern Indian vernaculars had a disruptive effect on all the literary and critical arts, but the proscription on human representation in Islam effectively relegated performance for several centuries to the traditional, devotional, folk, and intermediary genres of the countryside. The revival of urban Indian theatre during the British colonial period therefore marked a movement away from the more recent past, and the recovery of an older past through methods that were informed by a complex new cultural dynamic and altered relations of power.

THE USES OF TIME: THE VARIETIES OF MODERN HISTORIOGRAPHY

A "systematic" historiography of Indian theatre begins under Western auspices at the end of the eighteenth century, for the first time introducing a unique interplay of "Western" and "Indian" perspectives that has permanently altered the approach to theatre-as-historical-subject in the subcontinent. In hindsight this body of writing reveals three distinct strains. The first, foundational strain was firmly Orientalist. In 1789 the colonial administrator and Sanskrit scholar Sir William Jones published his English translation of Kalidasa's *Abhijnanasakuntalam* (titled *Sacontala, or, The Fatal Ring: An Indian Drama*), along with a preface that announced his "discovery" of the Sanskrit language and its dramatic literature to Western readers who had been hitherto unaware of both. Jones's imagination was seized by the "immemorially ancient" existence of drama in India, the mythic story of its invention by the sage Bharata, and the revelation that the Sanskrit genre of the *nataka* was very close to the Western "play." Jones viewed Kalidasa as the "Shakespeare of India" and his play as "a most pleasing and authentick picture of old Hindu manners, and one of the greatest curiosities, that the literature of *Asia* has yet brought to light."[15] In the next generation, Jones's fascination with Sanskrit drama was not only sustained but carried much further by another scholar-administrator, Horace Hayman Wilson, whose two-volume *Select Specimens of the Theatre of the Hindus* (1827) contained a celebrated "Treatise on the Dramatic System of the Hindus" as well as translations of six major Sanskrit plays and excerpts from twenty-three others.[16] Two generations later, over the 1890–1924 period, the history of Sanskrit theatre attracted academically trained Sanskritists and Indologists such as Sylvain Levi, Ernest Philip Horrwitz, Sten Konow, and A. B. Keith. The distinguishing trait of this Anglo-European philological tradition was that it dealt exclusively with Sanskrit theatre and sought to establish it as the "true" Indian theatre. Since the mid-twentieth century, however, despite substantial work by Sanskritists such as Barbara Stoller Miller and H. W. Wells, Sanskrit theatre has been displaced as the privileged subject of Western historiography. The focus in Indology has shifted to the two Sanskrit epics, the Ramayana and the Mahabharata, and sacred texts such as the Vedas and Upanishads, while in theatre studies the scholarly triad of Farley P. Richmond, Darius L. Swann, and Phillip Zarrilli has produced the first comprehensive albeit uneven history of Indian theatre from the classical period to the present.[17]

The second major strain in modern historiography consists of theatre histories by Indian authors, which began to appear in the 1930s. These studies concerned themselves from the beginning with the classical past *as well as* the emergence of modern theatre in about fourteen different languages. Over the last eight decades such studies have produced complex correspondences between the subject matter being investigated and language (both the language of the scholar and the language or languages of the theatrical works). English is the most prominent medium for totalizing studies of "Indian theatre" which attempt to encompass all of theatre history from the mythic moment of origin in antiquity to postindependence times. In the case of histories of individual "regional" language theatres that have a much shorter chronology, however, English and Hindi, the two national link languages, are less common but equally important media for the scholarship.

The collective cultural investment in these works of historiography, especially those written in English, can be gauged from the list of authors, which includes prominent writers, playwrights, critics, and scholars such as Mulk Raj Anand, Utpal Dutt, Balwant Gargi, Adya Rangacharya, Nemichandra Jain, Rustom Bharucha, and Shanta Gokhale. Far more numerous, however, are histories of regional theatres in their respective languages (histories of Bengali theatre in Bengali, Marathi theatre in Marathi, and so on) that have more limited geographical circulation than the nationally accessible works in English or Hindi but exercise great influence in their respective regions. K. Narayan Kale and V. B. Deshpande in Marathi, Prabhat Kumar Bhattacharya and Sudhi Pradhan in Bengali, Kirtinath Kurtkoti in Kannada, Venkat Swaminathan in Tamil, and Hasmukh Baradi in Gujarati are among the historians and critics who are regionally positioned but nationally visible.[18]

The third strain in historiography is the most recent (beginning in 1970) and shows an important move in postwar Western scholarship away from the legacies of nineteenth-century Orientalism. Studies by Euro-American area-studies specialists, performance theorists, and historians of religion have established new disciplinary perspectives in which the focus shifts from the classical to the postclassical or premodern period, and "performance" displaces "drama" or "theatre" as the operative term. Norvin Hein, John Stratton Hawley, Richard Schechner, Kathryn Hansen, and Phillip Zarrilli, among others, have scrupulously historicized (in relation to time, place, audience, and effect) specific genres of nonurban or quasi-urban performance that are an important part of the ritualistic, religious, or social life of particular communities. Hein and Hawley are concerned with miracle-plays and pilgrimage dramas from the Mathura-Brindavan region; Schechner with the Ramlila of Ramnagar, an environmental form that is religious in content but sustained by aristocratic patronage; Hansen with Nautanki, an "intermediary" form of entertainment at the cusp of urban-rural contacts in the north Indian Hindi belt; and Zarrilli with Kathakali, a classically derived form of ritualistic "dance drama" in Kerala that enacts traditional narratives but also has been assimilated to experimental urban performance.[19] This scholarship, moreover, complements the intense interest in Indian myth and tradition that has been a conspicuous part of the intercultural theatre theory and practice of leading contemporary directors such as Peter Brook, Jerzy Grotowski, and Eugenio Barba: the latest forms of Western engagement with Indian theatre thus circumvent both the *classical* and the *modern* in favor of the *premodern*.

Within these complex trajectories of modern history writing, I want to focus on temporal concepts in three divergent models. The first consists of Orientalist histories in which "Indian theatre" denotes only drama and performance in the Sanskrit language and the timeline concludes around 1000 CE. The second model encompasses nationalist macro-histories in which "Indian theatre" includes everything from the classical period to the present, but mainly as the cumulative sum of activity in fourteen or sixteen modern Indian languages. The third consists of regionalist micro-histories in which "Indian theatre" vanishes behind the narrative of theatre in a single language, usually from the time of its emergence in the precolonial or colonial period to the historian's present moment.

The first model is culturally "extrinsic" while the other two are culturally "intrinsic," but all three are dialectically related and ideologically determined. Conditioned by colonialist views of race and culture, the Orientalists locate a common Indo-European heritage as well as an essential civilizational identity for India in ancient Hinduism and Sanskrit and privilege the classical period above all subsequent history. In a directly contrary move, postcolonial cultural nationalists use the validating event of political independence in 1947 to connect the bimillennial history of theatre with the teleology of the long-imagined and newly realized Indian nation. In yet another act of repositioning, proponents of individual regional languages downplay independence and nationhood as pivotal events and assert a "natural" regional identity shaped by centuries of settlement and continuous creativity against "artificial" constructions of the nation, especially those scholarly works that employ the two national link languages of English and Hindu. The three models can be described as representing, respectively, "civilization time," "nation time," and "region time." That all three coexist in the present moment indicates the arbitrariness as well as elasticity of temporal frameworks. As I show through selective examples below, the demarcation of time in "Indian theatre history" depends to an unusual extent on the historian's subjective perspective, not on a consensually determined chronology of events.

"CIVILIZATION TIME" IN COLONIAL HISTORIOGRAPHY

Sir William Jones's preface to *Shakuntalam* (1789) and A. B. Keith's *Sanskrit Drama in Its Origin, Development, Theory, and Practice* (1924) represent the two terminal moments of a process whereby the Anglo-European engagement with Sanskrit theatre (and literature more broadly) develops from the excitement of discovery to full-fledged scholarly historiography. The synonymy between Sanskrit/Hinduism and India in this evolving tradition, which assimilates the philological scholarship of Leopold von Schroeder, Richard Pischel, Sir William Ridgeway, Heinrich Luders, Sten Konow, and above all Max Muller, leads to two questions about the historians' demarcation of their subject: why create "civilization time," and why end it at a moment so far removed from the present? In other words, why did India's classical past become worthy of reverential European attention at a time when India was an embattled subject nation? And why did European interest in India's rich cultural heritage end with the decline of the Sanskrit world instead of continuing into the present?

The answers to these questions involve the full range of historical, philological, intercultural, racial, and aesthetic judgments that Orientalism brought to bear on Sanskrit as both a language and a literary medium. With the category of literature including not only poetry and drama but also works in other disciplines such as religion, philosophy, and law, "Sanskrit literature" made a monumental entry into the traditions of world literature around the mid-nineteenth century. Philologically, Sanskrit contained "irrefragable evidence" (Muller's phrase) of a common Indo-European heritage that connected India's ancient language to Greek and Latin, and Indian to European classicism, leading to a significant revision of world history that gave European commentators a new "scientific" platform from which to view ancient and contemporary India. As Pollock explains, part of the fascination with India had to do with "Romantic Europe's preoccupation with origins and lines of descent, and in the mirror of this preoccupation, India came to be regarded as the cradle of Europe's own civilization."[20] As the language of Hindu antiquity Sanskrit was also seen as embodying the essence of Indian civilization, and the image of a pristine classical past offered both European Orientalists and Indian cultural nationalists a welcome counterpoise to a debased colonial present. Furthermore, the paradigm shifts accompanying the Islamic conquest allowed European commentators to posit a "natural" moment of rupture in the twelfth century, which they embraced all the more eagerly because of their antipathy toward the Muslim rulers they had dethroned in the later eighteenth century. Caught up fully in the self/other dialectic, the Europeans showed qualified and conditional interest in India: they embraced Sanskrit but dismissed the cultural formations of the postclassical world as inessential and secondary.

The selectiveness of civilization time has an even closer application to drama, because if Sanskrit literature is the privileged component within Indian literature, Sanskrit drama has a privileged position in relation to all the other genres of literary antiquity. In his preface to *Select Specimens of the Theatre of the Hindus* (1827), H. H. Wilson comments that in the study of an "ancient dialect . . . there is no one species which will be found to embrace so many purposes as the dramatic," making drama the genre "pre-eminently entitled to the attention of the philosopher as well as the philologist, of the man of general literary taste as well as the professional scholar."[21] Wilson's description of Sanskrit drama as "the national theatre of the Hindus" is also a deliberate anachronism, calculated to secure for this theatre the same careful attention commanded by the national theatres of Europe. In *Le Théâtre Indien* (1890), Sylvain Levi considers theatre in general "the highest expression of the civilization which gives birth to it" and Sanskrit theatre in particular "the Indian theatre *par excellence*," due in large part to a playwright such as Kalidasa, who "has gained his place in the pleiad [*sic*] in which every name sums up a period of the human mind. It is the series of those glorious names which constitutes history."[22] A. B. Keith, in *The Sanskrit Drama in Its Origin, Development, Theory, and Practice* (1924), continues this line of appreciative criticism by describing Sanskrit drama as "the highest product of Indian poetry, and as summing up in itself the final conception of literary art achieved by the very self-conscious creators of Indian literature."[23]

Having created a privileged object of inquiry in Sanskrit/Indian drama, however, the European commentators such as Jones, Wilson, Levi, and Keith go on to acknowledge, implicitly or explicitly, the impossibility of rational historiography in a "forgetful India" because of the indeterminable chronology of authors, works, events, and historical contexts. Levi's two-volume study *Le Théâtre Indien* is the most revealing example of the historians' attempt to impose a Western sense of causality on a disorderly field of evidence and to formulate strategies for devising a coherent narrative out of radically unstable timelines.[24] Levi's introduction sets up the problem, and his problematic solution for it, so succinctly that it deserves to be quoted at length:

> The literary history of India, like her political history, is so little known that every name becomes an object of controversy. However, we have tried to establish a complete system of chronology. . . . The state of our knowledge of Indian literary history clearly invites us to use the inductive method. The documents concerned with the formative period are too rare, too vague and too obscure to yield a well-defined picture; on examination, they prove to be so contaminated by imagination, prejudice and preconceived ideas that they have little chance to reflect the exact truth. If, on the other hand, one takes the trouble to observe minutely the better known periods, one may find a clue to what happened in the mysterious past. Literary development has its own implacable logic; successive stages are joined by a relation of causality. If a group of effects is clearly known, then the search for causes should not be too difficult. In literary history, the series of cause and effect is so closely knit that the same period seems to repeat itself at regular intervals.[25]

Armed with the inductive method, Levi appears confident about dealing with troublesome issues such as the origins of Sanskrit drama in Vedic and epic performance, the question of foreign (especially Greek) influences, the chronology of major playwrights, and the reconstruction of actual performances.

Yet in the body of his history, despite his confidence, Levi refers repeatedly to the lacunae that frustrate causal sequencing and undermine the sense of an orderly historical progression. He is confronted with a field of evidence that lacks "chrono-logic" at strategic points in time. One of Levi's persistent complaints is that major Sanskrit playwrights are thoroughly "familiar to literature" but "foreign to the history of literature."[26] His desire to establish the teleological progress of Sanskrit drama "towards the perfection of the *nataka*" is frustrated,[27] because India allowed the celebrated precursors of Kalidasa "to disappear without leaving any trace," with the odd result that "dramatic literature enters history like a miracle, offering at once perfect masterpieces."[28] To rationalize the scantiness of information about play production, Levi presents an egregiously circular argument: he comments that dramatic theory usually offsets the "counter-evidence of dramatic production," but Indian drama "presents the almost unique spectacle of a theory being accepted without question and being slavishly followed for a duration of fifteen centuries."[29] This reasoning allows him to "read" theoretical precepts as evidence about performance, entirely begging the question of an objective ascertainable relation between theory and practice. An analysis of the structure and content of Levi's study, in fact, points to a trait that all substantial European histories of Sanskrit theatre share. They consist not in a chronological or period-sensitive narrative of the intersecting trajectories of "drama," "theatre," and "performance" but mainly in *descriptive re-presentations* of the origin myths, taxonomy, theory, poetics, aesthetics, and criticism of Sanskrit drama, along with generous plot summaries and extended discussions of form, style, and language in individual plays. Much of the content of this history is derived either directly from the relevant Sanskrit sources or from previous histories in European languages, so that individual works of Orientalist theatre history echo each other to a disconcerting extent.

The 1924 history by A. B. Keith, who held the Regius Chair in Sanskrit and Comparative Philology at Edinburgh University, is thus the only colonial-era study with a methodology suited to its resistant subject. The leading Indologist of his generation, Keith incorporates nearly a century of previous philological scholarship in his discussion, as well as important new discoveries that warrant "a fresh investigation of the origin and development of the drama."[30] His history is qualitatively different from earlier works not so much in terms of content but in the organization, clarity, and authority of the presentation. The first two parts of the study, dealing with the origin and development of Sanskrit drama, proceed from a discussion of dramatic elements in Vedic and post-Vedic literature to individual chapters on the major playwrights, concluding with a discussion of the decline of Sanskrit drama and its achievements. They are followed by a shorter discussion of dramatic theory and even briefer speculations about theatrical practice. Keith thus separates his reconstructed chronological history from the discussions of theory and speculative practice, unlike Levi, who deals simultaneously with all these elements throughout his study. In dealing with chronology, moreover, Keith does not propose a teleology of dramatic forms or impose metanarratives of causality and literary logic on the cultural forms of fifteen centuries. Rather, he presents the available textual evidence and makes informed cultural inferences, leaving it to the reader to deal with the gaps. That Keith's history also contains generous plot synopses confirms that drama-as-literary-text is the cornerstone of any European historiography of Sanskrit drama. But his tone is objective, not romantic, and "civilization time" appears for once as a plausible if somewhat erratic progression of cultural forms along the axes of time and space.

"NATION TIME" AND "REGION TIME" IN POSTCOLONIAL HISTORIOGRAPHY

The movement toward and beyond the event of political independence in 1947 reorients Indian theatre historiography in two crucial ways: the authorship of history shifts from Anglo-European Sanskritists to Indian practitioners, critics, cultural commentators, and (after 1980) a few academic scholars; and the exclusive focus on Sanskrit gives way to a diametrically opposite framework in which the operative term—"Indian theatre"—encompasses the entire history of theatre in India, from the classical Sanskrit period to the present. Postcolonial Indian historiographers therefore concentrate on recuperating precisely those postclassical, premodern, and modern histories of "vernacular" theatre and performance that the European Orientalists had erased by arguing aggressively that a unified and continuous civilization underlies the imagined community of the modern Indian nation. The new "national/ist history" is also constructed almost exclusively in the medium of English—a practice that suggests not a continuing neocolonial dependence on the West but the rapid domestication of English as an *Indian* link language. With a handful of exceptions, however, the works in question are not examples of scholarly or professional theatre history but belletristic, polemical, even idiosyncratic narratives that often adopt what Sheldon Pollock calls the "purely serial" mode of temporality, "whereby texts follow each other over the centuries (as if sequence were somehow meaningful in itself, or were somehow safely situated beyond meaning)."[31]

An unbroken succession of such works since 1934 used the terms "Indian theatre," "Indian drama," and "the Indian stage" to define "nation time" in theatre history, following a variety of structures. One common strategy of periodization appears in noted Kannada playwright Adya Rangacharya's *The Indian Theatre* (1971), which begins with a discussion of the origins of drama and the Sanskrit tradition, recognizes the 1200–1800 period as an "Interlude" sustained by the "folk stage," and concludes with "the search for a new theatre" in the modern period that has entered an even newer phase in "independent India."[32] Another playwright, Balwant Gargi, bases his discussion of *Theatre in India* (1962) on both chronology and form, first separating the past and present genres of "Traditional Theatre" from the "Modern Theatre," and then analyzing the latter variously on the basis of language (Bengali, Marathi, English, and so forth), location ("Regional Theatres"), form ("Ballet," "Opera," "Children's Theatre"), or material organization ("Amateur Theatre").[33] Such contradictory categories apparently matter not at all.

The second dominant postindependence model of historiography is one in which "nation time" intersects with "region time," demonstrating that a "national" theatre history is inseparable from the histories of theatre in the modern Indian languages. In *Indian Drama* (1956), a collection published by the Ministry of Information and Broadcasting, an introductory overview and an essay on Sanskrit drama set up the cultural, aesthetic, formal, and textual foundations of Indian theatre, while "post-independence trends" in the period after 1947 show how Indian theatre as a whole is coping with the aftermath of colonialism and Westernization. The substantial middle, however, consists of more or less detailed descriptive histories of theatre in thirteen languages, arranged alphabetically from Assamese to Urdu, with the exception of Hindi, which appears first as the majority language.[34]

The third model, represented by the PEN volume on *Drama in Modern India* (1961) and another collection titled *Indian Drama* (1974), downplays the classical and contemporary frames still further and presents "Indian theatre" simply as the aggregate of theatre in sixteen modern languages.[35] The rationale for this structure is that an authentic national perspective can emerge only when it accommodates regional cultural identities. But the fragmentation of theatre history by language and region, the absence of any sustainable analysis of the relations between regions and nation, and the basic avoidance of diachronic developments over the ages greatly hinder and limit this approach to Indian drama and theatre. Perhaps most tellingly, it reveals a studied avoidance of comparative methodology in a theatre culture that constantly demands comparisons.

A different kind of contest involving time and history unfolds over the question of whether the urban commercial theatre that appeared in cities such as Bombay and Calcutta during the British colonial period "belongs" in nation time. Historians who take a holistic view of Indian theatre regard the Western influences on colonial theatre as elements that may have been alien at the beginning but were valuable in themselves and were rapidly assimilated into a continuous and syncretistic tradition. Javare Gowda notes, for example, that the contemporary Indian playwright has simultaneous access to classical, folk, and Western traditions and that "the really creative writer can use all these three influences and make a distinctively

Indian drama. This is the task . . . before the writers in India."[36] In contrast, cultural-nationalist critics such as Nemichandra Jain and Suresh Awasthi regard Western-influenced urban theatre as an alien imposition on indigenous theatre forms. Jain thus insists that Indian theatre had developed for more than two millennia "according to *our own* world-view, on the basis of one or the other aspect of *our culture*, and under compulsions of *our own* social and political conditions."[37] The Western-oriented modern theatre of the nineteenth century disrupted this unity by imitating an "alien theatre, fundamentally different in its world-view and aesthetic approach," and succeeded only because a growing middle class of English-educated Indians strove to mimic and please the colonial rulers.[38] The end of colonialism presents a long-awaited moment of restitution when the older "natural" theatrical traditions can resume their rightful place in national culture. The Orientalist idea of an essential, uncontaminated Indian (Hindu) identity as the defining ingredient in Indian history thus reappears in the polemic of the postcolonial cultural nationalists, now aimed at erasing not postclassical cultural forms but the modern urban tradition in its entirety.

These ideological contests have taken place mainly in polemical histories written in English by historians who are concerned with the cultural purity, authenticity, and Indianness of a new "national theatre." By comparison, the delineation of "region time" in historiography is a far less contentious process because the exclusive attention to a single language and region seems to create a ready-made chronology, brackets the problem of national perspectives, and sidesteps the troublesome issues of interlingual and interregional connections. Kironmoy Raha's *Bengali Theatre* (1978) follows a typical structure in this respect. In one direction, he establishes Sanskrit theatre and the intermediary *jatra* form as the classical and premodern (indigenous) precursors of theatre in Bengali; in the other, he sets up an exact correspondence between the British conquest of Bengal and the beginnings of modern theatre in Calcutta, yoking the rest of his descriptive theatre history to the chronology of colonial and postcolonial events *only* in Bengal. The event of national independence in 1947, inextricably linked to the violence of partition, merits half a sentence in Raha's study, and he does not mention a single theatre, author, or work outside Bengal.[39]

In *Playwright at the Centre: Marathi Drama from 1843 to the Present* (2000), Shanta Gokhale attempts to avoid provincialism. She acknowledges that Bombay and Calcutta are "the two leading cities in India with a professional theatre [and] the histories of the two theatres are marked by as much concurrence as divergence."[40] Her more ambitious work also is not organized exclusively by chronology but by qualitative issues such as the centrality of the playwright and the prime significance of the text in Marathi theatre. Yet Gokhale's focus remains unwaveringly on the many facets of the Marathi tradition, even within the multilingual metropolis of Bombay. For instance, during the colonial period the Bombay-based Parsi theatre companies created the first popular theatre that commanded a national audience and involved three major languages (Hindi/Hindustani, Gujarati, and Urdu), and since independence Bombay has sustained theatre not only in Marathi but in Hindi, Gujarati, Konkani, and English. Similarly, theatre in Bengali continues to be dominant in Calcutta, but the city is also an important venue now for practitioners in Hindi and English. Nonetheless, historians such as Raha and Gokhale prefer to focus exclusively on theatre in the majority "regional" language, because maintaining its discrete identity is an intrinsic and deliberate aspect of language-based histories—a way of valuing and protecting region time in a polyglot nation.

CONCLUSION: REFIGURING TIME IN A NEW HISTORIOGRAPHY

In "Some Critical Remarks on Theatre Historiography," Erika Fischer-Lichte suggests that "a partial perspective is a condition of the possibility of a history of theatre. All historians must limit the subject area of their theatre history in accordance with their specific epistemological interests and scholarly competence, select the events that are likely to be productive in terms of the questions they are asking, and construct their histories from their examination of the documents related to these events."[41] Such a judgment is possible because the (Western) historiographer, though also confronted with basic problems in representing and narrating the temporal and spatial dimensions of theatre history, can take for granted many of the conditions that enable her craft, including the existence of a professional discipline of theatre history, the availability of archives (often well organized), established methodologies for connecting history-as-event to history-as-record and history-as-account (to use Thomas Postlewait's careful categories),[42] and epistemologically sound criteria for the delimitation and identification of historical subjects.

Indian theatre history, by contrast, often lacks these foundational conditions. The scholar struggles to do justice to the historiographical challenges. Some studies, still largely preoccupied with totalizing views of "Indian theatre," grope for strategies to connect region with nation. Likewise, Orientalist histories produced during the colonial period are too exclusionary, Indian histories written in the postcolonial period too inclusive, and most histories of regional theatres too insular. In the absence of a dominant commercial center for theatre (such as New York, London, or Paris), a competitive marketplace, or a professional community of theatre historians and critics within or outside the academy, theatre-as-performance remains—even in contemporary India—a precarious event, as yet unconnected in dependable or predictable ways with the activities of archival documentation, reception study, cultural commentary, criticism, and historical scholarship.

In a larger comparative perspective, India also does not fit into the dominant Western schema that S. E. Wilmer, for instance, outlines for constructing national theatre histories on the basis of geography, language, ethnicity, or aesthetics.[43] The territorial boundaries of "India" have shifted constantly in the modern period due to British colonial occupation, the creation of Pakistan in 1947, and the reorganization of states after independence (a process that is still continuing). But with twenty-two official languages recognized in the national constitution, no common or unifying language can counterbalance this territorial instability.

The difference between India and the West is striking in this respect: a language such as English crosses national boundaries to serve as a vibrant theatrical medium in far-flung countries such as Britain, Ireland, Canada, the United States, Australia, New Zealand, and South Africa. And for a number of other countries, from Norway, Sweden, Denmark, and Finland to Israel, English is a pervasive second language. But in India no single language—not even Hindi or English—defines, let alone dominates, theatre within the country's borders. India has no designated "National Theatre," and its political capital—New Delhi—is not the theatrical capital (that role is shared by Bombay and Calcutta, now Mumbai and Kolkata). Also, though Hindi is the majority language and Hindi and English serve as the two national link languages, India has no designated "national language." Cultural differences within the country involve not primarily race, religion, and ethnicity (except in northeastern states such as Assam and Manipur) but regional identities based on a shared cultural and political history and a common language. Each major state within the Indian union is therefore comparable to a mid-sized European nation-state. Finally, the country's multifoliate performance culture does not support convenient binaries such as elite/popular, written/oral, textual/performative, classical/folk, urban/rural, modern/traditional, secular/religious, realistic/antirealistic, indigenous/foreign, and professional/amateur.[44] Because of the postcolonial preoccupation with the "recovery" (or invention) of tradition, all significant performance practices of the classical, premodern, and colonial pasts have come to coexist in, and intersect with, the theatrical present.

Inevitably, it is in the work of a handful of academic scholars that new methodologies for representing national and regional theatre histories have begun to appear, with the movement from colonialism to postcolonialism along the matrix of a syncretic modernity serving as a principle of chronological as well as qualitative organization. Sudipto Chatterjee's *The Colonial Staged: Theatre in Colonial Calcutta* (2007) is one recent example of how radically the concepts of "history" and "time" change when a single language—which is one of the two oldest and strongest theatre languages in modern India—is approached through the lens of critical theory, performance studies, and postcolonial theory. Chatterjee's declared objective is to connect the history of Bengali theatre to the contexts and issues of colonialism. The alternation between history and analysis for Chatterjee becomes "more complicated . . . when the concern is not only the specific history of theatre but the larger theatre of colonial history itself."[45] With theatre serving as the figural mise-en-scène for the performance of a hybridized colonial culture, Chatterjee's analysis effortlessly turns Calcutta and Bengali into microcosms for colonial India and Indian-language theatre, respectively.

Nandi Bhatia covers some of the same ground in *Acts of Authority, Acts of Resistance: Theater and Politics in Colonial and Postcolonial India* (2004); but as the subtitle suggests, she is concerned specifically with theatre as a political instrument, on both sides of the colonial divide. This dual perspective allows her to discuss antigovernment plays in 1870s Calcutta as well as the emergence of a nationwide people's theatre movement in the 1940s and to chart the multiple Indian mediations of Shakespeare in languages such as Marathi, Bengali, Hindi, and English over nearly a century. In contrast with Bhatia's colonial-postcolonial continuum, my own study *Theatres of Independence: Drama, Theory, and Urban Performance in India since 1947* (2005) approaches the event of independence as a moment of symbolic and real rupture with colonial formations in all the major languages.[46] This study examines the postindependence decades as a historically demarcated, unprecedented period in modern Indian theatre. I argue that political autonomy and new nationhood create new forms of authorship, textuality, production, reception, and multilingual circulation that did not exist earlier. And I investigate the complex new thematic formations that can be charted across multiple languages and regions. In the process, I consider both theory and practice in postindependence theatre as an inextricable fusion of historiographical forms and categories, including Indian and foreign, original and adapted, traditional and modern.

The decisive principle of chronological differentiation in the studies described above is the idea of "modernity"—that historical conjuncture of colonialism, European (mainly British) influences, and accelerated change. All of these factors established commercial urban theatre as an entirely new kind of cultural institution in mid-nineteenth century India and have continued to shape theatre in the decades since independence. Chatterjee, Bhatia, and I believe that the movement from colonialism to independence and beyond created the Indian "nation" as an inescapable referent in the political and cultural spheres. Accordingly, all three of us address in our respective ways the assimilation of theatre to the demands of anticolonial nationalism and cultural self-discovery. Beyond this, the methodologies and temporal frameworks diverge. Chatterjee is concerned with the cultural effects of colonialism over a finite period; she focuses on the region and language that appeared in the vanguard of the nineteenth-century "Indian Renaissance" and witnessed the first significant urban formations in theatre. Bhatia considers theatre as an important form of intervention in the politics of race, class, gender, and culture over an expanded time frame that includes colonial, postcolonial, and neocolonial configurations in several venues and languages. My work, which deals with eight important modern and contemporary theatre languages (all but two of which are "regional" by definition), is therefore centrally concerned with the relation of the regional to the national in theatre practice. "Region" and "nation," I argue, have emerged as interdependent rather than mutually exclusive categories in India, especially in the postindependence period. The possibility of a new historiography now lies in conceptions of a "national theatre" that attend to the intersecting trajectories of nation time and region time and are descriptive and inclusive rather than prescriptive and exclusive in nature.[47]

I began this essay by observing that Indian theatre historiography shares its crisis of representation with other forms of modern history writing in India: the reorientation of history as a discipline, especially through the Subaltern Studies initiative, can therefore be an equally energizing model for theatre historiography. Launched in 1982 to counterbalance colonialist British and bourgeois-nationalist Indian histories of India, Subaltern Studies adapted the methodology of "history-from-below" to Indian conditions in order to accomplish a wide-ranging recuperation of processes ignored by elitist history. Ranajit Guha, a founder-member, argued that colonial British historians such as James Mill had reduced Indian history to a highly interesting portion of British history, "which is why . . . it was up to the Indians themselves to try and recover their past by means of an Indian historiography of India."[48] Twenty years after the project's beginning, Partha Chatterjee summed up its effects in terms that have equal resonance for theatre history:

> what is distinctive about this moment is . . . its intense awareness of the place of history in the present and its willingness, indeed its urge, to rethink the constitution of that place. Its mode of inquiry is mainly methodological, critically examining the historian's practices and assumptions rather than putting forth another history. Its concern is to find a set of historiographic practices that are more truthful as well as more ethical. Its desire is to find a way out of the self-constructed cage of scientific history that has made the historian so fearful of the popular, virtually immobilizing him or her in its presence.[49]

What the term "popular" signifies in scientific history the terms "enduring," "plural," and "heterogeneous" signify in Indian theatre history. The relevance of Subaltern Studies to the historiography of Indian cultural forms lies not so much in the notion of the subaltern, which does not fit the bourgeois urban forms of colonial and postcolonial theatre, but in the call for a revisionist historiography that fits the peculiarities of India-as-historical-subject, connects the local and the global, and is alert to the difference between narratives of modernity in India and the West. The "history of Indian theatre" has not yet been written or even conceptualized: it can begin to take shape only when theatrical "forms" of all kinds are situated within changing material circumstances, without arbitrary strategies of exclusion or *a priori* judgments about value. The historian of Indian theatre, in turn, has to devise viable methods of chronological and thematic delimitation that move beyond reductive Orientalist or indigenist frameworks for dealing with more than two millennia of performance practices.

NOTES

1. For a classic denigration of India as a prerational "land without history," see G. W. F. Hegel, *The Philosophy of History*, trans. J. Sibree, introd. C. J. Friedrich (New York: Dover, 1956). For a critique of Orientalist reductions of Indian history and society, see the introduction to Ronald B. Inden, *Imagining India* (Oxford: Blackwell, 1990).

2. Hegel, *The Philosophy of History*, p. 163.

3. Romila Thapar, "Time as a Metaphor of History," in *History and Beyond* (New Delhi: Oxford University Press, 2000), pp. 5–6.

4. Ibid., pp. 9, 31.

5. Ibid., p. 6.

6. G. N. Devy, *"Of Many Heroes": An Indian Essay in Literary Historiography* (New Delhi: Orient Longman, 1998), p. 11.

7. Romila Thapar, "Interpreting Early India," in *History and Beyond*, p. 138.

8. Ibid., p. 151.

9. Ranajit Guha, *History at the Limit of World-History* (New Delhi: Oxford University Press, 2002), pp. 51, 52.

10. Sheldon Pollock, "Sanskrit Literary Culture," in *Literary Cultures in History: Reconstructions from South Asia*, ed. Sheldon Pollock (Berkeley: University of California Press, 2003), p. 79.

11. Ibid.

12. Ibid., pp. 79–80.

13. Rakesh H. Solomon, "When Did Brahma Create Theatre? and Other Questions of Indian Theatre Historiography," in *Writing and Rewriting National Theatre Histories*, ed. S. E. Wilmer, Studies in Theatre History and Culture (Iowa City: University of Iowa Press, 2004), pp. 201–202.

14. M. R. Kale, ed., *The Abhijnanashakuntalam of Kalidasa*, 10th ed. (Delhi: Motilal Banarsidas, 1969), p. 9.

15. Sir William Jones, *Sacontala, or, The Fatal Ring: An Indian Drama* (Calcutta: Joseph Cooper, 1789), p. 4.

16. Wilson's interest in Sanskrit drama was part of a multifaceted engagement with the classical language that included a Sanskrit-English dictionary (1819); an introduction to Sanskrit grammar (1841); translations of the Vishnu Purana (1840), the Rig Veda (1850), and two poems of Kalidasa (*Megha-duta* and *Ritu-samhara*); essays and lectures on Hinduism (1861–1862); and essays on Sanskrit literature (1864–1865).

17. Farley P. Richmond, Darius L. Swann, and Phillip Zarrilli, *Indian Theatre: Traditions of Performance* (Honolulu: University of Hawaii Press, 1990).

18. The newest trend in "Indian" theatre criticism, which both complements and contrasts with the post-1930 traditions of theatre history, is a small but growing body of criticism by academically trained scholars of Indian origin who are positioned within the Western academy. In the past decade the scholarly field of modern Indian theatre studies has begun to coalesce around publications (essays, articles, and books) by Rakesh Solomon, Nandi Bhatia, Vasudha Dalmia, Sudipto Chatterjee, and me. These studies, however, are not "theatre history" in the conventional sense but methodologically bold, thematically diverse amalgams of history, theory, and critical interpretation focused on single or multiple languages. The studies are discussed selectively in the concluding section of this essay.

19. Norvin Hein, *The Miracle Plays of Mathura* (New Haven: Yale University Press, 1972); John Stratton Hawley, *At Play with Krishna: Pilgrimage Dramas from Brindavan* (Princeton: Princeton University Press, 1981); Richard Schechner, *Between Theater and*

Anthropology (Philadelphia: University of Pennsylvania Press, 1985); Kathryn Hansen, *Grounds for Play: The Nautanki Theater of North India* (Berkeley: University of California Press, 1992); and Phillip Zarrilli, *Kathakali Dance Drama: Where Gods and Demons Come to Play* (London: Routledge, 2000).

20. Max Muller, *A History of Ancient Sanskrit Literature*, rev. 2nd ed. (London: Williams and Norgate, 1860; rpt. New York: AMS Press, 1978), p. 3; Sheldon Pollock, introduction to *Literary Cultures in History*, ed. Sheldon Pollock (Berkeley: University of California Press, 2003), p. 3.

21. H. H. Wilson, *Select Specimens of the Theatre of the Hindus*, vol. 1, 3rd ed. (Calcutta: Trubner, 1871), pp. ix–x.

22. Sylvain Levi, *Le Theatre Indien*, 2 vols. (Paris: Buillon, 1890); trans. by Narayan Mukerji as *The Theatre of India*, 2 vols. (Calcutta: Writer's Workshop, 1978), vol. 1, pp. 3, 141. All subsequent references to Levi are to this translation and appear in the text.

23. A. B. Keith, *The Sanskrit Drama in Its Origin, Development, Theory, and Practice* (Oxford: Clarendon Press, 1924), p. 276.

24. Sylvain Levi's complaint is typical of the Western impatience with Indian neglect of history: "Forgetful India has not kept the memory of the genius who gave to the drama its final form" (*The Theatre of India*, vol. 2, p. 45).

25. Ibid., vol. 1, pp. 6–7.

26. Ibid., vol. 1, p. 173.

27. Ibid., vol. 1, p. 12.

28. Ibid., vol. 2, p. 12.

29. Ibid., vol. 1, p. 132.

30. Keith, *The Sanskrit Drama*, p. 5.

31. Pollock, introduction to *Literary Cultures in History*, p. 12.

32. Adya Rangacharya, *The Indian Theatre*, 2nd ed. (New Delhi: National Book Trust, 1980).

33. Balwant Gargi, *Theatre in India* (New York: H. Wolff, 1962).

34. *Indian Drama* (New Delhi: Publications Division, 1956; rev. ed. 1981).

35. *Drama in Modern India and the Writer's Responsibility in a Rapidly Changing World* (Bombay: PEN [Poets, Essayists, and Novelists] All-India Centre, 1961); *Indian Drama: A Collection of Papers*, ed. H. H. Anniah Gowda (Mysore: Prasaranga, 1974).

36. Javare Gowda, preface to *Indian Drama*, ed. Gowda, p. x.

37. Nemichandra Jain, *Indian Theatre: Tradition, Continuity, and Change* (New Delhi: Vikas, 1992), p. 63 (emphasis added).

38. Ibid., p. 64.

39. Kironmoy Raha, *Bengali Theatre* (New Delhi: National Book Trust, 1978).

40. Shanta Gokhale, *Playwright at the Centre: Marathi Drama from 1843 to the Present* (Calcutta: Seagull, 2000).

41. Erika Fischer-Lichte, "Some Critical Remarks on Theatre Historiography," in *Writing and Rewriting National Theatre Histories*, ed. Wilmer, p. 3.

42. Thomas Postlewait, "Introduction," in *The Cambridge Introduction to Theatre Historiography* (Cambridge: Cambridge University Press, 2009), pp. 2–5.

43. S. E. Wilmer, "On Writing National Theatre Histories," in *Writing and Rewriting National Theatre Histories*, ed. Wilmer, pp. 17–28.

44. Although it is popular among scholars today to complain about binary thinking, many of these basic oppositions and divisions help to set up and frame fundamental categories of understanding. In order to get beyond some reductive binaries, we need, in the first place, the primary polarities that initiate thought. We need to show how they are interdependent rather than mutually exclusive categories. See Aparna Bhargava Dharwadker, *Theatres of Independence: Drama, Theory, and Urban Performance in India since 1947* (Iowa City: University of Iowa Press, 2005).

45. Sudipto Chatterjee, *The Colonial Staged: Theatre in Colonial Calcutta* (London: Seagull, 2007), p. 10.

46. Nandi Bhatia, *Acts of Authority, Acts of Resistance: Theater and Politics in Colonial and Postcolonial India* (Ann Arbor: University of Michigan Press, 2004); Dharwadker, *Theatres of Independence*.

47. Dharwadker, *Theatres of Independence*.

48. Guha, *History at the Limit*, p. 1.

49. Partha Chatterjee, "Introduction: History and the Present," in *History and the Present*, ed. Partha Chatterjee and Anjan Ghosh (Delhi: Permanent Black, 2002), p. 19.

3 Space

Space and Theatre History

Theatre as an artistic and cultural activity has been the subject of academic speculation ever since the Greeks, but it was not until the beginning of the twentieth century that European and American scholars institutionalized a field of theatre studies. A significant part of this new field's self-definition involved a clear splitting away from traditional literary studies, within which theatre had previously had its academic home. The entire Western tradition, from the Greeks onward, considered the drama primarily as a branch of literature (the other basic divisions being the epic and the lyric). Traditionally theatre scholarship was based upon the literary text (Aristotle's apparent indifference to spectacle is an early and notorious example of this bias), and the actual process of the physical realization of this text, while not entirely ignored, was a matter of considerably less interest.

Two pioneering theatre scholars presented a radical challenge to this orientation at the turn of the twentieth century, Brander Matthews in the United States and Max Herrmann in Germany. Their new perspective, which was bitterly resisted by many of their colleagues in both countries, was not to reject the study of literary drama but to insist that such study was incomplete unless one went beyond the literary text to consider the physical conditions of performance, the spatial realization of that text. Thus it is no exaggeration to say that the foundation of modern theatre studies was grounded upon a spatial reorientation—from the linear reading of drama to the three-dimensional staging of it. Herrmann was particularly interested in audiences and what would later be called reception theory, while Matthews, who in 1899 was named the first professor of dramatic literature in an English-speaking university, was more particularly interested in a spatial concern, the shape of historic theatres and the relation of that space to the plays presented in them. In *A Study of the Drama* (1910), he stated this fundamental principle in these terms: "It is impossible to consider the drama profitably apart from the theatre in which it was born and in which it reveals itself in its completest perfection."[1] The scale models of historical theatres built to illustrate performance spaces by Matthews and his students may still be seen at Columbia. In a very fundamental way, the new orientation introduced by Herrmann and Matthews still serves as the most widely accepted model for historical research in theatre, as may be seen in a very recent articulation of the aims of the discipline by one of its leading scholars, Robert D. Hume. In a survey article on the "Aims, Materials, and Methodology" of theatre history in his period of specialization, 1660–1800, Hume observes: "I would suggest that one crucial function of the theatre historian is *To demonstrate how production and performance circumstances affected the writing and public impact of plays*."[2] One could hardly ask for a clearer or more concise statement of the Herrmann/Matthews project.

It is also important to understand in what ways the new orientation proposed by Matthews and Herrmann was revolutionary and in what ways it was not. Although the establishment of theatre history as a discipline offered a new methodology and new sources of investigation, its object for most of the twentieth century remained essentially the same as that of the tradition of dramatic literature in which it was grounded. That object was to provide a fuller and deeper understanding of the largely European works of the traditional canon. As the field developed in Europe and America, it focused its attention not upon the history of theatre in general but upon the original performance conditions of those plays already established as the focus of literary study. It thus maintained a consistent if unacknowledged position as an adjunct to literature. The basic purpose for studying theatre history, as Matthews and Herrmann saw it, was to provide important insights into the understanding of canonical literary figures like Shakespeare, Schiller, and Molière.

A quick glance through almost any standard theatre history text up to the present confirms this orientation.[3] Theatre history has been dominated by the history of how canonical plays were originally performed. Opera is generally omitted almost entirely, and the few nonliterary forms given serious attention, most notably the *commedia dell'arte*, are included because of their clear influence on major canonical authors like Shakespeare and Molière. Within this main tradition of theatre history scholarship, space is an important matter, but largely for these literary reasons. This is why the single spatial investigation in the field of theatre history that has inspired by far the most scholarship is the question of what exactly was the physical stage upon which Shakespeare worked.[4] One of the first classic texts of theatre history in America, George R. Kernodle's *From Art to Theatre* (1944), attempted to explain the spatial configuration of the English and Dutch Renaissance stages by studying spatial configurations in Italian Renaissance painting, a methodology which has inspired far too little imitation in subsequent theatre historical research.[5]

Before pursuing the development of theatre history from its beginnings and how its practitioners have considered spatial matters, however, it might not be amiss to provide some brief commentary on what role spatial considerations might play in the literary tradition of drama from which Matthews and Herrmann theoretically separated themselves. As I have suggested, their reform was in large part involved with introducing spatial concerns to the study of drama, but we should not forget that space has played an important role even in the linear literary drama. The fictional character in drama, like fictional characters in epic or lyric literature, is situated in a space, sometimes referred to as the "imaginary world" of the fiction, which is evoked in the mind of the reader as a part of the receptive process. The imaginary world of the dramatic character is phenomenologically more complex in actual staging because part of it, often a tiny part but always a part central to the dramatic action, is present as a real space visible to the audience, while the rest, like the entire imaginary world of the novel or poem, is normally evoked through language (the adverb "normally" is an important qualification to which I will return).

At this point I wish to address only this latter, usually larger space, the imaginary unseen space in which the visible activity of the play is embedded. While the actor inhabits only the playing space, the character also imaginatively inhabits this alternative world. Within the theatre, this alternative world is normally referred to as "offstage" space, although that term is not widely found in theatrical theory. In the early days of semiotics, Keir Elam called this space *diegetic* space; he was following Plato and Aristotle, who made a basic distinction between mimesis, the showing of an action, and diegesis, the narration of it.[6] Much Western drama relies extensively upon such diegetic spaces, from the space where three roads meet that saw the fatal encounter of Oedipus and Laius, through the riverbank where Ophelia died, to the house of Aunt Ester that appears mimetically in August Wilson's *Gem of the Ocean* and diegetically in several other plays in his cycle, most notably in *Radio Golf*.

Unfortunately the term "diegetic" can no longer be used unambiguously, as Aristotle and Elam used it, to designate this sort of theatrical space, because of its development in film theory. Within traditional film theory the action depicted in the film is considered a special form of narration; accordingly, the term "diegetic" has been utilized to describe music actually generated within that narration, as opposed to the unsourced background music so ubiquitous in traditional film. As modern criticism of musical comedy developed, this usage from film theory was widely adopted; it helped to make the useful critical distinction between, on the one hand, music that is a part of the onstage action, created by onstage musicians (or, for that matter, songs consciously sung as songs by the onstage actors) and, on the other hand, the more general music that is provided by the orchestra as background to the action. Thus in musical theatre criticism the term "diegetic" refers to something onstage, in this case onstage music, instead of something offstage; this modern application of the term results in a direct reversal of the Platonic and Aristotelian usage.

Some years ago, attempting to avoid this semantic problem, I suggested using another common pair of semiotic terms, derived from C. S. Peirce: *iconic* space and *indexical* space—the former being what actors call onstage space, where everything seen is iconic, a chair serving as a sign for a chair, a human body serving as a sign for another human body, and so on.[7] Offstage space would thus be indexical, since it is not seen but is indicated or pointed to by the onstage narrative. The lack of a standard critical term for this important sort of theatre space indicates how little specific critical attention it has received. This situation is currently changing, however, largely due to the work of Una Chaudhuri and her pioneering study *Staging Place: The Geography of Modern Drama* (1995). Chaudhuri's basic thesis that the study of spatial relationships "can yield a new methodology for drama and theatre studies," although concerned primarily with the use of space and metaphors of space in the written drama, provides a clear demonstration that more attention should be paid to questions of how different cultural and historical theatres have treated the imaginary but very significant space and spaces within the literary text itself.[8]

Chaudhuri's "new methodology" involves both iconic and indexical space, since it concerns the entire imaginary world, seen and unseen, of the play. It thus involves both the concerns of the literary historian (metaphors of space) and the theatre historian (use of space). Since our present concern is with space and theatre history, let us focus on the latter. An important attempt to articulate an analytic vocabulary of onstage and offstage spaces was offered in a 1989 essay by Tim Fitzpatrick, "The Dialectics of Space-Time Dramaturgical and Directoral Strategies for Performance and Fictional World."[9] Here Fitzpatrick argues that so-called offstage space is in fact composed of many different kinds of space, beginning with the division into what he calls "localized off" and "unlocalized off" (pp. 60–62). "Localized off" refers to spaces that are physically contiguous to the viewed setting, immediately accessible through a window, perhaps, or a door, while "unlocalized off" refers to more remote spaces, existing only through linguistic reference, such as Moscow in *Three Sisters*. Fitzpatrick's system is particularly useful in the analysis of the entirely new critical and practical perspective on offstage space opened in recent performance by the introduction of modern electronic technology (a subject to which I will return near the end of this essay).

Important as offstage space is in the imaginary world created by the theatrical performance, the central space of that performance is of course the one actually occupied by the performers and observed by the spectators. We might therefore think that this space and its operations during performance would have been the central preoccupation of theatre history, but that is not in fact the case. The main tradition of theatre history has been to devote primary attention to plays, playwrights, actors, and scenic design, especially the tangible features of it such as the Torelli innovations in stage machinery, the permutations of the wing and drop system, or the development of the box set. An excellent example of such scholarship is Richard Southern's classic *Changeable Scenery: Its Origin and Development in the British Theatre.*[10] Important as work of this sort has been, it focuses not upon the actual use of space onstage but upon those elements which impinge upon, shape, or condition it, such as scenic elements or wings and borders.

An even more critical spatial concern has been largely neglected by theatre historians: the way that the bodies of the actors and other scenic elements move about within the defined stage space, the spatial patterning that is called "blocking" in modern English and American theatre. Although we have almost no historical record of it, spatial blocking somewhat like our modern conception of it surely existed in theatres before the late Renaissance, although it largely disappeared when the European theatre moved primarily indoors. In his book *The Seven Ages of the Theatre* Southern speaks of this spatial move as "revolutionary."[11] His use of this term is clearly justified, because no other change since the creation of the theatrical form itself had so profound an effect on every element of performance. This revolution was of course primarily a spatial one, creating a new conception of the relationship between space and performance on both the macrocosmic and microcosmic level. On the macrocosmic level, perception changed from thinking of theatre as the product of placing the two spaces of performer and spectator face to face to thinking of it as a third, overarching spatial structure which surrounded and enclosed those two earlier spaces of confrontation (I will return to that level and some of its historical implications). On the microcosmic level, that of the two originating spaces, some form of proscenium arch soon appeared to serve as an architectural dividing element separating audience space from performance space. On the audience side the creation of an overarching architectural structure allowed the development of the architectural subdivisions of space (which I will consider presently). First I want to continue with a consideration of what most observers would view as the indoor theatre's core space: that in which the actor appears. Somewhat surprisingly, for all its visual advantages, the move to an indoor theatre resulted in a serious diminishment in the ability of performers to exploit the potentials of the space traditionally provided for their activity.

The creation of permanent indoor theatre spaces allowed for the development of elaborate scenic backgrounds, first in Italy and then throughout Europe, but this increase in visual spectacle was at the cost of the performers' previous flexibility within the stage space. With movement indoors, illumination assumed an importance unknown in previous performance situations, and all the ingenuity of the Renaissance and baroque designs could not create an adequately illuminated stage space that would allow actors the freedom of movement within that space that they had enjoyed in open-air production. Almost the only illumination for the acting area came from the chandeliers that illuminated the auditorium. While the development of footlights provided more visibility for the actors' space, actors who wished to be seen still had to move within a long, narrow band at the front of the stage. The required prompter's box down center provided another element to reinforce this. The result, as can be seen in the few seemingly reliable sketches and engravings of pre-nineteenth-century performance, was that the actors normally lined up across the stage, utilizing very little of the space open behind them, which was dedicated to movable scenery.

From the start of the modern indoor theatre in the Renaissance until the beginning of the nineteenth century, then, the stage space (although in fact dimensional) was from the audience's point of view, and the actors' use of this space was more like a painting or at best a bas-relief. With the development of significant projectable and controllable lighting, however, performers could once again fully utilize stage space for desired effects to an extent that had been possible before the theatre moved indoors. Although the idea of the proscenium arch framing an essentially flat "stage picture" was still common throughout the nineteenth century, theatre practitioners from the Romantic period on began to see stage space in a different way, first fully articulated in theory by Adolphe Appia at the end of the century. He characterized the stage space not as an animated painting but as a cubic, three-dimensional space, with the living forms within it defined by light.

The actual utilization of stage space by the bodies of the actors—an activity which would seem to be absolutely central to the phenomenon of theatre—has, quite surprisingly, so far attracted almost no attention from theatre historians, despite the relatively great attention they have given, for example, to the scenic background of this activity. This is clearly an area where a greater interest in the spatial operations of theatre should inspire future historical research. A vast amount of material is available for analysis in the countless promptbooks and visual records preserved from the past two centuries. The process of arranging the bodies of the actors within the stage space that in English is now called blocking begins to appear in the early nineteenth century in the notes and sketches of Johann Wolfgang von Goethe and in the first published promptbooks in France. By mid-century the number of preserved records of such sources is enormous. Such material has not been totally ignored by theatre historians. In recent times a few detailed analyses of particular promptbooks have appeared, especially, of course, for notable Shakespearean productions,[12] but almost no general work has been done on what would seem to be a fundamental concern of theatre history—how actors and directors actually utilized their performing spaces. Our theatre histories provide at least some information, even if sometimes rather impressionistic, on acting style and on changing modes of costuming or scenery, but they still say almost nothing about the actual use of stage space or whether it can be used to characterize the work of certain directors, theatres, periods, or dramatic traditions.[13]

Even if theatre historians limited themselves to the available records of the past two centuries in order to study the varying utilizations of onstage space, this investigation would be an undertaking of considerable importance. But in fact the historical study of stage space need not be so confined. Why not investigate how stage space was used in earlier European periods or in other cultures, where modern Western-style promptbooks do not exist and where pictorial records of productions are scant or unreliable? We have strong evidence that we need not give up on research into these areas as well. As usual, much of the study of stage space is provided by Shakespearean scholarship, which remains the most extensive and highly developed area of historical research in theatre. Several imaginative and innovative Shakespearean scholars headed by Andrew Gurr have provided fascinating and often convincing reconstructions of specific blocking patterns on the Elizabethan stage. Gurr's recent study *Staging in Shakespeare's Theatres*, co-authored with Mariko Ichikawa,[14] bases these reconstructions both on what we know of the overall features of that stage and on what can be deduced from the careful close reading of the surviving texts. Much can be learned about Elizabethan performances by a critic sensitive to such matters as sight lines and spatial semiotics. Given the continuing dominance of Shakespeare in theatre studies, it is hardly surprising that such research has been pioneered in this area, but it is still somewhat puzzling that the sort of analysis developed by Gurr and others has not been applied more fully to other historical periods and other theatrical cultures to see what insights into the organization and manipulation of onstage space they might provide. Here again a clear strategy and area of investigation has been indicated for future theatre historians.

Although the space onstage is obviously of central interest to theatre historians, the attention paid by pioneers of the discipline like Herrmann to theatre audiences (and their place within performance settings) guaranteed that audience spaces also would receive at least some attention as the field developed. Although Matthews and his students were much more focused upon questions of staging, their reconstruction of historical theatres led them also to consider from the beginning the implications of the obvious spatial differences in audience arrangements of the classic Greek theatre, the Elizabethan stage, and the clearly socially divided audiences of the eighteenth century theatres.

I have already mentioned Richard Southern's highly innovative *The Seven Ages of the Theatre*, which attempted as early as 1961 to provide a fresh approach to theatre history that challenged the two most distinctive features of previous major works in the field, the standard pattern of periodization (the Greeks, the Romans, medieval theatre, the Renaissance, and succeeding centuries in chronological order) and the strong bias toward the literary canon, primarily that of England, France, and Germany. His book did not in fact seriously affect these well-established biases, as the enormous success a few years later of Oscar Brockett's widely accepted textbook clearly demonstrated. But Southern still provides a useful alternative perspective.

Southern begins his book by attempting to reduce theatre to its essence, which he divides into "seven ages." The first age (or stage of development) he finds in the encounter between Player and Audience. "Take these apart," he concludes, "and you can have no theatre."[15] This confrontation of actor and spectator has been accepted as the basis of the theatre experience by theorists from Aristotle to Eric Bentley. This returns us to the matter of spatiality at the most fundamental level of theatre studies. Up to this point we have been considering how the idea of theatre history developed from a consideration of the play as performed in space. Southern points out that theatre consists of not only the space of embodiment, occupied by performers, but also — and equally essential — the space of observation, occupied by the witnesses to this embodiment.

Herrmann and his German followers were, as I have noted, particularly interested in the analysis of audiences from the very beginning of their work. Many tools, of course, have subsequently been employed in audience analysis, but a basic one (and often one of the first considered by theatre historians) is a consideration of how the space the audience occupies is articulated and utilized. Indeed, somewhat surprisingly, rather more historical work has been done on audience space than on actor space. Almost all of this work appeared in the later twentieth century and was concerned, directly or indirectly, with how the spatial arrangements of the auditorium reflect social status. The obvious social implications of such spaces as the Elizabethan pit or the royal and aristocratic boxes were noted by theatre historians as soon as Matthews and his students began to study physical theatres, but such analysis became more important later as some theatre historians, in examining nonliterary aspects of theatre, became interested in theatre as a social rather than an artistic phenomenon. A relatively early example was James J. Lynch's 1953 book subtitled *Stage and Society in Johnson's London*. Its main title significantly looked to the spatial arrangement of audiences as the basic representation of this social orientation: *Box, Pit, and Gallery*.[16] The rise of a specific sociology of theatre, pioneered by Georges Gurvich and Jean Duvignaud in France in the 1950s and 1960s, encouraged more of this sort of historical analysis. Thus, for example, Timothy Murray in "Richelieu's Theatre: The Mirror of a Prince" (1977) suggests how the spatial arrangements of this key historical structure expressed and reinforced a whole system of social power relationships.[17] Joseph Donohue's *Fantasies of Empire* (2005) uses the controversies surrounding the arrangement of audience space in the Empire Theatre of Varieties in London's Leicester Square to illuminate a broad spectrum of social, political, moral, and legal questions in late Victorian England.[18]

It should also be noted that the dominance of interest in Shakespeare in the tradition of theatre scholarship has resulted in a significant number of modern studies on Shakespearean audiences, beginning with A. C. Bradley's "Shakespeare's Theatre and Audience" (1909).[19] On the whole, however, these studies have concentrated on the social composition of these audiences, whether they were essentially popular or elite,[20] with little analysis of space beyond the repeated observation that the less privileged "groundlings" stood around the stage, while more privileged spectators sat in the boxes and later, in private theatres, on the stage.

Although much work remains to be done on audience space in different societies and historical periods, from existing scholarship we could trace a fairly complete history of the changes in audience space and the significance of such changes at least in the European theatre from the Renaissance onward. Without questioning the importance of theatre audience spaces as reflectors of social status, however, we must also remember both that this is not the only possible use of space in the public areas of theatre buildings and also that the public spaces of theatres are by no means the only spaces that could be investigated. The generally neglected backstage spaces, important as they are to the functioning of what the public sees, have been rarely studied or even mentioned in our historical studies; yet they also not only reflect social status but provide all manner of additional information about the actual physical creation and operation of the performance. Gay McAuley's *Space in Performance* (1999), to the best of my knowledge, is the only modern attempt (aside from technical architectural studies) to consider these neglected spaces in the front and back of the theatre house in any detail. She designates the former as audience space and the latter as practitioner space, neither of course so fully documented or studied as stage space. Indeed McAuley also considers an even less known or documented space: rehearsal space, which, though never seen by the public, "can have a significant impact on the final production."[21]

Not all of the spaces so far discussed (those of the performer, the spectator, and, in the case of a theatre building, the space which unites and includes these other spaces) have been considered with equal attention by theatre historians, but together they have made up the central spatial concerns of traditional theatre history. Naturally they shared the often unacknowledged biases of that tradition, most notably an interest in the theatre of Europe and the United States to the almost total exclusion of the rest of the world and an interest in the staging of canonical plays to the almost total exclusion of so-called popular or minor forms. During the 1970s and 1980s, however, these biases began to be widely exposed and challenged. Many things contributed to this major shift in the field of theatre studies, but probably the most distinct and the most clearly involved with these challenges was the rise of the new approach that came to be known as performance studies.

In a number of respects performance studies may be seen as an American development of some of the views on art in general and theatre in particular by French sociologists like Gurvitch and Duvignaud. One of the first major theoretical statements of the aims of performance studies appeared in the introduction to a special issue of the *Drama Review* in the fall of 1973 by Richard Schechner, significantly entitled "Performance and the Social Sciences." Openly drawing upon recent work in sociology and anthropology (as elsewhere in his subsequent writings), Schechner called for a broader and deeper consideration of the phenomenon of performance as a cultural activity. This included a very broad range of activity: casual social gatherings, sports, play, ritual, and public events of all sorts. Schechner characterized traditional theatre as "a very small slice of the performance pie."[22]

Few researchers who would characterize themselves as theatre historians would attempt to consume all of Schechner's performance pie, but the emergence of performance studies has certainly contributed to a significant enlarging of the theatrical slice. Other cultural changes added further impetus to this change. One clearly was modern globalization, creating a worldview in which theatre history could no longer casually ignore whole continents like Africa, South America, or Australia or confine its study of Asia to a handful of manifestations, mostly Japanese. Another was a rise in interest in popular culture, forcing attention to the vast array of popular forms of theatre hitherto ignored by the high art bias of the tradition. Both of these were also reinforced by a major change within the study of art itself, especially the performing arts. Just as the study of theatre had from the beginning been dominated, and somewhat distorted, by critical models derived from literary studies, so the study of the performing arts in general had operated on a model derived from the plastic arts and the concept of the art object. A key expression of the change that took place in this attitude during the 1970s was Gerald Hinkle's book *Art as Event* (1979). Hinkle argued that critical understanding of the performing arts has been hampered by the application of strategies evolved in the plastic arts and literature, where performance is not essential. Theatre should be viewed "more as an event than an object in perception."[23]

A combination of these and related shifts in perspective resulted in a far more wide-ranging and flexible understanding of how theatre history might be considered. Were we to create a definition of theatre history as it was conceived a half-century ago, it might be something like this: "the study of the evolution, primarily in Europe and America, of the process of enacting literary dramatic texts." Today, as a result of these changes, a very different sort of definition might be more appropriate, perhaps something like "the study of particular theatrical events, or groups of such events, and how they operate within their cultural contexts." This more flexible definition avoids the now much discredited emphasis upon an evolutionary narrative, the still powerful if increasingly challenged emphasis on the European tradition, and replacement of the literary emphasis, dominant in European theatrical theory ever since Aristotle, with a more general concern with theatre as a cultural activity.

Looking beyond the spatial assumptions of the European literary theatre encourages the theatre historian to be conscious of performance spaces more prominent in other cultures and of their very different histories and association. A 2008 essay that I co-authored with a Moroccan scholar provides a sample of such research, based on the circular performance space, the *halqa*, widely found in traditional Arab culture and recently taking on a new meaning as a postcolonial reaction to European performance spaces. Aside from the postcolonial dynamic of this spatial choice, the essay considers the relationship of the *halqa* to various cultural traditions of North Africa and the Middle East; its use in folk festivals, in popular gatherings, and in the tradition of the traveling storyteller; and finally its mystic and religious associations.[24]

This different perspective opened many new ways of looking at space and the theatrical event in various historical contexts. The focus was no longer upon the embodiment of a particular dramatic text but upon the whole social and physical context of the event. To the best of my knowledge, the first theatre historian to utilize this new perspective was Michael Hays, who began his book *The Public and Performance: Essays in the History of French and German Theater, 1871–1900* (1974) with an essay entitled "Theater Space as Cultural Paradigm." It opens with this striking spatial observation: "Until recently, the social value and function of the buildings, the architectural forms which enclose the theater event, have remained largely unexplored territory. Critical investigation has instead focused attention on the smaller space of the stage or on the actor and the director." Hays goes on to assert that the location and shape of the performance area potentially provides the information "which first allows us to propose a connect between the ordering principles of the theater event and those of society at large."[25] Although his application of this insight is largely to the somewhat restricted cultural world of his study, it is clear that he is proposing a socioeconomic analytical model which could be usefully employed in a wide variety of historical situations.

Richard Schechner was another pioneer in such analysis, though from a more anthropological than sociocultural direction. In his major essay "Toward a Poetics of Performance" (1975) he observes: "Too little study has been made of the liminal approaches and leavings of performance—how the audience gets to, and into, the performance place, and how they go from that place."[26] To take a single famous example, clearly the necessity of crossing the Thames by boat to reach the marginal, quasi-respectable entertainment district of Southwark, where some of the major Elizabethan public theatres were located, was a significant part of the mental contextualization of attending those theatres. The study of such space has now become a standard part of historical analysis. As Susan Bennett observes in *Theatre Audiences* (1st ed. 1990), "The milieu which surrounds a theatre is always ideologically encoded" and thus "shapes a spectator's experience." She uses this insight to analyze the geography of Joan Littlewood's Theatre Workshop and a variety of other nineteenth- and twentieth-century theatres.[27]

Ric Knowles's *Reading the Material Theatre* (2004) suggests this new orientation even in its title. In his introduction he explains: "This book attempts to develop a mode of performance analysis that takes into account the immediate conditions, both cultural and theatrical, in and through which theatrical performances are produced, on the one hand, and received, on the other."[28] In examples drawn from large and small theatres in a number of countries, Knowles demonstrates how the analysis of space both within and outside the theatre provides significant insights into these cultural and social processes. David Wiles's more wide-ranging *A Short History of Western Performance Space* (2003) looks primarily at actor-audience configurations in both traditional theatres and nontheatrical performances to explore how meaning is created by space.[29]

My own book *Places of Performance* (1989), much influenced by recent event-oriented analysis of performance, utilizes a semiotic-based analysis to consider a variety of ways in which performances in different cultures and historical periods could be understood in part by their spatial surroundings.[30] It not only examines how space has been utilized within traditional European theatre structures but also moves outside these locations to discuss how the amount and kind of space these structures occupy and their location within the mental spatial map of a community or a city have affected the public attitude toward them. Much work remains to be done on this aspect of space and historical theatres. Most theatre students who study Shakespeare are at least generally aware of the significance of the English liberties and how important the geographical space occupied by the early public theatres in England is in understanding the history of those theatres; yet, as usual, far more work on urban spaces has been done on Shakespeare's era and setting than on any other era or location. Traditional histories provide almost no information about the comparable geographical positioning of the early public theatre in France or Spain, to mention only two prominent examples. The same lack of information still characterizes most theatre histories about the rest of European theatres. And of course when we move beyond Europe and the United States, where theatre scholarship has focused most of its attention, the lack of such studies is almost complete.

As I was revising this essay a striking example of the effect of such public space upon a performance was provided by the most publicized event in the closely followed tour of presidential nominee Barack Obama to Europe and the Middle East: his massively attended speech in Berlin. Central to this speech was a call to tear down the walls that today separate members of different religious faiths. Presented in the heart of Berlin, this speech inevitably evoked images of the Berlin Wall and America's strong support for the isolated city, including the Berlin airlift, President John Kennedy's "Ich bin ein Berliner" statement, and President Ronald Reagan's "Mr. Gorbachev, tear down this wall." A number of commentators noted, however, how much more daring and politically dangerous exactly the same speech would have been if it had been delivered in today's most famously divided city, Jerusalem, where the United States position on a political wall is considerably more troubled.

These thoughts about the spatial significance of Berlin and Jerusalem reinforce for me some of the reasons why theatre historians need to develop a more sophisticated understanding and methodology for studying theatre in terms of all its spatial codes—aesthetic, semiotic, social, political, geographical, and ethical. The ways we think not only *about* space but also *with* the ideas of space are crucial to our historical investigations.

For the final section of this essay I turn to new types of theatre space, unknown to previous eras yet already making major changes in the field of theatre history and certain to play an ever greater role in the future. The growing use of live video and digital imaging creates new spatial dimensions and even new concepts of space. This is obviously an enormous potential subject, and I can only suggest here certain aspects that are of particular importance to the study of theatre history. I first address the growing use of live video and of digital images within the theatre and some of its spatial implications and then conclude with some of the ways in which digital technology is impacting the concept of space within the study of theatre history itself.

Film, of course, has been with us now for over a century and almost from its beginning was utilized by experimental theatre artists. Although a film onstage clearly presents an image of another space, it remains simply that—an image, not actually a space. Here we see the validity of film theory referring to the film as diegetic rather than mimetic. If, for example, instead of the Queen's narrative in *Hamlet* describing the physical location of Ophelia's death ("There is a willow grows aslant a brook"), we should see at the back of the stage a film of this space, it would still remain an essentially absent, narrated space for audiences watching the performance. It would be the visual equivalent of the kinds of narrated and imaginary spaces that Una Chaudhuri and other theorists have considered. Thomas Irmir has usefully designated such filmic images as "second level" images, not fully integrated into the scene onstage but operating rather more like "footnotes to the stage picture."[31] Their primary use has nothing to do with the extension or elaboration of the scenic spaces but rather, as Patrice Pavis suggests, has been "to provide background or ironic comment on the stage action."[32]

A very different visual space is created by the ever-increasing introduction of live video into the performance area. A few experimental groups in the United States (such as the Wooster Group and Collapsable [*sic*] Giraffe) have provided important examples of this process, but it is far more elaborately developed in Europe, perhaps most notably in the work of German directors like Frank Castorf and René Pollesch. In a series of productions beginning in the late 1980s such directors began to use live video as a way of creating a new sort of theatrical space, a real space located somewhere between onstage and off. As one of its practitioners, Jan Speckenbach, has explained: "The paradoxical nature of the process of bringing the means of live transmission into a space that is involved in nothing other than transmitting a selection of this space makes filmic explorations possible that are not possible either in traditional film or video."[33] The constant renegotiation between the mimetic and the diegetic, which in the most extreme cases involves not only onstage and offstage space but audience spaces, lobbies, and even dressing rooms, poses significant new challenges to theatre historians seeking to chronicle and explain the experience such work offers. Only a few, mostly German historians such as Thomas Irmir have so far attempted to provide a history of such work.[34]

A quite different spatial challenge is presented by the growing utilization of what has been called virtual space in modern experimental dance and theatre. In some modern dance work, for example, dancers simultaneously performing in widely separated spaces are brought together, seemingly dancing with each other in a physically nonexistent electronic space; audiences may observe this space alone or in conjunction with one of its various components.[35] A related kind of experimentation is represented in the work of the American experimental company Big Art, which creates images in an electronic space presented onstage alongside the actors. These images are assembled out of elements from other onstage spaces captured by live video—props, elements of scenery, even parts of actors' bodies. The group's founder, Caden Mason, calls this blending "Real-time film." Attempting a historical study of this sort of work, as I have done in a recent essay in the *Journal of Dramatic Theory and Criticism*, requires dealing with a new kind of theatrical space and therefore developing a vocabulary which both relates it to and contrasts it with the kinds of spatial configurations traditionally dealt with by theatre historians.[36]

These examples indicate some of the new ways of thinking about space that new technologies are forcing upon theatre historians of the present and the future as their subject of study continually changes and evolves. Of even more direct concern to our current consideration of space and theatre history, however, are the ways in which modern technology, especially the coming of the digital age, is providing new analytical tools and ways of presenting research to theatre historians. Particularly important has been the development of virtual space, which offers the theatre historian a powerful new way to re-create and study historical performance spaces, the twenty-first-century equivalent of the three-dimensional model theatres of Brander Matthews.

An important pioneer in such work in America was Professor Jack Wolcott at the University of Washington, who in 1984 began to work on the Olympus Project, involving the digital reconstruction of a seventeenth-century English court entertainment, *Florimene*. This was created in a three-dimensional digital space utilizing an early form of CADD (Computer Assisted Drafting and Design) software. This kind of program can be used to create the enormously detailed environments containing moving figures that are so familiar in today's world of computer games. Wolcott went on to develop three-dimensional digital models of several historic theatres, such as the Hellenistic theatre at Pergamon. These models were discussed in a 1990 article in *Theatre Design and Technology* called "Learning Theatre History in the Third Dimension."[37] Wolcott's work anticipated a far more ambitious project of this same type that was launched in Europe in 1998, developed by a consortium of European scholars and computer experts led by members of the University of Warwick in England.[38] This project, Theatron, to date has created virtual models of sixteen major European theatre spaces, from Greek theatres to twentieth-century performance spaces such as the Vieux Colombier in Paris. Unlike actual full-sized reproductions such as the London Globe, virtual reconstructions can be readily modified in the light of changing scholarly opinion or adjusted to reflect conflicting interpretations of historical evidence. Equally important, they can be distributed worldwide, simultaneously and collectively experienced by users separated by real space.[39]

So far Theatron, like the Washington *Florimene* project, has been concerned only with the creation of virtual theatrical spaces, but other projects have built upon such work to create much more complicated and ambitious projects in the digitalization of theatre history. Again Wolcott at Washington provided an early model of such work. He followed the *Florimene* project in the late 1980s with the much more ambitious Philadelphia Project, which re-created the interior space of the historic Chestnut Street Theatre in Philadelphia, along with eight short "scenes" involving actors wearing historically accurate clothing. At the beginning of the twenty-first century the sort of work pioneered by early researchers like Wolcott, now called Live Performance Simulation, is becoming one of the most ambitious and exciting areas of contemporary research in theatre history.

An outstanding current example of this sort of research is the Virtual Vaudeville project headed by David Z. Saltz, the founding director of the Interactive Performance Laboratory at the University of Georgia. This project was designed to re-create historical performance in a virtual space similar to that of a 3-D computer game, within which the spectator is free to move about. Virtual Vaudeville re-creates the interior space of the Union Square Theatre in New York in 1895, along with its patrons, performers, and staff. Four actual vaudeville acts of the period are digitally re-created, which can be experienced in two ways. One provides a conventional spectator's view from various parts of the auditorium. The other, the "invisible camera" mode, allows a viewer to move through 3-D space to observe the performance from any angle, even from onstage. These projects and others of a similar nature are reported in the proceedings of the first major international conference on theatre research in a virtual environment, held at Lincoln Center in 2003. One of the articles is significantly entitled "The Virtual Revolution in Performance History."[40]

The widespread experimentation with such electronically based expansion of the concept of performative space in contemporary theatre and dance clearly indicates that future theatre historians concerned with space in the theatre are likely to look back upon this era as inaugurating another revolution in the way in which space is conceived and used. This promises to become a revolution with effects on our concepts of performative space as wide-ranging as anything we have yet witnessed. At the same time, the digital revolution has given theatre historians major new tools for the study of historical performance, the full implications of which are clearly still to be seen. Space remains a basic concern for theatre historians, but it is a more varied and complex space today than at any previous time in the development of the discipline.

NOTES

1. Brander Matthews, *A Study of the Drama* (New York: Houghton Mifflin, 1910), p. 3.

2. Robert D. Hume, "Theatre History, 1660–1800: Aims, Materials, and Methodology," in *Players, Playwrights, Playhouses: Investigating Performance, 1660–1800*, ed. Michael Cordner and Peter Holland (New York: Palgrave Macmillan, 2007), p. 12 (emphasis in original).

3. The pattern was set by the foundational works in the field, Allardyce Nicoll's *The Development of the Theatre* (New York: Harcourt, Brace, 1927), Sheldon Cheney's *The Theatre: Three Thousand Years of Drama, Acting, and Stagecraft* (New York: Longmans, Green and Co., 1929), and George Freedley and John Reeves's *A History of the Theatre* (New York: Crown, 1941), and reached its apogee in the most widely read and influential text in the field, Oscar Brockett's *History of the Theatre* (Boston: Allyn and Bacon), first published in 1968 and appearing in its tenth edition in 2007, now co-edited by Franklin Hildy.

4. John Cranford Adams's *The Globe Playhouse: Its Design and Equipment* (New York: Barnes and Noble, 1961) was a leading early example, but books and essays on the subject are now legion, encouraged, of course, by the recent physical re-creation of an imitation of the theatre near its original site in London.

5. George Riley Kernodle, *From Art to Theatre: Form and Convention in the Renaissance* (Chicago: University of Chicago Press, 1944).

6. Keir Elam, *The Semiotics of Theatre and Drama* (London: Methuen, 1980), p. 111.

7. Marvin Carlson, "The Iconic Stage," *Journal of Dramatic Theory and Criticism* 3 (Spring 1989): 3–18 and "Indexical Space in the Theatre," *Assaph* 10 (1994): 1–10.

8. Una Chaudhuri, *Staging Place: The Geography of Modern Drama* (Ann Arbor: University of Michigan Press, 1995), p. xi.

9. Tim Fitzpatrick, "The Dialectics of Space-Time Dramaturgical and Directoral Strategies for Performance and Fictional World," in *Performance: From Product to Process*, ed. Tim Fitzpatrick (Sydney: Frederick May Foundation 1989). pp. 49–112.

10. Richard Southern, *Changeable Scenery: Its Origin and Development in the British Theatre* (London: Faber and Faber, 1952).

11. Richard Southern, *The Seven Ages of the Theatre* (New York: Hill and Wang, 1961), p. 21.

12. See, for example, Charles Shattuck's *William Charles Macready's King John: A Facsimile Prompt-Book* (Urbana: University of Illinois Press, 1962).

13. Some years ago I created two articles suggesting how material from promptbooks could form the basis of such analysis: "*Hernani*'s Revolt from the Tradition of French Stage Composition," *Theatre Survey* (May 1972): 1–27 and "French Stage Composition from Hugo to Zola," *Educational Theatre Journal* (October 1972): 363–378. But to the best of my knowledge there has been no other such systematic historical study of blocking or movement patterns in the European theatre or elsewhere.

14. Andrew Gurr and Mariko Ichikawa, *Staging in Shakespeare's Theatres* (Oxford: Oxford University Press, 2000).

15. Southern, *The Seven Ages of the Theatre*, p. 21.

16. James J. Lynch, *Box, Pit, and Gallery: Stage and Society in Johnson's London* (Berkeley: University of California Press, 1953).

17. Timothy Murray, "Richelieu's Theatre: The Mirror of a Prince," *Renaissance Drama* n.s. 8 (1977): 275–297.

18. Joseph Donohue, *Fantasies of Empire: The Empire Theatre of Varieties and the Licensing Controversy of 1894* (Iowa City: University of Iowa Press, 2005).

19. In A. C. Bradley, *Oxford Lectures on Poetry* (London: Macmillan, 1909).

20. The position that they were essentially popular was most notably taken by Alfred Harbage in his *Shakespeare's Audience* (New York: Columbia University Press, 1941). For the view that they were essentially elite, see, for example, Ann Jennalie Cook, *The Privileged Playgoers of Shakespeare's London, 1576–1642* (Princeton: Princeton University Press, 1981).

21. Gay McAuley, *Space in Performance: Making Meaning in the Theatre* (Ann Arbor: University of Michigan Press, 1999), p. 70.

22. Richard Schechner, "Performance and the Social Sciences: Introduction," *Drama Review* 17.3 (1973); Richard Schechner, "A New Paradigm for Theatre in the Academy," *Drama Review* 36.4 (1992): 10.

23. Gerald Hinkle, *Art as Event: An Aesthetic for the Performing Arts* (Washington, D.C.: University Press of America, 1979), p. 40.

24. Khalid Amine and Marvin Carlson, "*Al-halqa* in Arabic Theatre: An Emerging Site of Hybridity," *Theatre Journal* 60.1 (March, 2008): 71–86.

25. Michael Hays, *The Public and Performance: Essays in the History of French and German Theater, 1871–1900* (Ann Arbor: UMI Research Press, 1974), p. 3.

26. Richard Schechner, *Essays on Performance Theory 1970–1976* (New York: Drama Book Specialists, 1977), p. 122.

27. Susan Bennett, *Theatre Audiences*, 2nd ed. (London: Routledge, 1997), pp. 126–130.

28. Ric Knowles, *Reading the Material Theatre* (Cambridge: Cambridge University, 2004), p. 3.

29. David Wiles, *A Short History of Western Performance Space* (Cambridge: Cambridge University Press, 2003).

30. Marvin Carlson, *Places of Performance: The Semiotics of Theatre Architecture* (Ithaca, N.Y.: Cornell University Press, 1989).

31. Thomas Irmir, "Das Theater der neuen Sehens: Zum Einsatz von Video und Film bei Frank Castorf, Rene Pollesch und Olaf Nicolai," *Quadratur: Kulturbuch* 5 (2003): 22.

32. Patrice Pavis, *Theatre at the Crossroads of Culture*, trans. Loren Kruger (London: Routledge, 1992), p. 130.

33. Jan Speckenbach, "Der Einbruch der Fernsehntechnologie," in *Einbruch der Realitat: Politik und Verbrechen*, ed. Carl Hegemann (Berlin: Alexander, 2002), p. 80.

34. See, for example, Irmir, "Das Theater der neuen Sehens," pp. 20–24.

35. Johannes H. Birringer has written extensively on this type of experimental work.

See his "Contemporary Performance/Technology," *Theatre Journal* (special issue on "Theatre and Technology") 51.4 (1999): 361–381; *Media and Performance: Along the Border* (Baltimore: Johns Hopkins University Press, 1998); and *Performance on the Edge: Transformations of Culture* (London: Athlone, 2000).

36. Marvin Carlson, "Mixed Media and Mixed Messages: Big Art Group's Exploration of the Sign," *Journal of Dramatic Theory and Criticism* 22.2 (Spring, 2008): 119–132.

37. Jack Wolcott, "Learning Theatre History in the Third Dimension," *Theatre Design and Technology* 26.4 (Fall 1990): 25–36.

38. See http://www.theatron.org (accessed July 10, 2009).

39. Hugh Denard, "Performing the Past: The Virtual Revolution in Performance History," in *Performance Documentation and Preservation in an Online Environment*, ed. Kenneth Schlesinger (New York: Theatre Library Association, 2004), p. 59.

40. "The Virtual Revolution in Performance History," in *Performance Documentation and Preservation in an Online Environment*, ed. Schlesinger, pp. 54–70.

DAVID WILES

Seeing Is Believing The Historian's Use of Images

For the practice of theatre history, "What did audiences see?" is a far more productive question than "What did playwrights create?"[1] Stephen Orgel's polemic introduces a recent collection entitled *From Script to Stage in Early Modern England*. Orgel's goal is one that I share with all contributors to this volume: to understand the lost theatrical event, where the playwright was but one contributor. Plays were once deemed to happen *inside* theatre spaces, but it is now increasingly recognized that the theatre event *is* the creation of a relationship in space. Space is therefore not the container but the substance of theatre. So far, so good.

I balk, however, at Orgel's unspoken premise that seeing is a privileged point in the sensorium and our primary means of accessing that spatial relationship which is the performance. Modern theatre architects pride themselves on giving the spectator uninterrupted sightlines and spacious comfortable seats—but their priorities stem from a cultural preoccupation which belongs to the present and is a product of history. Seeing the play and experiencing the play are two very different things. Images projected onto the retina are but one route to apprehending space. A blind person may be much more aware than a sighted person of what resonating sounds tell us about our environment. Most premodern theatres were crowded places, with knees touching backs and shoulders touching shoulders or standing bodies pressed against each other, engendering an osmosis among weeping, desiring, or laughing spectators that made theatre-going a less individualized affair than it is today. The air we inhale may once have been more humid, sweat-laden, deoxygenated thanks to tallow candles, impregnated with tobacco or saffron incense in Roman times. The kinesthetic sense was involved in following a medieval wagon or craning forward in the opera box to catch a favorite aria. While the modern spectator may be content to go to *see* the play, the premodern spectator went rather to inhabit a theatrical place.[2]

In lieu of a sensory analysis of performance space, the historian may prefer to dwell on the social dimension.[3] Attending a performance might involve physical movement out of a secular environment into a temple of the gods or a temple of art. A theatre may be a place where people of consequence choose to be seen or a place for sexual liaisons where it is preferable not to be seen; it may be a place where social hierarchy is mapped in the organization of the auditorium or a place for erasing social distinctions. Performers may be slaves, excommunicated as un-Christian, or idolized as celebrities and objects of sexual desire. Such social relationships map onto spatial relationships, as games are played with the permeability of whatever boundary line separates the performers from the space of the audience.

Theatre historians represent a performance space that exists in their imagination, and pictures have usually had a role to play in this task. Though pictures like words are simply ink-marks on a page, it is often assumed that images in some unmediated way communicate the reality of the historical space. This tendency to place images outside the domain of theoretical reflection owes much to patterns of academic training. In this essay I open up two areas of contention. I point out the gaps, often subtle, between pictorial representations of theatrical space and the actual experience of seeing in theatres; and I point to the implications of privileging vision as the supreme means of apprehending performance space. In regard to privilege, note that Renaissance princes enjoyed masques because they demonstrably enjoyed the optimum view of an expensive perspectival set; and in modern auditoria the richest continue to sit closest. The other senses of sound, smell, touch, and kinesthesia have proved more egalitarian, more likely to engage everyone in the auditorium on equal terms.

When we think carefully about the process of seeing—whether paintings in a gallery, photos in an archive, or landscapes through the train window—we come up against a fundamental question: do we see what is there, or do we see what our culture has taught us to see? Suppose I look at an ancient tomb painting which depicts dancers and looks as fresh as the day it was painted. Do I see the same thing an Etruscan or an Egyptian did, because I am of the same biological nature? Or am I cut off from the social and religious meanings that truly matter? Is the image on my retina processed by my brain in a completely different way from the image processed by an ancient brain? One attractive theory current among art historians proposes that artists of different periods abstract a set of perceptual data different from what the biological eye sees, like the play of light for impressionists, perspective for early Renaissance painters, or color for sixteenth-century Venetians.[4] These artistic fashions in turn condition the perceptual processes of those who view art. This theory concedes a constant human nature, while allowing for the culturally defined nature of visual perception.

Let me offer a concrete example of how seeing underwent historical change. When the Polish theatre director Tadeusz Kantor told of "the storming of the Winter Palace of Illusion," he related the emergence of cubism and constructivism to the Russian Revolution. The abolition of the aristocratic *ancien régime* went hand in hand with a new way of seeing which picked out the materiality of objects, not the decorative nature of facades. In theatre this emphasis on three-dimensional materiality entailed erosion of the proscenium, which turned the stage image into a picture.[5] After 1917 people *saw* differently. For us today, soaked in Pablo Picasso's modernist mode of seeing the world and his particular abstraction of the visual process, it is hard to recover an older way of seeing and appreciate the lost pleasures of pictorial theatre. The historian can help us once we have recognized that a problem exists and that our value judgments relate perforce to modern tastes.

In this essay I focus upon old theatre, because historical remoteness allows us to recognize cultural otherness, beginning with one of Britain's oldest performance spaces, Stonehenge. The principal British excavator of Stonehenge collaborated in the 1990s with an archaeologist from Madagascar, who pointed out that European archaeology had been obsessed for generations with the geometry of Stonehenge. From his Malagasy perspective, the interesting thing about Stonehenge seemed instead to be the texture of stone, which in his island symbolized the indestructibility of ancestors. His experience of standing stones in Madagascar yielded a persuasive account of why stone was carried all the way from the Pembrokeshire hills to Wiltshire, when local timber might have served.[6] We glimpse the cultural roots of our modern obsession with visuality and our tendency to prioritize seeing over, say, touching. We can trace this geometric cast of mind back to the Roman engineer Vitruvius, whose treatise on architecture included an influential account of theatre space.[7]

The theatre of Greece in the fifth century BCE offers a vivid case study of how historians project onto the past an idea of performance space that legitimates theatre practices in the present. The excavations of Wilhelm Dörpfeld in the 1880s yielded a primitive dancing circle that appealed to the romantic sensibilities of the late Victorian era and to the academic movement known as the "Cambridge ritualists." Ernst Fiechter abandoned primitivism and concocted a monumental stage building in the era when fascism invoked Greece as the fount of Aryan culture. Postwar tastes have been increasingly minimalist, in accordance with our modern theatrical sensibility. Rectangular seating blocks used for privileged seats have be-

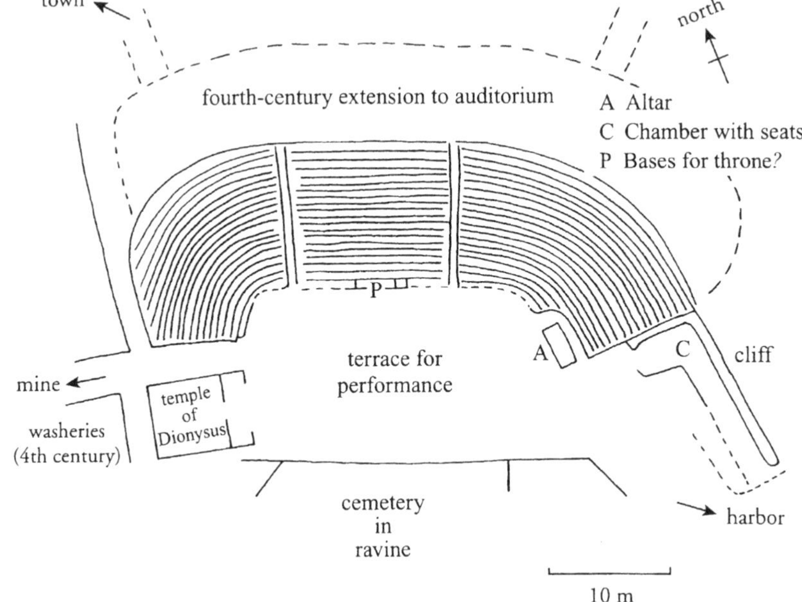

1. Ground plan of the theatre at Thorikos. Drawing by Gayna Wiles; reproduced from David Wiles, *Tragedy in Athens* (Cambridge: Cambridge University Press, 1997).

come the center of attention. In recent years a vigorous debate has taken place between traditionalists (like myself) subscribing to a version of Dörpfeld's circle and those persuaded by a fashion in German and Italian archaeology which holds that theatre was "rectilinear" before it was "circular."[8] Notice the geometric focus of this debate, which in recent years has centered on Thorikos, an Athenian mining town which possesses the only surviving stone auditorium dating from the age of Sophocles. The ground plan looks something like figure 1.

The question is, how do we see this shape? Is it a failed rectangle or a squashed circle or does it have a completely different formal logic? Two recent popular accounts leave the reader in no doubt. The new edition of Brockett's *History of the Theatre* states that Thorikos displays a "rectangular origin" and invites the viewer of the ground plan to "note the modified rectangular shape."[9] And in the Routledge *Theatre Histories* we learn that the theatre at Thorikos with its "rectangular *orchestra* curved at the edges" provides strong "evidence for a trapezoidal *orchestra*" in Athens where the canonical tragedies were performed.[10] The conduit between European archaeology and U.S. theatre scholarship was Clifford Ashby, who explained: "A long straight section of slightly curved seating (as at Argos) faces a rect-

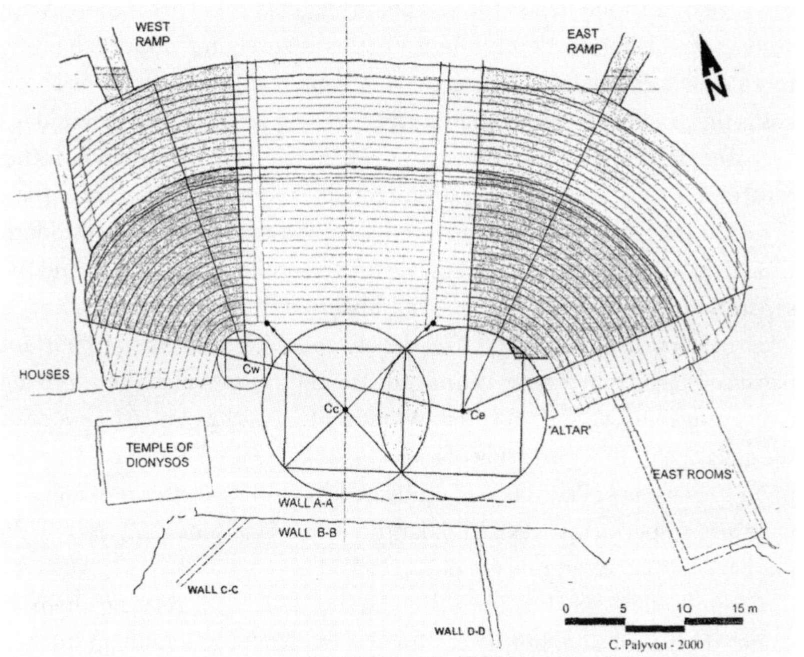

2. Diagram of the theatre at Thorikos. Reproduced by kind permission of Clairy Palyvou.

angular performance area; additional seating wraps around the sides." Ashby aligned his camera to take a shot along the front rows of seats to emphasize the long straight line and minimize the impact of the curves.[11] To his credit he spotted that the supposed straight line is a trompe l'oeil, because the Greeks found pure rectilinearity (as famously in the base of the Parthenon) offensive to the eye; but he manipulates language to suggest that the curved sides were a later addition. We have no archaeological evidence for this or for the "rectangular" performance area somehow existing independently of the shape defined by the auditorium. Ashby makes no reference to the asymmetry which is so conspicuous a feature of Thorikos and of the Theatre of Dionysus in Athens but which offends modern notions of what classical architecture ought to be.

A recent examination of the geometry of Thorikos encourages us to see its plan through different eyes.[12] The Greek archaeologist Clairy Palyvou identifies three virtual circles used to plan the layout (fig. 2). When these circles are supplied, we see at once that this is neither a failed rectangle nor a flattened circle. If the righthand side is wrapped around an altar, then perhaps the left was once wrapped round a statue removed from the temple. And what of the statue in the temple? The axis line produced by the gaze of a statue inside the temple takes us to the "east rooms." With seats carved laboriously into the rock, this is surely not a mere dressing room for actors but a space of ceremonial significance. The shape of Thorikos is the product of careful planning, according to a logic that now eludes us, based upon lost religious practices. We do not know how to look at this theatre. The best the theatre historian can do is warn us of the danger that, if we look through modern eyes, we shall see a modern theatre. Modern theatrical spaces are predicated on symmetry, optimum sightlines, and the separation of art from religion—and historians are too often content to take these norms for granted. The debate about Thorikos is so important because it determines how we imagine the theatre in which the surviving Greek tragedies were performed. Was it a ritual performance in honor of the gods or a frontal mirroring of a sociopolitical reality? So much depends upon how we see. Palyvou was motivated to see circles through cultural exposure to performances at Epidaurus, while U.S. scholars typically do not have the same reference point.

Ground plans speak volumes to those practiced in relating them to stones on the hillside; but if the aim of historians is to stimulate the historical imagination, plans are not enough. And a photograph of a ruin will always look like a ruin. Architectural training allowed Richard Leacroft to create precise isometric drawings that project ground plans into three dimensions, with the occasional human introduced for scale.[13] More recently Richard Beacham has created interactive computer-generated models of ancient theatres;[14] these allow us to construct unexpected angles of vision, but, as in perceptions of Stonehenge, geometry wins out over texture. A 2002 publication designed to popularize modern German archaeological findings uses another technique, photographing a handmade model. Christian Shiekel's models from the Theatre Museum in Munich translate into attractive graphic images and avoid the illusion of scientific objectivity. Unlike the isometric drawing and (as yet) the computer, they also incorporate the audience. The three hundred odd brightly painted clay figurines who watch performances of *Ajax* or *The Frogs* are the epitome of good order, with no hint of surrender to collective emotion. When we see *Agamemnon* being played in Thorikos, we notice that the unfortunate irregularities of the auditorium have become almost invisible.[15] Such models are useful tools to think with, but we must not be seduced. Historians need to learn to see differently, not to have seeing done on their behalf. Modern technologies have shaped modern ways of seeing, so their use by historians is perforce problematic.

From classical Greece, I pass to another mainstay of theatrical history, the theatre of Shakespeare. My case study is a tiny wood engraving, part of the frontispiece to a tragedy called *Roxana* (fig. 3). The play was written by William Alabaster, a theologian and mystic, who in 1632 decided to exhume this product of his student days, performed in Cambridge some forty years earlier. Christopher Balme describes a "referential dilemma" facing theatre historians in their use of well-known early images and asks: "Do such pictures index a 'theatrical reality,' an actual performance, or are they the product of iconographical codes, largely divorced from theatrical practice?"[16] This is a pertinent question to ask of the *Roxana* engraving. The image does not directly portray a scene from the play, where violent action happens offstage in accordance with classical convention. Victor Albright in 1909 was certain it represented a university stage of the Elizabethan era, while John Cranford Adams in 1942 believed that the engraver found his model in the fashionable private Salisbury Court playhouse; Glynne Wickham in 1972 argued for the octagonal Phoenix theatre.[17] Against these notions, John Astington in 1991 maintained that the *Roxana* plate was simply "a confection of iconographic conventions" and that the image of a stage was concocted from the study of Renaissance engravings of the comedies of Terence—though he conceded grudgingly that the railings around the stage might be based on direct observation. Astington's argument collapsed almost immediately with the discovery of the foundations of the Rose Theatre, which revealed that the stage in both versions of the Rose was of the same tapered shape as the *Roxana* stage.[18] The case for referentiality gained a fresh lease of life.

Happily I was able to consult a copy of the 1632 edition and hold in my hands this intricate specimen of seventeenth-century artistry. If I wish to reproduce the image (as for example in this book), however, then I have a dilemma. If I choose to reproduce the whole plate, then affordable technology means that I will lose detail and lose my reader's attention. If, on the other hand, as a historian of *theatre* I choose to isolate the theatre vignette and quadruple its scale, then I shall create a very different viewing experience. The image will pass all too easily for the equivalent of a newspaper photograph, referencing a performance in some specific time and place. When Cambridge University Press borrowed Wickham's redrawing of the *Roxana* vignette for the cover of the second edition of Andrew Gurr's *The Shakespearean Stage*, we come full circle: an image designed to sell one book has been reprocessed in order to sell another book.[19]

The copy I consulted belonged to the eighteenth-century antiquarian Francis Douce, who wrote on the first page: "The frontispiece to Roxana is extremely curious for the representation of the interior of the playhouse at

3a. Frontispiece to *Roxana* by W. Alabaster (a), with detail (b). Reproduced by permission of the Bodleian Library, Oxford: Douce A.399(1).

3b. *Roxana* detail.

that time; being 40 years earlier than another in 'Kirkman's Wits or sport upon sport,' with which it nearly agrees."[20] This was written before the discovery in 1888 of a Dutch drawing of the Swan theatre (fig. 4), which would define how the twentieth century visualized Elizabethan theatre. By contrast with the *Roxana* vignette, where much is crowded into a tiny frame, the Swan drawing creates a sense of grand scale with its elongated verticals and receding galleries. Though Adams championed the *Roxana* stage as the best source for the Globe stage,[21] the Swan definitively won the argument in the postwar period, thanks to the efforts of scholars like Richard Hosley and John Orrell.[22] Glynne Wickham in *A History of the Theatre* (1985) typically passed over *Roxana* and confined himself to reproducing the Swan drawing as the "only depiction of the interior of a playhouse used by actors within Shakespeare's lifetime."[23]

Following the discovery of the Rose foundations, Reg Foakes questioned this orthodoxy, arguing that the Swan stage was a removable structure in a multipurpose space, and found no good evidence for the Globe stage being square.[24] It is now generally felt that the Elizabethan theatre reconstructed on London's South Bank is too large, but John Orrell's mathematical arguments were persuasive because the scale which he proposed

4. The Swan theatre. Drawing by J. De Witt, copied by A. van Buchel. Bristol University Theatre Collection, reproduced by permission of Utrecht University Library.

seemed in accord with the Swan drawing. The new "Shakespeare's Globe" adopted the huge square stage of the Swan drawing, and the Royal Shakespeare Company is building a similar stage (minus the intrusive columns) in Stratford. So much hinges upon the power of a drawing for contemporary theatre practice.

It is a sign of changing fashions that Martin White, in order to represent an Elizabethan stage in *The Cambridge History of British Theatre* (2004), passed over the Swan drawing in favor of the 1640 frontispiece to *Messallina*, an image of secure theatrical provenance influenced by *Roxana*.[25] White also used C. Walter Hodges's reconstruction of the Rose.[26] For half a century Hodges's drawings have dominated our visual conception of what the Elizabethan stage *really* looked like;[27] when images are recycled often enough, they take hold of our consciousness. The aerial perspective, cutaway format, and quaint half-timbering of his Rose drawing reassure us that we know and understand, from a comfortable position of scientific detachment. When I sought to obtain this image from the Museum of London for the present essay, I learned that Hodges had recently died, with complications in his estate. The drawing is set to become a commercial asset. I was not sorry to be thwarted, hoping the drawing will be priced high so that scholars will have to seek more modernist eyes through which to see the past. An interesting feature of the Wanamaker Globe is the impossibility of photographing the performance space. In capturing what spectatorship feels like, a typical photo, such as the one in the Routledge *Theatre Histories*, renders the perspectival lines as drawn in fig. 5.[28] The Swan drawing responds to an impossible perspectival challenge by rendering three superimposed layers independently. Historians who want to restore a unified perspective and help readers imagine that they are seated in the gallery rather than up in the sky often conveniently eliminate the faint circle and text at the base of the Dutch drawing.

Michael Baxandall maintains that the art historian must develop a "period eye" in order to acquire the "cognitive style" of another era.[29] To view the *Roxana* frontispiece as a totality must be our first step when we strive for such a period eye. While Cambridge University Press marketed Gurr's volume with the implicit visual message "This is what Shakespearean theatre actually looked like," Alabaster's volume carried a different message, appropriate to the work of an elderly theologian: "Tragedy corresponds to divine law." The prototype for Alabaster's plate was the frontispiece to Ben Jonson's *Dramatic Works*, published in 1616. The title inscription is framed by personifications of Tragedy on our left (a regal male) and Comedy on our right (female and rustic), and in the center is a

5. The interior of Shakespeare's Globe theatre.
Drawing by Gayna Wiles, after a photograph by John Tramper.

Roman playhouse topped by some chaotic structures that recall an Elizabethan tiring house. Jonson adds for good measure the tumbrel of Thespis and a choral dance to evoke the origins of theatre, for his aim was not to represent his own theatre but an idea of what theatre essentially is. It matters nothing that Thespis and the dancers are in Jacobean costume.

A similar governing opposition of left and right structures the Alabaster engraving (fig. 6). At top center we see a classicized version of the last trumpet. Top left we see an emperor representing temporal power crushed by the pope, and on the right a pagan cosmic scene: Mars seduces Venus; but Mars also lies buried, with Venus reduced to a skull. Center left and right we have a pair of figures that we could read in the classical idiom as Tragedy and Comedy but in the Christian idiom as a sober youth praying to heaven and a decadent woman pointing to herself. In the bottom register we have tumbling crowns and scepters on the left (the side connected with power and kingship), while on the right (the side associated rather with sexuality) a young man in semiclassical dress consorts with a bare-breasted courtesan. The riddling logic here, for me at least, whets the appetite to read the play. The theatre scene, like the call to judgment day, unites the two sides.

The classical column dividing the balcony is aligned with the curtain divide in order to encourage a bipolar reading of the tiny image. The man is attracted to the woman, forgetting that death stalks him. While the woman

6. Two images from the *Roxana* frontispiece: (a) upper-right image of Mars, Venus, and other gods; (b) lower-right image of the lovers. Reproduced by permission of the Bodleian Library, Oxford: Douce A.399(1).

is framed by light, a dark interior stands behind the killer. Although the scene does not represent the actual staging of Alabaster's play, it could relate to the final act, after Roxana has been killed by the jealous Queen. The King kills the traitor Bessus, who has made love to the Queen, leaving the King and Queen locked in guilt and recrimination. The binary oppositions of the frontispiece relate neatly to the symmetry of the plot, and the pictorial space correlates with the play as it is conceptualized. It is not the plight of innocent Roxana to which we are directed, but the consequences of the King's illicit love.

This theatrical vignette is positioned at the base of the frontispiece, representing the *base* world of the flesh in contrast to the *higher* world of the divinities. When we focus on the vignette, we again need to look for symbolic vertical registers and not let our modern eyes set off on a fruitless quest for perspectival unity. The engraving was never a blueprint for reconstruction, so it is futile to ask whether the spectators above the stage have enough legroom and whether the lower spectators are sitting in a gallery or standing in the pit. The frontispiece construes tragedy as a metaphor for earthly life, and life in the Christian and classical conception is always overseen. In Alabaster's play, Roxana's dead father, in the manner of a Senecan ghost, overlooks the action along with the figures of Death and Suspicion. Accordingly, these onlookers may be read both as privileged human spectators and as cosmic participants. In the bottom register, the space of the common audience, the lefthand figure pointing at the stage wears a Turkish headdress, the central figure has a monkish or peasant cowl, and the righthand figure has a cloak that could be classical. All human life is here, witnessing a heroic scene played out by monarchs. The audience is certainly not that of a fashionable Stuart playhouse.

When Wickham wanted to demonstrate that the *Roxana* vignette illustrated the Cockpit theatre, refurbished by Christopher Beeston in 1616 to become the Phoenix, he had the scene redrawn and made a few discreet adjustments. He modified the hatching and added hints of a door behind the curtain, to support the idea that the tapered stage belonged to an octagonal building. The copyist blurred the front spectators and gave more facial expression to the upper spectators; but most importantly, he regularized the erratic geometry of the stage rail, so the image could feed neatly into Wickham's diagram of a reconstructed Phoenix. Astington, while praising Alabaster's artist John Payne as "one of the most accomplished contemporary engravers," lamented the "structural irrationality" of the stage. The "design falters badly," he wrote, "clumsy in its representation of structure" and offering a "geometric impossibility"; Payne, he concluded, must have been more interested in the human life of the figures.[30] This imputation of incompetence makes no sense, for Payne was perfectly capable of drawing straight geometric lines and had astonishing technical skill. Viewed in the context of the whole frontispiece, with its nine precise rectilinear panels, the crudely drawn depiction of the stage and the refusal to create parallel lines yield a sense of energy, so the stage itself seems to be in movement. The angle of the tumbling scepters echoes the stage sides, while the billowing curtain echoes the fabric provocatively raised by the courtesan. It is the space and not the human figures that makes the image live. In much the same way, Hodges's tidy reconstruction of the Rose drains that space of the energy that we discern in the simple plan of the foundations, where precise geometric symmetries are conspicuous by their absence.

Payne aimed at the essence of a tragic performance, not a photographic snapshot—and to this extent Astington was right to say that the vignette offers us the "imagined theatre of classical humanism."[31] But he was wrong to deny the importance of memory and observation. The *Roxana* stage resembles the Rose more than it resembles any illustration of Terence, and the dated costume of the woman recalls how Elizabethan women used to dress, so the scene has some overt value as an index of a vanished reality. But the iconographic codes at work are to my mind more revealing, helping us to move from *what* the Elizabethans and Stuarts saw to *how* they saw. The classical humanists who engraved imagined performances of Roman comedy were far bolder than Payne in their experiments with the perverse logic of perspective.[32] Alabaster was not a humanist, any more than most of his contemporaries, even though he based his dramaturgy on Seneca; his cast of mind was more analogical, metaphorical, and metaphysical. The historian's challenge is to help us see the world through such different eyes. The circular Elizabethan playhouse contained no privileged point of vision from which the whole could be seen and known (and potentially photographed). When we use two-dimensional images to comfort our readers with a sense of objective knowledge, we distort the historical object under investigation. How far the Globe was a "humanist" space or a space packed with metaphysical symbolism is an important matter for debate, but if we apply perspectival geometry to the evidence, then we predetermine the answer in favor of humanism.[33]

My third case study is an oil painting generally held to be the first English representation of a specific scene on a specific theatrical stage. John Gay's *The Beggar's Opera* was a celebrated public event in 1728, and William Hogarth's rendering has become an iconic image in histories of British theatre (fig. 7). A. M. Nagler in his *Sources of Theatrical History* (1952) used William Blake's engraved copy made in the late 1780s, doubtless because of its reproductive quality. He identifies the scene with the moment of Polly's song in act III, scene 11, and places it amid a text from the 1760s about the iniquities of spectators onstage. Brockett's *History* follows Nagler and invites the reader to "note the spectators on the stage."[34] David Thomas also used Blake in his contribution to the Cambridge series Theatre in Europe: A Documentary History in 1989, in a section on "stage presentation." For Thomas the picture "makes it quite clear that the opera used conventional scenic devices"; he believed he could identify "two pairs of wings and a back shutter" in the upstage prison set and describes the satyr at the base of the proscenium as "a distinctive feature of the stage at Lincoln's Inn Fields."[35] The referential status of the painting, accurately representing a particular place and moment, is never in question. When Thomas comments on the asymmetry of the wings in terms of design,

7. *The Beggar's Opera*. By William Hogarth (British, 1697–1764), 1729. Oil on canvas. 23¼ x 30 inches (59.1 x 76.2 cm). Yale Center for British Art, Paul Mellon Collection. B1981.25.349.

the reader is unlikely to think about the complex games that Hogarth is playing with strict Renaissance perspective to create a view that may be coming from both right and left of center, denying strict geometric logic in order to energize the pictorial space.

Thomas also reproduces a burlesque print by Hogarth (fig. 8), which shows a comparable grouping of actors on a mountebank stage. Behind them and to the left we see the boxes, proscenium, and wings of Gay's theatre, while on the right we see an opera singer being halted as she sings. Thomas simply captions this "The interior of Lincoln's Inn Fields theatre in 1728," with no reference to the fair in the foreground or to the King's Theatre in the Haymarket, where we might expect a frustrated Italian opera singer to be located. In lieu of guiding the reader in how to read this tripartite image, Thomas simply provides statistics about the size of the theatre.[36] *The* Revels *History of Drama in English* (1976) likewise used the burlesque print without mediation or commentary as a depiction of

et cantare pares et respondere parati
Harmony
THE BEGGARS OPERA.
Brittons attend — view this harmonious Stage,
And listen to these notes which charm the age.
Thus shall your tastes in Sounds & Sense be shown,
And Beggars Operas ever be your own.

8. *The Beggar's Opera.* Print by William Hogarth. Bristol University Theatre Collection.

Lincoln's Inn Fields. The format of the Revels series carries to an extreme the conceptual separation of the authored play from its spatial context or container. In the "staging" section of the volume, Richard Southern asserts that the Hogarth painting represents Covent Garden, to which *The Beggar's Opera* transferred, and not Lincoln's Inn Fields, apparently because of the enhanced scale of the stage; meanwhile, in the section on the authored play, A. H. Scouten denies that Italian opera was the main butt of Gay's opera but makes no reference to the print in which this is the overt theme.[37] The section of plates is a decorative appendage and forms no part of an argument.

Glynne Wickham was more adventurous in using an early version of Hogarth's painting, which depicts a more intimate space and a stage audience that surrounds the action. He wanted to create a narrative link to Bertolt Brecht's *Threepenny Opera* and thus to stress the burlesque nature of the play, whose popularity helped drive the government to introduce the Licensing Act to censor such productions.[38] Simon Trussler was able to use color in his *Cambridge Illustrated History of British Theatre* (1994) and reverted to the canonical Tate Gallery version, with its luxuriant reds for the temporary boxes and Macheath's highwayman coat, spread across a large-format page. Trussler argues in his text that *The Beggar's Opera* is "a theatrical equivalent of a Hogarthian print—so rich in incident, interpolation and low-life impropriety as to upset conventional expectations of dramatic art, but, like the best caricature, thought-provoking in its simultaneous likeness and unlikeness to life, even as it delights with its detail and dark corners." It is admirable that Trussler should recognize a correlation between pictorial space and theatrical experience but ironic that he should choose to reproduce not a print which illustrates his argument but a luminous oil painting with a classical composition. His choice makes for a more sumptuous book, however. His caption sticks to tradition, noting the exact song, the presence of spectators "casually interacting," the wings and back shutter, and the satyr that was part of the playhouse.[39] Trussler notes in his introduction that if we had a video of a performer like David Garrick we would find it at worst alien, at best a curiosity—but he does not extend the logic of this remark to his own historiography.[40]

In this conspectus of popular histories, the referential status of Hogarth's painting has gone unchallenged, its transparency assumed. Let us reexamine it.[41] The earliest version of the image we have is a pencil sketch executed on blue paper (fig. 9), which suggests a wish to be inconspicuous as Hogarth sat sketching amid the audience.[42] The sketch shows temporary boxes packed with spectators encircling the actors, so it must have been executed when the play was at the height of popularity. At the back is a hanging over what could be a central door or could be the gallows. To the sides we see vertical lines that indicate four wings which operated on the old-fashioned sliding shutter principle.[43] In the rapid process of sketching, the artist could not have captured a complicated tableau in a single freeze. It makes much more sense to think of Hogarth sequentially creating Macheath's articulation of a dilemma about which wife to choose, Polly's plea to her father, and then Lucy's plea to her father. While photographs capture moments, paintings typically construct narratives.

Hogarth used this sketch to generate three similar paintings. He introduced a curtain to suggest the line of the proscenium, though we may question its placing upstage of the spectators. He eliminated the wings, substituting real prison walls and windows to create an image that has moved into the world of our imagination. The spectators became fewer in

9. *The Beggar's Opera*. Drawing by William Hogarth. Collection © 2008 Her Majesty Queen Elizabeth II, the Royal Library, Windsor Castle.

number and are rendered as upper-class caricatures, yielding a satiric message: the morality of thieves echoes the morality of London's elite. Polly's handkerchief extended toward Macheath is at the center of the image to suggest the sentimental emotions of the scene, ignored by the spectators. John Rich, the owner of the Lincoln's Inn Fields theatre, bought one of these satiric paintings and then commissioned a fresh version, the one that became iconic thanks in part to Blake's engraved copy. A duplicate of this final version was made for a wealthy Member of Parliament and subsequently found its way to the Tate Gallery, a fitting work for a great national collection because it deploys the grand visual language of history painting.

The changes are profound in the final version. The canvas is now bigger, and the interior space of the prison is monumental rather than claustrophobic. The elite are more attentive to the play, and individualized so that contemporaries could recognize their features. The spectators to the rear of the action have vanished, replaced by the rabble who enter with Macheath at the very end of the play, so the illusion of a particular stage moment is gone, while the distinction between high and low society is emphasized. Hogarth has not sought to replicate the distorted perspective created by upstage figures on a raked stage. Polly has been set on a carpet, as part of a strategy to make her rather than Macheath the protagonist of the painting. Numerous diagonal lines point toward her, including the finger of the leader of the rabble, who stands at the honor point of the perspective. Discarding perspective, we may prefer to scan the painting from left to right, recalling that Hogarth became famous for his rendering of linear progresses. We would then see the gaze of Lockit and Macheath leading us to Polly, shining on her carpet; Polly's gaze, however, leads us not to her father, Peachum, but to the Duke of Bolton, who holds the script of the play on the extreme right and returns her gaze. The elopement of Lavinia Fenton, the actress who played Polly, with this married but infatuated aristocrat was a notorious public scandal in 1728. Robert Fagg, standing behind Peachum, was a rival for her affections. The elopement cost John Rich his star performer but contributed to the publicity of his production.

Yet another option is to read the painting in terms of Christian iconography. Lockit in a pose of denial has the keys of St. Peter, Macheath is like Christ tormented by his jailers, the rabble might be entering the Garden of Gethsemane, and Peachum adopts a *noli me tangere* pose in relation to Mary Magdalene.[44] The theme of the Magdalene as redeemed prostitute was pertinent to Lavinia Fenton, condemned as a whore by some yet idolized by others because she embodied the dream of the lower-class girl making good. The stone staircase introduced to the right of the painting suggests social and spiritual ascent, while the diabolic satyr points downward toward the duke. A final mode of viewing which the historian might reconstruct sets the painting within a code of genres; through casting this work as a history painting, Hogarth locates the play as a parody of high Italian opera.

This painting is not a rendering of what Gay's audience saw in the theatre in any technical or material sense, for the set, the stage, and the audience have been radically transformed. Yet the painting can initiate us into a historical way of seeing the world and help us apprehend a theatrical culture where the audience's world and the world of the play were intermeshed. We glimpse why the presence of spectators onstage created a social dynamic that, far from being a problem, enriched the theatrical experience. Our history books interpret the painting as a rendering of Gay's play, but Gay was not being flippant when he wrote in March 1728: "I am in doubt whether her fame does not surpass that of the Opera itself."[45] The cult of Lavinia was a social phenomenon, in which the personality of the singer merged with the role she played.[46] The effacing of the performer in favor of the author and manager in our historical narratives has obvious gender implications.

We should reflect upon why John Rich commissioned this painting. Perhaps it represented a spatial ideal that he would seek to realize when he built Covent Garden. Perhaps, indeed, he intended to hang the painting in the back rooms of Covent Garden, so elite playgoers with access to the female performers could reflect on what this privilege might promise. When photographic images are scaled up or scaled down in order to be reproduced as documents of theatre history, they are stripped of their initial material context in a printed volume or a beaux arts frame. We may then forget that they are a record of physical objects embedded in a social world. An eighteenth-century oil painting reached one class of viewer, a print reached another, and the messages, dreams, and pleasures that each medium provided were very different. Hogarth's images did not simply reflect the world of 1728; they also helped create that world. Peter Brook famously wrote that words fade but "it is the play's central image that remains, its silhouette, and if the elements are rightly blended this silhouette will be its meaning, this shape will be the essence of what it has to say."[47] Perhaps Hogarth's grouping of five figures recalled some essential silhouette; however, it is more certain that Hogarth's image shaped the spectators' memories of what they had seen. The performance as it actually was is an ever-elusive goal.

Christopher Balme introduces a useful dichotomy when he critiques Cesare Molinari's distinction between *monumenti* and *documenti*.[48] As monuments, Hogarth's images and Payne's wood-engraving have a texture, scale, and social function that we lose when the theatre historian translates them into historical documents. While historians are obliged to create documents, they need not and should not assume that any document speaks for itself without interpretation. I have argued here that seeing is historically conditioned and that different cognitive styles, different ways of seeing, characterize various periods. The historian needs to escape a tricky hermeneutic circle: we see the past through eyes conditioned by the present; and our vision of the past affirms the authority of what we do in the present. The ease with which historians persuade us that we see wings in a painting from which they have been eliminated reveals how malleable human vision can be. Pictures are influential, and I have suggested how interpretations of the Thorikos ground plan and the *Roxana* vignette bear on the work of modern directors.

I have argued in this essay that space was once seen by theatre analysts as the container within which the play itself happened; that understanding of theatre has shifted, and space is now recognized as the basic stuff of which a performance is made. The old Revels formula is no longer intellectually tenable. Yet the methodologies of theatre historians have not kept track of this new apprehension of the discipline. A performance space is still often taken as an untheorizable datum, which we can describe in terms of its mere geometry. Because of our familiarity with Renaissance laws of perspective, and the mechanism of cameras, we readily assume that pictures furnish an accurate record of those geometries. I have sought to show in this essay that converting a contingent, three-dimensional event into a two-dimensional image on paper is not a self-evident process. The viewer of a 2-D image cannot be inside the image, yet the viewer of a performance is always inside the performance, as one who helps create the theatrical event. When the historian tries to construct a viewing point up in the sky, looking into a cut-out model of the Rose or the Swan, then that historian enters a virtual environment which corresponds to no reality that was ever lived or experienced.

NOTES

1. Peter Holland and Stephen Orgel, eds., *From Script to Stage in Early Modern England* (London: Palgrave, 2004), p. 2.

2. Iain Mackintosh, *Architecture, Actor and Audience* (London: Routledge, 1993), contains many valuable insights on this subject.

3. On Henri Lefebvre's conception of social space, see David Wiles, *A Short History of Western Performance Space* (Cambridge, Cambridge University Press, 2003), pp. 9–13.

4. John Steer, "Art History and Direct Perception: A General View," *Art History* 12 (1989): 93–108. Steer is developing J. J. Gibson's theory of direct perception.

5. Tadeusz Kantor, *A Journey through Other Spaces: Essays and Manifestoes, 1944–1990*, ed. and trans. Michal Kobialka (Berkeley: University of California Press, 1993), pp. 221–222.

6. M. Parker Pearson and Ramilsonina, "Stonehenge for the Ancestors: The Stones Pass on the Message," *Antiquity* 72 (1998): 308–326.

7. See David Wiles, *A Short History of Western Performance Space* (Cambridge: Cambridge University Press, 2003), pp. 181–183.

8. See David Wiles, *Tragedy in Athens: Performance Space and Theatrical Meaning* (Cambridge: Cambridge University Press, 1997), pp. 44–52; J. Ch. Moretti, "The Theater in the Sanctuary of Dionysus Eleuthereus in Late Fifth-Century Athens," *Illinois Classical Studies* 24.5 (1999–2000): 377–398.

9. Oscar G. Brockett and Franklin J. Hildy, *The History of the Theatre*, 10th ed. (Boston: Allyn and Bacon, 2007), pp. 22–23.

10. Bruce McConachie in Phillip B. Zarrilli, Bruce McConachie, Gary Jay Williams, and Carol Sorgenfrei, *Theatre Histories: An Introduction* (London: Routledge, 2006), p. 87.

11. Clifford Ashby, *Classical Greek Theatre: New Views of an Old Subject* (Iowa City: University of Iowa Press, 1999), p. 36.

12. Clairy Palyvou, "Notes on the Geometry of the Ancient Theatre of Thorikos," *Archäologischer Anzeiger* (2001): 45–58.

13. See Richard Leacroft and Helen Leacroft, *Theatre and Playhouse: An Illustrated Survey of Theatre Building from Ancient Greece to the Present* (London: Methuen, 1984).

14. See Richard Beacham, "Playing Places: The Temporary and the Permanent," in *The Cambridge Companion to Greek and Roman Theatre*, ed. Marianne McDonald and J. Michael Walton (Cambridge: Cambridge University Press, 2007), pp. 202–226.

15. Susanne Moraw and Eckehart Nölle, eds., *Die Geburt des Theaters in der griechischen Antike* (Mainz: Philipp von Zabern, 2002). Pöhlmann's plan is figure 44.

16. Christopher B. Balme, "Interpreting the Pictorial Record: Theatre Iconography and the Referential Dilemma," *Theatre Research International* 22 (1997): 190–201, especially 190–191.

17. Victor E. Albright. *The Shakesperian Stage* (New York: Columbia University Press, 1909), p. 44; John Cranford Adams, *The Globe Playhouse: Its Origins and Equipment* (Cambridge, Mass.: Harvard University Press, 1942), p. 94; Glynne Wickham, *Early English Stages, Vol. 2, 1576–1660, Part 2* (London: Routledge and Kegan Paul, 1972), pp. 87–89.

18. John R. Astington, "The Origins of the *Roxana* and *Messallina* Illustrations," *Shakespeare Survey* 43 (1991): 149–169; a partial recantation followed in "Rereading Illustrations of the English Stage," *Shakespeare Survey* 50 (1997): 151–170.

19. As Astington notes in "The Origins of the *Roxana* and *Messallina* Illustrations," p. 149; Andrew Gurr, *The Shakespearean Stage, 1574–1642*, 2nd ed. (Cambridge: Cambridge University Press, 1980).

20. William Alabaster, *Roxana* (London, 1632): Bodleian Library Douce A.399. For "40" he should have written "30."

21. Adams, *The Globe Playhouse*, pp. 92–93.

22. Richard Hosley, following C. Walter Hodges and Richard Southern, argues for the essential similarity of the two spaces: J. Leeds Barroll, Alexander Leggatt, Richard Hosley, and Alvin Kernan, *The* Revels *History of Drama in English, Vol. 3, 1576–1613* (London: Methuen, 1975), pp. 121–196. John Orrell's theories informed the Wanamaker Globe. See, for example, *The Quest for Shakespeare's Globe* (Cambridge: Cambridge University Press, 1983).

23. Glynne Wickham, *A History of the Theatre* (London: Phaidon, 1985), p. 125. Cf. C. Molinari, *Theatre through the Ages*, trans. C. Hamer (London: Cassell, 1975), pp. 208–209.

24. See most recently R. A. Foakes, "Henslowe's Rose/Shakespeare's Globe," in *From Script to Stage in Early Modern England*, ed. Holland and Orgel, pp. 11–31.

25. Martin White, "London Professional Playhouses and Performances," in *The Cambridge History of British Theatre, Vol. 1: Origins to 1660*, ed. Jane Milling and Peter Thomson (Cambridge: Cambridge University Press, 2004), pp. 298–340, fig. 23. On *Messallina*, see Astington, "The Origins of the *Roxana* and *Messallina* Illustrations."

26. The color version appeared in Hodges's postscript to Julian Bowsher, *The Rose Theatre: An Archaeological Discovery* (London: Museum of London, 1998).

27. C. Walter Hodges dismissed the prowlike *Roxana* stage in *The Globe Restored: A Study of the Elizabethan Theatre* (London: Ernest Benn, 1953), p. 26.

28. Phillip B. Zarrilli, Bruce McConachie, Gary Jay Williams, and Carol Fisher Sorgenfrei, *Theatre Histories: An Introduction* (New York: Routledge, 2006), figure 4.10. Original photo by John Tramper.

29. Michael Baxandall, *Painting and Experience in Fifteenth Century Italy: A Primer in the Social History of Pictorial Style* (Oxford: Oxford University Press, 1972), esp. pp. 29–30.

30. Astington, "The Origins of the *Roxana* and *Messallina* Illustrations," pp. 161–162.

31. Ibid., p. 158.

32. See T. E. Lawrenson and H. Purkis, "Les Éditions illustrées de Terence dans l'histoire du théâtre," in *Le Lieu théâtral à la renaissance*, ed. Jean Jacquot (Paris: CNRS, 1964), pp. 1–23.

33. John Orrell argues the case for humanism in *The Human Stage* (Cambridge: Cambridge University Press, 1988).

34. A. M. Nagler, *Sources of Theatrical History*, subsequently republished as *A Source Book in Theatrical History* (New York: Dover Books, 1959), p. 378; Brockett and Hildy, *The History of the Theatre*, p. 226.

35. David Thomas, ed., *Restoration and Georgian England, 1660–1788*, comp. David Thomas and Arnold Hare (Cambridge: Cambridge University Press, 1989), pp. 122–123.

36. Ibid., pp. 78–79. For the size of the theatre, Thomas cites an unpublished thesis; for alternative dimensions, see Robert D. Hume, ed., *The London Theatre World, 1660–1800* (Carbondale: Southern Illinois University Press, 1980), pp. 45, 65.

37. John Loftis, Richard Southern, Marion Jones, and A. H. Scouten, *The* Revels *History of Drama in English, Vol. 5, 1660–1750* (London: Methuen, 1976), pp. 116, 236, plate 18.

38. Wickham, *A History of the Theatre*, p. 166.

39. Simon Trussler, *Cambridge Illustrated History of British Theatre* (Cambridge: Cambridge University Press, 1994), pp. 163–164. The caption also mysteriously identifies a gallows.

40. Ibid., p. x.

41. My principal sources for documentation and interpretation are Ronald Paulson, *Hogarth, Vol. 1: The "Modern Moral Subject," 1697–1732* (Cambridge: Lutterworth Press, 1992), pp. 172–195; and David Bindman and Scott Wilcox, eds., "Among Thieves and Whores": *William Hogarth and "The Beggar's Opera"* (New Haven: Yale Center for British Art, 1997). Marvin Carlson, "A Fresh Look at Hogarth's *Beggar's Opera,*" *Educational Theatre Journal* 27 (1975): 30–39, remains useful, particularly on the engraving.

42. Reproduced in A. P. Oppé, *The Drawings of William Hogarth* (London: Phaidon, 1948), plate 20.

43. See Jennifer L. Roberts, "Inscrutable Space: Hogarth's *The Beggar's Opera* and English Stage Design," in "*Among Thieves and Whores,*" ed. Bindman and Wilcox, pp. 25–33.

44. The Magdalene pose is identified in Paulson, *Hogarth*, p. 174.

45. J. V. Guerinot and Rodney D. Jilg, *The Beggar's Opera* (Hamden, Conn.: Archon Books, 1976), p. 163.

46. Documentation is collected in William Eben Schultz, *Gay's Beggar's Opera: Its Content, History and Influence* (New Haven: Yale University Press, 1923), pp. 23–35.

47. Peter Brook, *The Empty Space* (London: MacGibbon and Kee, 1968), p. 136.

48. Balme, "Interpreting the Pictorial Record," p. 192.

When "Everything Counts" Experimental Performance and Performance Historiography

In 1973 an artist named Mierle Laderman Ukeles presented a series of fifteen performances in conjunction with exhibits of her work at a range of U.S. museums and galleries. In one such iteration, *Hartford Wash: Washing Tracks, Maintenance Inside* at the Wadsworth Atheneum in Hartford, Connecticut, Ukeles descended to her hands and knees to wash the inside floors and exterior steps of the museum. She engaged continuously and for hours in the repetitive motions of crouching, squeezing, scrubbing, standing, dumping, crouching, squeezing, scrubbing, standing, and dumping that constituted her avant-garde experimental practice of "maintenance art."

In 1998 the Wooster Group first opened its production of *House/Lights* at the Performing Garage in New York City, presenting a show that would tour in Germany, Belgium, Canada, France, Scotland, and Norway before being revived again at St. Ann's Warehouse in New York in 2005. Joining the routinized plots and gestures of the brothel depicted in Joseph P. Mawra's 1964 film *Olga's House of Shame* with the looping phrases and scenarios of Gertude Stein's 1938 text *Doctor Faustus Lights the Lights,* the production coordinated a system of words, actors, and mediating machines to create a house and playhouse that were decidedly off-kilter.

I am interested in these performance practices in part for what they say to each other. Both have female performers at their center. Both engage in a dynamic construction of space, whether we understand their movements to extend within or beyond an aesthetic frame; neither performance seems to have a fixed ending point. Both invoke the metaphor of the "household"—of playing house and a house at play—even if together they straddle the two opposing poles of female stereotypes embodied in the cleaned house tended by a wife and the unclean whorehouse tended by its mistress. Both make productive use of repetition, whether to comment socially on female labor or to unhinge linguistic referentiality via the tropes of female modernism. Whatever these performances share thematically and formally, however, they are also each imbricated in art histories and theatrical histories that differ from each other. It is that difference and the relationships across their differences that most concern me in this essay. In brief, I consider how and whether a spatial turn in experimental art of the late twentieth century is allied with a spatial turn in late twentieth-century theatre history scholarship. Located in a collection on the "historiography of performance," which follows from and supplements the important earlier collection *Interpreting the Theatrical Past*, these examples also represent two different domains (though by no means all domains) in which the vocabulary of "space" and "experimental performance" might apply.[1] I want to think through some of the conceptual parallels and conceptual puzzles that different disciplinary methods bring to bear on the site of performance, exploring methods of theatrical history, art history, and cultural history where varied groups of scholars have reckoned with the politics of location. My use of words such as "site" and "location" is not coincidental, for I am most interested in exploring what I have elsewhere called the "hypercontextual" nature of theatre and performance, an enmeshment in site and location that always seems to make the notion of "situated performance" something of a tautology.[2]

In what follows, I present and compare different kinds of scholarly approaches to "sitedness" in performance, using two contemporaneous publications as touchstones for my presentation: theatre scholar Ric Knowles's *Reading the Material Theatre* (2004) and art historian Miwon Kwon's *One Place after Another: Site-Specific Art and Locational Identity* (2002; paperback 2004).[3] I then use the fact of their shared language to tease out some of the conceptual convergences within theatrical and visual art-historical methods at our present moment. At the same time, I also explore their conceptual differences to foreground the methodological tensions in an interdisciplinary performance historiography more generally. If, following Louis Mink, "space" is a key term in the production of historical understanding, spatial understanding for performance historiography is particularly intriguing, moving as it does across Mink's distinctions between concepts we think *about*, concepts we *use*, and *a priori* concepts we think *with*.[4] If, for Mink, space is one of those *a priori* concepts with which we encounter the world, it is also one that performance consistently redefines as *a posteriori*, as arising from experience rather than preceding it. Performance makes the process of *thinking with* space into a process of thinking about space and a process of using it. In so doing, performance brings the contingency of spatial knowledge into higher relief, asking us to notice our own situating habits as well as the changeable ways in which we locate ourselves. As it happens, different artistic practices and scholarly methods can vary in their sense of spatial contingency. Hence, before we can devise a spatially nimble performance historiography, we first have to situate how we situate.

MATERIALIST CATEGORIES

In the same decade that saw the publication of *Interpreting the Theatrical Past,* progressive scholarship in the humanities, social sciences, and the history and philosophy of natural science took seriously, vociferously, if also variously, the politics of situated identity. In what would retroactively be homogenized under the phrase "identity politics," scholars and activists called attention to the gendered, classed, raced, and homophobic discourses that structured our habits of interpretation and tacit exclusion. The vocabulary and conceptual frames of identity-based scholarship varied enormously; indeed, many questioned the stability of anything like a volitional, self-intending entity like "identity." This prompted an internal rift among varieties of feminist, antiracist and queer scholarship, often repolarized as a debate between essentialist and antiessentialist concepts of identity. Proponents of the latter argued that the former reproduced hegemonic identity categories by claiming to speak as woman or as black. Meanwhile, the essentialists accused the antiessentialists of evacuating the political efficacy of identity by questioning the stability of its material existence. Within this mix of positions, it is no coincidence that the language of "site" and "situation" emerged to sustain progressive critique. Probably one of the most well-circulated essays on feminist location came from Donna Haraway, who used her unusual position as a feminist critic of science to forward the concept of "situated knowledges."[5] In these and related scholarly movements, the concept of "site" helped scholars and activists navigate some of the perils and contradictions of identity-based critique. By pointing to the sited construction of identity, one could theoretically embrace a sense of identity's instability and constructedness while simultaneously analyzing the concrete material location in which that construction occurred.

While the progressive debates of the 1980s and 1990s gave a particular urgency to the methodological tasks of contextualization in theatrical analysis, it would be imprudent to assume that the "identity turn" invented the situating methods of theatre scholarship. Indeed, the hypercontextual form of the theatre has meant that theatre scholarship has long been preoccupied with the situatedness of its events, even if the techniques and politics of how that situating happens to have changed over time. In early twentieth-century iterations of the discipline of theatre studies, emerging scholars mimicked and adapted the epistemological conventions of their time to contextualize the theatrical event. In most cases, a reference to the limitations of the hermetically sealed dramatic script became the foil on which an expanded theatrical field rested. As scholars and artists argued for the necessity of considering performers, design, buildings, and audiences in addition to the dramatic text, the language used to analyze these other situated registers varied. Some employed philological conventions of fact-based contexualization and Darwinian preoccupations with genus and species to chart theatre's evolutionary expansion.[6] Proponents of Cambridge anthropology adapted models of ritual to interpret drama within a network of event-based processes.[7] Scholars of medieval and Renaissance theatre knew full well that the deepest resonances of the form only came forward with knowledge of its embodied gestures, guilds, wagons, churches, and street-layouts—what a later generation of scholars would call its material conditions.[8] Earlier American institutional figures, meanwhile, formulated their own kind of situated discipline by promoting the artistic act of performance production as essential to the understanding of a play-text.[9]

All of these quite different approaches can be understood as attempts to "situate" theatre, albeit with quite different vocabularies and visions of scholarly discipline. Additionally, at various moments in the scholarly pendulum, all these gestures contended with other scholarly movements that argued for the importance of autonomy in art and art criticism, whether in the New Formalism of the mid-twentieth century or further back when Joel Elias Spingarn, defending his critical compatriot Benedetto Croce, grumpily declared that to analyze the *production* of drama was akin to incorporating "a history of the publisher's trade" into analysis of poetry.[10]

As Ric Knowles shows in *Reading the Material Theatre*, scholarship in theatre studies has drawn from other approaches over the twentieth century to reckon with the extended nature of the form. Working toward what he calls a "materialist semiotics" for theatre studies, he cites two more trajectories for situated analysis. One lies in the "cultural materialism" of the theories of cultural production of Antonio Gramsci, who, Knowles reminds us, referred to the "theatrical industry" as early as 1917.[11] The other lies in the mid-century adaptations of Prague-school semiotics to theatre studies methodology, a preoccupation with signifying systems of production and reception that propelled highly influential European and Euro-American theatre scholarship such as that of Keir Elam, Patrice Pavis,

Marco de Marinis, Michael Quinn, André Helbo, and Marvin Carlson.[12] While Knowles refers to a certain methodological exhaustion with the taxonomic tendencies of semiotics, he adapts its categories to Gramscian-inspired movements in cultural studies and new historicism through the late twentieth century. He cites scholars who, in the words of one collection, sought to "redraw the boundaries of literary study."[13] Indeed, Spingarn's earlier admonitions became prognostications, for it was in the context of new historicist and cultural materialist literary criticism that many a scholar did in fact begin to consider the role of printing presses, "the publisher's trade," and other forms of material writing in the analysis of poetry.[14]

Knowles also goes on to expand beyond the Renaissance-based scholarship of new historicism to cultural studies scholarship on twentieth-century forms of popular production and reception to notice the relationship between Stuart Hall's models of "encoding/decoding" and the inherited models of theatrical semiotics.[15] Knowles adapts the graphic habits of theatre semiotics to offer a chart that "fleshes out a triangular model" for reading the material theatre: 1. Conditions of Production (Encoding), 2. Performance Text, and 3. Conditions of Reception (Decoding). All work "in concert or in tension both within their own 'corner,' and along the axes that hold the poles together in tension with one another. 'Meaning' in a given performance situation—the social and cultural work done by the performance, its performativity, and its force—is the effect of all of these systems and each pole of the interpretive triangle working dynamically and relationally together."[16]

Thus, in creating triangular frameworks for a "materialist semiotics," Knowles gathers and modifies a vocabulary for the situation of performance that places the myriad dimensions of a site into divided if relationally defined categories for making a text, for receiving a text, and for identifying the text itself. So productive and entrenched is this theatrical triangle that we might find it difficult to notice the hermeneutic act that such a spatializing of space entails. First of all, in adapting Jonathan Dollimore and Alan Sinfield's disquisition on the necessity of considering the production and reception of texts, Knowles inserts his own bracketed statement to be sure that we know that "texts" are to be considered performances. In their statement Dollimore and Sinfield insist that we should see "texts [including, here, performances] as inseparable from the conditions of their production and reception in history; as involved, necessarily, in the making of cultural meanings which are always, finally political meanings."[17] Despite the apparent ease of Knowles's bracketed phrase, it is worth noting that the elements of "performance" might well qualify as elements of its extratextual situation for a differently positioned scholar. While some theatre scholars might locate the designed set of a play within the diegesis of the "performance text," the scholarly habits of another might position that same component as an exegetic element of a dramatic text, better located as part of its "conditions of production." Both scholars may claim to be equally committed to "situating" theatrical texts, but they may possess different disciplinary habits for gauging which elements of theatre belong to the "text" corner of a material semiotic triangle and which to the "production/encoding" corner.

It is certainly not the case that Knowles and the scholars he cites are unaware of this hermeneutic contingency. Indeed, when Knowles quotes one of Tony Bennett's essays to say that "neither text nor context is conceivable as entities separable from one another," he invokes one of the most significant contributions of new historicist methodology: that is, the conceptual sense not only that texts need contextualization but that the text/context division is itself a contingent construct.[18] Even that recognition, however, does not in itself bypass the fact that differently positioned scholars locate the space of the text/context implosion in different places, for the barometer for "redrawing the boundaries of literary study" between text and context, between performance and situation, depends upon inherited generic assumptions of where those boundaries were in the first place.

By looking more closely at some of the ways that Knowles defines the elements of the interpretive models, we can get an even better sense of how fragile and contingent methodological dispositions can be. Under Performance Text, Knowles places "script, *mise en scène*, design, actors' bodies, movement, and gestures, etc. as reconstituted in discourse." Consider the relation between these elements and those that are placed under Conditions of Production, such as "actor," "director," "training," "working conditions," "stage and backstage architecture," and "historical/cultural moment of production." The categories require a curious separation between "actors" and "actors' bodies"; meanwhile they must uphold a firm boundary between *mise en scène* and "working conditions." The conceptual difficulties continue with the extended definitions of other points on the triangle, such as when "conditions of production" also include "backstage architecture and amenities" that are presumably distinguished from other elements that appear under "Conditions of Reception," such as "publicity" or "front-of-house, auditorium, and audience amenities."[19] The spatial elements of a theatrical building are thus placed in different semiotic registers; the auditorium is naturalized as part of a front-stage reception and distinguished from backstage architectural features. In turn, "publicity" is something received rather than something produced. And a scholar would have to make a determination about which "amenities" qualify as production and which as reception.

SITE-SPECIFICITY

Around the same time that Knowles composed his manuscript for *Reading the Material Theatre,* another scholar in the field of art history was simultaneously composing hers. While Knowles developed his "materialist semiotic" frames whose "theoretical rigour and located reading" could "provide a model for site-specific performance analysis that takes into account the specifics and politics of location,"[20] Miwon Kwon's *One Place after Another* adopted a subtitle in quite similar terms: *Site-Specific Art and Locational Identity.* Filtered through an alternate disciplinary lens, the same words ("site-specific" and "location") were differently loaded and differently expansive for Kwon, whose project was in fact to scrutinize and compare the range of sensibilities and goals that had collected under the notion of site-specificity. Concerned that the term had been "uncritically adopted as another genre category by mainstream art institutions and discourses," she wondered with other critics whether the "unspecific (mis) uses of the term 'site-specific' are yet another instance of how vanguardist, socially conscious, and politically committed art practices always become domesticated by their assimilation into the dominant culture."[21] At the same time, she also wanted to track the resistance of some site-specific artists to institutional absorption, noting that others had formulated still new terms—"context-specific, debate-specific, audience-specific, community-specific, project-based"—to "forge more complex and fluid possibilities for the art-site relationship."[22]

Like that of many other scholars grounded in the field of visual art history—Hal Foster, Rosalind Krauss, T. J. Clark, and Benjamin Buchloh along with other art historians expressly concerned with performance/live art, such as Amelia Jones, Jane Blocker, Rebecca Schneider, and Adrian Heathfield—Kwon's terminology and her concerns overlap with those of theatre and performance studies scholars.[23] With terms like "context-specific" and especially "audience-specific," it seems that visual art experiments are reproducing and perhaps reinventing theatrical art traditions. At the same time, the intellectual and artistic trajectories supporting Kwon's project and positioning her implied interlocutors are part of a different set of artistic coordinates and movements. In titling her book *One Place after Another*, Kwon echoes and plays with a phrase from Minimalist sculptor Donald Judd, whose 1965 essay "Specific Objects" tried to give a vocabulary to the redefinition of visual art at work in the period. Distinguishing what he called "three-dimensional work" from previous painting and sculpture, Judd argued that he and allied artists wished to challenge the inherited material and spatial constraints of traditional visual art forms, especially painting. "The main thing wrong with painting is that it is a rectangular plane placed flat against the wall. A rectangle is a shape itself; it is obviously the whole shape; it determines and limits the arrangement of whatever is on or inside of it."[24]

Integral to the Minimalist gesture, then, was a resistance to the framed flatness of the painting frame and, by extension, the bounded limits placed on the conventional props, plinths, and pedestals of sculpture. Key to this resistance was an engagement with an extended spatiality. "Three dimensions are real space. . . . Obviously, anything in three dimensions can be any shape, regular or irregular, and can have any relation to the wall, floor, ceiling, room, rooms or exterior."[25] Frank Stella was one of the many artists invoked by Judd to help him articulate the effects of "specific objects." "Stella's shaped paintings involve several important characteristics of three-dimensional work. The periphery of a piece and the lines inside correspond. The stripes are nowhere near being discrete parts. The surface is farther from the wall than usual. . . . The order is not rationalistic and underlying but is simply order, like that of continuity, one thing after another."[26] The serial proposition of "one thing after another" was thus Judd's phrase for articulating a certain kind of boundary reorganization in the visual arts, one whose parameters neither reproduced traditional visual distinctions nor utilized traditional material infrastructures for the support of the aesthetic object, thereby reworking distinctions between background and foreground, canvas and wall, core and periphery, under and above, inside and outside.

For Judd and others to disparage "the main thing wrong with painting" was at this time for him to challenge not only a *longue durée* of European masters but also a more contemporaneous context of modernist art practice and criticism. In developing a critical vocabulary for the nonrepresentational explorations of Abstract Expressionism and modernist painting, powerful visual art critics such as Clement Greenberg and his former student Michael Fried famously called for a mode of formal criticism that took seriously these painters' engagement with the intrinsic qualities of their medium. For Greenberg, this medium of pure engagement respected the classical definition of the spatial, juxtapositive, and nondurational nature of the plastic arts, a respect for the all-at-once encounter that for G. E. Lessing and Joshua Reynolds had distinguished painting and other static arts from the durational arts of poetry and drama.[27] Crucially (especially for a spatially complex performance historiography), painting's spatiality was nondurational and highly circumscribed by the essentially flat medium of the canvas, as Greenberg insisted: "It quickly emerged that the unique and proper area of competence of each art coincided with all that was unique to the nature of its medium. . . . It was the stressing . . . of the ineluctable flatness of the support that remained most fundamental in the processes by which pictorial art criticized and defined itself under Modernism. Flatness, two-dimensionality, was the only condition painting shared with no other art, and so Modernist painting oriented itself to flatness as it did to nothing else."[28]

The focus on flatness as a condition of modernist legitimacy prompted such critics to value paintings that replicated the wholly present encounter of classical painting via a meditation on the flatness of the canvas. By extension, for both Greenberg and Fried, modernist painting required a criticism that did not engage either with the corruptions of other media or with the historical contingencies of its social conditions. Significantly, such an intrinsic criticism did not consider itself to be uninterested in criticality but understood the modernist engagement with its medium to constitute its own form of "self-criticism." The younger Fried spent a good deal of time grappling with and defending his mentor's scholarly method. "[I]n general, criticism concerned with aspects of the situation in which it was made other than its formal context can add significantly to our understanding of the artists' achievement. But criticism of this kind has shown itself largely unable to make convincing discriminations of value among the works of a particular artist."[29] For modernist critics like Fried and Greenberg who were well-aware of situating and contextualizing methodologies in art historiography, modernist art had the label it did because of its wholly present, formal resistance to social contingency; hence it required a criticism that understood that gesture.

As complicated and powerful as intrinsic modernist art criticism was in the period, it became in many ways a convenient foil for artists and art critics who would go on to celebrate an expanded and "situated" field for art practice. For pro-Minimalist (or "three-dimensional") artists and their supportive critics, modernism's medium purity functioned much as "dramatic literature" did for the field of materialist theatre, as the internally focused foil on which externally minded appeals to spatial situatedness could rest. Michael Fried would go on to write a polemic against the theatricality of Minimalist art in "Art and Objecthood," an infamous essay that only propelled the aesthetic expansion it sought to forestall. Fried's decision to align Minimalism's "literalism" with "theatricality" came from his sense of its concern with "actual circumstances" in "*a situation*" that "*includes the beholder*," even "the *beholder's body*."[30] As with Spingarn's "publisher's trade," this was another moment when admonition became prognostication. Fried's italicized disdain only emboldened situated art practice, even as it implicitly supported (albeit negatively) the sense of theatricality as a figure for hypercontextuality, for situatedness, and for dependence upon a spectatorial "receiver"—that is, exactly the registers that have been so central to the materialist and semiotic study of the theatre. Moreover, as Kwon's substitution of "place" for "thing" suggests, artists and critics began to offer new kinds of answers to the question of how far an artistic work could engage its situation. Could "place" be made as specific as an object: that is, with its fundamental registers exposed and its inherited barometers, boundaries, and supporting infrastructures reorganized? Those varied answers are at the heart of what it means to produce and to analyze "site-specific art" and "locational identity" from within the field of visual art history.

In giving a history and a vocabulary to the site-specific turn in contemporary art, Kwon recounts some of the familiar Minimalist gestures and public art controversies around works such as Robert Smithson's *Spiral Jetty* and Richard Serra's *Tilted Arc*.[31] At the same time, site-specific art encountered a paradox as artists and curators faced new questions about what exactly "the material context" contained and whether implicit conceptual boundaries had existed within those early boundary-breaking calls. Moving beyond Judd and Serra to consider artists such as Michael Asher, Marcel Broodtheaers, Daniel Buren, Hans Haacke, and Andrea Fraser, Kwon analyzes a mode of practice that began to engage not only the phenomenological registers of the art object and the gallery walls but also the social and institutional forces that shaped the space of presentation. Repeating what is now a familiar art historiographical move "from Minimalism to institutional critique," she considers how Mel Bochner's *Measurement Room*, Hans Haacke's *Unfinished Business* and Andrea Fraser's *Museum Highlights* pushed the Minimalist envelope, extending its engagement with situation beyond the *materials* of the artistic environment to the *materialist* processes of the artistic institution. While Judd had celebrated the many possible "relations" of "three-dimensional work" to "the wall, floor, ceiling, room, rooms or exterior," institutional critique began to push the concept of site to ever new "exteriors," considering not just the walls and the ceilings but the institutions, funding structures, real estate deals, and construction contracts that built the walls in the first place. As a result, minimalism's phenomenological reaction to medium purity began retroactively to look "pure" itself.

CONVERGENCES

Each of the theatrical and art historical trajectories tracked thus far includes a persistent interest in the material sitedness of the art work. At the same time, in each of these trajectories the parameters for dividing or imploding divisions between art and site shift historically amid debates and confusions about what elements constitute a "site" and where divisions between intrinsic texts and extrinsic engagement lie. Much as theatrical historians have made assumptions about whether the production of drama was intrinsic or extrinsic to the dramatic text, so art historians have made assumptions about the diegetic or extradiegetic status of a painting's canvas, its paint, and its wall. Moreover, spatial boundaries have changed with different sensibilities and innovations. The wall is the beginning of "context" from one vantage point but is incorporated into the artwork from another. The "performance" is part of "conditions of production" from one vantage point but is incorporated into the concept of "text" from another. Additionally, every situating gesture has met different critical resistances from those who object to deautonomizing methods in both art and criticism, whether in Croce's and Spingarn's critical avoidance of stage architecture, audiences, and printing presses or in Greenberg's and Fried's scandalized reaction to finding themselves "in a situation," that is, amid artworks "where *everything counts*."[32]

As much as variations in contents and boundaries of site change within discrete art histories, it is my sense that those variations become more ubiquitous and differently defamiliarizing when we begin to combine the formal and analytic habits of more than one field into the interdisciplinary pursuit of performance historiography. An implicit question arises: how much does a given work understand itself to be site-specific versus how much site-specificity is something a critic finds in it? In other words, for whom is "space" a form of *a priori* knowledge and for whom is it something to use? Moreover, how do the parameters of space extend and retract for differently positioned artists and scholars? For Knowles, the language of materiality and site-specificity emerges most often to describe the work of the scholar who assembles information around various registers of textuality, production, and reception to understand the total theatrical event, often deploying such registers to offer interpretations that theatre-makers had not always anticipated themselves. In Kwon's world, the language of materiality and site-specificity most often describes the goals of artists who consciously try to reorient their work away from the framed painting or pedestaled sculpture and into the extended environment of production and reception. Along the way, artists encounter elements of the situation that they might not have anticipated—and Kwon goes on to analyze institutional and community experiments where such surprises occurred—but the artistic impulse toward situated engagement is one that the artwork seeks to create, construing heretofore contextual elements of a site into the art itself. Indeed, it is in this kind of site-specific work that we see a contemporaneous artistic version of the new historicist trope, an ever expanding attempt to recast context as text and to unsettle any desire to re-institute the boundary between them.

We would be completely misguided if we did not notice that certain theatrical artists also actively seek situated engagement, understanding situatedness to be the material of their work and not only the materialism that a theatre scholar finds in it. Brechtian techniques of alienation clearly extended the boundaries of the theatrical situation, as did, in different ways, movements in environmental, feminist, protest, and community theatre. What becomes interesting to me, then, is how we bring the formal vocabulary for understanding site-specificity in visual art history into conversation with theatrical history and a performance historiography. What can we learn from each other's preoccupations with site? And how might each one's analytic habits and medium-specific knowledges embolden the other as well as foreground the medium-specificity of the spatial concepts we deploy? Does the "street" in street theatre have a different valence if we think about it through the lens of a site-specific artist? Does the body in theatre resonate differently when we think about it as a material akin to clay, wire, or oil paint? Conversely, does the post-Minimalist preoccupation with the receiver get a more sustained kind of attention if joined to theatrical scholarship on the role of audiences? Does the current curatorial habit of letting artists create not only displayed artworks but also engagements in the lobbies, shops, cafés, and promotional material of the museum look different to a theatre historian who specializes in the analysis of "amenities"?

In many ways, a number of scholars and historians have been posing different versions of similar questions, whether or not a cross-disciplinary conversation between theatre and the visual arts was explicitly engaged. Nick Kaye's work on site-specific art tracks a Minimalist genealogy from the visual arts in order to contextualize different kinds of environmental theatre, building on the work of Henry Sayre and Jon Erickson.[33] Scholars of live art, ranging from Adrian Heathfield to Amelia Jones to Rebecca Schneider to Jane Blocker, have approached the body of the performer as a material, an approach that differs significantly from a theatre historian's approach to "actor training." At the same time, we might wonder about forms of rapprochement that have yet to occur explicitly: say, a conversation on *place* between New York art historian Rosalyn Deutsche's *Evictions* and New York theatre scholar Marvin Carlson's *Places of Performance* or another conversation that might join Patrice Pavis's *mise en scène* to Nicolas Bourriaud's *esthétique relational*.[34]

To focus this wider, defamiliarizing cross-disciplinary conversation, I would like to return to the opening of this essay. What does it mean to place Mierle Laderman Ukeles and her maintenance art next to a troupe like the Wooster Group and its *House/Lights*? As it happens, Kwon includes Ukeles in her disquisition on institutional critique, and in fact her decision to do so shows how earlier feminist reactions to Minimalism give the history of institutional critique a distinctly politicized genesis. Ukeles's maintenance performances actually accompanied photographic exhibitions of her maintenance art as a wife and mother at home, framing documentation of her dressing children, washing diapers, and cleaning the house as a brand of devalued everyday art. The Washing Track series showed the reliance of not only the household but also the institution of the museum on daily forms of gendered, classed, and raced labor. Ukeles thus acted as an institutional critic of the museum, exposing the labor required to keep the walls of the gallery white and its stone steps clean. As Kwon argues, "she forced the menial domestic tasks usually associated with women—cleaning, washing, dusting, and tidying—to the level of aesthetic contemplation."[35] In the language of theatre historiography, Ukeles moved "working conditions" into the territory of the *mise en scène*.

What is interesting, then, is how Kwon goes on to analyze the significance of work such as Ukeles's within her larger attempt to give a vocabulary and specific history to the changing orientation of site-specific art, an argument that is worth quoting at length:

> [T]he site of art begins to diverge from the literal space of art, and the physical condition of a specific location recedes as the primary element in the conception of a site . . . it is rather the *techniques* and *effects* of

> the art institution as they circumscribe and delimit the definition, production, presentation, and dissemination of art that become the sites of critical intervention. Concurrent with this move toward the dematerialization of the site is the simultaneous deaestheticization (that is, withdrawal of visual pleasure) and dematerialization of the art work. Going against the grain of institutional habits and desires, and continuing to resist the commodification of art in/for the marketplace, site-specific art adopts strategies that are either aggressively anti-visual—informational, textual, expositional, didactic—or immaterial altogether—gestures, events or performances bracketed by temporal boundaries. . . . In this context, the guarantee of a specific relationship between an art work and its site is not based on a physical permanence of that relationship (as demanded by Serra, for example) but rather on the recognition of its unfixed *impermanence*, to be experienced as an unrepeatable and fleeting situation.[36]

First, as we move here from a discrete notion of a *work* of art to a process-based notion of the *work* it takes to make art, I find it interesting to think about Ukeles and this analysis in relation to the triangulated frameworks of theatre historiography. In many ways, Ukeles seems to be exposing the "conditions of production" for visual art. She trains the attention of the receiver away from the framed canvas or the Minimalist block in the center toward the institutional processes and material conditions required to maintain the walls and floors that support them. As much as the attempt to expose production resonates with what we might call Brechtian techniques of theatre-making, this performance also confounds theatrical conventions for delineating its object. First of all, such site-specific performance does not usually uphold the divisions of labor we find in the theatre; principles that would divide actor from director from designer erode in the face of work where spatial design, conception, and performed execution are credited to a single artistic intelligence. Furthermore, Ukeles's performance is in some ways less easily located on the "performance text" portion of theatre historiography's analytic triangle. As someone trained as a sculptor and craftsperson, Ukeles's turn to performance was an extra-diegetic move away from sculpture's diegetic form; the movements and motions of performance were very explicitly the vehicle for enabling her "contextual turn." In other words, what might look like a "performance text" to a performance critic was in fact an attempt to unhinge the "text" corner of the analytic triangle, perhaps to unhinge the semiotic logic of any triangle that would imagine even a fragile boundary separating performance text, production, and reception. It seems to me quite significant that performance is understood here less as its own medium or text and more as a vehicle for exposing visual art's conditions of production and reception.

This kind of framing also informs Kwon's language of "dematerialization," a term that became ubiquitous in visual art history in conjunction with post-Minimalist art movements. Used early on by art critics Lucy Lippard Chandler and John Chandler, the language of "dematerialization" has been used subsequently to mark the movement of artistic preoccupation away from discrete objects and toward situations and processes.[37] Kwon's disquisition on the dematerialization of site in turn invokes the language of ephemerality and impermanence, reminding us of the art historical genealogies that support Peggy Phelan's theorizing of performance's ontological ephemerality.[38] At the same time, I think it is important to ask: to whom does Ukeles's crouching, squeezing, and scrubbing appear "dematerialized"? By what logic is this "gesture" and its institutional critique "immaterial"? This seems to me an important place to notice the medium-specific knowledge that supports an analysis, for it is by measuring this performance's distance from painting and sculpture that its processes come to appear "antivisual" and receive the label "dematerialized." To another kind of theatrical eye accustomed to the durational and gestural language of stylized theatre, the everyday tasks of washing might look hypermaterial; they might be read as an explicitly concrete enactment when measured within and against a theatrical medium that happens to think of durationality and embodied gesture as essential materials.

The theatrical eye might also offer a different take on performance's role in enabling a contextual engagement. I cannot help but wonder whether Ukeles, while breaking with the medium purity and formal integrity of painting and sculpture, found herself reckoning with the conventions and skills required of another medium—a theatrical one. She may not ever have had "actor training," but did she nonetheless find herself cultivating some attributes of the "actor's body"? Did she develop a performing persona (or try not to)? Did she participate in bodily training, stretching, and breathing to sustain her endurance? Did she cultivate reflexive skills for managing her own reactions to audience involvement? In other words, by resisting the modernist definitions of the medium she inherited, Ukeles might well have found herself adopting the medium-specific definitions of a new one. The extrinsic engagement of visual art needed the intrinsic elements of theatrical performance.

 Having reengaged Ukeles and Kwon through a theatrical lens, what happens when we try to reverse the lens to consider how visual art history might engage materialist theatre historiography? One of the most intriguing examples of materialist semiotics in action occurs in Knowles's analysis of the text, production, and reception of The Wooster Group's *House/Lights*. Starting off with "an unlocated, formalist reading," we learn that *House/Lights* places a 1964 cult lesbian bondage flick, *Olga's House of Shame*, into "productive contact" with Gertrude Stein's *Doctor Faustus Lights the Lights*, mixed together with filtered voices, bodily prosthetics, and sound and video bites drawn from *I Love Lucy*, *Young Frankenstein*, Esther Williams, Yiddish theatre, classical ballet, and Cantonese Opera.[39] Such a mix of disparate references is characteristic of The Wooster Group's oeuvre and one of the central reasons it was dubbed "a postmodern theatre company" by both scholars and journalists. That attribution, however, becomes somewhat troubled through the course of Knowles's analysis, beginning with his interest in the importance of "landscape" both to Gertrude Stein and to The Wooster Group's compositional aesthetic. He quotes Elinor Fuchs's sense of The Wooster Group's landscape-based creations of "the multi-focal scene" as well as her argument that "landscape to Stein was wholly present to itself, simple and un-anxiety-provoking to the spectator."[40]

Significantly, this inherited sense of landscape offers its own kind of hermetic encounter, creating, in Peter Sellars's words, "a classical repose . . . beneath the busy surface level." Whether appearing in pastoral depictions of the natural or later in Steinian and Wooster Group creations of a busier but wholly present encounter, the impulses toward landscape are in fact not to be confused with the impulses toward site-specificity. Indeed, the refusal of the referential and material contingencies of the world outside the depiction is part of its signature. When Kate Valk acknowledges that the Stein "landscape is as abstract as the landscapes we make," she provides Knowles with a justification for attributing the modernist label to the Wooster Group; "it is the very abstraction of Stein's landscapes—their lack of social referent—that made her work recruitable for high-modernist formalism."[41] What might appear to be postmodern *multi*-referentiality turns out to be modernist *a*referentiality instead. Here is a place where different concepts of space collide, paradoxically, where the classically antidurational, all-at-once encounter of visual art appears in a theatre space that seeks not to engage the "situatedness" of theatre's extended hypercontextuality. Despite the shared use of a spatial metaphor, to create a landscape is not to engage a social situation. Within this frame, the Wooster Group's *House/Lights* has far less kinship with the site-specific performances of Mierle Laderman Ukeles and far more kinship with the wholly present encounters and internally critical ambitions of modernist painting.

Once we begin to think of The Wooster Group's work within the formalist, asocial, wholly "present" discourse of modernist painting, the intervention of Knowles's materialist analysis of the group is brought into higher relief. In interviews, Elizabeth Le Compte and Kate Valk resist the idea that there is anything iconically "American" about their work, even as it is marketed as the quintessential example of an American avant-garde in the publicity for all their tours. In reacting to the referential readings that some give to their work, Le Compte firmly recircumscribes its parameters, saying that it is a theatre made only from "who we were in the room."[42] "They replied that they didn't think of themselves as having . . . even a New York orientation, but thought of themselves as quite specifically located in Manhattan, and more particularly lower Manhattan."[43] That lower Manhattan is, of course, specifically SoHo (South of Houston), a "location" that is most notable for transforming from an artists' community to a high-end district of expensive lofts and boutiques. Analyzing SoHo tourist guides, Knowles finds that such "amenities" also claim The Wooster Group as part of the SoHo location, advertising the group's experimental cult-status as part and parcel of its tourist appeal.[44] Here is a materialist framing of The Wooster Group unanticipated by the group itself, oriented from the people "in the room" to new "exteriors" that suggest their enmeshment within an expanded site of economic and real estate development. The noncontingent, *a priori* understanding of the Wooster Group space becomes highly contingent, fettered by an extension of its spatial parameters. The cheekiness of Knowles's analysis lies in his decision to locate a theatre company that seeks not to be locatable.

LOCATING LOCATION

Throughout this essay, I have tried to highlight the disciplinarity and medium-specificity of what space can mean for performance historiography. As performance historiographers draw from methods in a variety of disciplines, our cross-disciplinary engagements and medium-impure experiments might be more medium-specific than we realize. The forms that we find ourselves historicizing are embedded in medium-specific genealogies that differ not only in "content" but also in form. Such differences in form affect how we understand the parameters of words such as "space," "site," and "location," fretted as such terms are with implicit assumptions about what is interior and exterior to an art object. In the end, a located historiography in performance means coming to terms with different ways of locating location. It means contending with the degree to which an analysis of materials might differ from a materialist analysis. It means contending with the degree to which the situated art event may or may not seek to engage its context. It means thinking about the degree to which certain projects refuse a boundary between art and situation and the degree to which others adamantly seek to uphold it. It also means deciding on our role as scholars of such practices and what conceptual boundaries and frames we bring with us when we analyze. It means deciding whether we understand the materialist critic's job to lie in locating another context unanticipated by the contextualist gesture, another exterior to even the most externally engaged art or performance practice. It means tracking the vacillation of spatial concepts among different registers of historiographical understanding—as object or as tool, as *a priori* knowledge that precedes experience or as *a posteriori* knowledge that derives from it. Meanwhile the ways we conceive background and foreground, art and apparatus, text and context, and inside and outside vary with medium-specific histories and disciplinary locations. If, as Michael Fried said, contending with theatricality means contending with forms where "everything counts," a locational historiography of performance requires vigilance about how we interpret, categorize, and sometimes implicitly circumscribe that "everything."

NOTES

1. Thomas Postlewait and Bruce A. McConachie, *Interpreting the Theatrical Past: Essays in the Historiography of Performance* (Iowa City: University of Iowa Press, 1989).

2. Shannon Jackson, *Professing Performance: Theatre in the Academy from Philology to Performativity*, Theatre and Performance Theory (Cambridge/New York: Cambridge University Press, 2004).

3. Ric Knowles, *Reading the Material Theatre* (Cambridge: Cambridge University Press, 2004); Miwon Kwon, *One Place after Another: Site-Specific Art and Locational Identity* (Cambridge, Mass.: MIT Press, 2002).

4. Louis O. Mink, *Historical Understanding*, ed. Brian Fay, Eugene O. Golob, and Richard T. Vann (Ithaca: Cornell University Press, 1987), p. 205.

5. Donna Haraway, "Situated Knowledges: The Science Question in Feminism and the Privilege of Partial Perspective," in *Simians, Cyborgs and Women: The Reinvention of Nature* (New York: Routledge, 1991), pp. 183–202.

6. Brander Matthews, *The Development of the Drama* (New York: C. Scribner's Sons, 1903).

7. Shelley Arlen, ed., *The Cambridge Ritualists: An Annotated Bibliography of the Works by and about Jane Ellen Harrison, Gilbert Murray, Francis M. Cornford, and Arthur Bernard Cook* (Metuchen, N.J.: Scarecrow Press, 1990).

8. See, for instance, E. K. Chambers, *The Medieval Stage* (London: Oxford University Press, 1903); Richard Southern, *The Medieval Theatre in the Round: A Study of the Staging of the Castle of Perseverance and Related Matters*, 2nd ed. (London: Faber, 1975); Richard Beadle, ed., *The Cambridge Companion to Medieval English Theatre* (Cambridge/New York: Cambridge University Press, 1994); A. M. Nagler, *Theatre Festivals of the Medici, 1539–1637*, trans. George Hickenlooper (New Haven: Yale University Press, 1964); Ronald W. Vince, *Renaissance Theatre: A Historiographical Handbook* (Westport, Conn.: Greenwood Press, 1984).

9. Wisner Payne Kinne, *George Pierce Baker and the American Theatre* (Cambridge, Mass.: Harvard University Press, 1954); Susan Harris Smith, *American Drama: The Bastard Art* (Cambridge/New York: Cambridge University Press, 1997); Jackson, *Professing Performance*, pp. 40–78.

10. Benedetto Croce, *Guide to Aesthetics/Breviario Di Estetica* (South Bend, Ind.: Regnery/Gateway, 1979); Benedetto Croce, Remo Bodei, and Hiroko Fudemoto, *Breviary of Aesthetics: Four Lectures* (Toronto/Buffalo: University of Toronto Press, 2007); Joel Elias Spingarn, *Creative Criticism and Other Essays* (New York: Harcourt Brace and Company, 1931), p. 31; noted also in Marvin A. Carlson, *Theories of the Theatre: A Historical and Critical Survey from the Greeks to the Present*, expanded ed. (Ithaca: Cornell University Press, 1993), p. 312.

11. Knowles, *Reading the Material Theatre*, p. 11.

12. Ibid., p. 12. See Keir Elam, *The Semiotics of Theatre and Drama* (London/New York: Methuen, 1980); Patrice Pavis, *Languages of the Stage: Essays in the Semiology of the Theatre* (New York: Performing Arts Journal Publications, 1982); Marco de Marinis, *The Semiotics of Performance* (Bloomington: Indiana University Press, 1993); Michael Quinn, *The Semiotic Stage: Prague School Theatre Theory* (New York: Peter Lang, 1995); André Helbo, *Les mots et les gestes* (Lille: Presses Universitaires de Lille, 1983); Marvin A. Carlson, *Theatre Semiotics: Signs of Life* (Bloomington: Indiana University Press, 1992); and Erika Fischer-Lichte, *Semiotics of Theater* (Bloomington: Indiana University Press, 1992).

13. Stephen Greenblatt and Giles B. Gunn, *Redrawing the Boundaries: The Transformation of English and American Literary Studies* (New York: Modern Language Association of America, 1992), p. 4.

14. Jeffrey Masten, Peter Stallybrass, and Nancy Vickers, *Language Machines: Technologies of Literary and Cultural Production*, Essays from the English Institute (New York: Routledge, 1997); Jeffrey Masten, *Textual Intercourse: Collaboration, Authorship, and Sexualities in Renaissance Drama* (Cambridge/New York: Cambridge University Press, 1997); Meredith L. McGill, *American Literature and the Culture of Reprinting, 1834–1853* (Philadelphia: University of Pennsylvania Press, 2003).

15. Stuart Hall, "Encoding, Decoding," in *The Cultural Studies Reader*, ed. Simon During (New York: Routledge, 1999), pp. 507–517.

16. Knowles, *Reading the Material Theatre*, p. 19.

17. Jonathan Dollimore and Alan Sinfield, *Political Shakespeare: New Essays in Cultural Materialism* (Manchester: Manchester University Press, 1985), p. ix; quoted in Knowles, *Reading the Material Theatre*, p. 12 (bracketed phrase added by Knowles).

18. Knowles, p. ix.

19. Ibid.

20. Ibid., p. 12.

21. Kwon, *One Place after Another*, p. 1.

22. Ibid., p. 2.

23. See, for instance, Hal Foster, *The Return of the Real: The Avant-Garde at the End of the Century* (Cambridge, Mass.: MIT Press, 1996); Rosalind E. Krauss and Marcel Broodthaers, *A Voyage on the North Sea: Art in the Age of the Post-Medium Condition* (New York: Thames and Hudson, 2000); T. J. Clark, *Farewell to an Idea: Episodes from a History of Modernism* (New Haven: Yale University Press, 1999); B. H. D. Buchloh, *Neo-Avant-Garde and Culture Industry: Essays on European and American Art from 1955 to 1975* (Cambridge, Mass.: MIT Press, 2000); Amelia Jones, *Body Art/Performing the Subject* (Minneapolis/London: University of Minnesota Press, 1998); Jane Blocker, *What the Body Cost: Desire, History, and Performance* (Minneapolis: University of Minnesota Press, 2004); Rebecca Schneider, *The Explicit Body in Performance* (London/New York: Routledge, 1997); Adrian Heathfield, ed., *Live: Art and Performance* (New York: Tate Publishing, 2004).

24. Donald Judd, "Specific Objects," in *Donald Judd: Complete Writings, 1959–1975* (Halifax: Press of the Nova Scotia College of Art and Design, in association with New York University Press, 1975), pp. 181–182.

25. Ibid., p. 184.

26. Ibid., pp. 183–184.

27. Gotthold Ephraim Lessing, *Laocoon: An Essay upon the Limits of Painting and Poetry* (New York: Noonday Press, 1957); Joshua Reynolds, *Discourses on Art* (New Haven: Published for the Paul Mellon Centre for Studies in British Art [London] Ltd. by Yale University Press, 1975).

28. Clement Greenberg, "Modernist Painting," in *The New Art: A Critical Anthology*, ed. Gregory Battcock (New York: E. P. Dutton and Co., 1973), pp. 68–69.

29. Michael Fried, "Three American Painters, Kenneth Noland, Jules Olitski, Frank Stella: Fogg Art Museum, 21 April–30 May 1965," in *Art and Objecthood: Essays and Reviews* (University of Chicago Press, 1998), p. 215.

30. Michael Fried, "Art and Objecthood," *Artforum* 5 (1967): 153 (emphases in original).

31. Kwon, *One Place after Another*, p. 12.

32. Fried, "Art and Objecthood," p. 53 (emphasis in original)

33. Nick Kaye, *Site-Specific Art: Performance, Place, and Documentation* (London/New York: Routledge, 2000); Henry M. Sayre, *The Object of Performance: The American Avant-Garde since 1970* (Chicago: University of Chicago Press, 1989); Jon Erickson, *The Fate of the Object: From Modern Object to Postmodern Sign in Performance, Art, and Poetry* (Ann Arbor: University of Michigan Press, 1995).

34. Rosalyn Deutsche, *Evictions: Art and Spatial Politics* (Chicago/Cambridge, Mass./

London: Graham Foundation for Advanced Studies in the Fine Arts/MIT Press, 1996); Patrice Pavis, *La mise en scène contemporaine: Origines, tendances, perspectives* (Paris: A. Colin, 2007); Nicolas Bourriaud, *Esthétique relationnelle* (Dijon: Presses du Réel, 1998).

35. Kwon, *One Place after Another*, p. 23.

36. Ibid., pp. 19–24 (emphases in original).

37. John Chandler and Lucy Lippard Chandler, "The Dematerialization of Art," *Art International* (February 20, 1968): 31–36.

38. Peggy Phelan, *Unmarked: The Politics of Performance* (London/New York: Routledge, 1996).

39. Knowles, *Reading the Material Theatre*, pp. 148–149.

40. Ibid., pp. 152–153; quoting Elinor Fuchs, "Another Version of Pastoral," in *The Death of Character: Perspectives on Theater after Modernism* (Bloomington: Indiana University Press, 1996), pp. 92, 95.

41. Knowles, *Reading the Material Theatre*, pp. 149 (quoting Sellars), 152 (quoting Valk).

42. Robert Coe, "Making Two Lives and a Trilogy," *Village Voice*, December 11, 1978; quoted in ibid., p. 155.

43. Ibid., p. 159.

44. Ibid., p. 155.

4 Identity

CATHERINE M. COLE

History's Thresholds Stories from Africa

"Who are you? And why are you here?" I have been asked these questions often in my research, far more often, I assume, than if I had chosen to study Broadway musicals, Restoration playhouses, international arts festivals, Shakespeare's dramaturgy, or archaeological remains of ancient Greek theatres. I have conducted historical research for over two decades in both Ghana and South Africa—two very different regions of a continent that is three times the size of the United States and is home to one-third of the world's living languages. I am a woman of mixed European heritage (Scottish, English, German), born in Detroit at the tail end of the baby boom, and my family has lived in the United States for many generations. But in Ghana in the mid-1990s I usually answered these questions by saying simply that I was a student from America or *aburokyir* (overseas) who had come to research my doctoral dissertation. That seemed to satisfy most inquirers. In South Africa seven years later I received the same questions, to which I responded with a slight variation: I was a professor from America writing a book on the Truth and Reconciliation Commission (TRC). But rarely are declarations of identity static. Being an American in 1995 was not the same as in 2002. Bill Clinton's America was not George W. Bush's, and the difference between these presidents was not lost on my African interlocutors.

"Who are you?" is a question about identity. But what is identity? It is an elusive concept fraught with contradictions. To name but one, identity is simultaneously about sameness and difference. The *Oxford English Dictionary* (*OED*) first defines identity as "the quality or condition of being the same in substance, composition, nature, properties, or in particular qualities under consideration; absolute or essential sameness; oneness."[1] Yet the next definition privileges individuality over commonality, difference over sameness: identity is "the condition or fact that a person or thing is itself and not something else; individuality, personality." Thus identity is simultaneously about sameness and difference. We know our sameness only by knowing our differences.

Another contradiction is that identity is both fixed and changing. The *OED* first posits that identity is static: "The sameness of a person or thing at all times or in all circumstances." So much for Clinton's versus Bush's

America: an American is an American. Yet the dictionary's ninth entry throws a spanner in the works. Titled simply "S. Afr.," this parsing, unlike the other nine entries on identity, has no explanation at all but guides the reader to an example: Edgar Harry Brookes's 1924 publication *The History of Native Policy in South Africa*: "Most modern thinkers on the Native question argue as if there were no *via media* between the principle which refuses to acknowledge any real difference between Europeans and Natives, the policy of identity as we may call it, . . . and the principle which insists on the subordinate position of the Native in the body politic, the policy of subordination."[2] In other words, "identity" was a policy rather than a substance, composition, or nature in South Africa in 1924, a policy that supported the inherent sameness of Europeans and Africans (or Natives, to use the historically appropriate nomenclature). Opposing the policy of identity was subordination, which held that Natives and Europeans were not only different from each other in kind but also in value, power, and esteem within the body politic. Between these two positions, Brookes tells us, thinkers of his era could imagine no middle ground, no *via media*. Yet somehow by the 1960s identity had become subordination, inasmuch as the word "identity" became central to the legislated racial segregation and white supremacy known as apartheid. Those formerly called Natives were now categorized and segregated into different tribes, and their identities were inscribed in passbooks which not only announced who the bearers were, but what they could do (where they could travel, work, and live and with whom they could sleep). And Native bearers of identity cards could certainly *not* live, mingle, or sleep with Europeans. The "S. Afr." *OED* entry concludes abruptly, even cryptically: "The earlier British policy of identity broke down." Broke down indeed! As we can see, identity is an inherently unstable concept, even if identity is supposed to be the "sameness of a person or thing at all times or in all circumstances."

A curious feature of the questions "Who are you? And why are you here?" is that I almost always get asked them in this order. Is this succession significant? The first question demands that one identify oneself, and the second solicits a declaration of motive or intent. Should we infer that identity determines motive? Do we need to know identity before we can understand motive? Furthermore, who gets to ask these questions? Who deserves an answer? And who has a right to demand an answer? Which answers are adequate, which are not, and why? These are classic "identity politics" questions of the 1990s. And yet historians have always had to deal with questions of identity, inasmuch as we must discern historical subjects as agents who operated within a particular time and place and within a culture that had overarching and overlapping categories of personhood, be these categories of gender, class, seniority, reproductive status, royalty, vocation, religion, sexuality, race, or nation, to name but a few. And, as we have seen, these categories change over time. The historical record clearly shows that persons once called "Natives" in South Africa were at other times called "Africans." Then they were divided into "Zulu," "Xhosa" and "Ndebele" tribes. After that, Natives decided to define themselves rather than be defined, and they identified as "Black," a terminology that asserted an essential sameness with African Americans and a commonality and solidarity with the Civil Rights Movement in America.

Given the changing terminology and taxonomies of identity over time and space, historians must ask specific and nuanced questions: who was this person within his or her own time? By what salient categories of identity would she have identified herself or been identified by others? Why did this person do the things he did? Who was John Wilkes Booth, and why did he kill Abraham Lincoln—and do it in a theatre, of all places? If we learn more about who Wilkes was, will we gain insight into why he did what he did?

Questions about identity and motive are common among historians. But the usual direction of such questioning is unilateral: the historian asks questions of the past and specifically of archival records about the past. The past does not usually get to ask the historian: "Who are you? And why are you here? Why are you investigating my era? Why are you mucking around in my diaries, correspondence, and tax records?"[3] But when the historian studies past and present in Africa, these questions often get asked. The "S. Afr." *OED* entry about identity is deceiving in its simplicity, for it represents a very large story about the stakes in questions of identity, historiography, and the production of knowledge in and about the African continent in the nineteenth, twentieth, and twenty-first centuries. In the study of African history, we are forced to grapple not just with conventional questions of the identity and motives of historical agents but also with how our access to Africa's past has been and continues to be mediated by colonialism, prejudice, and grossly asymmetrical power relations.

African history, as a field of study, first had to struggle with a Eurocentric denial that Africa had any history at all or that it could be known. Historians of Africa inherit the unfortunate legacy of intellectual forbears such as G. W. F. Hegel, who pronounced in *The Philosophy of History* that Africa has "no historical part of the World; it has no movement or development to exhibit. . . . What we properly understand by Africa, is the Unhistorical, Undeveloped Spirit, still involved in the conditions of mere nature, and which had to be presented here only as on the threshold of the World's History."[4] Even as Europeans perceived Africa as an unhistorical place, a wild, uncultivated world that had not yet achieved civilization but rather stood at its threshold, they were erecting archives in Africa that enshrined certain histories, very particular categories of thought, European teleologies of progress, and presumptions about Africa's backwardness.

Then came Jan Vansina's pioneering work on oral history that rescued African voices and testified to a viable, important, and knowable African past.[5] But Vansina championed oral tradition within what subsequent researchers found to be a narrowly positivist approach and conventional frame.[6] Furthermore, his merging of historical and anthropological methods caused African history to inherit the troubled legacy of ethnography, which had long been the handmaiden of colonialism. Indirect rule relied on colonial agents understanding who the native peoples were and how and why they organized their societies the way they did. European anthropologists asked questions of "local informants" to gain such information, and the very word "informant" conveys an important clue about the utilitarian objectives that often lurked behind the interview. Nevertheless, the use of oral sources became widely accepted among African historians. In 2003 Eric Allina-Pisano said that "over the past decade oral testimony has moved from common to compulsory in the writing of African social history. One would be hard-pressed to find support for a project that examined the past century of African history and did not employ oral historical material. Its use has become a methodological orthodoxy, especially among Africa-based scholars but also in the United States and other countries."[7] Abdullahi A. Ibrahim reminds us, however, that despite the ubiquity of oral sources in African historiography we cannot forget that "the will to know and the will to surveil and administer" were intertwined at the birth of the interview in Africa. Interviews were instruments "for the regulation of data in order to better know and govern the colonized."[8]

Despite these caveats, oral sources liberated historians of Africa to tell a wider range of stories about a greater diversity of historical actors, for they were no longer dependent upon the problematic and limited material held in colonial archives. Some wrote histories "from below," inserting into narratives of the past African voices that had long been excluded, a historiographic turn inspired in part by Subaltern Studies in India.[9] A socialist and materialist history of Africa emerged that enshrined "resistance" and aimed to render Africans as historical figures with agency, even if these agents operated within tightly circumscribed realities of systematic exploitation and asymmetrical power relations. As with European and

American historiography, a gradual shift occurred, from telling history as a story of great men, the rise and fall of empires, and the exploits of war to writing about other people—laborers, women, children, market vendors, miners, the disabled—and a greater range of life experiences, including private lives, subjectivity, and African concepts of personhood.[10] Liberated by postmodernism from an obsession solely with "what really happened," African history then began to encompass rumor, gossip, partial truths, and the productive work of truth claims. Luise White, for instance, looks at how rumor and gossip can be used as primary sources in the writing of African history. What, for instance, can ubiquitous stories of blood, bloodsucking, and vampires reveal about African concerns about colonial power? What can vampire stories say not about colonial worlds but about how the speakers "imagined and saw their world"?[11] In a similar vein, David William Cohen examines the many trajectories of investigation and testimony that arose in the wake of the murder of Kenyan minister of foreign Affairs Robert Ouko in 1990. As is clear from the title of his article "In a Nation of White Cars . . . One White Car, or 'A White Car,' Becomes a Truth," Cohen explores the "power of incomplete and unfinished accounts, the power of intermediate and indeterminate knowledge, and the power not so much of 'a truth' or 'the truth' but of, rather, *a claim to truth*."[12]

My highly compressed survey of African historiography must also include the moment when intersubjectivity entered the field of African history, when the interdependence between the researcher and the researched was acknowledged, the moment when the formerly ignominious first person made its entry into academic prose, just as it has entered mine in this essay. History is ultimately the telling of stories. A pact—explicit or implied—exists between the author and the audience. At the same time there is a pact—acknowledged or denied—between the author and the sources. For researchers who work with oral sources, as many do in Africa, disclosing one's identity and intentions is central to the methodological process. Indeed, it is not possible to get research clearance from Institutional Review Boards[13] without this, and it is likewise difficult to get the cooperation of oral "informants" or "interview partners" without such self-disclosures.

To announce who you are as the researcher and why you are there in Africa (if Africa is not your home or place of birth) is a prerequisite to conducting research. In the rest of this essay, I explore some of the ways that these prerequisites that shaped my research in two different parts of the continent (Ghana and South Africa) in two different decades (the 1990s and the 2000s). I then extend an analysis of the identity of the researcher and the researched to include an analysis of the identity of the archive. Archives too have identities. They are not just passive repositories but can be productively examined as historical actors that exert power and influence. Over time institutions built during one era accumulate within their walls sedimented layers of records, ideologies, testimonies, and epistles generated by previous generations. Archives can exert influence on the research process in ways that may contradict the will of their present-day human custodians, the archivists. The records themselves—their nature, taxonomy, and language—may have their own ways of demanding from researchers very particular answers to the recurring questions that inaugurated this essay.

THE RESEARCHER'S IDENTITY IN QUESTION

The Akan culture of Ghana places a high priority on offering hospitality to strangers. Doors opened to me during my research far more often than they closed. Indeed the only resistance I ever faced was in official government sectors of the society, and usually for bureaucratic reasons. I encountered plenty of other obstacles: broken vehicles, lack of water, intermittent electricity, floods, bouts of malaria and "running stomach," lack of easy communications via cell phone (at the time). Another condition of my research was managing the intricate web of material obligations and expectations with which any person of even modest resources in this country must contend. Ghana has little history of social welfare, and the overall per capita income is extremely low. Yet one sees very few beggars on the street—a testament to the integrity of the social fabric of family, clan, and communal systems of interdependence. By entering this society to conduct research, the researcher is ensnared in that web, like it or not.

Obstacles to research were rarely about my identity, however. Ghanaians are proud of their culture. Most people with whom I dealt seemed to perceive my journey across the world to study their culture as a further confirmation of what they already knew: Ghanaian culture had integrity, complexity, and sophistication and was entirely worthy of scholarly attention, even from those from *aburokyir*. Ghana was formerly a British colony, but its experience of colonization involved relatively few colonial settlers and few of the gross violations seen in other African colonies such as Kenya and South Africa (passbooks and forced removals). My skin color in Ghana led people to associate me in a generally positive way with foreign tourists, nongovernment organization (NGO) workers, missionaries, or the ubiquitous American popular culture rather than negatively with an unresolved colonial past.

Being mistaken for someone spreading the word of God or distributing funds to build new wells could be problematic, but I generally felt that I could divest myself of inaccurate assumptions about my identity, especially as I strove to use and improve my Twi language. Language was the gateway to indigenous ways of operating, networking, and knowing. Akan customs of hospitality have a formulaic and conventional protocol for discerning the purpose of any visitor's arrival. This is *amanneɛ* (custom). Anyone who arrives at a house as a visitor is welcomed and given a seat and a full glass of water. Then the host shakes the visitor's hand, sits down, and says in Twi: "Here everything is quiet. How is the road?" Rather than be so blunt as to ask "Who are you, and why are you here?" Akan protocols demand indirection (*akutia*). *Amanneɛ* greatly facilitated my research in Ghana, as a culturally appropriate and codified way to show up in a town or village, approach almost any stranger, announce my purpose, and be fairly confident that I would receive some level of assistance.

Not until I shifted my research focus to South Africa did questions about the purpose and motivation of my research take on a different tone. When I began a project on the performative aspects of South Africa's Truth and Reconciliation Commission in 2002, my descriptions of the project to South Africans often produced a polite but strained smile, perhaps with a flash of condescension. Or was it skepticism? In either case, an absence of additional follow-up questions and, not uncommonly, an abrupt change of subject were quite typical, especially among whites. Such experiences early in the research process gave me an indication of the cloud of ambivalence that hangs over the TRC in South Africa. While my identity has been a factor in the research, it would be solipsistic to think it determined how people behaved toward me. South Africans' ambivalence about the commission arises from the perceived failures of the commission and/or the government to act on its promises as well as the perpetuation of gross socioeconomic disparities in the new South Africa.[14] Some people believe that the TRC was a deal made between the former apartheid state and the African National Congress, one that benefited those who least deserved it: many perpetrators still live today in freedom and prosperity, while many "victims" continue to live in poverty.

Another factor in the reluctance of South Africans to speak about the TRC, however, was their exasperation with the inundation of American researchers who are both obsessed with South Africa's "miracle" and confident that this miracle was wrought by the TRC. Over the six years when I conducted this research, from 2002 to 2008, the strained smile on the faces of South African interlocutors faded into a stare or even a frown, perhaps followed by questions about my own country's behavior in Iraq or queries about my opinions about President Bush or pointed comments about America's state-sanctioned (and state-denied) gross violations of human rights through torture. Shouldn't we be busy mounting our own rendition of a truth and reconciliation commission?

A curious reversal has occurred in South Africa, especially in relationship to America: whereas white South Africans were the pariahs of the world during the apartheid days—judged more often by their national identity and skin color than by their personal beliefs or actions as they traveled internationally—Americans such as myself are now surrogates in that role. As Joseph Roach has led us to understand, surrogation "rarely if ever succeeds": collective memory works selectively, imaginatively, and perversely.[15] The results are curiously uneven. Consider the following two anecdotes. A white, English-speaking South African actress playing the role of Martha (apparently both onstage and offstage) in a South African revival of *Who's Afraid of Virginia Woolf?* (complete with carefully coached American accents) asked me at a dinner party, "*Why* are you here!! I mean *really?!*" Swirling her tumbler of whisky and ice, she leaned closer: "Why the F#@K are you here??!!" The question was rhetorical, and I demurred and deflected, knowing there was probably no way to win with this woman. (I was clearly no longer in the land of Akan indirection!) My most pointed barb of the evening was to say that many of us in America felt during the Bush years as many white South African liberals did during P. W. Botha's rule: that our country had been hijacked. For Martha, my most salient identity feature was my nationality—not my race, age, gender, profession, or physical condition. During the period between my Ghana and South Africa research projects I had become disabled (a leg amputee due to cancer) and a mother. In Ghana both of these conditions would have shaped perceptions of my identity profoundly. But in South Africa what registered with most people with whom I interacted was either my nationality or my race—identity categories that have historically been of paramount importance to this country.

Yet my second anecdote provides a useful corrective to the first. Earlier in the day before my run-in with Martha I visited the home of a middle-aged black, Xhosa-speaking translator who lives in a modest township outside Grahamstown. I had come to his house to collect transcriptions and translations from an interview we had conducted together with a woman who had testified before the TRC. He wanted to know more about my project and why I had come to South Africa. In the process of answering, I told him about my prior experiences in West Africa. He was keen to know more about Ghana, for such knowledge of other African countries was cut off during the apartheid years. He carefully wrote down some Twi words I taught him, including his "day name" in Akan, "Kwabena." He said that on his next birthday he would publish a notice in the paper using his Ghanaian name. Before I left, he asked permission to pray. He rose, bowed his head, and thanked God for the end of apartheid, because now people from other places in the world can come freely to South Africa and we can learn about one another. The world will be a better place because of such connections, he said. He thanked God for sending me. For this Xhosa man, the notable feature of my identity was neither race nor nationality. Rather my status as a foreigner, a non-South African, was most important, for my arrival was seen as yet another confirmation that apartheid was really over. For decades South Africa had been diplomatically, economically, politically, and psychologically isolated from the African continent and the world, but now his country was open to visitors like me from elsewhere, who brought new knowledge and were keen to learn about South Africa in a reciprocal process of exchange.

Whether I am perceived in South Africa as an unwelcome intruder or a messenger sent by God or in Ghana as a stranger from the "road" to be welcomed, I must routinely explain in the course of my research who I am, what I want, and for what purpose I want to use the information I am seeking. Some people might say that this need to answer basic questions is the plight of any researcher who works on subject matter that is contemporary as opposed to historical. Yet neither my research in Ghana nor my research in South Africa has been contemporary. I have written about performed practices from Africa's past, whether that past is ten or a hundred years ago. In Ghana the inception of the concert party dated back to the first two decades of the twentieth century. I traced the history of the concert party from its beginnings through the early days of independence in the 1960s. In South Africa I studied the country's Truth and Reconciliation Commission, a government-sponsored ritual of state transition set up in the mid-1990s. That commission, which had largely concluded by the end of the 1990s, is already becoming remote in collective memory. My research frequently requires me to declare my identity, articulate my intentions, and prove my integrity not because of the temporal focus of the research (past versus present) but rather because of the politics of the production of knowledge in Africa.

THE IDENTITY OF ARCHIVES

Unexamined assumptions about the superiority of written versus oral sources or the reliability of texts over the vagaries of memory are severely undermined by African historiography. Archives throughout Africa are highly suspect. Their holdings often include papers that were key instruments of oppression and colonization: the authorization of land seizure, records of indentured labor, the active suppression and disparagement of indigenous cultural practices, the invention and distortion of chieftaincies using indirect rule, and legislative control of the distribution and sale of alcohol. As Ann Laura Stoler argues, "Whether the 'archive' should be treated as a set of discursive rules, a utopian project, a depot of documents, a corpus of statements or all of the above is not really the question. Colonial archives were both sites of the imaginary and institutions that fashioned histories as they concealed, revealed and reproduced the power of the state."[16] The foundations of Africa's archives, built on the continent's colonial legacy, remain in place today, even in the so-called postcolonial world. Much of Africa has been free of formal colonization for four decades now, yet the zeitgeist of old orders haunts new regimes. It also haunts research projects and those who conduct them.

A colonial inheritance is perhaps more palpable in South Africa than in any other place on the continent because of both the centuries-long European occupation of this country and its quite recent liberation from apartheid rule. As with many state buildings in South Africa, the National Archives Repository in Pretoria was undergoing renovations in 2005 when I first arrived there hoping to conduct research on South Africa's Truth and Reconciliation Commission. Though uncertain whether I would be able to gain access, I came in person, which is the way I have accomplished much of my research during the past fifteen years: by showing up in person and negotiating my way verbally through embodied, performed, face-to-face interactions with all kinds of people, including archivists, the keepers of texts. I knew that, at the conclusion of the TRC commission's work, the collection had undergone a rocky transfer from the commission's offices in Cape Town to the Department of Justice and finally to the custodianship of the National Archives. In the process thirty-four boxes of sensitive files on chemical and biological warfare went missing, and several lawsuits about access to this archive had already come before the courts.[17]

While I did not know if I would be granted access to TRC records, I was fairly certain I would be able to get access to the National Archive building.

In addition, I hoped to meet in person someone responsible for the collection to whom I might explain my mission and receive a candid assessment of the current state and likely future of the TRC archive. Yet, after a journey of many thousands of miles, I was alarmed to discover at the site of the National Archives not a building but a pile of dirt. Next to this mound was a monolith of stone with small black lettering indicating that this was indeed the location of the "National Archives Repository." A plume of red dust wafted in the air, evidence of the earth-moving equipment toiling in the belly of the work site. The property was flanked on either side by two other government buildings, the Department of Agriculture and Department of Commissions. These buildings were also undergoing renovations, and no one seemed to know anything about the National Archives or where it might have gone. ("What is an archive?" asked one worker.) Only when I entered the work site, scaled open trenches, and ducked under electrical wires temporarily lofted through trees did I discover that the old National Archives building was in fact still there, located at the back of the property and protected by a brick wall and iron gates. As I lifted the caution tape and approached the entrance, I noticed a security guard watching me through a small glass window. I felt like I was a visitor at a prison. And perhaps I was.

Throughout the built environment of Pretoria, the ideology of the previous government is viscerally expressed. Pumla Gobodo-Madikizela, who worked for the TRC, describes Pretoria, the former center of the apartheid state, in this way: "A city filled with too many of apartheid's symbols—the Union building, the seat of apartheid's parliament, the statues of Afrikaner heroes, prison cells, and buildings of torture where many opponents of apartheid, black and white, had died or disappeared or mysteriously committed suicide. Pretoria was the heart and soul of apartheid, and I had no desire to set foot there."[18] Some Pretoria buildings are grand and imposing, others graceless and forbidding. Almost all are inhospitable to the average person. Streets are wide, with many lanes of traffic, and pedestrians are an afterthought. Apartheid was a government of the minority, established to ensure and protect the rights and privileges of that minority at the overwhelming expense of the majority.[19] While South Africa became a nonracial democracy in 1994, the vestiges of the prior regime cannot easily be legislated away. The legacy of the past is literally carved in stone, in the edifices that now house the new government. That legacy is also embedded in long-standing behaviors that constitute the government's repertoire of enactment, the way its civil servants do their jobs.[20] We must remember that part of South Africa's "deal" for transition was an agreement that career civil servants would not be fired. Thus institutions like the National Archives today have many layers of socialization. It is not uncommon to find that all-white, largely Afrikaner senior staff members socialize and greet each other in isolation from the more recently hired black staff. Renovations of the physical and social environment are ongoing and incomplete. The past and present rub shoulders, not always amicably.

The postapartheid legislation that is supposed to ensure open access to information like the TRC archive is the "Promotion of Access to Information Unit," administered by the Department of Justice (DOJ). While it would seem logical that the DOJ would be prepared to receive and process requests for access to the TRC archive, the individual in this unit to whom I was directed by the TRC's own website thought otherwise: "Kindly take note," I was told through an e-mail before I ever went to the archives in person, "that the TRC is no longer in operation and there is no committee which is in existence at this stage. Therefore, we are unable to assist you with your query. However, you may contact . . . the National Archives of South Africa."[21] Yet inquiries to the National Archive prompted the following reply: "The Truth and Reconciliation Commission records are housed at the National Archives of South Africa. The Department of Justice however is the owner of the records and all requests for access must be directed to them."[22]

Well-honed bureaucratic methods of obstruction have developed: no one ever says "no" to the request. Instead the petitioner is worn down with endless deferrals, delays, circularity, and red tape. This experience evokes South Africa's past. The thousands of TRC testimonies heard before the Human Rights Violation committee clearly reveal how individuals living under apartheid faced an impenetrable thicket of bureaucracy, systematic lethargy, and outright incompetence masquerading as invocations of procedure when trying to find out information about missing relatives or missing papers. Likewise, in my years of research on the truth commission in the "new" South Africa, it was abundantly clear that a sort of administrative zeitgeist from the old order still pervades the new one.

Throughout its tenure, the TRC upheld the premise that a new human rights culture could only be built on a foundation of truth, transparency, and freedom of information. Censorship is entirely contrary to the goals of the commission, an enterprise that privileged the production of information over the administration of justice.[23] So why is the TRC's archive now locked away in the "new" South Africa? As with anything in South Africa, the answer is complex. Shortly after the TRC finished its work, public access to its archive was challenged by lawsuits claiming that the information revealed about some of the persons named in nonpublic statements was too sensitive to be revealed. Subsequent legal decisions, however, affirmed that the TRC archive should be open. Yet in practice it is not. We know that the files were moved at the conclusion of the TRC from its headquarters in Cape Town to the National Archives. The staff there has been instructed to refer all requests for information to the Department of Justice, which retains control over access to TRC information. The person at the Department of Justice to whom I was first directed never responded to my inquiries over three years. I tried to work through other DOJ representatives but got nowhere. I then began contacting other researchers of the TRC to see if any had been successful either in submitting a request to the Department of Justice or in gaining access. So far I have met no researchers other than those who work for the Department of Justice who have successfully gained access to the classified portions of the archive, which are in fact the vast majority of it.

In 2006 the TRC archive was the subject of a lawsuit brought against the Department of Justice by the South African History Archive on behalf of the filmmaker David Forbes. He was making a documentary about the well-known Cradock Four community leaders, who were murdered by the state during the apartheid era.[24] The Pretoria High Court ruled in 2006 that Forbes could get access to the relevant files for thirty days. But the story did not end there. Nomonde Calata, the wife of Cradock Four member Fort Calata and a participant in the suit, received a phone call from her local municipality in Cradock saying that "some people" from Pretoria wanted to see her about her request. Calata agreed to a meeting the next day, for she assumed the officials would need time to fly to Cradock from Pretoria. Much to her surprise, several men in suits emerged from state-issued vehicles not twenty minutes later and descended on her house.[25] "Are you Mrs. Calata? Can we see you privately?" She took them into her living room, where they explained that the TRC files that David Forbes had requested, contained some "sensitive information." They asked her, "Do you want to see these files?" They took out a "bunch of bags" and opened them. "Do you want to see the files?" they repeated. Calata recalled during our interview:

> At that moment I was not ready to see the files. I don't know, when will I be able to be ready to see those files, because what I think, whatever is in those files, I don't want to see it. I want to remember my husband as I know him. Because I heard at the inquest about how he was beaten by dogs, his fingers were off, his tongue was pulled, his hair was pulled.

> I don't . . . I don't want to see those things. OK, I heard it. But I don't want to *see* it. Because I only want to remember my husband the way he was. So these people made me to sign affidavits and things like that.

Pressured, intimidated, and emotionally manipulated, Calata signed an affidavit that the men had already prepared, rescinding her request on behalf of Forbes to see the TRC files. She had wanted the information there to be given to Forbes because she believed his documentary was "a good thing, it's for the community." But as a traumatized widow she could not bear to look at what the files held. In our interview Calata said she most feared the likelihood of viewing graphic, gruesome images of her husband after he had been tortured. She would derive no benefit from having these images seared into her thoughts, eclipsing happier memories of Fort Calata as a robust, healthy young man. The experience of having government officials suddenly descend on her home was haunting, reminiscent of the old apartheid state. Home invasions were a routine part of her married life with Fort:

> The way they came here, it really reminded me of the old days when the Security Branch used to come to my house, you know, coming into your house without expecting them to come to your house, because I thought maybe the lady from the municipality phoned—neh?—and maybe they are going to phone and confirm time, and ask me when am I going to be ready to see them so that I can prepare myself to see them. I didn't know that they are going to instruct the people from the municipality to phone me and all of a sudden, here they come. You know? And it shocked me in this . . . in this new era that people are still acting in that same way. I was surprised.

In this new era, Calata says, people are still acting in the same old ways, but are they the same people? Are the racial dynamics of this encounter, for instance, the same as under apartheid? Calata is colored, which in South African parlance means "mixed race," an identity that resides uncomfortably between the polar extremes of black and white that apartheid created. Tensions between coloreds and blacks are still prevalent in new South Africa. Yet Calata's bona fides in the antiapartheid struggle are well established through the prominence of the Cradock Four and the profound and traumatic loss she sustained during the struggle years. As for the state officials who arrived at her door in both the old and the new South Africa, they were multiracial. Apartheid needed a racially and ethnically diverse security force in order to enforce white control over an overwhelmingly black population that spoke many different languages. The extent of black involvement in apartheid police work was made abundantly clear in the racial demographics of those who sought amnesty through the TRC, with blacks being the vast majority. As for the "new" South Africa, multiracial staffing of the government is a mandate. But was racial identity a dominant theme in Calata's recent brush with security forces? These are valid questions, but they are beyond my focus here, which is instead the nature of the interrogative exchange: "Do you want to see these files?" What lies behind such questions posed by the owners of the archive to this woman whose dead husband is represented in that archive?

After the state officials left her house, Calata consulted with family members and lawyers and eventually completed a second affidavit granting David Forbes the right to see the TRC files relevant to her husband's case. Yet the episode dramatizes how fraught the content of the TRC archive remains, even when derived from cases that were highly publicized and had open hearings. In the new (as in the old) South Africa even the victims and prominent witnesses who appeared and gave oral testimony before the TRC cannot look at their own records.

How do we understand South Africa's current ambivalence and suppression of information about a process that was intended to promote transparency, democracy, and respect for human rights? It is not entirely clearly why the archive that the TRC created has become inaccessible. Some attribute the sorry state of the TRC record to incompetence. The Department of Justice has neither sufficient resources nor adequately trained staff to determine which information in the archive would be considered too sensitive to release. It is easier to say no to all requests than to grant selective access. Others claim that withholding access to the TRC archive protects these records for use in potential future prosecution. After all, those perpetrators of past human rights violations who did not gain amnesty through the TRC process are now potentially subject to prosecution. The TRC's investigative evidence may be more admissible in court if access to it now is highly controlled. But Nomonde Calata's story perhaps reveals some other elements at work: it suggests that the stakes are extremely high in the issue of right of access to this archive. Her case was a high-profile one; should she gain access to her files, this would set a precedent. Some parties are clearly quite apprehensive about what this precedent might unleash.

I read the refusals to grant access to the TRC archive as part of the commission's and the country's repertoire, to use Diana Taylor's term. "Repertoire" refers to how "people participate in the production and reproduction of knowledge by 'being there,' being part [or not part] of the transmission."[26] Archives are themselves part of that repertoire, and the identity and motives of the archive change over time, as for all historical actors. Internal contradictions between past practices and present mission can play out in spectacular, baffling, and infuriating ways. The National Archives and Records Service of South Africa came about through a Parliamentary Act (Act No. 43 of 1996 as amended). Passed after the first democratic elections in 1994 during the very year in which the TRC began its work, this act transformed the former State Archives Service, which was a central apparatus of the apartheid state, into a National Archives and Records Service (NARS). The new archive's mission, function, and structure are supposed to "reflect the South African democratic political order and imperatives. In essence, the mission of the National Archives and Records Service is to foster a national identity and the protection of rights."[27] The NARS website goes on to say that archival records help us to understand "who we are, either as individuals or as organizations." So what national identity was fostered for Calata through her experience trying to gain access to her own TRC records? Whose rights were being protected? What did she learn about herself as an individual or about the identity of organizations in the new South African state?

These stories about experiences trying to gain access to the TRC archive might be characterized as the historian's version of a wild goose chase. I tried for years to gain access to an archive that would seem to be central to my project. I tried via e-mail, faxes, phone calls, in-person visits with the Department of Justice and the National Archive, and working through other researchers, archivists, and even those classified as "victims" who had given evidence before the TRC. Nearly all my attempts were repelled. But that does not mean that I came away without any valuable knowledge. We can learn a great deal about the *identity* of a wild goose by chasing it—perhaps more than by catching the goose.

"Who are you? And why are you here?" are questions that reverberate between the researcher and archives and state institutions that may continue to perform an old totalitarian order even in a contemporary world busily immersed in the construction of a new, democratic, nonracist state. If ever a place undermined the idea of disinterested knowledge, it is Africa. Knowledge about the past is always *interested*. At the thresholds of Africa's history is an active questioning: Who are you? Why are you here? Do you want to see these images? Are you sure? What do you want to do with the knowledge you seek? What *will* you do? What have you done? Such exchanges between researcher and researched, between visitor and host

("Here everything is quiet. How is the road?"), between the owners and custodians of archives, between the living and the nonliving, between the past and present, and between memory and forgetting ("I don't want to see those files") reverberate through African historiography. These negotiations evidence the intellectual's fundamental complicity and responsibility or "responsibility-in-complicity," as Mark Sanders has so thoughtfully theorized.[28] The intellectual who chooses to go digging around in the past—any past, but particularly Africa's past—must reckon with the connections of humanity. Deep in the heart of empirical research is the history of empire. But is African historiography as I have described it here really so exceptional? Might not all historical sources and investigative processes be subject to interdependency, reciprocity, and a negotiation of identity and motive? Might not all history writing enfold the historian in a web of complicity and responsibility? What would happen if all historians had to answer repeatedly the questions: "Who are you? And why are you here?" How would our histories be different?

NOTES

Research for this essay has been made possible by funding from the National Humanities Center, the National Endowment for the Humanities, the American Association of University Women, the University of California Regents Humanities Fellowship, and University of California–Santa Barbara's Interdisciplinary Humanities Center and Academic Senate. Portions of this essay were presented in seminars at Northwestern University, Yale University, and the University of Michigan.

1. *Oxford English Dictionary* online, http://www.oed.com (accessed March 22, 2009).

2. E. H. Brookes, *The History of Native Policy in South Africa from 1830 to the Present Day*. 2nd rev. ed. (Pretoria: J. L. van Schaik, 1927), p. 82.

3. Some individuals enjoy the power and/or resources to control access to archival records by future researchers, but rarely was this the case for Africans represented in colonial archives.

4. Georg Wilhelm Friederich Hegel, *The Philosophy of History* (New York: Colonial Press, 1899), p. 99.

5. Jan Vansina, *Oral Tradition* (Chicago: University of Chicago Press, 1965), later republished as *Oral Tradition as History* (Madison: University of Wisconsin Press, 1985).

6. For overviews of Vansina's work and its reception, see David Newberry, "Contradictions at the Heart of the Canon: Jan Vansina and the Debate over Oral Historiography in Africa, 1960–1985," *History in Africa* 34 (2007): 213–254; Anne Reef, "African Words, Academic Choices: Re-Presenting Interviews and Oral Histories," *History in Africa* 35 (2008): 419–438.

7. Eric Allina-Pisano, "Resistance and the Social History of Africa," *Journal of Social History* 37.1 (2003): 191.

8. Abdullahi A. Ibrahim, "The Birth of the Interview: The Thin and the Fat of It," in *African Words, African Voices: Critical Practices in Oral History*, ed. Luise White, Stephan F. Miescher, and David William Cohen (Bloomington: Indiana University Press, 2001), p. 104.

9. For an overview, see Allina-Pisano, "Resistance and the Social History of Africa," pp. 187–198. For examples of monographs in this vein, see Jonathan Glassman, *Feasts and Riot: Revelry, Rebellion, and Popular Consciousness on the Swahili Coast, 1856–1888* (Portsmouth: Heinemann, 1995); Paul S. Landau, *The Realm of the Word: Language, Gender, and Christianity in a Southern African Kingdom* (Portsmouth: Heinemann, 1995); and Allen Isaacman, *Cotton Is the Mother of Poverty: Peasants, Work, and Rural Struggle in Colonial Mozambique, 1938–1961* (Portsmouth: Heinemann, 1996).

10. See Susan Geiger, *TANU Women: Gender and Culture in the Making of Tanganyikan Nationalism* (Portsmouth: Heinemann, 1997); Stephan F. Miescher, *Making Men in Ghana* (Bloomington: Indiana University Press, 2005); Julie Livingstone, *Debility and Moral Imagination in Botswana: Disability, Chronic Illness, and Aging* (Bloomington: Indiana University Press, 2005); and Charles van Onslen, *The Seed Is Mine: The Life of Kas Maine, a South African Sharecropper, 1894–1985* (New York: Hill and Wang, 1996).

11. Luise White, *Speaking with Vampires: Rumor and History in Colonial Africa* (Berkeley: University of California Press, 2000), p. 50.

12. David William Cohen, "In a Nation of White Cars . . . One White Car, or 'A White Car,'" Becomes a Truth," in *African Words, African Voices*, ed. White, Miescher, and Cohen, p. 265 (emphasis in original).

13. Institutional Review Boards (IRBs), governed by the American Code of Federal Regulations, are charged with protecting the rights and welfare of people involved in research (otherwise known as "human subjects"). Such boards review, in advance and during the course of a research project, the methods and ethics used by the researchers. Their aim is to ensure that fully informed and voluntary consent has been obtained from research subjects and that these individuals are capable of making such choices. IRBs also attempt to maximize the safety of human subjects once they are involved in a study. These boards, which often reside on individual university campuses, are regulated by the Office for Human Research Protections within the U.S. Department of Health and Human Services. More information can be found at http://www.hhs.gov/ohrp/.

14. For more on the TRC, see Catherine Cole, "Performance, Transitional Justice, and the Law: South Africa's Truth and Reconciliation Commission," *Theatre Journal* 59 (2007): 167–187; Catherine Cole, *Performing South Africa's Truth Commission: Stages of Transition* (Bloomington: Indiana University Press, forthcoming).

15. Joseph R. Roach, *Cities of the Dead: Circum-Atlantic Performance* (New York: Columbia University Press, 1996), p. 2.

16. Ann Laura Stoler, "Colonial Archives and the Arts of Governance: On the Content in Form," in *Refiguring the Archive*, ed. Carolyn Hamilton, Verne Harris, Jane Taylor, Michele Pickover, Graeme Reid, and Razia Saleh (London: Kluwer Academic Publishers, 2002), pp. 89–90.

17. Kate Allen, interview with the author, Johannesburg, September 9, 2005; Verne

Harris, "'They Should Have Destroyed More': The Destruction of Public Records by the South African State in the Final Years of Apartheid, 1990–1994," in *Archives and the Public Good: Accountability and Records in Modern Society*, ed. David A. Wallace and Richard Cox (Westport/London: Quorum Books, 2002); Piers Pigou, "There Are More Truths to Be Uncovered before We Can Achieve Reconciliation," *Sunday Independent* (Johannesburg, South Africe), April 23, 2006, p. 9.

18. Pumla Gobodo-Madikizela, *A Human Being Died That Night: A South African Story of Forgiveness* (Boston: Houghton Mifflin, 2003), p. 2.

19. For an overview of South African history, see Leonard Thompson, *A History of South Africa*, 3rd ed. (New Haven: Yale University Press, 2000).

20. On the relationship between archives and repertoires, see Diana Taylor, *The Archive and the Repertoire: Performing Cultural Memory in the Americas* (Durham: Duke University Press, 2003).

21. William Kekana, Promotion of Access to Information Unit, Department of Justice, South Africa, personal electronic communication, February 7, 2005.

22. Gerrit Wagener, Head, Client Services, National Archives Repository, South Africa, personal electronic communication, February 28, 2005.

23. If South Africa had engaged in a full criminal and civil prosecution for past atrocities, the courts would have been completely overwhelmed for years. The TRC provided a different model of justice. It gave incentives for individuals to come forward and bring into the public light information that had been hidden, specifically information about disappearances, torture, and murders. The underlying concept was one of "restorative justice" rather than retributive justice. The TRC produced information and gave victims of gross violations of human rights the possibility of finding out what had really happened to them or to their loved ones. This production of information was deemed to be preferable to the administration of justice through prosecution, judgment, and retribution via incarceration or civil damages.

24. The Cradock Four (Matthew Goniwe, Sicelo Mhlauli, Sparrow Mkhonto, and Fort Calata) were killed in June 1985 by security police. Their bodies were mutilated and burned. This high-profile case received much attention at the TRC.

25. Nomonde Calata, interview with Liza Key and the author, Cradock, July 2, 2007; Kate Allen, interview with the author, Johannesburg, September 9, 2005. All subsequent quotations from Calata come from this interview.

26. Taylor, *The Archive and the Repertoire*, p. 20.

27. National Archives and Records Service of South Africa, http://www.national.archives.gov.za/aboutnasa_content.html (accessed March 20, 2009).

28. Mark Sanders, *Complicities: The Intellectual and Apartheid* (Durham: Duke University Press, 2002), p. 11.

The High Stakes of Identity Lorraine Hansberry's *Follow the Drinking Gourd* and Suzan-Lori Parks's *Venus*

> How do we negotiate between my history and yours? How would it be possible for us to recover our commonality, not the ambiguous imperial-humanist myth of those shared human (and indeed also most divine) attributes that are supposed to distinguish us absolutely from animals but, more significant, the imbrications of our various past and presents, the ineluctable relationships of shared and contested meanings, values and material resources? It is necessary to assert our dense particularities, our lived and imagined differences; but can we afford to leave untheorized the question of how our differences are intertwined and, indeed, hierarchically organized? Could we, in other words, afford to have entirely different histories, to see ourselves living—and having lived—in entirely heterogeneous and discrete spaces? — Satya P. Mohanty, *Literary Theory and the Claims of History*, 1997

In a 1961 *Village Voice* essay, the late playwright Lorraine Hansberry provocatively asserts that perpetuation of separate and unequal American racial politics has depended on the complex interactions between identity and narrative. Over the course of history, she claims, the stories told of racial difference have profoundly impacted the attitudes and behaviors of black and white Americans: "White America has to believe not only that the oppression of the Negro is unfortunate (because most of white America does believe that), but something else, to keep its sense of the unfortunate from turning to a sense of outrage. . . . White America has to believe that Blacks are different—and not only so, but that, by the mystique of this difference, they actually profit in certain charming ways."[1] The white belief in this fictional narrative, "the mystique" of racial difference, Hansberry forcefully points out, has enabled white economic advancement at the expense of any moral outrage and collective social advancement. By extension, we could argue that this narrative of black difference has informed and justified legal codes such as "separate but equal," Jim Crow, and of course chattel slavery. Narratives, historical and fictional, have consequence.

Accordingly, American historians generally and African American theatre historians most particularly need to observe and to interrogate where and how ideas of identity function in the telling of the past. For what Parks asks us as theatre historians to understand is that a causal and referential relationship exists between one's sociohistorical location in time and space and one's identity. Examining questions of identity, consequently, can inform our readings of African American history, as narratives of identity have informed how these African Americans not only perceived themselves but were perceived. For the African American theatre historian, then, it is not just a matter of exploring how plays have historically constructed African American subjectivity but of examining how existing narratives of identity inform the construction of each particular play. Such an emphasis on identity produces a history that focuses on people as historical agents, that studies the actions of individuals as history producers, rather than just recording historical moments or events that seem to produce individuals. It also recognizes what Satya Mohanty points out in this essay's epigraph: historiography can provide us access to alternative histories that are complex, contested, and imbricated.

It is just such a process of historiography that I intend to explore in this essay by examining two works, Lorraine Hansberry's *Follow the Drinking Gourd* (1960) and Suzan-Lori Parks's *Venus* (1996). These plays deal with significant historical incidents of black subjugation: slavery in the days before the Civil War and the infamous exploitation of the Hottentot Venus in the early 1800s. In *Venus*, Parks revisits the history of Saartjie Baartman, the "Venus Hottentot," brought from South Africa to London England in 1810 by a white doctor, William Dunlop. Baartman was exhibited in both London and Paris as an exotic and erotic freak until she died in 1815. Hansberry's *Drinking Gourd* considers the relationship of slavery to the Civil War by focusing on events on a southern plantation on the eve of that monumental conflict. *Follow the Drinking Gourd* and *Venus* raise important questions about how narrative and identity can intersect in the representation of blackness. Confronting historical subjects, Parks and Hansberry show how play-making serves as a form of historiography and how identity operates as a critical source of meaning. Accordingly, by analyzing these works we can inform ourselves on how theatre can contribute to the production of race.

Theatre historians, by negotiating the processes of theatre historiography, have to delineate what is at stake in maintaining certain identity positions and in sustaining certain narratives of race. They also must identify the significant stakeholders. Notably, these two plays by the two most celebrated African American women playwrights both have been the subject of controversy because of their particular conjunctions of historical and fictional narrative and their alternative approaches to questions of identity, particularly as these questions relate to black women. The two playwrights present black female characters that subvert conventional expectations and thereby raise questions as to who is allowed to narrate black women's history and what such narratives should be able to say.

In 1961 the National Broadcasting Company (NBC) commissioned a teleplay from Hansberry to be the opening sequence in a five-part series of ninety-minute television dramas commemorating the centennial of the Civil War. The network executives, however, soon decided not to produce *Drinking Gourd* and to scuttle the series. Evidently, NBC deemed Hansberry's rendering of the "Peculiar Institution" too provocative to air.[2] The act of preventing *Drinking Gourd* from reaching a television audience speaks to the investment that key players at NBC had in preserving or protecting certain narratives of slavery.

In the case of Suzan-Lori Parks's representation of the Venus as well as the actual life story of Saartjie Baartman, the woman's body became a text on which others wrote their own scripts to serve their own ends. Georges Cuvier, who had been Napoleon's surgeon, dissected her body after her death. His experiments on her body allowed him to lecture widely on what he theorized to be her aberrant physiology. How could a play be written about this horror? Critics have attacked Parks for not giving enough weight to Baartman's racial abuse or to the violence enacted on her body. Scholar Jean Young argues that Parks's depiction of Baartman "reifies the perverse imperialist mindset, and her mythic historical reconstruction subverts the voice of Saartjie Baartman."[3] According to Young, Parks's play reinforces the denigrating stereotypes of black womanhood. By subverting Baartman's voice, the play has had a wider, residual impact on the voice and self-image of black women. At issue for opponents of both plays, yet for different reasons, is an uneasy fear that these two plays narrate identity in troubling ways that could have real consequences in and for American racial politics.

What is identity? Paula Moya understands identity as both being real—having actual consequence—and being constructed. She writes that identities "can be politically and epistemically significant, on the one hand, and variable, nonessential and radically historical, on the other."[4] And it is this quality of identity that has particular significance in defining how race, history, and identity function in these two works. The social events and critiques that have circulated around *Drinking Gourd* and *Venus* testify to the power of identity as well as the social force of narrative.

PLAYWRITING AND HISTORY MAKING

My first critical questions for this historiographical investigation concern the playwright as a stakeholder. How does racial orientation inform the playwrights' art? How do Hansberry and Parks negotiate their dramaturgical interests in creating effective dramatic art with the ingrained social expectations of white and black audiences around certain racialized histories? Significantly, neither playwright portrays a simple picture of oppressive whites and exploited blacks. Rather, within their narratives confronting historic cruelties in the 1800s they find space for alternative perspectives on agency and complicity in the face of racial oppression. They disrupt stereotypical depictions of black and white identities. Hansberry and Parks resist conventional expectations due, in part, to the nonlinear structures of their plays. In *Venus* as in *Drinking Gourd*, the playwright's form is critical to her content. Parks challenges traditional storytelling entirely by having the play's chronicle told in reverse. The death of the Venus is announced and then the scenes work backward, retelling the history of her travel from Africa, her exploitation in Europe, and her death. Because of this nontraditional form, the historical exploitation of the Venus is Parks's subject but not her principal focus. Hansberry is equally uninterested in uncomplicated exegeses of racism. She destabilizes chronology and troubles the relationship between the historical and the fictional narratives as she employs a white Union soldier—slated by NBC to be played by Henry Fonda—to narrate the play's story. His identity as a white Union soldier—a potentially empathetic figure to the largely white viewing audience—proves crucial to how Hansberry unfolds her story. Appearing at the beginning and end of the play, at once inside and outside the frame, both real and imagined, this narrator frames the action and underscores its contemporary significance for the intended TV audience. Talking directly to the audience, he situates the play's events in time present with an awareness of time past and future.

By representing historical conditions of the late 1850s, Hansberry was very much concerned with how such representations were perceived a hundred years later. Consulting the New York Public Library and the Schomburg Collection on African American studies in Harlem as well as transcripts of the prewar *Congressional Record*, Hansberry immersed herself in the period in order to write *Drinking Gourd*. Still, even as she studied this history, she felt that she basically had to "dismiss" it when it came time to write her play: "What I think a dramatist must do is to thoroughly inundate himself or herself in an awareness of the realities of the historical period and then dismiss it. And then become absolutely dedicated to the idea that what you are going to do is to create human beings whom you know in your own time, you see."[5] In this play, accordingly, Hansberry identifies the tensions between the diachronic and the synchronic. She argues against constructing stock historical figures and for creating fully imagined humans that have relevance across time to the present. Playwriting, Hansberry suggests, requires the creation of such characters in order for the work to function as empathetic and engaging art.

Yet Hansberry is also extremely interested in the social efficacy of her art and how her playwriting might address the absences she had observed in American history in the case of African American experiences. At a symposium on "The Negro Writer in America" in 1961, Hansberry pointed out that "it is now possible to get enormous books on the Civil War and to go through the back of them and not find the word 'slavery,' let alone 'Negro.'"[6] *Drinking Gourd* serves as her dramaturgical response to this problem. With this play Hansberry sought not only to address the dearth of historical scholarship on African Americans but to contest the misrepresentations of slavery that she found prevalent in American culture. In writing her play, Hansberry remembers and employs conversations with her grandmother, who was born a slave. On a trip down south as a child one summer, Hansberry visited her grandmother: "she was born into slavery and had memories of it and they didn't sound anything like *Gone with the Wind*."[7]

Hansberry's recollections of her discussions with her grandmother about slavery underscored her awareness of the power of historical and artistic representations of identity. Films such as *Gone with the Wind* and others within the public sphere can have a significant influence on our understanding of the past and, as a result, on our comprehension of racial identities in the present. By countering the popular representations of slaves as happy, loyal "darkies" (images that dominated popular culture for a hundred years), Hansberry's *Drinking Gourd* offers an alternative vision of the identities of African Americans. Consequently, for a theatre historian who is interested in matters of race, identity, and history, the task of assessing the achievement of *Drinking Gourd* requires methods of historical analysis and research beyond the traditional archival recording of box office success, critical reviews, or interviews with artistic personnel. After all, the play was not even produced; NBC canceled its production. Unfortunately, Hansberry's intended narrative joined the silences, absences, and invisibility that existed for African Americans.

Suzan-Lori Parks's *Venus*, like Hansberry's play, takes a revisionist approach to matters of history and her function as a playwright. In an interview with dramaturg Shelby Jiggets, Parks explains her own concept of history through an invocation of William Faulkner: "Faulkner has this great thing: he talks about is and was, or was and is. History is not 'was,' history 'is.' It's present, so if you believe that history is in the present, you can also believe the present is in the past."[8] The notion that history "is" for Parks suggests that history functions always in the now. Moreover, her understanding of history not only situates it in the present but leads her to identify an activist role for the individual and the playwright in the creation of history. History *is* in the individual. In an interview about *The America Play*, Parks states: "I take issue with history because it doesn't serve me—it doesn't serve me because there isn't enough of it. In this play, I am simply asking, 'Where is history?', because I don't see it. I don't see any history out there, so I've made up some."[9] This statement, like the earlier comments by Hansberry, speaks to the conventional silences of American history, the practiced omission from critical histories of the past events in various communities, particularly people of color.[10] She argues that history as it has been told, has neglected or misinterpreted the presence of black people and so fails to "serve" her in the present. History, as currently constituted, reflects a bias that is not in her interest. Functioning in her own self-interest, she makes up events and performs her own history.

I see an important connection between Parks's statement on history and that of James Baldwin, who proclaims: "History is the present. . . . You and I are history. We carry our history. We act our history."[11] Far from being a disinterested process that is supposedly free of biases and only concerned with finding facts, history, for Baldwin and Parks, calls for imaginative and malleable perceptions open to interpretation. To the theatre historian, self-conscious about finding the truth and committed to knowledge production, a concept such as that espoused by Parks and Baldwin may seem antithetical to the project of historical location and discovery. Yet only through the process of interpretation do facts come to meaning, and this meaning is always subject to the politics of time and location. I do not believe that Baldwin and Parks are arguing for an approach to African American theatre history that is overly presentist, imposing present values onto the past, but rather for writing or making history for the present moment. They urge us to recognize the given "interestedness" of any official history and thus the right of others to participate in the writing of history, whatever their self-interests and racial interests, especially as compensation when they have been written out of the master histories.

Parks's notion of "making some up" grants to the playwright or playmaker the imaginative power to construct historical narratives, most particularly new narratives of blackness that bring African Americans out of the shadows of history. She writes: "Theatre, for me, is the perfect place to 'make' history—that is, because so much of African-American history has been unrecorded, dismembered, washed out, one of my tasks as a playwright is to locate—through literature and the special strange relationship between theatre and real-life—the ancestral burial ground, dig for bones, find bones, hear the bones sing, write it down."[12] Not limited by fixed ontological definitions of blackness, Parks, as theatrical archaeologist, seeks to unearth the complexity of African American experiences. Provocatively, she suggests that the process of history can be one of imaginative creation; that history is not simply found but made; that the playwright as playmaker can make some history up. "Making some up" does not infer that theatre can itself constitute "real" history; rather it recognizes the unique relationship of the theatre to the "real" as well as the power and value of this creative process of representation. Parks insists on the very theatricality of the project of writing history.

As both Parks and Hansberry attest in their writings, the playwright's positionality is critical to the process of history making. Conscious of past misrepresentations of African American history, they self-consciously understand themselves as historical actors in the creation of history. Their location and experiences in history influence their writing of history. With *Drinking Gourd* and *Venus*, Hansberry and Parks devise an imaginative archaeology in service to their endeavor not only to uncover the past but also actually to participate in its construction in the present.

COMPETING NARRATIVES OF IDENTITY

The playwrights, however, are only part of this story, for this tale has other important stakeholders. Critical to this engaged historiographic reading of *Drinking Gourd* and *Venus* are the competing narratives of identity that surround and inform the plays. The story of *Drinking Gourd*'s censorship reflects not only on Hansberry's attempts to construct the past, but on how others, most significantly the NBC executives who canceled its broadcast, interpreted her work as a potential threat to racialized identity positions in the present. NBC had imagined its Civil War series as one of the most important events of the 1961 television session. In a move designed to return serious drama to television, the network decided to commission well-known dramatists to write the scripts.[13] The network selected Dore Schary, the socially committed theater producer, to produce the series. In turn, he picked Hansberry, who had just been awarded the Drama Circle Critics' Award for *Raisin in the Sun*, to write the opening script. The network was quite wary of Schary's selection of Hansberry. Schary remembers how the response of the network executives to his choice of Hansberry foreshadowed the demise of the project as a whole: "There was a long moment of silence. And then the question was asked: 'What's her point of view about it—slavery?' I thought they were pulling my leg, and so I answered presently, gravely; 'She's against it.' Nobody laughed—from that moment I knew we were dead."[14] This anecdote, with its double punch lines ("She's against it" and "Nobody laughed"), is quite amusing but also quite revealing. It points out that these network executives could not recognize the nature of Schary's retort because they were quite uneasy about hiring a black writer. For them the choice of Hansberry was a point of controversy. To trust her, given her interpretation of slavery, represented for these executives a decision fraught with potential difficulties.

Schary himself believed that the horrors of slavery were non-negotiable and represented a historical condition that demanded to be told truthfully. But the executives wanted the program to deemphasize slavery, as Schary explained to a reporter: "They [NBC executives] want to call it the War Between the States. I would rather call it the War of Rebellion. . . . The slaves were subjects of an evil. They wanted freedom."[15] Schary recognized that the title "War between the States" would designate the Civil War as a matter of states' rights. Such a narrative not only omitted slavery as a primary cause; it removed the slaves as agents in this history. By contrast, his notion of "the War of Rebellion" positioned the slaves as participants and situated this rebellion within the context of other American struggles against oppression for liberty. His view, however, was not shared by the network.

The Drinking Gourd would not air as planned, because NBC executives—functioning as social arbiters—squelched the show out of concerns for its potential to stir racial conflagration. While Schary was adamant about the need to confront the cruel legacy of slavery with frankness, the network was fearful of ratings and of raising the rancor of southern viewers in the 1960s. At the dawn of the Civil Rights Movement—a time of entrenched Jim Crow policy—NBC hesitated and stalled when Schary presented them with Hansberry's treatment. Believing in Hansberry's text, Schary continued to press the network to go forward with the project. NBC, however, soon terminated not only the project but also Schary's contract. So he returned to the theater. On August 30, 1960, Hansberry first learned of the termination of the series not from NBC or from Schary but from a headline in the *New York Herald-Tribune*: "Dore Schary Tells Why TV Shies from Civil War."

NBC's decision to shut down the Civil War Project initiated a chain reaction: both ABC and CBS immediately followed suit and canceled their own plans for programming to commemorate the Centennial anniversary of the war. They all concluded that the times were too rife with tension around questions of race to honor one of the most important events in American history. At this point in history—more than forty years before the nine-part Ken Burns documentary *The Civil War* aired on the Public Broadcast Service—slavery and the Civil War constituted territory too perilous and contentious for representation in the public sphere. For the NBC executives, the tensions around the topic of race, palpable in the surrounding 1960s social environment, influenced their readings of and decision to suppress Hansberry's script. Accordingly they deemed Hansberry's revised narrative of slavery a threat to established identity positions. Her rendition, they feared, could spur black unrest. So, by preventing its airing, they maintained the status quo.

The history of Saartjie Baartman, the Hottentot Venus, reveals the constant assertion and reassertion of identity positions in order to subvert or preserve the status quo. Baartman's body has repeatedly served as a text upon which individuals, ethnic groups, and even nations have sought to write their own historic narratives of race and sexuality. Baartman, the South African !Kung or Khoi-Khoi or Khoisan tribeswoman brought to London and displayed in a sideshow as the "Venus Hottentot," was "led by her keeper" and exhibited like "a wild beast," according to Robert Chambers's *Book of Days*.[16] The derogatory designation "Hottentot Venus" presents us with a telling concatenation of meanings. Venus, Roman goddess of erotic love, source of desire, and seductress, but signally European, is set off against the Hottentot, sign of the primitive, promiscuous African. The names join elemental desire and beauty with exoticism. Hottentots (so called by the Boers) were distinguished by Europeans and from Europeans by their protruding, fatty buttocks (or steatopygia) and their color. European viewers fetishized the buttocks as the location of Hottentot sexuality and clamored for the opportunity to marvel at this spectacle.

To the European spectators of that time, then, Baartman represented exotic difference and abnormal sexuality. As Tavia Nyong'o notes, Baartman "embodied a primeval, African essence that contrasted powerfully with civilized European bodies."[17] By means of this bodily distinction, Europeans promoted white beauty over African grotesqueness. When Baartman died in 1815, her body was both figuratively and literally invaded. Henri de Blainville and Cuvier published autopsies in 1816 and 1817, respectively. The Cuvier autopsy notes figure prominently in Parks's play. Cuvier preserved Baartman's genitalia and constructed a plaster cast of her body. Through these body parts she was again put on display. As recently as 1994 the Museum de l'Homme in Paris displayed Baartman as part of an exhibit that documented "the harsh, racist portrayal of aboriginal peoples by 19th century Europe's painters and sculptors."[18] Despite this attempt to rationalize her exhibition under the guise of exposing oppression, Baartman still served after her death as an object of prurient interests. Harvey Young reports that in some cases the act of just viewing the remains "awakened the sexual desires of the tourists and occasionally erupted in the form of visitors groping the cast, masturbating in the (public) presence of the cast, or attempting to assault tour guides" after having seen the cast of Baartman.[19]

Yet the manipulation of the representation and the cultural meanings of Baartman's body has not been solely the domain of white Europeans. In the mid-1990s, with the end of apartheid in South Africa, the Khoisans, descendants of the original Khoisan peoples of the Western Cape, have sought to reclaim Baartman as part of their own ethnic narrative and claims for identity. In May 1996, two months before *Venus* premiered on the stage of the Public Theater in New York, the members of the Khoisan National Council of the newly constituted South Africa, petitioned the Museum de l'Homme in France for the return of Baartman's dismembered body to her homeland for burial. A spokesman for the Griquas (Khoisan people), Mansell Upham, justified this demand by stating that Baartman is "a potent symbol of the dismemberment and dehumanized of the original people of South Africa. She's a human being who has been denied the right to dignity after death."[20] The Khoisans, grouped under the label "Coloured" during apartheid, have sought to express their own specific indigenous identity in the postapartheid era, when such labels have been further eroded of political meaning. More important than the "Coloured" political designation for the Khoisans is the preservation of the cultural and ethnic heritage as symbolized by Baartman. Nyong'o explains: "While Khoisan peoples today exist across the South African racial spectrum, including many who were considered Black under apartheid laws, Khoisan leaders still consider their rights to collective representation as the modern-day descendants of the 'Hottentot' threatened."[21] Accordingly, the return of Baartman's remains to the Khoisans symbolizes their struggle for recognition as a distinct people, the first indigenous peoples of South Africa.

On May 6, 2002, Baartman's remains were returned to the Cape Town, where the Khoisan National Council interred her "body parts" in a ceremony that used history to foreground Khoisan identity politics in the new South Africa. In a move that potently symbolized her South African roots and her indigenous identity, the National Khoisan Council placed Baartman in a coffin wrapped with the postapartheid South African flag. To all those who witnessed, the flag symbolically reinforced her South African origins. Moreover, the celebration of Baartman's historic homecoming ritualistically put an end to her personal history of degradation and dehumanization, as it marked a new beginning for the Khoisans. Her retrieval served the Khoisan political efforts to create recognition for their own separate ethnic identity. Interviewed at the event, Joseph Little, the chairperson of the Khoisan National Council, commented on the significance of Baartman's public burial for the Khoisans: "She's brought to the fore that we need to be proud of our identity instead of hiding behind the classification of 'Coloured' which was given to us by the racist apartheid regime."[22]

The Khoisans have seized upon Baartman's history for its meanings in the present. They have constructed a particularly self-interested historical narrative that they have employed to shape not only their current social context but their future. Free of the imposed label "Coloured," the Khoisans have sought to claim through Baartman a distinct sense of self-determination; they insist upon recognition of their right to an ethnic past as well as to contemporary entitlement. Matty Cairncross, a member of the Khoisan community, remarked at the services for Baartman: "She's a symbol of our history that's been taken away from us. We have a rich history and culture which needs to be revived and shown to the world. We need to hear more stories about forgotten people like the Khoisan in books and theatre to correct the imbalances created by the previous system of apartheid."[23] Cairncross's comments on Baartman foreground the power of representation to right and rewrite history.

Significantly, Cairncross named the theatre as critical to this process of historical recuperation. For, as evidenced by both *Venus* and *Drinking Gourd*, the theatre is a site for constructing narratives and identities capable of both supporting and subverting the status quo. In addition, the fears of NBC executives concerning the televising of a narrative about slavery and the demands of the Khoisans concerning the return of Baartman's remains provide historical contexts for these works and for how the playwrights shape and construct history.

HISTORY ON TRIAL, RIGHTING, WRITING HISTORY

In *Venus* and *Drinking Gourd* the playwrights respond to and critique the place allotted to black women in historical records and studies. Parks discovered "the woman called Hottentot Venus" at a cocktail party when she overheard a conversation in which a friend, director Liz Diamond, mentioned Baartman. Parks recounts: "As I listened bells started going off in my head and I knew this Saartjie Baartman woman was going to end up in a play of mine. She was a woman with a remarkable bottom, a woman with a past."[24] In *Venus* Parks cleverly riffs on the sordid connotations of both the word "past" and the mythic figure of Venus, as she presents Baartman as a woman of sexual agency confined within a sexual history. It is equally significant that, through her representation of Baartman, Parks challenges the very notion of why it is a slur for a woman to have "a past."

Parks constructs a history that explores what it means for her Venus to have a past and in so doing challenges the space for and definitions of blackness. In Parks's portrayal the identity of the Venus character is not fixed or completely constrained by circumstance. Purposefully, Parks avoids portraying this Venus character as a simple victim and consequently resists simplistic representations of blackness. "I could have written a two-hour saga with Venus being the victim. . . . But she's multifaceted . . . as black people we're encouraged to be narrow and simply address the race issue. We deserve much more."[25] Accordingly, her Venus is both a desiring subject and subject to the exploitative, perverted desire of the Baron Docteur—a surrogate, at least partially, for the actual Doctor Cuvier who bought her and dissected her body parts upon her death. As Parks chronicles the narrative from Venus's arrival in London to her death in Paris, she presents a story in which the conflict is not merely reduced to a condition of white hegemony but also concerned with systems of representation in which the character of Venus is implicated. To be sure, such a portrait of Venus, even as it refutes the suppression of pastness for black women, garners the rancor of critics, such as Jean Young, for reinscribing stereotypes of black women. Yet Parks's strategy is to construct a character and a dramatic action that complicate existing categories of racial identity.

Still, Parks's *Venus* inevitably must engage past and present discourses about Baartman's body and its exploitation. Even as Parks exposes the horrors of Venus's exhibition, she is herself implicated in these bodily dynamics. Parks puts Baartman onstage in a cage. Before the audience, Parks has her keeper, the Mother-Showman, display the Venus. Her Venus functions as a taboo site of desire for the Baron Docteur, who masturbates at her side. An actor, a black woman, must don a body suit with an enlarged butt to play the figure. The actress and her costume become the site of spectoral fascination. The actor as Venus is a black woman on display. As she portrays a black woman who was objectified, she becomes a black woman objectified. The actor is not Venus but not "not Venus." Ghosted by the history of Baartman's bottom and its resultant meanings, the past is at once present.

Yet, Parks's *Venus* reveals not simply how the past haunts the present but how historical narratives have consequences in the present. The Venus is put on trial in the play, just as an actual trial was held in London in 1813 to investigate the circumstances of the Venus Hottentot's public exhibition in a cage. Perhaps out of coercion or concern for her own survival, Baartman testified at this affair that she performed of her own free will and was not exploited. Kate Cloete, the secretary of the Griqua (Khoisan) Conference, subsequently has defended Baartman, her ancestor, with the claim: "She had to earn some money. She was a human being, not an animal."[26] In her play Parks repeats and revises these historical events by having the trial scenes in *Venus* revolve around the writ of habeas corpus, a law that literally requires the presence of a body. Although the writ of habeas corpus originated in English Common Law in 1305 as a means of providing defendants access to the king's justice, in contemporary United States federal cases this law now serves to protect defendants against unlawful imprisonment at the hands of the government. Ironically, then, in this current understanding of the term the Venus is both the accuser and the accused. She must testify against herself. The Venus possesses the body, but the play reveals that the politics of representation are actually beyond her control and distinctly racialized. In this courtroom possessing the body is not an asset but a liability. Speaking for herself, not before a "jury of her peers" but rather in front of a room full of white voyeurs, only serves to reinforce their perceptions of her deviance. Parks uses the Venus's inevitably unsuccessful self-representation to critique the supposed blindness of Western justice and its protection of individual rights regardless of race. Within this context, justice is overdetermined and does not protect the Venus.

Moreover, in this courtroom scene where the Venus must testify for and against herself, Parks asks: what happens when you bring historical actors into the present to defend themselves? She shows the peril of having historical actors speak for themselves in the present without the necessary contextualization or mediation of the historian. When the Venus rises in her own defense at the trial, she mouths an internalized racism that associates blackness with deviance and whiteness with goodness: "If i bear thuh bad mark what better way to cleanse it off? / Showing my sinful person as a caution to you all could, / in, uh, the good Lords eyes, be a sort of, repentance / and I could wash off my dark mark. I came here black / Give me the chance to leave here white."[27] This narrative that the Venus offers does not reveal any inner truth but only perpetuates the racial status quo. Purposefully, her plea has an ironic ring to it: Parks uses this moment to comment on the historic power of whiteness in Western culture, where white equates with purity while black connotes contamination. In Western culture these foundational racial paradigms have produced an identity politics of white supremacy and black inferiority. Ironically, Parks has the Venus appeal to this racial logic for her acquittal. In so doing Parks answers Jean Young's critique that she does not give the Venus a voice. Venus does speak. Parks argues, however, that providing voice to historical actors may not produce the results that you seek.

While Parks's *Venus* contests Western authority over who can represent history, it also makes a case for the creative license and mediating role of the historian interpreting that history. Near the conclusion of the play the Venus, speaking directly to the audience, narrates the "history of chocolate." Rather than detailing her own story or reflecting directly on her exploitation, she lectures on chocolate. She explains how chocolate has been detested and desired in Western culture. Venus notes chocolate's evolution from being the food of the gods to serving as the gift of love to becoming a source of body fat and pleasure. Her chocolate discourse foregrounds the parallels between the history of her own chocolate-colored, fatty body and her treatise on the history of the cacao bean. Within this chronicle, as she delineates the varied subjectivities that chocolate has occupied within Western cultural hegemony, she alludes by extension to her own fate and that of black women more generally. Yet such an informed reading of this chocolate narrative surfaces only as a result of what Walter Benjamin would call "reading history against the grain":[28] relating this history of chocolate to the entire narrative of the Venus Hottentot that the audience has just experienced. At the end of the play Venus turns to both the Baron Docteur and the audience and cries out: "*Kiss* me *Kiss* me *Kiss* me."[29] Her words function as both a challenge and enticement to perceive her as more than just her body and behind.

In *Drinking Gourd* Hansberry also attempts to challenge historic representations of black women and the role of historians in perpetuating those representations. The screenplay revolves around three families: those of the white slave master Hiram and his son Everett, the lower-class white farmer turned slave overseer Zeb, and the house slave Rissa and her son Hannibal. Initially, Hansberry presents Rissa in ways that seemingly conform to the stereotype of the happy yet subservient house slave, suggestive of "Mammy" as portrayed by Hattie McDaniel in the film *Gone with the Wind*. Hansberry describes Rissa as a woman "*who overhears everything that is ever spoken on the plantation.*" She thus seems to be a busybody, more concerned with the affairs of the house and the master than with the conditions of her own family. Hansberry crafts the relationship of Rissa and Hiram as one of apparent interdependence, comfortably established over the years on the plantation. The relationship changes, however, when Rissa learns that Hiram's son Everett has punished her son Hannibal by having his eyes gouged out—a punishment for the crime of learning how to read. From that point on, she takes a decidedly different course of action. Rather than tending to the dying Master Hiram after he collapses outside her cabin, pleading for her assistance, Rissa attends to the blinded and bloodied Hannibal. Socially awakened and angered by Everett's cruelty and Hiram's complicity, Rissa purposefully allows her master to die. She subsequently steals the master's gun and gives it to Sarah, the woman in love with Hannibal. Rissa wants to aid in the escape of Sarah, Hannibal, and their child Joshua. Hansberry's filmscript states that Rissa "*thrusts the gun into Sarah's other hand.*"[30] With this action she empowers Sarah. The resolution of *Drinking Gourd* features these two women galvanized into a revolutionary consciousness that represents a stark contrast to the conventional image of slave womanhood. Hansberry, like Parks, uses her narrative to expand the representation of black women in history.

Like Parks, Hansberry does not portray black characters simply as victims. With her depiction of Rissa's son Hannibal, Hansberry offers a character who attempts to construct an identity outside of the constraints placed upon him by the facts of his birth and the inhuman conditions of slavery. Early in the play Hannibal explains to his mother why he will not follow the rules and expectations of a field slave and must buck the authority of the overseer: "I am the only kind of slave I could stand to be—a *bad* one! Every day that come and hour that pass I got sense to make a half step do for a whole—every day that I can pretend sickness 'stead of health, to be stupid 'stead of smart, lazy 'stead of quick—I aims to do it. And the more pain it give *your* marster and the more it cost him—the more Hannibal be a man."[31] Aware that bondage limits his capacity to be human, Hannibal resists and equates manhood with this resistance of the master and slavery. Here Hansberry gives the historical record a specifically personal significance. At the time of slavery the U.S. Constitution valued a slave at three-fifths of a man. A slave, as Orlando Patterson notes, was a "quasi-person."[32] Thus Hannibal's statement critiques such callous denials of slave humanity at the same time as it suggests that by not serving the master he serves himself and claims the remaining two-fifths of manhood.

Significantly, Hannibal's resistance to slavery is not the expected violence but rather withholding. He withholds his labor by making a "half step do for a whole," by not committing his whole body and mind to the field work, by pretending "sickness 'stead of health." All slaves recognized that a prime factor in how they would be treated and how much more work they would have to do in the future was how long it took to complete that particular task. As evidenced by Hannibal, laziness or slowness became a calculated method for the slave to steal back time; such acts represented a form of what Saidiya Hartman terms "stealing away." As Hartman explains: "Stealing away involved unlicensed movement, collective assembly and an abrogation of the terms of subjection in acts as simple as sneaking off to laugh and talk with friends or making nocturnal visits to loved ones."[33] The act of stealing away, no matter how seemingly small, was an act of resistance that asserted self-identity in defiance of the master and the system that constituted the slave as property. "Through stealing away, counterclaims about justice and freedom were advanced that denied the sanctity or legitimacy of property rights in a double gesture that played on the meaning of theft."[34] For Hannibal this "double gesture" of stealing away allows him to become whole.

By adopting the identity of a bad slave, Hannibal refuses the normal conditions of identity formation on the plantation. Under the conventions of servitude, the "conventional" slave becomes a nonbeing, whose very existence depends on the master. As Orlando Patterson argues, "In his powerlessness the slave became an extension of his master's power. He was a human surrogate recreated by his master with god-like power in his behalf."[35] As a human surrogate, the slave operates not with individual agency but rather only with the ability to carry out the master's bidding. The "god-like" master attempts to construct the slave in his own image. Hannibal, however, does not accept this limitation on his self-identity; he protests by attempting to learn to read and by stealing time. He rejects any association with and reliance on the master. In fact, Hannibal distances himself from any participation in the master-slave relationship by referring to Hiram not as *his* master but only as his mother's master: "And the more pain it give *your* marster and the more it cost him."[36] What is equally significant in this statement is that Hannibal understands that the master must rely upon his labor in the economy of slavery and that his tactic of resistance costs the master economically.

In *Drinking Gourd* Hansberry, as historian, posits that the economics of slavery are inextricably tied to matters of social location and identity. She shows that Zeb, a poor white farmer hired as an overseer by Hiram's son Everett, is equally caught up in the economics of slavery. A preacher who visits Zeb and his family argues that the free labor of slavery has undermined their ability to farm and forced them into poverty. The preacher bemoans that the white farmer has no place within the system that produces cotton. Zeb, however, does not want to accept his status as poor white and wishes to position himself differently: "Zeb Dudley aims to own himself some slave and be a man—you hear."[37] Hansberry contrasts the white Zeb's perspective on manhood with the black Hannibal, who believes his resistance to the white master's authority will produce manhood. But Zeb maintains that embracing the economic capital of slavery ownership will make him a man. Hansberry shows that the economic system of slavery corrupts notions of masculinity as it diminishes the humanity of both blacks and whites.

Through Zeb, Hansberry both personalizes and critiques the historical discord between the white and black lower classes. From slavery through Reconstruction and beyond, the white working class has been resistant to political coalitions with blacks. Despite their shared socioeconomic position, white workers have seen black advancement as a threat to their own status. Hansberry shows that Zeb defines himself through difference. He refuses to associate himself with enslaved blacks and with the conditions of blackness, even as he is exploited by the very same economic system. Everett goads his overseer Zeb to blind Hannibal for the crime of learning to read. Despite his trepidation, Zeb must serve his own masters and the economic system that keeps him poor. Zeb functions as both victim and victimizer. Hansberry's historiographic method humanizes and complicates the vision of oppression. The play ends with the return of the white Union soldier, the play's narrator, who laments the terrible price that the nation must pay for the economics of slavery: "Slavery is beginning to cost this nation a lot. It has become a drag on the great industrial nation we are determined to become; it lags a full century behind the great American notion of one strong federal union which our eighteenth-century founders knew was the only way we could eventually become one of the powerful nations of the world."[38] Rather than making a final appeal to the human and moral folly of slavery, Hansberry makes a case for the way in which America's endorsement of slavery has constrained the country from reaching its full maturity and stature as nation. Its identity has suffered, along with the many individuals who make up the country. Strategically, even as her play shows the psychological as well as economic damage to Zeb, the physical abuse of Hannibal, the death of Hiram, and the stern resistance of Rissa, the soldier's epilogue promotes not a picture of polarized racial identity but rather a call for a collective American identity around notions of a strong federal union.

CONCLUSION

With both *Drinking Gourd* and *Venus*, the playwrights have blended fiction and history to reenvision past relations and conditions in ways that impact our perceptions and even our possible actions in the present. We understand the past and our present by means of the construction of narratives. As Hayden White notes, "The conjuring up of the past requires art as well as information."[39] It is this art that some have tried to censor or have contested. Critic Jean Young attacks Parks for not being true to history: "Parks's blending of truth and fiction is both a distortion and an historical reconstruction, because Parks uses the distorted lens of gender and racial typecasting to portray Baartman."[40] Yet Young's notions of "distortion" and "reconstruction" play precisely into the matter of this essay: all history depends on the location and identity of the narrator telling that history and therefore inherently involves reconstruction. Dissatisfied with the histories and constructions of identities available, Parks has made some up.

For the theater historian, these concerns over identity raise important issues that need attention as we examine theatrical representations of historical moments and delve into the historical archive. Theatricalizations of racialized oppression, such as Hansberry's retelling of slavery or Parks's *Venus*, teach us that theatre historians need to consider the location and positionality of the artist as well as those of the artwork. We must situate the artwork in history and the history that is in the art. We also need to examine our own positionality and how it impacts on how we interpret these events and how we give them meaning in the present. By no means am I calling for a now outmoded politics of location that would limit historiography by race, where only black historians would write black history or Latino historians would write Latino history. Hansberry and Parks in their complex delineations of race demonstrate that blackness and its meanings have evolved over time. There is no singular or essential blackness as there is no singular black identity; instead we are confronted with identities. Possessing black skin does not bestow any special access or insight into African American theatre history. Accordingly, I know that the editors of this book did not commission me to write this essay on race and identity merely or principally because I am black. What I am suggesting, rather, is the need for sensitivity to and increased awareness of the materials at hand, enabling us to understand identity and its power within the historiographic scene. We must develop a progressive concept of history and history making that takes such matters of identity into account. With such a strategy we can and must observe more fully the battles over identity and identity politics that play out within the space and through the agency of dramatic text and performance.

NOTES

As always, my thanks to Michele Elam for her help in shaping this essay.

1. Lorraine Hansberry, "The New Paternalists," quoted in Robert Nemiroff, "*The Drinking Gourd*: A Critical Background," in *Lorraine Hansberry: The Collected Last Plays* (New York: New American Plays, 1983), p. 156.

2. The phrase was made famous by Kenneth Stamp's *The Peculiar Institution: Slavery and the Ante-Bellum South* (New York: Alfred Knopf, 1967).

3. Jean Young, "The Re-Objectification and Re-Commodification of Saartjie Baartman in Suzan-Lori Parks's *Venus*," *African American Review* 31.4 (Winter 1997): 700.

4. Paula Moya, "Introduction," in *Reclaiming Identity: Realist Theory and the Predicament of Postmodernism* (Berkeley: University of California Press, 2000), p. 12.

5. Lorraine Hansberry, interview with film director Frank Perry on the NET program "Playwright at Work," quoted in Nemiroff, "*The Drinking Gourd*: A Critical Background," p. 147.

6. Ibid., p. 145.

7. Ibid., p. 144.

8. Shelby Jiggets, "Interview with Suzan-Lori Parks," *Callaloo* 19.2 (1996): 317.

9. Suzan-Lori Parks quoted by Michele Pearce, "Alienation: An Interview with Playwright Suzan-Lori Parks," *American Theater* (March 1994): 26.

10. In my own life growing up in the late 1960s we never learned about Japanese American internment during World War II in our American history classes. My history books and teachers simply omitted that significant detail in America's past.

11. James Baldwin, "James Baldwin and Margaret Meade," in *A Rap on Race* (New York: Dell, 1971), quoted by Byron Kim, "An Interview with Glen Ligon," in *Glen Ligon Un/Be-*

coming. ed. Judith Tannenbaum (Philadelphia: Institute of Contemporary Art, University of Pennsylvania, 1998), p. 54.

12. Suzan-Lori Parks, "Possession," in *The America Play and Other Works* (New York: TCG Press, 1995), p. 4.

13. Nemiroff, "*The Drinking Gourd*: A Critical Background," p. 146.

14. Dore Schary quoted in Nemiroff, "*The Drinking Gourd*: A Critical Background," p. 147.

15. Ibid., p. 146.

16. Robert Chambers, *The Book of Days: A Miscellany of Popular Antiquities in Connection with the Calendar*, 2 vols. (London: W. and R. Chambers, 1888), vol. 1, November 26, 1869, at http://www.thebookofdays.com (accessed June 12, 2008).

17. Tavia Nyong'o, "The Body in Question," *International Journal of Communication* 1 (2007): 28.

18. Ibid.; Sudarsan Raghavan, "Body Becomes Symbol of Oppression," *Houston Chronicle*, February 11, 1996, Sec. A, p. 33.

19. Harvey Young, "Touching History: Suzan-Lori Parks, Robbie McCauley and the Black Body," *Text and Performance Quarterly* 23.2 (April 2003): 135.

20. Raghavan, "Body Becomes Symbol of Oppression," Sec. A, p. 33.

21. Nyong'o, "The Body in Question," p. 28.

22. Joseph Little quoted by Mohammed Allie, *BBC News*, May 6, 2003, http://news.bbc.co.uk/2/hi/africa/1971103.stm.

23. Matty Cairncross in ibid.

24. Suzan-Lori Parks, "About Suzan-Lori Parks," in *Venus* (New York: TCG Press, 1997), p. 186.

25. Parks quoted by Monte Williams, "From a Planet Closer to the Sun," *New York Times*, April 17, 1996, Sec. C. 1, p. 8.

26. Ben MacIntyre, "Hottentots Demand the Return of Their Venus," *London Times*, December 30, 1995.

27. Parks, *Venus*, p. 68.

28. Walter Benjamin, "Theses on the Philosophy of History," in *Illuminations*, trans. Harry Zohn (New York: Schocken Books, 1968), p. 261.

29. Parks, *Venus*, p. 140.

30. Lorraine Hansberry, *Drinking Gourd*, in *Lorraine Hansberry: The Collected Last Plays*, p. 217 (emphasis in original).

31. Ibid., p. 201 (emphasis in original).

32. Orlando Patterson, "Introduction," in *Slavery and Social Death* (Cambridge, Mass.: Harvard University Press, 1982), p. 4.

33. Saidiya Hartman, *Scenes of Subjection* (New York: Oxford University Press, 1997), p. 67.

34. Ibid., p. 69.

35. Patterson, "Introduction," p. 4.

36. Hansberry, *Drinking Gourd*, p. 201 (emphasis in original).

37. Ibid., p. 196.

38. Ibid., p. 217.

39. Hayden White, "Introduction: Historical Fiction, Fictional History, and Historical Reality," *Rethinking History* 9.2 (2005): 149.

40. Jean Young, "The Re-Objectification and Re-Commodification of Saartjie Baartman in Suzan-Lori Parks's *Venus*," *African American Review* 31.4 (Winter 1997): 702.

XIAOMEI CHEN

Fifty Years of Staging a Founding Father

Political Theatre, Dramatic History, and the Question of Representation in Modern China

On May 27, 1942, Chen Duxiu, a penurious fifty-three-year-old man, was buried in a lonely mount in a small Sichuanese town. Chen had died of poisoning from the Chinese herbs with which—because he had no professional help or access to money—he had been trying to treat his illness. Judging from the small group of attending family members and friends who had donated the piece of land and coffin for the burial, few people would have been aware that this poor, unfortunate man, newly buried in an obscure grave, was a founding father of the Chinese Communist Party (CCP) and from 1921 to 1927 had been the general secretary, presiding over five party congresses. During this period the CCP grew from a minuscule gathering of fifty-seven intellectuals and students at its first party congress in 1921 to a political movement large enough to assume a major leadership role in modern Chinese history. At that time, it had become allied to the Kuomintang (KMT, established by Sun Yat-sen and later led by Chiang Kai-shek) in waging a nationwide war against the Japanese army. In 1949, four years after the Japanese were defeated in World War II, the CCP triumphed over the KMT and established the People's Republic of China (PRC).

This burial of an old man seemed unimportant in 1942, during the national drama of Chinese resistance against Japanese invaders. Yet in recent decades the identity and reputation of Chen Duxiu have been reformulated repeatedly by the CCP in theatrical representations on stage, film, and television as part of an effort to connect a seemingly irrelevant past to the national and global strategies. Since the founding of the PRC, numerous party history publications, textbooks, and cinematic, dramatic, and literary accounts have depicted Chen Duxiu as a "rightist opportunist" active during the tragic "grand revolution of 1927," in which the CCP submissively collaborated with the KMT. He was thus saddled with the blame for the failure of the Republican revolution, the CCP's first major setback.

In order to show how historical narratives can be constructed and reconstructed, this essay traces five "revolutionary epic" performances that explored Chen Duxiu's life stories in plays, films, and a television drama series. These historical representations, developed by artists and intellectuals in league with the CCP, also reveal the societal anxieties that resulted from the various types of villains and heroes created as part of political culture from 1964 to 2001. Highly melodramatic, the performances had stock characters, such as the villain who posed a societal threat and the hero who eliminated the threat. One might argue that socialist China was exploring the didactic, moralistic, and ideological roles of traditional opera, which featured an array of character types such as "loyal ministers and ardent men of worth," who, as dutiful servants of the state, "rebuke treachery and curse slander." They stand for traits of "filiality and righteousness, incorruptibility and integrity" and express "grief and happiness at [scenes of] separation and reunion."[1] Almost all these figures are present in five performance texts, but how did revolutionary epic theatre's contemporary audiences stomach these echoes of bygone years' didactic, moralistic theatre? What were the cultural and ideological strategies that made them wildly popular, to the extent that some even became "national treasures of state art"?

These "morality plays" answered a persistent need for heroes and villains that could embody the values of the revolution and arouse sympathy for the suffering poor. The plays also engendered in the people the necessary ardor to sacrifice for the noble cause—qualities that the plays shared with their Western counterparts such as the chauvinistic or patriotic figures on the American stage and in film. Yet unlike the stock characters of some Western melodramas, the Chen Duxiu character embodied shifting, even oppositional, identities ranging from villain to hero that reflected drastically different national sentiments of the past half-century.

Chen was first portrayed as an archvillain in the high Mao culture of 1964 and retained that role during the Cultural Revolution (1966–1976), which saw fit to extol Mao Zedong as the supreme hero. In early post-Mao China previous villains, such as Liu Shaoqi (the former president of the PRC), were reclaimed as heroic figures, but Chen remained a villain. Even in the post-Mao era, when the regime had reasons for rehabilitating Chen, he remained a villain because the regime needed a scapegoat against which to pit new heroes. During those early post-Mao years the new government could not attack Mao for the Cultural Revolution's disasters and cruelties. Not until the political reorganizations of the CCP in the later 1980s and 1990s, resulting in an economic process of capitalization and globalization, did Chen emerge in the various stage and film representations as a complex, powerful figure, brilliant and far-sighted enough to rebel against foreign interference in the early course of the Chinese revolution. This calculated discovery of a new hero could work in multiple ways. His spirit could continue to inspire the Chinese people to stay the course set by socialist China, striving for the equality, freedom, and prosperity that the early revolutionary leaders had envisioned. This beneficent persona could also fan a deeply rooted Chinese nationalism and encourage the belief that whatever had gone wrong in the history of both the party and the nation was the fault of foreigners. The party could do no wrong, of course; and after all, "Aren't we all Chinese?" By keeping the CCP political figures on center stage, theatrical performance attested to the continuing relevance of the CCP in contemporary China, where capitalism had replaced socialism, communist idealism was passé, and foreigners were revered as successful entrepreneurs. The revisionist understanding of both the country and Chen stood in stark contrast to Chen's anti-imperialist agenda in the early 1920s, with which he tried to inspire the Chinese people to pursue revolution.

In the larger scheme of things, these epic productions of revisionist scripts of national identity and purpose revealed a problematic relationship of self, subject, agent, state building, and national others in contemporary China's production and reception of theatre performances. Chinese drama and performance thus served as an extended form of political theater that engaged critical issues of memory and commemoration. The popular theatre of modern times delivered a series of contested narratives of the CCP's history. Thus the CCP's political theatre, as realized in its calculated self-representations onstage, revealed some wide-ranging vital questions regarding cultural performance in cross-cultural contexts during the post–Cold War and postsocialist era. By examining these historical narratives, we can understand the theatrical nature of everyday life, both in the formation of political culture and in the shaping of the Chinese people's personal experiences. We would miss an important piece of history without understanding the dramatic culture of modern China and the theatre history that demonstrates this complex history.

In a socialist country, where public performance was censored and tightly controlled by various levels of art officials, the statements of artists, critics, historians, and producers all came from state-run official presses, newspapers, and journals. Artists and historians therefore did not and could not operate as individual subjects, in the manner typical of artists and historians in Western societies. In this restrictive context, the political, social, and psychological ideas of "historical identities" and "performed identities"—which in Western cultures today tend to suggest a great flexibility and even multiplicity of self-expression for individuals—are difficult, even inappropriate, concepts for formulating self-identities and sociopolitical behavior in the national culture of the PRC. Because the theatre producers, critics, and historians had to adhere to the CCP ideology, their published statements had to express the party line, not their own identities and views.

This shaping factor in the performance culture of the People's Republic of China does not necessarily mean that identity politics did not exist, however, even though the production of *The East Is Red* (*Dongfang hong*) in the 1960s was created, directed, and promoted by high-ranking CCP state and even military leaders. The complex relationship that developed between theatre productions and national identities within the PRC occurred as a series of compromises between the ruling party and the individual artists and historians. Nonetheless, several notable artistic productions were achieved under these circumstances. In the 1960s, when *The East Is Red* was created and performed, some of the artists and historians were able to embrace more readily the CCP's socialist blueprint for "an equal and democratic China free from imperialist dominations" (as a popular refrain of the time insisted). Their own political sentiments coincided with the optimistic and nationalist sentiments then associated with the state ideology. Indeed, many important writers and artists had already either led or been affiliated with the left-wing artistic circles before 1949 and had in fact helped to bring about a "new China" through their artistic activities in opposition to the KMT's corruption. Many of them became key players in pioneering socialist theatre before and after 1949.

For example, Lao She, who wrote exemplary socialist plays such as *Teahouse*, switched from fiction writing to playwriting after the founding of the PRC, because he believed that theatre was the most effective way to educate people and change society for the better. Besides this accommodation with the status quo in the PRC's early days, the intellectuals passionately desired to write, create, and perform, and their survival skills led them to find outlets for their creativity. The socialist theatre also provided artists with unprecedented mass audiences, huge stages, lifelong salaries funded by the local and central governments, and a glorified status of professional writers and performers: Lao She was crowned "The People's Artist." They no longer had to eke out a threadbare existence, like the intellectuals under the previous KMT rule.

With changes in regime in post-Mao China (1976 to the present), some intellectuals were able to challenge the official ideology in the limited space permitted them by that ideology. This capacity for independent thinking within ideological limits allowed them to express their individual subjectivities more freely while still playing along with the ruling party and its political program. In some cases these intellectuals and artists could genuinely welcome the new regime as another avenue for change. Nonetheless, the performance representations of past leaders changed slowly, as was the case with Chen Duxiu. Although judgments on some of the former revolutionary leaders were reversed in post-Mao official histories and subsequently in theatre productions, Chen Duxiu had to wait until 1991, when the zigzagging course of the party's histories finally led to his "liberation." The first positive depiction of Chen was in the film *Creating the New World* (*Kai tian pi di*). This and subsequent productions relating to Chen operated within the post-Mao official framework of redeeming party officials wrongly accused in the Maoist era.

The construction of Chen's new image expressed the artistic discontent with the failed aspects of the socialist experience, whereby the artists could attract and please audiences by recourse to embedded subversive sentiments. Various negotiations occurred within the limited cultural space that existed at the borderline between the official and antiofficial cultures within the PRC. These negotiations became a fundamental feature of post-Mao performance culture,[2] which still operated under strict censorship in public yet allowed for the rendering of complex identity politics. In modern Chinese life political identities remained fluid, interwoven, and multidimensional. Of course, the idea of political identity is always complex—and often contradictory—as the various negative and positive representations of Chen reveal. The changing positions of Chen and Mao as villains and heroes demonstrate that the identity representations of political leaders remained in flux within both the CCP and the PRC. Thus the historical and political spectacles from the 1960s to present times substituted in key ways for open historical books for the Chinese people. Over the decades historical truths were represented, yet these truths experienced changing identities. Accordingly, both political and cultural historians need to track and interpret the changing identities, in their several representations, as they transformed over the decades. It is crucial to examine epic performances as historical modes of representation that occurred as a series of complex negotiations between actual historical events and theatrical representation in their shape-changing relations. The problem of the idea of "political identity" when carried from current performance analysis in the West to the study of theatrical representation in modern China became even more complicated when the global politics of the late twentieth century endowed Chen with the political power of a new national hero to expose the corruption and privileges of other CCP leaders.

THE EAST IS RED

One of the most influential depictions of Chen Duxiu as a political villain on the twentieth-century Chinese stage occurred in the revolutionary dance and song epic *The East Is Red*, which premiered in Beijing on October 2, 1964, under the direct supervision of the Chinese state premier, Zhou Enlai. Nowhere else in world history of modern times was a similar theatrical event of such grand scale personally supervised by a head of state. Late in the evening of October 1, the National Day, Zhou Enlai received thousands of the epic's cast members in the Great Hall of the People to announce that Chinese military scientists had just successfully carried out their first atom bomb test without assistance from any foreign country. Zhou conceived of both events in terms of his political program. He revealed the local stage to be an intricate part of state politics and nation building in the battle against Western imperialists and socialist bloc countries such as the Soviet Union, which in the early 1960s had retrieved its scientists from China on the grounds of ideological differences.

Chinese national politics targeting the hegemony of the Soviet Union called for solidarities with other Asian socialist countries such as North Korea, whose own political theatre had inspired *The East Is Red*. In 1960, during his visit to the North Korean armed forces, Liu Yalou (the Chinese Air Force's general commander) attended a similar epic, *Three Thousand Miles of Motherland*, in praise of Kim II Sung's leadership of the Korean revolution. Impressed by the staging of the grand spectacle of 3,000 performers in the Korean army's large warehouse, Liu ordered song-and-dance ensemble personnel attached to his air force to go back to the Soviet areas in Hunan and Jiangxi Provinces and collect favorite Red Army folksongs of the revolutionary war period. Three months later Liu's troupe presented *A Song and Dance Ensemble of Revolutionary History Songs*, performed by a cast of 300 members with much media fanfare in Shanghai and Beijing. The Beijing performance caught the attention of Zhou Enlai.

Realizing the potential for converting such a stage performance into a national commemoration of the glorious party, Zhou called for a production on a much larger scale. He envisioned an epic spectacle involving more than 3,000 cast members who would offer brilliant singing, dancing, and poetry recitation, culled from 70 professional performing troupes all over China. Staged in 1964 and advertised as a major event to celebrate the fifteenth anniversary of the PRC's rise to power, the production was attended by Mao Zedong and other domestic and foreign leaders during the holiday season. A year later *The East Is Red* was made into a film to salute the PRC's sixteenth anniversary. Millions of Chinese people who lacked access to professional theatre, especially those in the rural areas, saw the film.

After the publication of several books on the spectacle, various theatre artists and politicians around the country caused more productions to be mounted in local theatres. From 1965 to 1966, for example, the Guangdong Province production of *The East Is Red* gathered a cast of 1,300 to put on 200 performances attended by 850,000 people. The process of rehearsing became a "party training school," wherein the cast studied Chairman Mao's works and revolutionary histories with a view to remolding their outlooks, which in turn helped them achieve this collective production under challenging circumstances.[3]

A book on the performance of *The East Is Red* in Guangzhou further dramatizes the role of these political performances in everyday life. In the audience, the book claimed, were revolutionary war veterans reliving their experiences through scenes in the epic. By means of the spectacle, they appreciated the wise leadership of Chairman Mao, who had led them through the life-and-death struggle to liberate the Chinese people from foreign invaders and domestic enemies. Throughout China people embraced the production as a timely reminder of the miserable past before 1949 and the happy and prosperous life that was supposed to exist in socialist China. In the Cold War era, when China was isolated from the rest of the "free world," *The East Is Red* also served to demonstrate the wisdom of Mao's leadership to people from the Third World countries. For example, a clerk from Argentina reported that the revolutionary epic he attended in Guangzhou not only was "one of the best dance productions in the world" but also drew a powerful lesson about the Chinese people's glorious history and their great leader Chairman Mao.[4] A young Chinese woman from Malaysia compared the miserable life of a Chinese peasant girl presented for sale to strangers in *The East Is Red* to her own childhood experience, when her impoverished parents felt compelled to sell her overseas; having experienced "the bitter past," the young woman proclaimed that she especially appreciated life in the brave new world of the People's Republic of China.[5]

The East Is Red blended, manipulated, and transformed historical "records," as provided by the party line of the PRC, into an imaginary theatre spectacle. An early attempt to construct a Mao cult (which reached its apex during the Cultural Revolution in 1966), *The East Is Red* begins with a prologue titled "Sunflower Turning toward the Sun," in which seventy female dancers in long, blue silk dresses wave silk sunflower props in time to *The East Is Red*'s theme song: "The East is red / The sun has risen / Mao Zedong has appeared in China / He is devoted to the Chinese people's welfare / He is the people's great savior." With grace and tenderness, they walk toward the radiant sun rising from the ocean, symbolizing "the vivid image of sunflowers growing toward the sun while the masses are guided by the CCP's leadership."[6]

To elaborate on the significance of Mao's "rising sun" image, the subsequent six scenes highlighted the main episodes in the grand drama of Chinese revolutionary history, all designed to portray Mao as indispensable leader. In scene 1, titled "Dawn in the East," a narrator urges the audience "living in the magnificent era of Mao" never to forget how much hardship the people had suffered before liberation. With the projected image of an American battleship anchored in Shanghai harbor as a backdrop, struggling dock workers contend with foreigners and their Chinese agents, who had tyrannized the Chinese people in "dark, old China."[7] The next song, "The October Wind Comes from the North," accompanies the narrator's celebration of the Russian October Revolution of 1917, "which spread Marxism and Leninism to China." As the result of the 1919 May Fourth movement, which had "raised the banner of anti-imperialist and antifeudalist agendas and helped disseminate Communist idealism, the great CCP came into being in 1921," the narrator declares. Thanks to "Comrade Mao Zedong," who "folded the theories of Marxism and Leninism into Chinese revolutionary experience," the "brilliant truth finally lit up the Chinese revolution's road."[8]

Scene 2, "The Spark That Sets the Prairie Afire," staged the sudden tragic split between the KMT and the CCP, when the KMT "massacred" several thousands of workers, CCP members, and their sympathizers in Shanghai on April 12, 1927. The narrator explains that "because of Chen Duxiu's defeatist policies" in regard to the KMT "the grand revolution failed." To drive home the dire consequences of Chen's mistakes, in the next and most memorable scene enacted on the PRC stage fearless revolutionary martyrs march side by side in chains toward the execution ground, singing the "Internationale," convinced that their deaths will awaken millions to the necessity of taking up their Communist cause. The contrast between Mao the savior and Chen the traitor is further developed in the next four scenes, dramatizing Mao's leadership in establishing "the first Soviet bases" in the Jinggang Mountains (1927), the Long March to escape the KMT's elimination campaigns (1935–1936), the anti-Japanese war (1937–1945), and civil war with the KMT (1945–1949). All these scenes lead to the climactic festivity: a celebration of the PRC's founding, with colorfully dressed schoolchildren and dancers and singers from multiethnic backgrounds singing the "Internationale," joined by the audience in rousing sing-alongs.

State-run theatre reviews reflected the party line stance by insisting that the greatest appeal of *The East Is Red* was its strict adherence to modern Chinese history. Yet the glaring distortion of a key episode in the scene "Dawn in the East" undermines any such claim of historical truth. When the poetic narrator announces the founding of the CCP in 1921, in response to the October Revolution, photos of the heads of Karl Marx and V. I. Lenin are projected onto the huge red background, together with two huge red flags, one picturing the head of Mao Zedong, the other with the CCP symbol of a hammer and a sickle. With this single stroke of theatrical setting, modern revolutionary history was fundamentally rewritten. It erased the contributions of Chen Duxiu, who co-founded the CCP with Li Dazhao; the two of them, not Mao, should have been the images paired with Marx and Lenin. A self-declared student of Chen and Li, Mao was one of the CCP's eleven members present at the first party congress but by no means its head. Seen in this light, *The East Is Red* became political theatre whose construction of stories of origins and teleology had an immeasurable impact on Chinese history in the 1960s. The spectacle, with its montage of historical representations shaped into a narrative of party history, could be viewed as a prologue to the dramatic political theatre of the Cultural Revolution (1966–1976), when the Mao cult whose seeds had been sown in *The East Is Red* grew into an essential part of political theatre. It also provides a typical example of Chinese intellectuals not only collaborating with the ruling ideology in theatre productions but, most intriguingly, discovering their own possibilities for self-realization in a state art that granted them a new elite status as revolutionary artists. Some of these elites wholeheartedly believed the party line, others halfheartedly embraced it, and others did not believe it, yet they all explored the rare opportunities to write, act, and perform the grand national spectacle.[9] These ambiguities of varying degrees of alliance with the government allowed the individuals to blend their ambitions with the public circumstances. Everyone participated in the national narrative. Whatever their beliefs and motives, they contributed to the complex process of artistic expression that affected the everyday lives of the people, who themselves shared a special relationship to state theatre culture.

EARLY POST-MAO REVOLUTIONARY HISTORY PLAYS AND FILMS

If *The East Is Red* misrepresented the historical conditions of Chen's activities and contributions during the PRC's first seventeen years (1949–1966) and during the Cultural Revolution's ensuing ten years, he should have enjoyed a "makeover" in early post–Cultural Revolution China, when Mao's absolute power was challenged and political enemies like Liu Shaoqi were rehabilitated in party narratives and theatrical representations. But the rehabilitation did not happen. Chen remained a villain in the artistic boom of spoken drama that emerged in early post-Mao China. The "revolutionary history plays," as the flourishing genre became known, were an important part of the political campaign to restore the Chinese revolutionary leaders' rightful places in history.[10] After the arrest of the Gang of Four in 1976, revolutionary history plays attracted many people to the theatres, to see onstage the downfall of new traitors while celebrating the nation's new "liberation." Earlier liberations included the battle against the Japanese and the defeat of Chiang Kai-shek and the KMT. The 1978 play *Newspaper Boys* (*Baotong*) celebrated a new hero, Zhou Enlai, and demonstrated his courage and wisdom in spearheading CCP activities in Chongqing during the war, when he effected the second CCP-KMT alliance that waged the national war against the Japanese invaders. *Eastward March* (*Dong jing, Dong jing!*), which premiered in 1978, and *Chen Yi Leaves the Mountain* (*Chen Yi chu shan*), which premiered in 1979, dramatized the war legends surrounding the generals He Long and Chen Yi, respectively. They were persecuted to death during the Cultural Revolution and rehabilitated as heroes again in early post-Mao political theatre.

The redemption of tortured leaders of the CCP required the creation of more villains in conformity with new party historical narratives, which had reversed verdicts of those persecuted during the Cultural Revolution but not those eliminated from the party's earlier days. Scriptwriters, playwrights, and theatre critics had to work cautiously within the limits of the party lines, expressing their anger against the Gang of Four while complying with existing condemnations of Chen Duxiu. This is another instance of intellectuals collaborating with the new authorities in the early days of regime change, without losing sight of opportunities to express themselves to the degree that the ruling ideology would allow. For example, unlike *The East Is Red*, where Chen Duxiu was merely mentioned as the intimidated traitor lacking vision and wisdom who had led the party astray, post-Mao plays and films presented Chen as a real dramatic character in order to sharpen the contrast with Zhou Enlai's political correctness. Chen emerged on the stage to set back the revolutionary campaign and even provoked great leaders such as Zhou and others openly to rebel against his misguided leadership in order to win major battles in the revolutionary warfare.

The 1981 play *A Generation of Heroes* (*Yi dai ying hao*) is a case in point. The play presents a crucial period of the Chinese Communist revolution, with thirty-four historical characters, including Chen Duxiu, Zhou Enlai, Zhu De, He Long, and Chiang Kai-shek (the commissar of the Northern Expedition Army). Portraying a series of historical events, the play features Zhou Enlai's successful leadership of the Shanghai workers' uprising in March 1927, when they defeated the warlords in anticipation of the arrival of Chiang Kai-shek's Northern Expedition armies in Shanghai. Next Chiang is shown forcing the workers' militia to surrender their weapons and disperse their troops; massacring thousands of workers, CCP members, and sympathizers; and driving the CCP, now his archenemy, into the underground.

After revealing the dire consequences of the CCP's setback, the play follows up with a youthful romance. Zhou Enlai's wife, Deng Yinchao, bids him farewell as he leaves Shanghai; although she has just lost their first child at birth, she is much more concerned with the CCP's future; "Have you considered that the CCP central committee might have made serious mistakes?" she asks Zhou. Zhou, who has already written Chen Duxiu requesting a reversal of his policies of relying heavily on the KMT for the revolution, replies that the CCP must declare war on Chiang's reactionary troops and establish its own armies to fight the reactionary forces.[11]

In a subsequent scene, various literary figures, actors, political activists, and military leaders gather in Wuhan, where they appeal to Wang Jingwei, the left-wing KMT leader, who has led anti-Chiang factions and pledged to join forces with the CCP against the new and old warlords. They excoriate Chen Duxiu for lacking the courage to stand up against Chiang and for his submissiveness to Wang. Ye Ting, his CCP General Secretary, says that Chen does "not even have the courage of a small child," since children had already joined the workers' and peasants' militia to fight Chiang.[12] To further appease Wang, Chen distributes a party resolution to dismantle workers' militia and other worker/peasant associations, ordering them to hand over their weapons to the KMT in order to show his sincerity in collaborating with Wang. Zhou Enlai, Chen Geng, and Nie Rongzhen (all later on persecuted during the Cultural Revolution as villains) denounce Chen's order as being equivalent to "a declaration of surrender" to the KMT.[13] When confronted with Zhou's argument that "only timely military uprisings can preserve the CCP and its revolutionary forces," Chen attempts to attack Mao Zedong's theory of "using revolutionary armed forced to fight against the reactionaries." In the play Chen dismisses this idea as nothing but disruptive to the united front with the KMT. "No one could talk about theory," Chen claims, because they were all his "students" back then, when he first started to spread Marxist theory throughout China before the founding of the CCP.[14] Chen even boasts that he successfully led the past five party congresses: "I would rather lose everything, even all the workers and peasants, than to lose Wang, in order to hold onto the current cooperation with the KMT."[15]

By the end of the play, in spite of Chen's tyranny, Zhou Enlai, He Long, and others succeeded in organizing the first military uprising against the KMT, known in Chinese history as the "August First Uprising of 1927." Here Chen's dramatic character played the role of a party "historian" to re-create Chen as a despot, thereby negating his previous reputation as a great liberal who heralded the May Fourth movement's drive for science and democracy. This is another typical case in which epic drama rewrote the political and intellectual history of modern China. The character of Chen, conveniently serving as the villainous tyrant, demonstrates that it was the "correct" policies of the wise and heroic leaders such as Zhou Enlai and others that saved the CCP and the country. By bringing Mao Zedong into the play, the playwright also confirmed that in the judgment of history Mao never failed in his role as the greatest leader to lead the Chinese revolution to victory in the most crucial period of the past party history, even though he and his followers persecuted Zhou and others during the Cultural Revolution.

Building on the popularity of Zhou Enlai, the 1981 film *Nanchang Uprising* (*Nanchang qiyi*), based on the play *The Storm of August First* (*Bayi fengbao*), exceeded the latter in popularity because it was more accessible to more audiences than the stage performance. Chen Duxiu appears only briefly in *Nanchang Uprising* as an antagonist, to enhance Zhou's credentials as the protagonist. Chen turns down Zhou's request that he pressure Wang Jingwei for the 2,000 guns he promised for the workers' militia, on the grounds that he does not want to provoke Wang. To persuade Wang to declare war on Chiang Kai-shek, Chen suggests dismissing the workers' militia and the peasant movement against rural China's rich landlords, whose interests the KMT represents. In his second meeting with Zhou, Chen accuses the Chinese peasants of being hooligans, mobs, and gangsters with no revolutionary qualifications, seeming to imply that he believes what the Soviets concluded from their experience: only a mature proletarian working class can constitute the primary force of the Communist movement.

Unlike *A Generation of Heroes*, with its national spectacles peopled by numerous political and literary figures, *Nanchang Uprising* focuses on a central question in the Chinese revolution. Can the Chinese peasants, whose lives and values derived from a semifeudalist society, become the major players for the "Chinese proletariat revolution," contrary to the teachings of Marx and Lenin and the experience of the Soviet socialist revolution, which had relied on the working class in urban uprisings? To authenticate the idea of the peasants as the backbone of the Chinese revolution, the film turns to tales of personal romance. A poor peasant wife joins her husband, fighting side by side with him in the Nanchang uprising, but then loses him on the battlefield before victory has been won.

In terms of the identity politics of the performers, it is important to point out that the poor peasants—and especially women characters on the stage and on screen—were played by glamorous, graceful performers, who did not act or speak as the rustic, uneducated rural poor characters they were supposed to be portraying. Whereas it is common in films and plays of other countries to use beautiful performers to portray poor people for dramatic effects, Chinese script writers and performers were taught by the CCP to use the identity politics of the common people to promote the values of the party. Constantly told to learn from members of the working class to represent them better, Chinese performers attempted to act like them in order to advocate their interests. In the name of "their" interest, however, script writers and performers in fact transcribed the party's demands for its people into loyal, terrified, and obedient dramatic characters at the expense of the real interest of the working class. This problematic mode of representation—in which the intellectual elite collaborated with the ruling ideology in using the image of the subalterns—has become one of the most consistent features of Chinese performances in the PRC.

CREATING THE NEW WORLD

Not until 1991 do we witness the first rehabilitation of Chen Duxiu's image as a new hero in the 1990s as the result of another round of revisionist history in the party literature. The revision of Chen—actually a historical reversal—occurred in the film *Creating the New World* (*Kai tian pi di*), made for the seventieth anniversary of the founding of the CCP. In the ten years from 1981 to 1991 the Chinese political, intellectual, and artistic landscape had undergone huge changes owing to post-Mao enlightenment. China's turn toward greater political pluralism challenged the dogmatic socialist legacy, especially the previously untouchable "CCP party narrative." In 1985, for instance, the CCP official journal *Party History Newsletter* published an essay, "On Evaluating Chen Duxiu's Life," that finally eliminated the previous four verdicts of Chen as "Japanese collaborator," "opportunist joining the revolution," "usurper of the top position of the CCP," and "KMT spy." Although the essay retained the other familiar accusations that Chen was "a representative of the rightists," "a defeatist," and "a Trotskyist who betrayed Marxism and Leninism"—all of which would be dismissed later—it articulated a new official view of Chen's life story brought about by the Research Office of CCP history under the jurisdiction of the CCP central committee.[16]

In subsequent years this change in the appraisal of Chen generated another event of political theatre. In a 2001 memorial work celebrating the life achievements of Hu Yaobang, the party general secretary in the new 1980s era of reform, historians recounted that Hu was dissatisfied with the first draft of the above-mentioned essay. He asked the historians to come up with a more comprehensive reevaluation of Chen Duxiu that did justice to him as the brilliant leader of the May Fourth movement and a co-founder of the CCP. The mistakes of the CCP in its early years, Hu argued, had less to do with Chen's leadership role than with the overpowering presence of the KMT and the impractical leadership of the Comintern, which failed to understand the Chinese reality. Hu's guidance in revising this work made it possible for the subsequent reassessment of Chen to be closer to what we now know about the man and his activities.[17]

Indeed, Hu acted as a "super historian" whose power as the top party leader led to an unprecedented period of political reform that challenged Mao's mistakes before and during the Cultural Revolution. Hu's powerful leadership urged party officials and historians to venture into an otherwise risky territory of rehabilitating countless people ruined by wrong verdicts such as the declaration of innocence of Liu Shaoqi, the former president of the PRC persecuted to death during the Cultural Revolution. Morever, Hu's revisionist campaign not only contributed to the new economic and political reforms in the 1980s but also resulted in a more relaxed and liberal public sphere that encouraged the intellectuals to put forward their demands. This activity cost Hu his top position, from which he was forced to resign in 1987. His sudden death in April 1989 triggered the June 4 student demonstrations against the party's corruption and his unfair treatment by the party. The Hu-supervised work on Chen, however, initiated the founding of the Chen Duxiu Research Association in 1989 and numerous essays, biographies, chronologies, and memoirs of Chen's life and career. These publications created a "redramatization" of Chen's life, which helped to boost the declining image of a Chinese regime that had posed both as the inheritor of the CCP-bequeathed legacy of representing the broad interests of the masses and as a new generation of leaders radically different from their Maoist predecessors.

In the new film entitled *Creating the New World* (1991), Chen is shown as a martyr willing to die for the political cause. This representation is poles apart from the depiction of Chen Duxiu as an opportunist and traitor in the previous three works. Numerous historical figures join Chen in the film to stress the difficulties and personal sacrifices they faced in the early years before and after the founding of the CCP. These sacrifices evoke the film's title phrase, *Kai tian pi di*, with its clear reference to the Chinese creation myth of the universe. In the myth, the world comes into being after Pan Gu has separated earth from heaven through his immense personal sacrifice, requiring him to grow one yard per day for 18,000 years to reach the height of the sky to prevent it from collapsing. Upon his death from exhaustion after the heaven and the earth had become separated, his body grew into an integral part of the universe, benefiting generations to come.

Despite the mythical distinctions between the story of Pan Gu and the history of the CCP's founding fathers, *Creating the New World* is essentially a story of the beginning, or the new beginning, of an old, dark world transformed into a brand new world according to the Communist ideal. Chen emerges as a visionary, dynamic leader who supported the Beijing University students in the May Fourth movement, edited the seminal intellectual journal *New Youth*, and fearlessly fought the vicious warlords, who imprisoned him for antigovernment activities. The nationwide "rescuing-Chen" movement as presented in the film fortified Chen's reputation as a national leader, as further attested by the efforts of Dr. Sun Yat-sen, the president of the KMT, to free him, a historical event that occurred in September 1919,[18] dramatically represented in the film with impressive scenes. The film shows Chen accepting the tenets of Marxism and Leninism during his 98-day imprisonment. In these particular scenes Chen savors his role as orator, speaking eloquently to the crowd outside the prison and to the oppressed workers in factories. These events can be traced in many scholarly essays and biographies of Chen published since the late 1980s. History was being renarrated, in accord with Hu's leadership, by intellectuals and artists alike, a partnership of accommodation with the CCP that had continued to operate since *The East Is Red*.

In contrast to the then familiar tropes that characterized Mao as "the great leader" and "great teacher" who inspired generations of revolutionaries in the party history, in a shocking and even unimaginably daring move at that time to reverse the past narrative the film presents Mao Zedong as an inspired student and admirer of Chen's revolutionary career. More closely following the most recent research on what had "really" happened in the past than the earlier party histories and performances, the film shows Mao in his capacity as the editor-in-chief of the *Xiang River Review* in Changsha city, courageously protesting the Beijing government's imprisonment of Chen in 1919. To drive home the point that the film offers a realist historical representation of the past, the script writers let their character Mao quote a few lines from an actual article that he had published in the local newspaper in 1919. The film's Mao proclaims of Chen: "He is a brilliant and shining star of the intellectuals" and "I wish the magnificent spirit of Mr. Chen a long, long life!" Such utterances, which credit Chen as the revered leader at the origin of the party, contrast sharply with the way in which both Chen and Mao were represented in numerous representations in arts and literatures during the period when the familiar popular slogan "Long live Chairman Mao!" was constantly heard.

Other episodes in the film could also more easily find their counterparts in the historical archives of the past. For instance, as a kind of elementary school teacher in Changsha, Mao gives his pupils this instruction: "It is Mr. Chen who has introduced Mr. Democracy and Mr. Science to us. These two gentlemen are really outstanding teachers." This representation of Mao praising Chen as the master teacher of the people was indeed shocking, considering the numerous movies and plays that had portrayed Mao himself as the great educator. Another episode shows Chen providing Mao with his galley proofs of Marx's *Communist Manifesto* in the first complete Chinese translation. Chen tells Mao that at his age he had also toyed with the idea of assassinating the empress dowager, studied abroad, edited newspapers, and served in prison, until he "finally discovered Marxism after seventeen years of searching for truth."[19] Having read Chen's copy of the *Communist Manifesto* overnight, Mao becomes so excited that he determines to bring Marxism to Hunan Province; he vows to heed Chen's teaching that only through class war can the workers seize political power from the bourgeois.

Thus, by repositioning Chen squarely above Mao as the true pioneer who introduced socialism to early twentieth-century China, the film altered the powerful image of Mao that had been spread by *The East Is Red*, which saw Mao as the sole pioneer of the Chinese revolution, on a par with Marx and Lenin. In that historical narrative the three of them were the Chinese trinity of revolution, comparable to the troika of V. I. Lenin, Joseph Stalin, and Leon Trotsky in the Russian version of the true leaders of the international socialist revolution. Even though some of these plots were rearranged and minor dramatic characters were created for the integrity and flow of the film, most of these events corresponded to the revisionist party history, biographies, memories, and oral narratives that had mushroomed since the late 1980s. It is obvious that Hu's intervention left fewer gaps between what really happened in the past and the latest revisionist version of Chen; but the film should not be seen as a more "reliable" documentary of historical truth, because it is also filled with the new party ideology of revisionist history in the 1990s, which removes Mao from the pinnacle of the CCP. What is important is the impulse toward revisionist history, as we see in the problematic and changing representations of Chen and other state leaders in the state media, no matter who is in power. In the modern Chinese performance scene, therefore, we need to be especially careful about the complexities, ironies, and subversive underpinnings in any kind of "historical representations."

Also, it is important to note that the dramatic structure of *Creating the New World* resembles that of both *A Generation of Heroes* and *Nanchang Uprising* in its genre traits. All of them use melodrama as the inevitable means for representing character, crisis, emotions, and historical turning points. The film depicts Chen as a strict but loving father. In a moving scene of family reunion, his two sons visit him in prison, where Chen encourages them to be brave and to follow his revolutionary idealism. The two sons later pursued studies in France, were elected to the CCP central committee, and subsequently were made heads of the CCP provincial committees. In 1927 and 1928, before and after Chen was ousted from the CCP leadership in the summer of 1927, his two sons were arrested, tortured, and murdered by the KMT, both betrayed by traitors from within the CCP organizations. His sons' martyrdom reminded audiences in 1990s China that—contrary to the charge that Chen was a traitor to the party—he had made great sacrifices and endured great losses in his own family, as had Mao, who lost six family members to the revolutionary cause. Chen and his family were indeed victims of real traitors from within the CCP, who had handed over his brilliant sons to be slaughtered by his enemies. The personal sacrifices required of Chen and Mao evoked those demanded of Pan Gu, the ancient hero in the creation myth.

Creating the New World caused a perceptible stir in China and also in Hong Kong, where Chen Duxiu's surviving son was reportedly excited to encounter the very first positive account of his father in the Chinese media. The Chinese Internet also hailed the great acting of Shao Honglai, who had played Chen Duxiu in both *Nanchang Uprising* and *Creating the New World*. Shao claimed that for the second film he had plowed through historical archives in order to understand and portray the "real" Chen: a profound thinker and a masculine, courageous, and upright man endowed with literary talents and moved by real emotions.[20] For obvious reasons, Shao did not go into his motivation and preparation for portraying Chen in an unfavorable light in the first movie. Multiple—and sometimes opposing—perspectives from performers, script writers, and audiences in performance art therefore reinforced Chen's positive image much more powerfully than did the party's political treatises, which in recent years have been deemed increasingly irrelevant by ordinary readers in contemporary China.

THE SUN RISES IN THE EAST

In 2001 the heroic image of Chen was developed even more substantially in the television series called *The Sun Rises in the East* (*Ri chu dongfang*). Going beyond the 1991 film *Creating the New World*, the popular television series of twenty episodes portrayed Chen as an anti-Stalinist hero, who stood against the popular trends of the socialist movements in the early twentieth century in order to pursue his own vision of the Chinese revolution. The most radical aspect of *The Sun Rises in the East* is this total redemption of Chen. The television drama depicts him not merely as a CCP founding father but also as a visionary hero who rebelled against the totalitarian Stalinist regime and the Comintern hegemony. The Comintern had dominated Communist movements all over the globe without comprehending the historical, cultural, ethnic, and ideological differences among the various countries and societies beyond Soviet borders. The supposed "failure" of Chen's leadership—and by extension of the Chinese revolution leading up to the tragic events of 1927—attested to the bankruptcy of Soviet approaches. In accord with the revisionist historical narrative, the first ten episodes focused on Chen and provided the historical details of the Comintern and CCP's secret decisions and activities, many of which were then unknown to the Chinese public. These new details in the television drama reflected recent research by Chinese party historians, who had traveled to Russia to examine the secret archives that included the correspondence between the Comintern and the CCP. In just one year leading to the failure of the grand revolution of 1927, Comintern wrote numerous letters to Chen, ordering him to follow Comintern policy, which he rejected as incorrect and impractical. This coverage gave the television series the weight of a new documentary, fortifying it with both "the spirit and scope of an epic" and "irreplaceable archival significance."[21]

To reflect this new light on Chen as the original thinker unwilling to follow foreign models, the first episode expressed Chen's doubts about foreign authority. In response to Li Dazhao's conversion to Marxism, as Li described it in his famous essay "My Marxist View" (1919),[22] Chen questions Li's claim that Chinese society would undergo great changes if only Chen were to add the word "Marxism" to his popular science and democracy banners. Chen wonders aloud: "Why a Soviet model for revolution? We are here in Beijing, in China!" With the rising soundtrack in the background heightening his heroic image, Chen pauses and reflects, in his passionate and determined fashion: "I still believe that we should not limit ourselves to any kind of 'isms'; the most urgent task for China is revolution."[23] When Li asks him to describe his vision for a new China devoid of a Marxist perspective, Chen replies with confidence and enthusiasm: "The future new society should be honest, positive, progressive, free, equal, creative, peaceful, kind-hearted, harmonious, beautiful, loving, mutually beneficial, work-oriented, and happy for everyone in the entire society. I hope that we diminish and even eliminate tendencies toward the hypocritical, negative, conservative, class-biased, restrictive, ugly, evil, lazy, depressive, war-ridden, and chaotic that have served the interests of the minority!" In this episode Chen quotes from his own famous essay published in *New Youth*. The China he envisioned differed from the blueprint given in the *Communist Manifesto*, which advocated setting up a proletarian dictatorship over the bourgeoisie and other exploiting classes.

According to this television version of past events, the sheer force of Chen's belief in a free, egalitarian, and happy society moved Li Dazhao, He Shi, and Chen's wife, as attested by the closeups of their admiring expressions. This scene thus reminded or taught the television audience that Chen was originally a liberal Chinese intellectual who reluctantly had to adhere to increasing Soviet pressures in the 1920s.

In the subsequent key moments of the Chinese revolution, Chen continued to doubt and reject foreign interference. In the third episode Li Dazhao tells him that Grigory Voitinsky, a Soviet representative sent by the Comintern to help to found the CCP, has recommended that they pay attention to the workers' living conditions and revolutionary desires. But Chen cautions Li: "What does a foreigner know about Chinese society? We should guard against blindly following in their footsteps." Chen's cautionary statement proved prophetical. As subsequent history would show, CCP leaders suffered a series of tragic defeats after they followed the Soviet model of relying on the urban working classes as the backbone of the proletarian revolution and threw themselves into organizing worker strikes and even uprisings in the style of the Paris Commune of 1871.

To enhance Chen's noble qualities, the television series stressed the dramatic conflicts between Chen and the Soviet agents. For instance, in the seventh episode, set in 1921, Chen accepts Li Dazhao's suggestion that they speed up efforts to convene the first CCP congress in Shanghai. Upon hearing that Lenin has sent Comintern agent Hendricus Sneevliet to investigate the feasibility of a CCP organization, Chen complains: "How can the CCP become a branch of the Comintern before it has even been born?" In the eighth episode, set after the first CCP congress, Chen argues fiercely against Sneevliet's assertion that all Bolshevik movements in the world should be led by the Comintern and that China is no exception. Chen insists that the CCP would accept guidance and suggestions from outside but not overt leadership. The ninth episode ends with Sneevliet delivering dramatic, deadly directives. Having met with Sun Yat-sen, Sneevliet proposes that the CCP join Sun's KMT to reform it. Sneevliet maintains that a small party like the CCP, with only a few dozen members, has no choice but to rely on KMT's existing might to advance its political agenda. Hearing this, Chen is so furious that he breaks his teacup, yelling: "As a veteran Bolshevik, you should know the crucial difference between the two parties. I do not allow you to look down upon us!"

To explain who was really responsible for the ill-fated KMT-CCP collaboration, another episode centers on the CCP "Western Lake special session" in 1922, when the Comintern's directive that the CCP make common cause with the KMT sparks off Chen's vehement objection. In the third CCP congress in 1923, Chen reluctantly gives in to Sneevliet: CCP members will join the KMT as individual members in order to promote the two-party collaboration, but only if the KMT will undergo democratic reform. By dramatizing the CCP party congresses and the 1924 KMT congress presided over by Sun Yat-sen and bidden to promote party reform and collaboration (an event that had never been portrayed in any other media before), the television series highlighted the Soviet agents' roles and the problematic relations between the CCP and the Comintern. As CCP party chief Chen fought repeatedly to repel the Soviet hegemony, only to be labeled the chief architect of *its* "defeatist" and "opportunist" policies—and, most absurdly, labeled as such by the Soviets. In this connection, a Chinese critic observed that the portrayal of dramatic conflicts between Chen and the Comintern in *The Sun Rises in the East* broke new ground in a better understanding of how Chen had preserved "the independent status of the CCP."[24]

In this sugar-coated version of Chen's democratic vision of a better China for everyone, we see several layers of representation at work. First, in a new era of globalization and capitalization the almost perfect Chen as the first heroic leader of the CCP again validates the significant role of the CCP. In the late 1990s the party had finally built China into a strong economic power on an equal footing with the rest of the world community, free from imperialist invasions and interferences from either the democratic West or the totalitarian East in the socialist bloc. Ironically, this wealthier China was achieved through capitalism, which produced a greater gap between the rich and the poor in the country, thereby moving in the opposite direction from the CCP's socialist approach, which had aimed at narrowing this economic gap. By representing Chen as an admirable anti-Soviet hero, the television series appealed to the neonationalist sentiments of the Chinese audience at the beginning of the twenty-first century, an appeal to a policy that aimed to protect China from foreign domination in a global economy. By celebrating the dream of an independent China, as supposedly envisioned and articulated by Chen eighty years ago, the television narrative contributed to the current Chinese government's need to claim the uniqueness of the Chinese revolution—unlike any other model in the world. These complex circumstances made it possible for the television script writers, producers, and critics to claim—quite safely—that the television drama provided contemporary audiences with a "vivid history textbook through artistic media" that they could use to celebrate the CCP's history for a free and independent China.[25] According to the critics, the television drama presented "a touching" history, "reflective" of the CCP from its miraculous birth to the historical turning point when "the CCP finally found its path to victory," a precious epic as "significant" for the Chinese people as "the sun rising in the East."[26] The changing image of Chen, which served the ruling ideology's new need to promote its current agenda, reflected the governmental adjustments to the changing contemporary conditions.

Second, *The Sun Rises in the East* benefited from a more relaxed public and intellectual life and a booming book and media market, exploring the mutual benefits among different genres. In the late 1980s and early 1990s television dramas, popular with people from various age groups and social backgrounds, began to predominate over films and stage performances. A number of television series adapted novels and stage plays from traditional and modern canons. Huang Yazhou, who wrote the television script of *The Sun Rises in the East*, also published his long biographical novel about Chen with the same title. As a popular writer, he was sensitive to the changing tastes and needs of the television audiences and readers. This practice of deriving a novel from a popular television series offered a new wrinkle on the more familiar process of adapting a television drama from a novel or other literary works. Writing the television drama script first allowed Huang to choose the most theatrical episodes; his subsequent writing of the novel clearly profited by using television-script techniques, such as "montage," "fluidities in space and time," and "the visualization of narrative language."[27] These techniques reached a wider readership by tapping not only the viewers of the television drama who wanted to read more on the topic but also the booming market in biographies and autobiographies of historical figures. The clever venture of publishing a novel based upon a well-received television show became popular in the 1990s because it could successfully attract audiences and readers via creative interactive multimedia. Historical representations of Chen in the television series, in this context of popular culture, took on literary and fictional characteristics aimed at more effectively appealing to audiences who were drawn to entertainment yet still sought information about current affairs and their historical past.

Third, *The Sun Rises in the East* reflected—and in turn promoted—the tremendous interests and painstaking efforts in new scholarship. Especially appealing were histories of the CCP and histories of intellectual and literary topics. Histories of international socialist and Communist movements were also popular. These studies were essential parts of global politics, Cold War histories, and colonial and postcolonial debates. Party history scholars confronted the damaging hegemonic policies of the Comintern, which was seen as a problematic episode in the global Communist movements. In the original archives of the Comintern, Chen Duxiu's name appeared 198 times on the issues of Chinese revolution between 1920 to 1927, the period when he was in charge of the CCP.[28] From 1923 to 1927 the Politburo of Stalin's Communist Party called 122 meetings to discuss issues and directions of the Chinese revolution, which resulted in 738 resolutions, an average of one resolution every two and a half days.[29] Chen's leadership experience overlapped substantially with the twenty-four years of existence of the Comintern, whose entanglement with Chen provided the party historians with key events and issues for representing early party history.

Writing from the revisionist perspective of the 1990s, historians argued that Chen was truly ahead of his times in not merely rejecting the Comintern during its "Trotskyist period" but also, most astonishingly, rejecting Trotskyism and other alternative theories of the Soviet experience. Accordingly, Chen was the first leader to advocate "socialist democracy" as the alternative approach to the "proletariat dictatorship"—both within the Chinese experience and in the global socialist movement. The documents reflected the Comintern's arbitrary demands for all socialist movements and Communist parties to follow the Soviet model and to sacrifice their own regional interests in order to serve the interests of the Soviet in the name of the final victory of the world revolution. This finally led Chen, in the last six years before his death, to reject not merely Stalinism but the very underlying system, which, if left intact, "would produce numerous Stalins in many other countries."[30] According to Pan Peixin (writing in 2001 for the *Journal of the Party Training School*, which was attached to the CCP Party Committee of Huangzhou City), Chen advocated "a socialist democratic system" for the masses in order to battle against personality cults, "proletariat dictatorship," power abuses, and both individual and group corruption; he wanted to narrow the increasing gap between the ordinary people and the bureaucratic ruling class.[31] Chen's critique was twenty years earlier than Nikita Khrushchev's 1964 secret report that denounced Stalin. *The Sun Rises in the East* thus revealed Chen's persistent demand for democracy, human rights, and a multiparty system in socialist countries. This portrait has become his political identity in recent years, especially for the Chinese people still in search of these fundamental rights that Chen had advocated decades earlier.

Fourth, in light of this new historical research, it can be argued that *The Sun Rises in the East* in effect re-created Chen as a free, liberal thinker, who valued his own independent thinking and indigenous Chinese approach much more than the dogmatic Marxist doctrines imposed by his Soviet boss. Thanks to historical circumstances beyond his control, however,

Chen was apparently swept into the CCP leadership and thus, in spite of his heroic resistance, was pushed to an inevitable downfall on the tragic wheel-of-fortune of party politics. Implicitly, the television drama raised an intriguing question. What would have happened if Chen and Li had not converted to Marxism but had persevered in the liberal approach to the Chinese revolution through peaceful means of social transformation? Is Marxism really capable of freeing China from its predicaments? Indeed, in 2006 some historians pointed out that Chen urged his friend to have Trotsky's *The Revolution Betrayed: What Is the Soviet Union and Where Is It Going?* (1936) translated from English into Chinese. Chen readily agreed with Trotsky's argument that there would be no democracy without the existence of oppositional parties; this position, which contributed to the tragic fates of both Trotsky and Chen, pointed to a crucial difference between a dictatorship and a modern democratic political system.[32]

These historical documents concerning Chen, recovered by contemporary Chinese intellectuals, reflected a continuing search for a free and democratic China—an alternative vision and history than that of the totalitarian socialist regime, which Chen had rejected as early as the late 1930s. Ironically, Chen has been rediscovered as an early pioneer who denounced the very socialist system that his co-founded CCP still defends and imposes. The rehabilitation of Chen allows for a return to his earlier call for a society of "science" and "democracy" during the May Fourth movement, a call that still rallies support in the people but is not fulfilled by the political system in contemporary China. The message of a liberal Chen is clearly subversive, for it potentially allows some readers and audiences to question authority even as they appear to follow the societal rules of the present day.

One wonders what Chen Duxiu would say if he returned to the twentieth-first century and observed China as it became the fastest-growing capitalist country, controlled by the one-party system of the CCP. What would Chen say about the increasing gap between the rich and the poor? It is highly unlikely that a script could be written and staged for this imaginative return of Chen. Yet *The East Is Red*, the Maoist classic, made a surprising return to the Chinese stage in the twentieth-first century. To express nostalgia for a "cleaner" society in the era of Maoist China, artists, amateurs, and retirees put together various productions of *The East Is Red* from 2004 to 2007. The venues were concert halls, parks, university campuses, and even tourist spots. None of these productions mentioned Chen as a villain. Indeed, many performances, besides eliminating the elaborate and costly dance scenes, omitted the narrator's part, which moralized about Chen's supposed failures, thereby turning *The East Is Red* into a mostly musical experience without any intrusive political discourse.

Interestingly, when citizens of Beijing gathered in the North Sea Park in the summer of 2006 to sing the songs from *The East Is Red*, they added a new poetic narrative that they themselves had composed. Seeming to embrace the old ways, they sang: "We present our songs to Mao Zedong / the savior of humankind." But they also sang: "Why are we looked down upon by others / who would respect the suffering of slaves? / Our lives have become difficult without the blessing of truth." The revised narrative articulated their nostalgia for a "peaceful, egalitarian, and selfless era" in which the workers and peasants were once again "masters of a socialist society" that was not stained by "corruption, bribery, and prostitution." As they ended their performance with the "Internationale," these stagings invoked Lenin's motto: "Those who forget the past are traitors." Thus the revival of *The East Is Red* called on the people never to forget the revolutionary martyrs who had given their lives for the founding of "our socialist country."[33]

In the course of half a century Chinese performance culture *seemed* to have come "full circle" with the return to *The East Is Red*, apparently reclaiming the original blueprint for the socialist state once devised by both Chen and Mao to seek a new way to address China's predicament. But of course this "full circle" is neither a simple nor a complex return to the past. Like all of the spectacles described in this essay, it is an illusionary representation that is simultaneously "true" and "false"; its narrative is significantly revealing of its moment yet inaccurate and misleading in its historical representation of the past. The restaging of *The East Is Red* almost fifty years after the first performances rehabilitated Mao by an act of reformulation. For the spectators it projected into the image of Mao a paradoxical longing for a return of his egalitarian programs for the poor, yet it also provided a convenient rejection of his totalitarian means of achieving those programs. In this contemporary representation the historical Mao is therefore once again removed from the performative version of him. The spectators—or some of them—must attempt to align these representations with their selective memories of Mao.

Likewise, the public restoration of Chen's status simultaneously negotiates past and present versions of modern Chinese history. As the latest representations seem to challenge the Maoist socialist theory and practice while embracing Chen's vision of a "socialist democracy" for China, free from foreign dominations, spectators must often make sense of seemingly contradictory narratives that contend for attention and belief (or at least calculated accommodation). Chen's "restoration," by the same token, is no different from the changing identity of Mao. Even after historians and performers have presented more balanced accounts of Chen Duxiu as a historic figure, the future representations of him will likely shift in response to complex political, social, and ideological changes.

Accordingly, as historians we need to proceed carefully and cunningly. While guarding against the post–Cold War and Orientalist mentality of dismissing Chinese theatre as merely the product of a suppressive political regime, we have to unpack the complex mixture of reliable and unreliable historical representations in the well-crafted political spectacles of the last fifty years. In the process of reconstructing the past, as it is displayed in these dramatic narratives, we should take seriously the identity politics that guide both the producers and audiences of the performance culture. We need to see the writing and performing subjects as historical agents who must negotiate their relations with both the present and the past. We need to understand how various factors and conditions contribute to the representations, including the shifting demands of various historical periods, the challenges of censorship, the interweaving role of political history and public spectacle, and the complex mechanics that allowed—and even encouraged—the creative acts of border crossing.

NOTES

I want to thank Thomas Postlewait for his legendary editorial skills and for insightful, detailed, and substantial comments on early versions of this essay from him and from Charlotte Canning.

1. Wilt Idema and Stephen H. West, *Chinese Theater, 1100–1450: A Source Book* (Wiesbaden: Steiner, 1982), p. 138 (discusses the twelve types of characters in traditional opera enumerated by Zhu Quan of the Ming dynasty).

2. For a fuller study, see Xiaomei Chen, *Acting the Right Part* (Honolulu: University of Hawaii Press, 2002), pp. 159–193.

3. *Dongfang hong* Guangdong sheng yanchu zhihuibu (The Headquarters of Guangdong Production of *The East Is Red*), "Paiyan yinyue wudao shishi *Dongfang hong* jiben jingyan" (Our Experience in Rehearsing the Song and Dance Epic *The East Is Red*), in *Mao Zedong sixiang de songge* (The Song of Mao Zedong's Thought) (Guangzhou: Guangdong Renmin, 1966), pp. 1–12, esp. p. 1.

4. Huang Hua, "Xiang taiyang" (Toward the Sun), in *Mao Zedong sixiang de songge* (The Song of Mao Zedong's Thought), pp. 61–86, esp. p. 64.

5. Ibid., pp. 66–67.

6. "*Dongfang hong* yinyue ju" (The Music Drama *The East Is Red*); available at http://lib.verycd.com/2005/02/08/0000038422.html (accessed August 18, 2007).

7. *Dongfang hong* (The East Is Red) (Hong Kong: Ta Kung Bao, 1966), p. 5.

8. Ibid., p. 6.

9. Many examples from the memoirs, biographies, and autobiographies of artists and writers would testify to the fluid, multidimensional, and varying degrees of the intellectuals' ambiguities and collaborations with the status quo, even as they began to harbor doubts about their own construction of the Maoist cult, which later proved disastrous during the Cultural Revolution.

10. For a fuller story, see Xiaomei Chen, "Introduction," in *Reading the Right Texts* (Honolulu: University of Hawaii Press, 2003), pp. 21–28.

11. Wang Jun et al., *Yi dai ying hao* (A Generation of Heroes), *Juben* 8 (1981): 7–38 (quotation on 14).

12. Ibid., p. 16.

13. Ibid., p. 22.

14. Ibid., p. 24.

15. Ibid.

16. "On Evaluating Chen Duxiu's Life," as discussed in Qiu Guanjian and Jia Gangtao, "Ershi shiji jiushi niandai yilai Chen Duxiu wannian sixiang yanjiu zongshu" (A Survey on the 1990s Research on the Thoughts of Chen Duxiu in His Later Years), in *Guizhou Shifan Daxue xuebao* (Journal of Guizhou Normal University: Social Science) 5 (2005): 71–76 (quotation on 71).

17. Zhang Liqun et al., eds., *Huai nian Yaobang* (Remembering Hu Yaobang), vol. 4 (Hong Kong: Yatai Chuban Gongsi, 2001), pp. 252–255.

18. Zhu Hong, *Chen Duxiu fengyu rensheng* (The Trials and Tribulations of Chen Duxiu's Life) (Wuhan: Hubei Renmin Chubanshe, 2004), p. 90.

19. For publications on Chen Duxiu's life with regard to Mao's relationship to him as a student, see ibid., pp. 100–101; Guo Huaqing, "Mao Zedong yu Chen Duxiu guanxi xulung" (On the Relationship between Mao Zedong and Chen Duxiu), *Guangzhou Daxue xuebao* (Guangzhou University Research Journal) 1.3 (2002): 1–10.

20. Lu Mingkang, "Zoujin mingren: Shao Honglai, 'ji guo-gong hezuo' yu yishen" (Approaching Celebrities: Shao Honglai, the Embodiment of "the KMT and CCP Collaborations"); available at http://www.slyswy.com/zjmr (accessed May 17, 2006).

21. He Zhenbang, "Zhuangmei de gemin shishi, youyi de yishu tansuo" (Magnificent Revolutionary Epic and Beneficial Artistic Experiment) *Xiaoshuo pinglun* (Fiction Review) 6 (2001): 49.

22. Zhu Wentong, *Li Dazhao zhuan* (Biography of Li Dazhao) (Tianjin: Tianjin Guji Chubanshe, 2005), p. 144.

23. The description of *The Sun Rises in the East* is based on the TV series. The quoted dialogue is identified by episode number in the text.

24. He Zhenbang, "Zhuangmei de gemin shishi," pp. 49–53 (quotation on p. 50).

25. Zhang Dexiang, "Cangmang dadi juan julan" (The Rolling Waves on the Boundless Land) *Zhongguo dianshi* (Chinese Television) 8 (2001): 5–6 (quotation on 6).

26. Ibid., p. 5.

27. He Zhenbang, "Zhuangmei de gemin shishi," p. 51. For the fictional version of this television series, see Huang Yazhou, *Ri chu dongfang* (The Sun Rises in the East) (Beijing: Renmin Wenxue, 2001).

28. Chen Tiejian, "Dai ren shou guo de Chen Duxiu—*Chen Duxiu yu Gongchan Guoji* shu hou" (Chen Duxiu, a Scapegoat for the Comintern—Reading *Chen Duxiu and the Comintern* by Li Ying), *Shixue yuekan* (Journal of Historical Science) 8 (2006): 59–67 (esp. 59). Li Ying argued in his book that during the six years of Chen's leadership as the head of the CCP for five terms since its founding the Chinese revolution was completely under the control of the Comintern in remote Moscow. Li Ying suggests that the relationship between the leadership of Chen and the manipulation of the Comintern provides a key to understanding many perplexing problems in the study of the early history of the CCP.

29. Feng Dongshu, "Zhonggong lishi shang di yi da'an—Chen Duxiu an" (The First Unjust Case in the History of the CCP—The Case of Chen Duxiu), *Jizhe guancha* (Reporters' Notes) 7 (2003): 12–14 (esp. 13).

30. Pan Peixin, "Chen Duxiu wannian lun Sulian" (Chen Duxiu on the Soviet Union in His Later Years), *Zhonggong Huangzhou shiwei dangxiao xuebao* (Journal of the Party Training School Attached to the CCP Party Committee of Huangzhou City) 5 (2001): 52.

31. Ibid., p. 53. Of note, Khrushchev's report was challenged by Palmiro Togliatti, the general secretary of the Italian Communist Party. Arguing against Khrushchev's critique of Joseph Stalin's personality cult as the root of the Soviet problem, Togliatti believed that the lack of democracy and a legal system was to blame for the Soviet regression into a corrupt society, which no longer served the interests of the proletariat. Togliatti insisted that his "Italian road to socialism" was preferable to violent revolution; he rejected the Stalinist concept of an internationally directed movement in favor of a democratically oriented and national one. This position repeated some of the same insights that Chen Duxiu had expressed two decades earlier.

32. Lu Xiaobo, "Lun Chen Duxiu wannian minzhu guan de sixiang ziyuan" (On the Intellectual Origin of Democratic Thoughts of Chen Duxiu in his Later Years), *Xuehai* (Learning Sea) 3 (2006): 54–61 (esp. 59).

33. "Tongchang Dongfang hong gao ge Mao Zedong" (Singing *The East Is Red* for Mao Zedong), http://www.xyzxsx.com/Article/Class4/2006061/7347.html (accessed August 10, 2009).

5 Narrative

Textual Evidances

ORGANIZING AND NARRATING DANCE'S HISTORY

DANCE'S ORIGINS

In 1682 Claude François Menestrier, a Jesuit writing on the history of dance, summarized its origins as follows:

> The dance that today serves as entertainment for all peoples and persons of quality was in its origin a kind of mysterious ritual and ceremony. The Jews, to whom God himself gave his laws and the ceremonies that they observe, introduced dance into their festivities, and the pagan peoples following them worshiped their gods in dance.[1]

Seventy-two years later Louis de Cahusac, author of several entries on dance and gesture for Denis Diderot's *Encyclopédie*, proposed this alternative beginning:

> Man had sensations at the first moment that he breathed; and the tones of his voice, the play of his features, the movements of his body, were simply expressions of what he felt. . . .
>
> The body was peaceful or agitated; the eyes flamed or smoldered; the arms opened or closed, rose toward heaven or sank to the earth; the feet formed steps slow or rapid; all the body, in short, responded by postures, attitudes, leaps, shudders to the sound with which the soul expressed its emotions. Thus song, which is the primitive expression of feeling, developed from itself a second which is in man, and it is this expression that we have named dance.[2]

For Menestrier, dance's murky origins are embedded in the social practices that constitute ritual and religion. His description evokes a group dance, both ceremonial and celebratory, and weighted with a symbolic significance passed down from one generation of performers to the next. The first records indicate that it was performed by Jews and subsequently by Egyptians and then Greeks, whose civilizations developed dancing over centuries. For Cahusac, dance's origin is both psychological and universal. His portrait of originary dance depicts a solo, a moment of discovery by a sensitive and responsive everyman moved by the power of feeling.

Dance thereby existed as an innate human response prior to any social conventions that came to govern it. For Menestrier the connection between dances past and present resides in the fact of their performance at both moments in history. Cahusac attributes such continuity to the enduring structure of the human psyche.

TABLES OF CONTENTS

Menestrier, whose work is widely acclaimed as the first extant history of dance, continues his description of dance's origins by listing the various instances of dance—by Moses and Miriam at the parting of the Red Sea, by the daughters of Silo, by David before the Ark of the Covenant—known to scholars through references in ancient texts. With the seeming spontaneity of a raconteur, Menestrier discovers each new topic or feature of dance nestled close to its predecessor. David's dance at the Ark reminds Menestrier of sacred Spanish dances, which remind him of something Lucian said about dance, and so forth. Each topic inspires the next by sharing some attribute of the dance with it.

Cahusac, who had studied Menestrier's text, describes these same dances, including much of Menestrier's commentary about them, but not before categorizing them with respect to their nature and function. In his history these dances occupy a particular place within a much larger taxonomic organization: first, they are examples of "Sacred Dances," and, within that broad category, they are instances of "Sacred Dances of the Jews." In much the same way that Cahusac's description of dance's origins segments the body, vividly cataloguing its repertoire of movements, so his history itemizes dances insofar as they conform to one of several main types. Thus he describes sacred dances of Jews, Egyptians, Greeks, Romans, Christians, and Turks, followed by an examination of the "Profane or Secular Dances" of these same peoples, and then concludes with a treatment of their "Theatrical" dance forms. The arrangement of the chapters on the pages renders the body of Cahusac's book as clearly jointed as the originary dancer he describes. White spaces and centered titles frame each chapter at predictable five- to seven-page intervals.

No such exoskeletal organization supports Menestrier's history. A glance at a section of the table of contents is sufficient to violate all categorizing sensibilities:

> On figures in the ballet.
> On movements.
> Criminals exposed to suffering and death in performance.

On harmony.
On paraphernalia.
On machines.
On costumes.
The Crowning of Petrarch.
Horse ballets.

Yet Menestrier leads the reader with ease from costumes to "The Crowning of Petrarch" to "Horse ballets": Petrarch's coronation made use of exemplary costumes and, as a procession, recalls other similar processions, some using horses, which in turn invites comments on horse ballets in general. And he moves just as convincingly through the entire history of dance from its earliest occurrences to the invention of the ballet to an analysis of different aspects of the ballet, with descriptions of specific ballets interspersed throughout. The chapter titles, appearing in the margins of an otherwise seamless text, simply add another level of commentary, marking noteworthy people, features of dance, or dances rather than junctures in a developing logic.[3]

STAGING HISTORIES OF DANCE

Menestrier's and Cahusac's histories, so deliciously, excruciatingly different from one another, frame the historical period in which European theatrical dance undergoes the processes of both professionalization and narrativization. During this period theatrical dance loses its cast of amateurs and promotes instead the highly skilled accomplishments of professional dancers trained in a codified and delimited repertoire of steps and gestures. Selected and salaried at the king's behest, these master dancers exert enormous influence over pedagogical, stylistic, and evaluative procedures. Their designation as specialists and the sheer number of hours they can devote to dance training set these performers apart. The skills they demonstrate, while clearly issuing from the aesthetic matrix of the social dance lexicon, increasingly exceed the amateur's grasp. The same period witnesses the first experiments with dance movement as a vehicle through which a coherent narrative can be conveyed. In these danced stories, characters enact soliloquies and dialogues using gesture, dramatic posture, and facial expression. Unlike the opera-ballets, where singing characters move the plot forward and danced interludes establish a corporeal and emotional ambiance for the story, these new story ballets attempt to shift from mimetic movements to the virtuoso vocabulary of ballet steps and back again. These experiments eventually allow theatrical dance to separate from opera and develop as an autonomous genre of spectacle.

The two dance histories likewise document the changing conceptions of the body which ensue from the challenge to absolutism undertaken during the Enlightenment. Menestrier's history, written at a moment of supreme monarchic control by Louis XIV, presumes a world of physicalized sociability which the king has helped shape. All social classes, but especially aristocrats, rely on systems of corporeal signification to convey status and identity. Louis's issuance of the patents that authorize a professional cadre of dancers only extends his authority over bodily discipline, a domain he has begun to regulate as early as the 1640s through his proscriptive behavior for proper comportment at court and his insistence on social dance occasions as performances. Cahusac's history, in contrast, participates in the Enlightenment privileging of the category of the individual human being over political and religious social formations. Enlightenment concern with expressive gesture, with gesture that depicts the intimate feelings of each character in a story, stems from its capacity to portray individual sensibilities rather than social standing. Gestural expression has the status of a kind of universal language to which all humans have equal access. Even the story ballet's use of gesture grows out of the fair theatre productions that were specifically designed as an affront and challenge to royal authority.

The shift from Louis XIV's absolutism to an Enlightenment humanism encumbers the body with a new and distinctive expressive function, and it also specifies a new relation between writing and dancing. In Menestrier's time both practices are conceptualized as forms of inscription. Each medium is equally capable of articulateness; each can represent many different things. Both forms of inscription circulate within a rigidly fixed social and political hierarchy. The chain of meaning that descends from god to king to social classes enables but also requires the body to speak. Its corporeality must be cultivated so as to ensure control over the contents of its communications. By the time Cahusac writes his history, words and movements, while each forming the vocabulary of a kind of language, are apprehended as unique in their expressive abilities. Words can translate directly into movements, as the scenarios for the story ballets demonstrate, yet movement's message appeals to heart and soul in a way that words cannot. The body's expressive movements thereby secure a private place, an incipient interiority for the individual, over which that individual exerts control.

Even though construed as a language in Enlightenment thought, the body's gestures begin to signify that which cannot be spoken. This unique role for gesture prepares the way for a complete separation between dance and text that occurs in the early decades of the nineteenth century. Dance becomes imbued with a dynamic charisma, and text is assigned the ability to interpret and theorize about the ephemeral yet magnetizing presence of the dance. So powerful is this attribution of mutually exclusive functions for dancing and writing throughout the nineteenth and twentieth centuries that its historical specificity has only recently been questioned. But what if we allow movement as well as words the power to interpret? What if we find in choreography a form of theorizing? What if in learning to choreograph, the choreographer learns to theorize, and in learning to dance, the dancer assimilates the body of facts and the structuring of discursive frameworks that enable theorization to occur? What if the body of the text is a dancing body, a choreographed body?

This essay responds to these questions by reading two historical texts, two classic dance histories, as a choreographer might, looking for evidence of theories of relationships between body and self and one body and another body that could be choreographed. What permits this reading is a general assumption that theories of representation can translate, even if imperfectly, from one form of discourse to another. That is, literary conventions that enable such maneuvers as the framing and organization of an argument, the delineation of a subject, or the indicating of an authorial presence have choreographic equivalents. Such conventions theorize relationships between subject and surroundings or between subject and mode of expression in the same way that choreographic conventions theorize the body's relation to subject and to the expressive act. For a given historical period, the contents of these forms often, although not always, move in unison alongside one another.

In order to express choreographic equivalents from these two historical texts, to press the texts for live and moving versions of themselves, I have treated them as if they were scores for dances. The act of comparing two such different textual forms with two such similar contents foregrounds the places where theory operates, and thus where a translation to choreography(-as-theory) could occur. The righthand column of text represents the effort at one such translation. In that column the textual stances taken in the two histories toward their subjects find choreographic articulation in sets of parameters for two dances, one corresponding to Menestrier's text and the other to Cahusac's. The abstract guidelines for dance-making that are set forth in the righthand text convert as literally as possible the text-making procedures discussed in the analysis of two histories conducted in the lefthand column of text.

Of course my interpretation of the histories as "scores" relies heavily on yet another set of "texts." These texts are the imaginary dances I have fabricated in response to fragmentary historical evidence that documents dances from the time of Menestrier and Cahusac and also in response to live concerts by choreographers attempting to reconstruct historical dances for performance in the present. Out of these texts, some written and some performed, I have developed my own imagined versions of the court ballets that Menestrier saw and directed and of the action ballets that Cahusac watched emerge during his lifetime. These imagined dances impinge on my efforts to detect the theoretical moves made in the histories, and they also influence profoundly the shaping of the corresponding choreographic directives. The righthand column thus responds choreographically to the histories but also performs as an intertext, a kind of choreographer's notebook filled with ideas that coalesce past and present images of dancing into the general features of two distinct dances, one choreographed in response to Menestrier's world and the other to Cahusac's.

SUBJECT-ING DANCE

CONSTRUCTING THE SUBJECT

Des ballets anciens et modernes recounts the actual history of dance in only 30 pages. The rest of the 332-page treatise is taken up with an examination of the ballet, using citations from classical and contemporary philosophers as well as descriptions of actual performances to illustrate the aguments. The text proceeds at a lively pace, shifting imperceptibly from theory to description to citation to opinion. Rarely is there any marking of the different kinds or levels of analysis. Comments of theoretical preeminence, such as the criteria for an adequate subject or the relationship between dance and painting, are often found buried, mid-paragraph, undistinguished from the descriptions

An evening-length dance incorporating various kinds of sources and involving different levels of abstraction. It presents surreal sequences of images, seemingly magical transitions from one landscape or set of characters to another. The performance progresses without developing toward an obvious climax; nor does it offer a summary, celebratory conclusion.

which surround them. Nor does Menestrier offer any summary or conclusion. The manuscript ends abruptly with the description of a newly invented Italian card game, part of the discussion of literary and other sources of subjects of ballets.

Cahusac's history, although equivalent to Menestrier's in length, is more ambitious historically and cross-culturally. He discusses dances of Mediterranean antiquity, including those of Egypt and Turkey, as well as Greece and Rome, and his treatment of ballet occupies only half the book. Chapters typically conclude with a few summary sentences or with Cahusac's opinions about the relative merits of the particular type of dance. The history follows in precise segments the development of dance until the last few chapters, where Cahusac considers briefly the main elements of ballets, in general—their actions and characters. He concludes with a summary plea for continued improvement in dancing and dance-making.

A five-act work unified by a clear plot consisting of a beginning, a middle created around a dramatic knot that moves the action forward toward a climax, and an ending. It may begin or conclude with a celebratory section that consists of portraits of distinct dance traditions, each of which is transformed into the homogeneous style of the production through an insistent emphasis on the visual characteristics that each dance form exhibits.

DEFINING HISTORY

Prefaces to the two histories place distinctive frames around their project. Menestrier's preface is taken up with lengthy descriptions of two ballets—one reprehensible for its indiscriminate presentation of profane and gaudy images, and the other, his own *L'Autel de Lyon* (1658), meritorious for the restraint and appropriateness with which it develops a single theme. Cahusac's preface, instead of examining dances or choreographic principles, refutes the aesthetic theories found in other dance histories, in particular that of Abbé du Bos's *Réflexions critiques sur la*

The performance is conceived and produced for a singular occasion. Because of its commemorative function, it draws members of the community into the dance and even the dance-making. They actively interpret the dance as it is composed, embedding its form with symbolic structures and redeciphering their meanings while it is performed.

poésie et sur la peinture. Cahusac's critique of his predecessor situates his own work within a tradition of inquiry whose purpose it is to reflect on the continuing failures and successes of dance. Where Menestrier sees in history the opportunity to reinterpret and restate a set of aesthetic principles of interest to both historians and choreographers, Cahusac casts himself as one of a group of specialists capable of evaluating "objectively" the intention of a given dance. In doing so, he sets history apart from choreography as an impartial documentation of its accomplishments and errors. History, an indispensable reference for choreographers who, because of the practical nature of their work, cannot take time to reflect on their own aesthetic decisions, creates a picture of dance's development for choreographers to evaluate.

The performance occurs as part of the institutionalized art offerings of the society, for general edification but not for any specific occasion. Dancers perform for viewers who are set apart in a related but separate sphere. Rather than interpret the performance, viewers evaluate its success using clearly specified aesthetic criteria. Just as dancers train to perform, so viewers educate themselves as to the levels of perfection a dance can attain.

Early in his first chapter Menestrier sets forth the principles of his historical method—to determine the origins of things with briefness and exactness through an examination of the names things have been given. A thorough consideration of these names, Menestrier argues, will establish the foundation of the art so that its various parts can be studied and related to the whole. Menestrier then proceeds to outline not the contents of the book but the source materials for this study. He proposes to treat with clarity and order the names given to dance by the Hebrews, Greeks, and Romans as well as the definitions offered by Aristotle, Plato, and others. These very definitions will lead to an understanding of choreographic practice.

Dance movements, like costumes, scenery, music, and dialogue, are selected for their metaphoric appropriateness. They should all relate harmoniously by each emblematizing the most essential elements of the subject being represented. Dance movement has the status of a name—a referent with a history and usage that are open to explication.

Cahusac, in contrast, assumes that the origins of dance are common knowledge, its history a set of incontestable facts. Historical research, the organization and comparison of facts about the past, needs no methodological justification. What does require comment, in Cahusac's estimation, is his own aesthetic evaluation of the dances he writes about. Where the Abbé du Bos argued that dancing in his time achieved complete perfection and also that it was different in every respect from dances of antiquity, Cahusac is concerned to show the continuity between classical and contemporary forms and also the superiority of the most recent developments in ballets. Cahusac thus separates, in a way that Menestrier does not, "historical" information about dances of the past from his own "didactic" views on the relative merits of dance in his own and earlier times. And he advises his readers that he has supplemented the facts with his own judgments, which are, he admits, the specific product of his own time.

Taxonomies constituted by the simple and complex and the true and false organize all dance movement. The selection of steps conforms to the guidelines for tasteful proportion and lively yet clear rhythmic and spatial articulation. Selection of gestures — detailed schemata for the representation of human attitudes and feelings — is based on how well the movements look like, even as they perfect, their quotidien referents. Gestures and steps, distinct categories of movement, all have the status of facts. They are incontestable; only their use can be evaluated.

RE-VIEWING THE DANCE

Differences in the overall structures of the two volumes are reinforced by the authors' distinctive approach to the description of a specific ballet. Both historians make detailed references to several of the same performances, always with consistent differences in emphasis. Where Menestrier is concerned to point up the symbolic significance of characters and acts, Cahusac focuses on the way things looked. Take, for example, their accounts of the ballet *Les montagnards* (1631), which, both argue, was sig-

All events and actions in the performance take place under the auspices of an unquestioned, overarching set of relations that reference a moral order of cosmic proportions.

nificant because it introduced a new kind of subject matter—concerned with peasant life—into the courtly tradition. Both texts begin their descriptions of the ballet with the same sentence: "The theatre depicted five large mountains" (Menestrier, 79; Cahusac, 3:5), and both continue by explaining that each mountain symbolized a type: windy; resonant because inhabited by Echoes; wooded; luminous; and cloudy. Cahusac adds to this observation that the middle of the stage constituted a field of glory recently seized by the inhabitants of all five mountains. According to both authors, Foolish Rumor, costumed as an old woman, then entered, riding an ass and carrying a wooden trumpet. Cahusac provides a footnote explaining her trumpet as an allusion to an old proverb; Menestrier notes the allusion in the text itself. Cahusac describes the old woman delivering a speech that revealed the subject of the ballet. Menestrier notes instead that the first part of her recitation was delivered to the animal she was riding and the second part to the audience. Menestrier then goes on to quote her speech in its entirety.

Events elaborate the logic of human reaction and interaction. Each action requires motivation and, in turn, provokes a response. The full sequence of actions creates a moving portrait of life.

At this point the styles of the two narratives diverge dramatically. Menestrier proceeds as follows:

All features of the production—dancing, text, music, costumes, scenery—carry equal weight, and all are sublimated to the project of representing a larger moral, political, and aesthetic order. Movement, sound image, texture, and mass all convey their messages equivalently.

> After this pleasant speech, the Winds came forth from the windy mountain carrying windmills on their heads and bellows in their hands that whistled like the Winds. Echo then gave a speech and led in the inhabitants of the resonant mountain, all dressed like bells. (80)

Cahusac describes the same action in these terms:

> Then one of the mountains opened and a whirlwind sprang forth. The quadrilles that composed this act were dressed in the color of flesh; all of them carried windmills on their heads and, in their hands, bellows that when shaken produced the whistle of the winds.
>
> The nymph Echo made the opening speech for the second act and led in the inhabitants of the resonant mountains. They carried tamborines, a bell as a head ornament, and their clothes were covered with small bells of varying pitches that together created a joyful and lively harmony. The ensemble adapted itself to the meter of the songs played by the orchestra, in following the cadences of the dance movement. (3:6)

The visual impression of the dancing, the way it looks, takes primacy over kinesthetic or aural forms of information. The visual has factual rather than hermeneutic value. Dancing illustrates, makes visible, both music and text.

Whereas Menestrier only provides information that would be helpful in interpreting the identity of the characters and the meaning of their actions, Cahusac emphasizes the visual appearance of the performance. His description contains many more phrases portraying the characters and also more active verbs indicating the quality of the movement. Furthermore, Cahusac is concerned to delineate structural features of the ballet—Echo's speech commences the second act.

The same kinds of differences reappear throughout the rest of the descriptions. Menestrier completes his report in three long sentences, one for each act; Cahusac requires five short paragraphs. Menestrier

Dancers work to fit into the ensemble, to make the overall statement evident through their careful and astute execution of the choreographic directions.

mentions only the main characters and actions and concludes with a comment on the new reputation for mountain people created by the ballet. Cahusac methodically lists first the act and then the principal characters, costuming, and actions. As his description proceeds, he also begins to introduce evaluative phrases: "ingenious steps," "this grand spectacle," and even a footnote commenting that "the wooden leg and dark lantern, props of the Lie, are two ideas quite new and amusing" (3:7).

Menestrier's version of the ballet records its main features in order to educate viewers as to the relationship between the ballet's subject, the enactment of that subject, and its moral impact. After quoting the opening *récitatif* as an overview of the ballet's intent, he seems concerned only to explain key symbolic figures and paraphernalia so that viewers can augment their understanding of the principles of representation. Cahusac, in contrast, replicates his history's functional division of information into chapters in his precise classification into acts of all the action. His description assembles the distinct elements presented onstage into vivid, discrete images. The meaning of these images is self-evident. Once they have been described in all their detail, it remains for the narrator to evaluate their originality and effectiveness. Menestrier offers a set of codes so that readers/viewers can live out and through danced ideas; Cahusac provides visual information so that his audience can compare and improve upon images of life.

Menestrier's account of *Les montagnards* occurs at the end of his discussion of

Dancers show themselves aware of performing before others. Their actions are shaped so as to be viewed from one perspective, and they deliver those actions with daring showmanship to the viewing eye.

Bodies have sculptural presence. They are round and dripping with emblems; they create masses of potential energy that release into kinetic trajectories that modulate between fast and slow, high and low, and quick and sustained.

Bodies look like two-dimensional cutouts frozen in picture-perfect tableaux that depict a touching scene. Then they suddenly exhibit extraordinary plasticity, darting through space as they display intricate coordinations of hands, feet, and head.

Characters reiterate a set of static structural relation-

three types of plot structure for ballets—philosophical, poetic, and romantic—and pivots the narrative into a comparison between dance and painting (for which there are also three types). Cahusac mentions the ballet in his chapter titled "Festivals in which dancing played a major part given at the French court between 1610 and 1643." He attests to the low aesthetic standards that had developed at court during this period as a result of the assumption that French ballets were superior to all others. For him the ballet's greatest significance lies in its reception—the initial derisive response of the snobbish nobility and the subsequent triumph of a ballet composed in the Italian style. His analysis of the ballet ends the chapter; it is followed in the next chapter by a discussion of similar festivals at other courts in Europe.

ships among types of characters. Individual actions link to evoke a harmonious balance between lively and sedate moods and good and evil presences. Characters' actions do not cause change in circumstances; rather changes occur as the action reaches designated moments in a preordained plan. Their form is lyric.

The dancer's identity resides in the interstices between the local choreographic moment and the larger moral, aesthetic, and political order of which it is a part.

DANCE'S FACTS AND FICTIONS

In Menestrier's history, *Les montagnards* exists as one among many stories of dances, some good and others inadequate, which can be told about this fine art. In Cahusac's history the ballet occurs at a particular moment in the narrative trajectory that follows the decline and subsequent regeneration of dance. The quality of dances, Cahusac points out, had deteriorated during the reign of Henry IV to the point where "pleasantries of the vilest and worst taste took undisputed possession of the Palaces" (3:4). *Les montagnards* signals the coming of a new era of choreographic genius which officially begins as Louis XIV takes the throne. This dramatic story replicates on the larger scale

Individual phrases of movement that rise and fall nest within larger sections of dance which likewise reach toward and then fall away from climaxes. Characters' aspirations and struggles reveal the unfolding plot. The overall narrative structure conforms to that of tragedy or comedy. Suspense is followed by resolution

of dance history: the initial glory of classical Greek and Roman dance is followed by the fall into decadence during the Middle Ages and the rise *toward* greater glory witnessed by the author and his contemporaries. Unlike Menestrier's history, extending seemingly without end into the flat, continuous terrain formed by past and present, Cahusac's history delineates epicycles of refinement and vulgarity as part of the single dramatic progress of civilization.

repeatedly. Variations on the simple plot trajectories show the choreographer's inventiveness, just as innovations in vocabulary usage demonstrate choreographic skill.

The epistemological assumptions that enable Cahusac to separate facts from opinions and to verify facts on the basis of visual appearance also permit him to posit a universal rather than a particular origin for dance. The *fact* of dance exists prior to the various social forms it has assumed. For Cahusac, dance results from a natural correspondence between gesture and all the feelings of the soul. Along with song, dance paints in an unequivocal though clumsy manner all the situations of the soul. The soul's feelings, although they dictate what the gesture will be, do not motivate the gesture. Instead Cahusac suggests a metonymical relationship between body and soul—they exist side by side. The body's gestural representations of the soul can thus be compared one with another and with an abstract visual image of the soul itself. The act of comparison takes place on the two-dimensional framed canvas, the site of the body's paintings, analogous in structure to the proscenium stage itself.

Whether the dancer transforms into the character and lives out the character's actions or, instead, learns to approximate perfectly the look of those actions becomes a question of acting technique.

For Menestrier, dance does not originate in the individual soul but in the social body. Dance as it was known in Menestrier's time developed out of ancient group practices, with their inherent political and religious as well as aesthetic connotations. The body's gestures thus represent aspects of social life rather than individual feeling. They reenact, rather than paint, life's events. They exist as social facts in a world to be interpreted by all who witness them. The body does not display the world but alludes to it in ways that can be likened to, but not measured against, one another.

The dance provides a map to assist the viewer in navigating through the rest of life. The dance surrounds viewers as much as they surround it. The dance is a commentary.

For Menestrier, dance's history consists of a body of stories, and the historian's art lies in the appropriate arrangement and interpretation of these stories so as to achieve a balanced and judicious account of the past. Cahusac's history, in contrast, adorns a body of facts with a refined set of opinions. More sociological than hermeneutic in orientation, the historian's project is one of comparing life and its images and presenting the best organization of images possible by selecting and arranging an existing body of knowledge. Although Cahusac might discover new facts, he would never admit responsibility for having created them. Facts remain neutral, aestheticized, and amoral within a past that separates the evidential from the evaluative so as to provide objective criteria for the ordering of historical events.

The production impresses and inspires with its brilliance, cleverness, and virtuosity. The dance's proscenium frame both isolates and factualizes the performance. The dance is an appraisal.

For Menestrier, the original dancing body cannot be separated from the dances it performed. In ancient times, as in his own, the dance, and not the body, is the medium of expression. Through the dance, all participants reinterpret their own life situations. In contrast, Cahusac's

The dance reconfigures images of life.

original dancing body learns to interact, to dance, with others so as to exhibit dance, which in turn provides society with a model for refined and decorous conduct. Menestrier's history, like Menestrier's dancing body, offers to choreographers, viewers, and readers the opportunity to peruse endless stories, some meandering and some coherent, in an effort to comprehend the rules that transform bodies into ideas and life into dance. Cahusac's conception of history offers instead a method for evaluating dance, one that sensitizes readers to the degenerate and enlightened elements of which it has been composed over the years. Cahusac's readers are thereby inspired to attain the sensibility necessary to distinguish between an imaginative performance and a lifeless one.

The dance re-presents images of life.

The dance relies on a universal code to create images appropriate to a particular context.

The dance employs a universal language to portray a particular situation.

DANCING THEORY

Bodies of texts, like dancing bodies, are subject to disciplinary actions that cultivate them in specific ways. These two dance histories and the dancing bodies they describe take shape in response to distinct distributions of power that impel their presentations' structure and content. Menestrier envisions his own role and that of dance as extensions of both religious and royal authority. The free play of interpretations invited by his text and its dances is enabled by the absolutist control of a king who embodies divine authority and a divinely inspired system of interpretation. Cahusac, in contrast, imbues artists and scholars with an individual ingenuity consonant with Enlightenment values, yet this emphasis on individual initiative is accompanied by new configurations of disciplining control. Individuals must internalize values of fact and fiction which authorize their distinction-making. It is as if the proscenium itself supplants the royal figure watching the dance and individual audience members use this prosthetic device to guide the organization of their viewing labor. The story ballets that they see displayed onstage, like the taxonomized treatment of dance's history, replace the opera-ballets' endlessly similar commentaries on dance and text. The segmented, carefully shaped body with its hierarchies of accomplishment takes over from the body capable only of innumerable analogies to other moving things.

In each of these choreographies of power the body retains a certain integrity. It functions neither as a sentimentalized disappearing act nor as an awesome source of magical inspiration. Both Menestrier and Cahusac evoke a body that has agency and that can participate actively in the production of meaning. Yet in the reduction of the body to fact Cahusac's history initiates a distinction between the verbal and the bodily in which bodies lose their capacity to theorize. For Cahusac, bodies cannot theorize relationships between time and space or individual and group; they can only pronounce the fact of those relationships. Cahusac's approach to history thus establishes grounds on which text can claim exclusive rights to theory.

The body of this text teaches itself to choreograph through its interactions with both dance histories. It throws itself into dancing alongside them and returns, ambidextrous, fragmented, replete with fantasized limbs and unusual boundaries. It has learned some new moves, the most intriguing of which is the ability to turn, to trope, from fact into metaphor and back again. In this turning it performs as evidence of theory and at the same time as evidence for theory. The choreography for this double-bodied dance, this dance by bodies of facts and bodies of fictions, gives theory new explanatory power just as it makes dancing theory more evident.

NOTES

1. Claude François Menestrier, *Des ballets anciens et modernes selon les règles du théâtre* (Paris: Chez René Guignard, 1682), pp. 8–9 (my translation).

Born at Lyon in 1631, Menestrier became a member of the Jesuit College as a scholar specializing in religious heraldry and ceremony. Like other Jesuits who recognized the educational opportunities afforded by performances, he became heavily involved in their study and production. He traveled widely throughout France and Italy, witnessing many ballets, weddings, festivals, banquets, tournaments, entries, and pageants of all kinds and, as a close friend of those Jesuits who had worked with Count Filippo D'Aglié San Martino at the Savoy court in Turin, heard about even more. Menestrier documented these performances in some 160 books and pamphlets, including two major theoretical works, *Des représentations en musique anciennes et modernes* (1681) and the companion volume considered here, *Des ballets anciens et modernes selon les règles du théâtre.* An authority on ceremonial symbolism, Menestrier was also in demand as a choreographer and composed numerous processions, ceremonies, and ballets, many of which are described in his writings. For a concise summary of Jesuit involvement in ballet, see Margaret McGowan, *L'art du ballet de court en France, 1581–1643* (Paris: Editions du Centre National de la Recherche Scientifique, 1963).

2. Louis de Cahusac, *La danse ancienne et moderne* (Paris: Chez la Haye, 1754), p. 17 (my translation).

More a devoted critic of dance than a practitioner or philosopher, Louis de Cahusac was born in 1706 at Montauban. He studied both law and literature before moving to Paris at the age of twenty-seven. Once there he began to write librettos for opera and dance. His most successful productions were collaborations with the composer Jean-Philippe Rameau: *Les fêtes de polymnie* (1745), *Les fêtes de l'hymen* (1747), *Zaïs* (1748), and *La naissance d'Osiris* (1754). His history of dance, *La danse ancienne et moderne* (1754), and his entries for the *Encyclopédie* are his only known scholarly works.

3. Exceptions to this general format are the chapter titles "On figures in the ballet," "On movements," "On harmony," "On paraphernalia," and, much later in the text, "On the number of parts in a ballet" and "On games and divertissements." These titles appear in capital letters, centered on the page, and have the effect of segmenting and emphasizing those portions of the text. They are not consecutive, however; nor do they seem more significant than other chapters, whose titles appear in the margins.

Narratives of Nostalgia Oriental Evasions about the London Stage

In the period between 1916 and 1921, during and immediately after World War I, a wave of Orientalist narrative and spectacle claimed great popularity in London's West End theatres. Of course, this was by no means the first manifestation of Oriental images, motifs, and clichés on the London stage; indeed, as Edward Ziter has traced, Orientalist themes, characters, and scenic spectacles were pervasive throughout the nineteenth century.[1] Especially because of the enormous popularity of W. S. Gilbert and A. S. Sullivan's *The Mikado* (1885), followed by a series of long-running musical comedies by George Edwardes, including *The Geisha* (1896), *San Toy, or The Emperor's Own* (1898), *The Messenger Boy* (1900), and *The Cingalee* (or *Sunny Ceylon*) (1903), Oriental topics, characters, costumes, and spectacular scenery were hardly an occasional fad in the West End theatres but in fact were one of their most distinguishing features. Some of these Orientalist productions regularly clocked up uninterrupted runs of nearly two years at their first outing, such as George Dance's *The Chinese Honeymoon* (1900) that surpassed the 1,000-performance mark. While dominating the theatre scene on both sides of the Atlantic, some of these productions even toured the world of the British Empire to Canada, Australia, New Zealand, South Africa, and India.

Orientalism triumphed. Indeed, it is easy to trace a continuous and quite various evocation and representation of the Oriental world in British society and sensibility, from the Renaissance forward. Versions of the Near and Far East gained great popularity on the stage, such as Christopher Marlowe's *Tamburlaine* and several of G. F. Handel's early operas. And from the eighteenth century onward, as Daniel O'Quinn has pointed out,[2] as British commercial interests spread eastward, Oriental images, themes, artifacts, and styles entered British culture. From early in the century Alexander Pope's poetry included teasing Oriental motifs, while the spreading market for *chinoiserie* in ceramics, furniture and textiles, and "Persian" rugs grew apace. Later *japonisme* emerged as fashions changed, and a fascination for the geisha in drawings, prints, and costumes developed. Both Lord Byron's poetry and the costumes he wore to evoke distant and dangerous lands conjured up an appetite for representations of the empire, which Rudyard Kipling continued to provide in his various reports from the "Orient" at the end of the nineteenth century.

The idea of the British "Orient" encompassed various aspects of the Near and Far East, including the Turks and the Ottoman world, Arab cultures, Persian civilization, India in its many identities, the shipping world of Indonesia (including Sumatra, Java, and Borneo), the civilizations of Japan and China, and the "mysterious" cities stretching from Constantinople to Beirut, Damascus, and beyond. Moreover, the various manifestations of the Oriental were not exclusive to British life and sensibility. Throughout Europe—as Edward Said and his commentators (as well as his critics) have documented, analyzed, and debated—a fascination with aspects of the Near and Far East shaped European sensibilities.[3]

Thus when the Oriental theme reemerged in 1916 in the West End theatres it was quite familiar, yet still capable of seducing (and occasionally offending) the British public. Tapping into its seemingly endless appeal, Oscar Asche (known primarily as a Shakespearean actor-manager) wrote, directed, and starred in two hugely successful London productions on Oriental themes, *Chu Chin Chow* (1916) and *Cairo* (1921). These two productions, which had long runs at His Majesty's Theatre, occurred during and soon after World War I, at a time of national crisis in British foreign policy in the Near and Far East; yet they had little or nothing to say or suggest about those political issues. Nonetheless, from a historiographical perspective, these two productions offer a rich and fascinating touchstone for understanding how historical narratives in theatre studies operate. From our viewpoint today we can trace the ways that popular culture, including the stage, represented aspects of race, sex, and class. Our understanding of "Orientalism" provides us with our own narratives, which are not necessarily the ones that emerged at the time of these two productions. We can uncover how these historical events were determined and understood by their own agents and how subsequent historical narratives have related (and are related to) these events. The productions were major events in the London theatre, praised by memorialists, such as Walter Macqueen-Pope, who championed the popular entertainment produced by West End actor managers and whose demise in the 1920s they equally lamented. Later historians, however, usually took a different view for a complex set of reasons. Some were severely critical of the populist ethos of the whole West End establishment and instead wrote histories of British theatre that celebrated a series of high moments in modernist avant-garde achievement. Others were severely critical of the popular theatre, decrying the sexist representations of women in the productions as well as the chauvinist celebrations of British imperialism. Yet others, committed to the supposed revolution of 1956, dismissed almost all theatre and drama of the first half of the twentieth century.

Born in Australia, Oscar Asche came to England in 1893 to start an acting career. In the first ten years he developed his craft with Frank Benson's company, working his way through the Shakespearean canon before joining Herbert Beerbohm Tree in 1902. Both of these men had a huge impact on Asche's own company that he established in 1904 with his wife, Lily Brayton. While Shakespeare's plays formed the backbone of his repertoire, Asche finally capitulated to the taste for Orientalism with a production of Edward Knoblauch's play *Kismet* in 1911. But it was during World War I that the vogue for the comfortable familiarity of Orientalism really found its place in the popular imagination. Asche wrote and produced one of the longest-running West End productions of all time (*Chu Chin Chow*) by reworking the *Arabian Nights* tale of "Ali Baba and the Forty Thieves," with endless scenes of local and sumptuous color, a strong love interest, and an ending in which evil is vanquished.

The emergent representation of this fictional Orient took place in a late-Victorian and Edwardian Britain that was experiencing enormous social unrest. The British had been left reeling at the tales of atrocities by their own administration in colonial South Africa during the Boer War (in which it transpired that approximately 20,000 women and children had perished in what were effectively concentration camps). Their revulsion was compounded because Britain ultimately lost that war. Political rhetoric that had filtered down into popular culture in the form of jingoism in the music halls and melodramas had its first serious challenge by that defeat. Russia and Germany were arming themselves at an alarming rate, and nearer to home the Home Rule campaign in Ireland was gathering violent momentum. Meanwhile at home the Suffragists had launched a series of attacks on public property in their demand for the right to vote and had engaged in hunger strikes upon their arrest. Furthermore, an unprecedented wave of strikes occurred in numerous key areas of employment, particularly in British ports. Samuel Hynes succintly sums up the period: "By the summer of 1914 the British Isles were an armed camp, armed for a war against the workers, a war against women, or a war against the Irish—for every war, in fact, except the one that was already begun on the far side of Europe."[4] The legacy of Victoria's reign throughout the first decade of the twentieth century was to propagate the myth of a nation and its empire being run in the form of patriarchal benevolence. Many of the commercial theatres of the time fed that myth with escapist fantasies of the Orient that evaded the narrative of British foreign policy.

Looking back on the period with a postcolonial understanding of the representation of Otherness in the form of Orientalism, we need to reflect carefully on the cultural practice on the stage at the height of empire. Fear was very much embedded in the national psyche: fear of the "Other" and a sense of supremacy engendered by the expansionist imperialist policies of government since the 1870s. Interpreting the theatrical "Othering" of the foreigner is further troubled because foreignness was not a lived reality for most Britons; thus stage representations of the Orient were essentially those of the imagination and of fantasy in particular. Contemporary historical narratives (from the 1900s to 1930s) of this Orientalist stage genre are few and far between. For the most part Orientalism was not only a popular cultural practice on numerous London stages but also an accepted attitude throughout much of British society. Subsequent historians until the 1980s largely ignored Orientalism on the London stage, primarily because of its practice in popular forms of entertainment. We have lost sight of Oscar Asche's dominance of the stage in the World War I era, in part because we no longer appreciate the appeal of his spectacles within the context of the British empire and also because of a deliberate erasure of popular entertainment from most theatre history narratives.

What are the most useful theoretical tools for the analysis of this period from a historiographical point of view and in relation to the idea of historical narrative in particular? Postcolonial theorists of Orientalism, as well as their critics, agree to a large extent that Orientalism usually expressed an "anxiety-desire" dialectic. This dialectic provides some possible ways to understand the historiographical problem of representing—from our perspective today—the historical identities of Otherness in earlier times. While the anxiety of the unknown "Other" is thoroughly understandable in an age of empire, the desire for what is feared is more complex. Desire in Orientalist terms is not simply a desire for the Other, since it is very much tied up with a concomitant fear of the Other. Desire for the Other is centered very much on a lack (or loss) in the Self, namely, a longing for a premodern world that the idea of the Orient provides. In the anxious conditions of the modern age the desire often evokes a longing (a wish fulfillment) for all of the supposedly lost comfort, security, and familiarity of a remembered (or imagined) past.

This nostalgia, which provides a principal aspect of the practice of theatrical Orientalism, is at the heart of Asche's two popular productions during World War I. The killing fields of France delivered an obvious and ongoing threat to the very fabric of British society. Nostalgia, as Susan Stewart reveals in her book *On Longing: Narratives of the Miniature, the Gigantic, the Souvenir, the Collection*,[5] operates in the present by using a remembered past (however fanciful it may be) to construct a desire for the future. This practice operates simultaneously in the three tenses of past, present, and future, and it is very similar to Paul Ricoeur's theory of "emplotment" in his study *Time and Narrative*.[6] Orientalism on the London stage during World War I was a specific practice of narrative emplotment, yearning for a future that was in fact a nostalgic past. As we shall see, the subsequent historical narratives that deigned to recall Asche's huge contribution to the London stage use nostalgic emplotment either to remember the productions and era fondly as a lost golden age or to reject and remove the practice of Orientalism in the theatre. Interestingly, the narratological form that various memorialists and theatre historians adopted and used in their reconstructions of Asche's Orientalist productions reproduced many of the cultural practices and assumptions that guided Asche.

Asche's two self-penned and extraordinarily successful productions based upon elements from the *Arabian Nights* tales were not just escapist fantasies from the political climate and social conditions of the era but were very much determined by that very context. The first, *Chu Chin Chow*, which opened on August 31, 1916, and ran for an amazing 2,235 performances, was a retelling of the "Ali Baba and the Forty Thieves" tale from the *Arabian Nights*. The action is set in Baghdad, in the sumptuous palace of despised merchant Kasim Baba, who is preparing a banquet for his Chinese counterpart, Chu Chin Chow. Bandit Abu Hasan, however, in an attempt to steal Kasim Baba's riches, has robbed, murdered, and assumed the identity of the Chinese merchant. Having hidden the stolen property in a cave that can only be opened by the secret code "Open Sesame," Hasan attends the banquet along with accomplices hiding in jars. But his criminal plan goes terribly wrong as the prized female slave Zahrat-al-Kulub (whose lover has been captured by Abu Hasan alias Chu) takes her revenge and kills the dastardly villain. The plot was extremely familiar as a popular children's story. Because most of the dialogue was sung, the production lurched from one appealing musical number to the next. But its success was enhanced by the great expense lavished on scenery and costumes. Asche took great pains to re-create a sense of Baghdad by staging extra market scenes that suggested local color. Furthermore, he filled the stage with animals for a bazaar scene. But it was the slave market scene that attracted the most attention, because it featured lines of seminaked women (admittedly in body stockings). These scenes sported highly fanciful designs based on a vague Oriental theme.

After *Chu Chin Chow* concluded its five-year run in London, it was succeeded by *Cairo* (which appeared first in New York in 1920 under the title *Mecca* then in London in 1921 under the modified title). *Cairo* went even further in lavishness, a myriad of revenge plots and double-crossings based on the theme of the theft of property and women. The production reduced the dialogue to a minimum and replaced it with large-scale action scenes, supported by a filmic musical score. The plot centers on Prince Nur-al-Din, who conspires to kill his brother the Sultan and assume power. He enlists the help of the wrestler Ali Shar (played by Asche) to murder the Sultan in a wrestling bout. But the plan goes wrong; the Sultan survives and captures the heart of Ali's daughter Zummurud (who had been abducted as part of a scheme by her own father to save her from the evil intentions of the Prince). The play concludes with Zummurud joining the Sultan's harem while Ali is banished and sent on a pilgrimage to Mecca to atone for his sins. The highlight (or to some the lowlight) of the production came in a feasting scene of bacchanalia which featured a chorus of men and women who danced around the stage in erotic abandon before collapsing (fig. 1). The curtain was dropped and raised moments later to reveal a scene of near-naked postcoital exhaustion. Some critics were outraged, and several moral-interest groups started a campaign to get the production stopped. But the more the protest gathered pace the more the audiences came in droves.

These two productions, as these descriptions suggest, displayed aspects of popular Orientalism as scenic and sensuous spectacle. Both productions represented the Orient in the form of stereotyped double-crossing foreign characters. The productions appealed to and depended upon an embedded Western prejudice about the Orient, as it had become part of the fabric of the social and political agendas of imperialism. By ignoring the realities of the Orient and representing it in the same way as popular storybook fiction, the productions not only tapped into an already existing cultural narrative of a fantastical Orient but also delivered a historical narrative of the all-pervasive power of the British nation over its empire.

Though reflecting and furthering already well-established cultural and political narratives, Asche's productions also evoked some of the major concerns for the home country that the audiences of the wartime (and ultimately postwar recession) felt. Many of the songs reveal those concerns; for example, "I Long for the Sun" called for an end to the war and "We Are the Robbers of the Woods" for the defeat of the enemy. These

1. The bacchanal scene from Oscar Asche's *Cairo*, His Majesty's Theatre, London (1921). By permission of the Harry Ransom Humanities Research Center, University of Texas at Austin.

two songs clearly capture the hopes and fears of the public in wartime. "I Long for the Sun," however, could have been understood in a totally different way. It was sung by a harem chorus—a group of women lacking freedom. If its trope of the nation as woman (a Britannia longing for freedom) was placed within the context of the prewar Suffragist campaigns, it might have been interpreted by some spectators as a call for the end to the domestic enslavement of women by the Suffragists whose campaign had been put on hold for the benefit of the national campaign against the enemy without. After all, in *Chu Chin Chow* it is the principal female character (Zahrat) who frees herself from entrapment and executes the revenge plot by an act of violence. What is important to highlight here is that musicals such as *Chu Chin Chow* were participating culturally in the war effort (and not just by providing escapist fantasy). For instance the production of *Chu* marked Armistice in 1918 with an additional patriotic liberation speech spoken by the female lead dressed as Britannia. Whatever the case, the narratives of songs and plot embedded implicit social reflections on the status of women and the corruption of the upper classes, albeit mapped onto a very thinly disguised imagined racial Other.

While the society and style magazines such as the *Tatler* and the *Sketch* nourished the production by devoting many pages to photographs of the spectacular costumes and scenic design, the middle-class daily newspapers (and the *Daily Mail* in particular) engaged in a campaign of vilification of Asche's spectacular entertainment that offended conservative taste and supposedly compromised conservative morality. The morally outraged used the letters pages of the newspaper to give vent to their anger at the tastelessness of the musical comedy that had displayed—and apparently sanctioned—an inappropriate sexualization of behavior, on and off the stage. This campaign was an extension of the moral debate that already had shifted some forms of popular entertainment out of the theatres and into the music halls in an act of class segregation.

Asche's production of *Cairo* in 1921–1922, with its near-naked scenes of bacchanalia, had exposed the myth behind Orientalism; far from representing any kind of reality of a foreign Other, it was actually using the Other as a cover for the licentiousness of the self. The media controversy that surrounded Asche's productions, and *Cairo* in particular, provided an opportunity for some conservative and religious groups to attempt a restoration of class order by what Jacky Bratton terms a "strategy of containment within the discourse of the popular."[7] Their criticism in the popular press did not call for the removal from the stage of Orientalist representations but for a refocus on and recovery of the earlier traits of Orientalism (as an extension of Romanticism in painting). That is, the critics claimed that they wanted the stage to represent the "real" Orient, as they understood it, rather than to create false images of fantasy and desire. Of course, their versions were also fantastic. This campaign meant that the critics in all guises (from letter-writers to newspaper editors to the official stage censor) focused on the anxiety of the Other rather than a desire for it. What they were calling for in fact was a return to the prewar narrative of empire (seen in the popular melodramas and pantomimes); they sought a return to a very simple binary of good and evil, us and them. By sexualizing the Orient, however, Asche was making foreignness too attractive and morally dubious.

A further and related historical narrative exists as a context for Asche's production: the competition for the control of the stage in the London theatres. Asche flourished in the actor-manager system that controlled commercial entertainment in the West End while a modernist agenda, led by Bernard Shaw, Granville Barker, and others, was simultaneously creating an alternative repertoire. Of course, both the West End managers and the new modernists (whose activities have generated two distinct historical narratives from theatre scholars throughout the twentieth century) were subject to the licensing system of the Lord Chamberlain's Office. In most instances, it sided with the aims of the actor-managers, who generally supported the system. Often the judgment and values of the censor were established at the expense of the modernist alternative theatre. For this reason, Shaw and critic William Archer had begun a campaign against the Office of the Lord Chamberlain—his power and collusion with the actor-managers—but the government, in its parliamentary reviews of London entertainment, always sided with the Lord Chamberlain and the West End managers (until censorship was finally removed in the 1960s).

Asche, who attempted to follow the theatrical model of Herbert Beerbohm Tree's repertoire, also sought to discover a new drama in the early years of his company; but commercial imperatives always carried the day in favor of conservative values and forms. And, as Thomas Postlewait notes, "during World War One the alternative theatre staled, as patriotism and chauvinism took over both country and stage."[8] One might assume, accordingly, that popular entertainment during the war years (such as Asche's *Chu*) would have the support of the Lord Chamberlain's Office, given its reputed collusion with the West End theatres. A close examination of the Lord Chamberlain's Correspondence Files, however, reveals that the relationship between the censor and one of the West End's leading managers was not as simple as the modernist critics would have it in their historical narratives, which usually attack or dismiss West End theatre as commercial entertainment while celebrating the revolts and resistance campaigns of the alternative theatre movement.

In these Correspondence Files, which offer archival sources that we often treat as primary evidence, we discover a wide range of epistolary narratives. Besides recording the censor's decisions, the files provide a perspective on Oscar Asche's activities as a producer, the views of the morally outraged (who usually were unidentified in their correspondence), and a vast array of letters, including those of religious leaders. Although *Chu*, the first and longest-running of Asche's spectacular productions, received complaints for its scantily clad dancers, the Lord Chamberlain's Office firmly and repeatedly endorsed it as good old-fashioned family entertainment and noted that the show attracted the very desirable middle-class audiences. Much of this correspondence seems to support the critical complaints of Archer and others about the hypocrisy of the licensing system, which regularly permitted sexualized musical entertainment while banning Ibsen's *Ghosts* and Shaw's *Mrs. Warren's Profession*.

Chu's sequel *Mecca/Cairo*, however, provides a narrative that troubles the historical versions of London theatre so prevalent today. A note of caution is needed as we consider the content of these files, for we could fall prey to a "longing" to privilege the documentary record as the primary historical narrative. Except for the theatre reviews and newpaper reports (and gossip), the Lord Chamberlain's Correspondence Files provide the only extant narrative contemporary with the historical events of Asche's productions. No other account, including Asche's autobiography, is a recording of the events as they unfolded; subsequent commentary on *Cairo* is always a remembering, a narrative reflection on and reconstruction of previous events of and for posterity. Consequently, the documentary record is crucial to our historical understanding and narratives, but we need to proceed with caution.

Foregrounding the files as a narrative of origin, I am mindful of how this narrative of interiority and authenticity from one of the agents of the historical action might itself be used to authenticate a past event. Privileging this originary narrative, of course, as Susan Stewart reminds us, "is not a narrative of the object; it is a narrative of the possessor" (in this case the historian now writing).[9] This narrative then needs to be set against other narratives operating in the "future past." The extent of the correspondence on *Mecca/Cairo* and the six-month delay beween application for a license and its eventual production as *Cairo* demand special attention, particularly in the light of how Asche was to downplay the controversy in his autobiography. There he dismissed the situation as a personal act of spite by a "single and rival author,"[10] though this claim is not corroborated by the extant correspondance.

The first report on April 30, 1921, by G. S. Street, a reader in the Lord Chamberlain's Office, clearly alluded to the "success in America" of *Mecca* and to its chief attraction being "in gorgeous Eastern scenes and dresses and unlimited local colour generally." But the last paragraph includes a cautionary note about a possible offense: "Possibly Mohammedans might object to the Mecca pilgrimage being taken lightly, but there is obviously no offence meant and no ridicule of sacred Mohammedan things. If any objection is taken to the performance it probably would be some question of dresses—and that cannot be foretold from the script. The harem scene does not seem to me at all unpleasantly suggestive. The slave-market scene involves a certain amount of brutality, but nothing beyond precedent. Recommended for Licence."[11]

The report signals possible concerns that had dogged the Lord Chamberlain's relationship with the production of *Chu Chin Chow*: the "tastefulness" (or lack thereof) of the exposure of flesh by scanty clothes. Possible objections on religious grounds are acknowledged by Street but are not viewed as a hindrance to a license. However, he was too sanguine in his judgment. After a complaining letter to the *Daily Mail* and also a letter from Mustapha Khan, a Muslim cleric from Woking who served as the editor of *Islamic Review and Muslim India* and objected to the license, a second report was drawn up in response. Contrary to Asche's reporting of the controversy, it is interesting that Street dismissed the objection almost completely and in fact was extremely supportive of Asche's fantasy play. Street's subsequent examination of the script from the point of view of offense to Muslims is extremely detailed and includes a list of points in defense of Asche's play, with the conclusion: "The only actual point to which, I think exception might be taken, is that the pilgrims drink wine. That is, no doubt, merely ignorance of the Mohammedan law. The assumption, therefore, that the play 'will ignore the feelings and the sentiments of the Moslems' etc., is unfounded and inspired only by the title. Perhaps this might be changed."[12]

The relationship between the Lord Chamberlain and Khan, the objector, was polite, and it is clear that a compromise among all parties was being sought. The Lord Chamberlain arranged a face-to-face meeting with the objectors, and a meeting with Asche was agreed upon. In a letter to the Lord Chamberlain, Khan expressed his gratitude "for the sympathy which you showed to the interest of the Muslims in connection with the safe guard of their religious feelings."[13] Despite Khan's perception of the Lord Chamberlain's display of sensitivity to religious feelings, we cannot ignore that the first report completely dismissed such feelings as not warranting a withholding of the license. The Establishment, as represented by the Lord Chamberlain's Office, was quite simply out of touch with the Muslim community, not least through a reference to Geoffrey Chaucer and Catholic pilgrims as a fitting analogy for the Mecca pilgrimage. It also appeared to be colluding with a socially and economically powerful actor-manager.

Subsequent to the initial exchange of correspondence, the protest gathered momentum. William Mansfield, Lord Sandhurst, who held the office of Lord Chamberlain, consulted leading Muslim figures in London, including the Aga Khan and senior figures from the major Muslim countries of the empire (Muslim India and Egypt). The protest was partially successful in that Asche finally agreed to a title change from *Mecca* to *Cairo*. The production opened on October 15, 1921, having received six months of free prepublicity about its possible offensiveness. As the religious debate subsided, a new though familiar controversy ensued as another religious group fought for control of the stage.

The new battle that ensued after the production finally opened was waged on the premise of decency rather than as a matter of religious offense. The censor was alerted to possible charges of indecency by the nu-

2. The reveal or "orgy" scene after the bacchanal from Oscar Asche's *Cairo*, His Majesty's Theatre, London (1921). By permission of the Harry Ransom Humanities Research Center, University of Texas at Austin.

merous critics who had complained of gross "sensuality" in a scene of bacchanalia. This scene has defined in great measure how many memorialists and historians have remembered or reconstructed the production, which was widely claimed to represent an orgy featuring approximately a hundred dancers. Their collapse on the stage, on pillows, rugs, or the bare floor, culminated in a curtain drop. Almost immediately the curtain was raised to reveal a scene of the dancers asleep in a pose of presumably postcoital exhaustion, or so the critics would have it (fig. 2). G. S. Street, who had initially reported on the script's innocuousness, changed his mind. He became adamant about the inappropriateness of the scene for the sensibilities of a middle-class audience: "the thing is so unseemly and likely to be a scandal."[14] But it was the orgiastic sexualization of racial Others that belatedly troubled the censor: "Girls dance frantically with dark-skinned men . . . the men fight for them." This apparent racial fusion stood contrary to the tenets of British imperial policy: the separation of races and cultures. As we read the revised report, a very clear sense of the Orientalism of empire can be detected.

This report, along with other documents and the decisions of the Lord Chamberlain's Office, endorses the historical narrative (prevalent today) that criticizes the contributions of both the government and the West End theatres to national chauvinism. Yet a note on a telephone conversation between Asche and the Lord Chamberlain's Office records Asche's claim of "unwarrantable persecution of him and his production by the Department." This evidence clearly suggests a lack of complicity between this populist manager and the censor. Indeed, the Lord Chamberlain's Office was apparently growing suspicious of Asche's motives and actions. In an unsigned internal memorandum, which related to a meeting at which Asche offered to change the title to *Cairo* (and, at the same time, the Lord Chamberlain attempted to mediate between the Muslim protesters and Asche), someone in the Lord Chamberlain's Office recorded the following statement: "I have no doubt our interview will appear in a distorted form in this evening's Press, though I told him we were talking in confidence."[15] The implication seems fairly clear: the Lord Chamberlain's Office was fully aware that Asche was using the controversy to fuel publicity for his production. Asche's mischief was not only confined to his manipulation of the media. Lord Chamberlain's Office reader E. Trendell was sent to assess the production in light of the criticisms. Trendell's visit to the theatre was "managed" by Asche and his actors to ensure that any possible offense was obscured from view, as is evident in the report: "I do not know if it was done on purpose, but it was rather strange that the seat reserved for me was the last one on the left end of the front row (facing the stage); the result was that when the dancing scene came on, my view was greatly impeded by one of the characters, sitting surrounded by his retinue, so that it was only by leaning sideways that I was able to see the stage properly."[16]

Contrary to our standard understanding that a collusive relationship existed between the Lord Chamberlain's Office and the West End theatre managers during this era, the originary documentation on the production of *Cairo* provides a different historical narrative. Though clearly in accord with the commercial desires of this celebrated West End producer and popular actor, the Lord Chamberlain's Office did not endorse Asche's position. Indeed, it showed some sympathy to objectors of various hues. Ultimately, though, the Lord Chamberlain's sympathy only extended to the point where it could successfully evade the issue of racial misrepresentation and religious offense by focusing instead on the sexual representations, which could be tempered. The Lord Chamberlain's Office, which in times of controversy preferred to see itself as a mediator between competing agents in a matter of theatre business rather than as a moral authority on matters of racial codes and religious beliefs, retreated to its institutional persona as a paternalistic national authority. In this detached yet sanctioned role it tapped a societal desire (or nostalgic longing) for a kind of British stability and authority that served the country in various aspects of governmental policy (such as the mandates that guided imperial policy). This self-serving identity and national narrative of benign leadership, though increasingly precarious after World War I, derived from a smug authority that might question and judge others but not itself.

Meanwhile the purification of the stage was to come in dramaturgical form and by those who sought to record their memories of those events. The purification was hastened by events not connected to a concerted campaign. Asche's marriage dissolved acrimoniously. After *Cairo* was hastily taken off the stage, he departed on a two-year tour of his native Australia with his "greatest hits." The vacuum created by the departure of this hugely successful producer of theatrical Orientalism, among the last of the actor-managers in the 1920s, permitted a new form of drama to emerge on the stage of His Majesty's Theatre, such as W. Somerset Maugham's *East of Suez* (1922) and James Elroy Flecker's *Hassan* (1923).[17] The various aspects of Orientalism did not disappear, but they did begin to change significantly.

One of the most important determinants in the choice of form and content after World War I was the demise of the actor-managers as a producing force and their replacement with syndicated managements of theatres. Syndication invariably led to the closing of many theatres and a controlled and controlling production practice. The artistic personnel no longer dictated the repertoire; this change led, at His Majesty's, to the rejection of musical comedy in favor of drama with an integrated plot, all the while cashing in on the vogue of Orientalism.

To compound the rout of Asche and his like by the new business syndicates as well as by critics of the theatrical establishment (such as Shaw, James Agate, St. John Ervine, and various others) who continued to wage a campaign against popular entertainment in the West End, new histories and studies of the theatre and drama were published in the 1920s. These publications came from theatre professionals (playwrights and critics) who sought to change, purify, or save the stage. Some sought to free the stage of its lower-class connotations; others sought an edificatory role for it as a form of entertainment. Others, committed to the emergence of modern drama and modern theatre, made the case for not only the new drama but also revisionist histories of British theatre (such as William Archer's *The Old Drama and the New* in 1923 and James Agate's *A Short View of the English Stage* in 1926).

Of special note, William Poel, actor-manager and founder of the English

Shakespeare Society, published *What Is Wrong with the Stage?* (1920), a history of the theatre that appeared at about the same time as Asche's *Cairo*. In this study, which set a benchmark for subsequent historical critiques on London theatre, Poel saved his vitriol for the contemporary period. He castigated the West End commercial system, whose sole aim was profit. In accord with its mission of maximizing profit, the West End theatres "trained" their audience in bad taste: "But it must be remembered that in London, with a population of 13,000,000 to draw from, a large number of theatres can thrive by catering for only one class of audience—a class whose taste has been systematically trained to appreciate a depraved quality of entertainment. And managers may find that they are obliged to continue the unwholesome productions which they have taught their public to like."[18] Poel thus both contributed to and extended a long campaign, led by Archer, Shaw, and others since the 1890s, to criticize the West End theatres for their excessive penchant for sex farces, melodramas, and musicals. The theatrical purist that was Poel went further than most others in his loathing of commercial theatre that sought long runs for popular productions to maximize box office returns, beyond their time-slot as seasonal entertainment. Although not working in tandem with Shaw or with the West End producers who emerged in the 1920s and replaced the actor-managers, Poel helped to articulate and put in place a historical narrative that aided and abetted those who sought, as part of their morality campaign, to cleanse the stage for other class-based reasons.

Two years after Asche left the London stage, playwright and critic St. John Ervine took up an argument similar to Poel's in another revisionist "history" of the contemporary stage, *The Organised Theatre: A Plea in Civics* (1924): "An audience of half-wits will not accept anything but a half-witted drama, nor will a man with a *Chu Chin Chow* mind easily be persuaded to patronize any other than *Chu Chin Chow* plays."[19] Of course, Ervine's own agenda in writing such a chronicle was driven by self-interest. One could easily dismiss Ervine (and indeed Poel) for promoting their own class-based interests in such vitriolic attacks on Asche's work, but these attacks are symptomatic of a battle in the theatrical establishment itself for the control of the stage. Thus Clive Barker and Maggie B. Gale in *British Theatre between the Wars, 1918–1939* (2000) have been careful not to dismiss Ervine, for instance, as a "figure of fun."[20] Ervine distorted the popular mythology of Asche's productions for his own ends. *Chu Chin Chow*, for instance, was rumored to have entertained the troops on leave. While no doubt some troops did attend the theatre, this narrative was created by Asche in the first place in an attempt to situate his production and theatre as patriotic supporters of the war effort. His campaign can be seen in his rewriting of the play for the Armistice and in his ability to keep the show going during air raids with reduced versions of favorite scenes. Calling attention to this suspect mythology, Ervine attempted to subvert it by ridiculing the pretentious play and production: "But the relief provided for them [the troops on leave] by their civilian friends was of such a character that they gladly went back to the trenches."[21] The purpose of these men of letters clearly was to consign Asche and his production to the historical dustbin.

So what happened to Asche's Orientalism, both on and off the stage, subsequent to the productions? Asche returned from Australia two years after *Cairo* closed and tried without success to revive both the genre and his career. By the 1920s the vogue for Asche's type of Orientalism shifted from theatre to film and brought its audience with it. In his 1929 autobiography Asche attempted to put in place his own narrative version of the productions and scandals. Yet in his historical construction of events he chose to glide over the very significant theatrical controversy about *Cairo* that had fueled and enlivened the popular press for months. Why should he do so? One answer could lie in Paul Ricoeur's notion of the "emplotment" of narrative through verbal experience, whereby "concordance mends discordance."[22] By narrating his own version of his theatrical past, Asche was not simply offering a present perspective and discourse on his lived past. He was also providing what Ricoeur, in his analysis of the methods and aims of historical narrative, calls an "emplotment between a stage of practical experience that precedes it and a stage that succeeds it."[23] This autobiographical account by Asche situates his Oriental musicals within a wider and more "legitimate" professional career of Shakespearean productions. Moreover, Asche's historical narrative, which makes much of the hugely successful Australian tours of his London productions, attempts to sanction his theatrical ventures by celebrating his own notable celebrity in both countries. Asche's tactics in 1929 eventually prove crucial in establishing subsequent narratives by other writers—theatre people and historians, especially in the 1950s and beyond. Asche and others look backward on the early decades of twentieth-century theatre with nostalgia, a longing that expressed not only a sense of self-importance and self-justification so typical of theatre autobiographies but also a desire to remember the past in specific ways that enhance the supposedly unique qualities of the lost era.

After the 1920s selective memories of *Chu Chin Chow* clearly lingered, as evidenced in a reference to it in Noel Coward's 1931 production of *Cav-*

alcade. During World War II, *Chu* was revived (1940–1941) when popular entertainment as light relief was recalled fondly. Apparently Asche had successfully planted the seed that the musical had been a successful wartime entertainment during World War I. The revival served as a cue for a series of historical remembrances of a bygone age of theatre that provided a new set of memorial histories of London theatre that pose an interesting historiographical problem. The first was Ernest Short's *Theatrical Cavalcade* (1942), a historical reflection that attempted to revive Asche's contribution to English theatre. Short used Asche's career to highlight the fact that many actor-managers started their artistic enterprises with often paltry savings from salaries and investments from admirers. Short celebrated the commercial success of Asche's Orientalist musicals and situated their popular appeal in their ability to cross genres: "sun-flooded and colourful scenery and pretty dresses worn by pretty women can give the theatre not a little of the allure of the ballet."[24] Short also enhanced the professional allure of Asche's career by highlighting his critically acclaimed productions of Shakespeare plays during the Edwardian period. Unlike Ervine before him, Short praised Asche's productions as part of an actor-management system which generated worthy productions within a commercial system that was guided by artistic personnel. He lamented that the demise of the actor-manager system was brought about by the syndicated business leaders who "controlled" the theatres and relegated artistic personnel to the role of hired help. This historical narrative, though partly an attempt to rehabilitate Asche by reminding readers of his Shakespearean credentials and critical success, primarily interpreted the artistic policy of the actor-managers (such as Beerbohm Tree and Asche) as cunning management. By piggybacking on commercial entertainment, the artistic managers were able to finance their less lucrative ambitions of discovering new authors for the stage and reinterpreting Shakespeare.

Perhaps the most notable theatre memorialist for the London theatre of the early century was Walter Macqueen-Pope, who churned out a series of popular theatre histories, including *Twenty Schillings in the Pound* (1948), *Gaiety, Theatre of Enchantment* (1949), *St. James's Theatre of Distinction* (1958), and, most famously, *Carriages at Eleven: An Account of the Theatre from 1897–1914* (1947). A theatre publicist turned "historian," Macqueen-Pope continued his reminiscences in his 1956 publication *Nights of Gladness*, in which he fondly remembered (or misremembered, we should say) the cultural contribution of *Chu Chin Chow* to the war effort. Unlike Ernest Short, Macqueen-Pope wallowed in nostalgia for a bygone era: "It was a piece of musical and stage magic, which started an era and struck a note."[25] Reflecting sentimentally on the era, he embraced the myths surrounding *Chu Chin Chow* that Asche had propagated in his 1929 autobiography. Macqueen-Pope then recycled them to justify his belief that in attracting people from all walks and classes of life *Chu* united the nation in a time of war. This type of history as selective memory has been critiqued by Jim Davis and Victor Emeljanow, who identify this particular type of historical narrative as a mode of "imperfect recognition." These kinds of "reviews, reminiscence, and surveys," which have often been accepted as documentary records, "provide part of the source material through which we investigate the theatrical past."[26] Macqueen-Pope's nostalgia, as Davis and Emeljanow point out (in a critique that is in accord with Susan Stewart's analysis of nostalgia), offers an ideological narrative: "the past it seeks has never existed except as narrative, and hence, always absent, that past continually threatens to produce itself as a felt lack."[27] This method of historical representation is of course predicated on the selective and distorted narrative that Asche helped to put in place.

Despite the example of Macqueen-Pope, reminiscence does not necessarily invoke nostalgia for a utopian past. In his 1945 publication *Before the Lamps Went Out*, Esmé Cecil Wingfield-Stratford articulated an altogether different kind of remembering that was not based on a longing to return to Asche's form of entertainment. As a counterpoint to Macqueen-Pope, Wingfield-Stratford published what could be described as a post-traumatic narrative of Asche's contribution to the stage. Remembering the production of *Chu Chin Chow*, which, he claimed, had "degenerated into such silliness and vulgarity that I could stand it no longer," Wingfield-Stratford offered an anxious narrative of fear for the future of class-based English society.[28] Like a number of other memorialists of London theatre, Wingfield-Stratford used the first person to authenticate a "feeling" of the period (while also implicitly expressing a concern for an uncertain future). He wrote history in much the same way as Asche's contemporary protestors had written their epistolary protests to the press and the Lord Chamberlain. These complaints personalized the offense that Orientalist musical comedy had caused them. He used his own "memory" of the production and the period as a "device for measurement," as Susan Stewart would say.[29] He thus constructed a calibrated narrative that presents itself as enriched by knowledge and status, while presenting the subject under review as impoverished entertainment.

J. C. Trewin, writing a decade later than Wingfield-Stratford, revisited the period in his book *The Gay Twenties: A Decade of the Theatre* (1958). He represented *Cairo* as the end of the genre as well as the culmination of Asche's career. The premature closing of the production, following the disproportionate nature of the scandal, had fueled rumors at the time of the demise of the musical genre. Yet, as Trewin notes, an examination of the box-office returns for the production easily counters that rumor. Setting the record straight with figures presumably gleaned from Asche's autobiography, Trewin proclaimed that "in spite of sour-grape rumours, [*Cairo*] made a profit of £12000."[30]

Nevertheless, while Trewin insisted that Asche was commercially successful, he speedily condemned Asche's brand of musical genre by proxy. His survey of James Elroy Flecker's poetic drama *Hassan* (one of the Orientalist plays that succeeded *Cairo* at His Majesty's Theatre) is notable because he concentrated on the failure of the production: "It was a pity, perhaps, that the theatre had to be His Majesty's. Memories of *Chu Chin Chow* and *Cairo* still tingled, and to put *Hassan* with these was a tempting piece of facile rudeness; detractors grasped it with delight."[31] Trewin failed to mention who these detractors were, thus implying that the theatre critics panned the play and production. But the critics were unanimous in their praise, highlighting that the play had an integrated plot. And the music by Frederick Delius had wide appeal. Yet despite this support the audiences failed to be attracted by *Hassan*. More recent commentaries, such as Phyllis Hartnoll's *Oxford Companion to the Theatre* (2nd ed., 1957) and Barker and Gale's *British Theatre between the Wars*, offered contradictory views on the production; the former cited it as an important example of poetic drama, yet the latter focused on its lack of popularity because of its poetic pretensions. Trewin was the first historian to attempt to make sense of the contemporary and historical responses to Orientalism in performance, but he had difficulty placing Asche's productions in a larger cultural and social context. Some people were attracted to it, while others were repelled by it. This difference in opinion divided according to the genre of entertainment under the microscope. Censorship of the stage was still ongoing, however, and the historical records of the Lord Chamberlain were apparently not available to Trewin. His consultation of newspaper archives also apparently led him to his conclusion about the lack of popularity of Orientalism on the London stage in the 1920s. Thus, despite a genuine attempt to reinstate Asche's contribution to the history of British theatre, Trewin also succumbed to "imperfect recognition."

Histories of the period that delivered and also depended on nostalgic memories persisted throughout the century. In his several books on London theatre, including *The Story of Pantomime* (London: Home and Van

Thal, 1949) and *Edwardian Theatre* (London: Arthur Barker, 1951), A. E. Wilson provided a sympathetic catalogue of people, plays, and productions that contributed to the popularity of London entertainment. He peppered his narratives with names, titles, and dates, often unrecorded in other theatre histories. Throughout his historical surveys he celebrated the lost era (though with less nostalgia than in Macqueen-Pope). But his historical method hardly extends beyond the cataloguing of information on West End theatre.

Raymond Mander and Joe Mitchenson also looked back on the century's popular entertainment with fond recollection. For example, in *Musical Comedy: A Story in Pictures* (1969) they celebrated (and elevated) *Chu Chin Chow*'s historical importance: "It gave the bleak war years from 1916, well into the almost as bleak first peace years up to 1920, a glamorous escape into a romantic alien world of make-believe."[32] In some ways Mander and Mitchenson, actors who had transformed themselves into collectors of memorabilia and historians of theatre since the Victorian era, are similar to all of their predecessors (from Poel and Ervine to Macqueen-Pope) in that they were part of the theatrical establishment. They were closely involved with the business of theatre at the very highest level of practice. This very much dictated their favorable inclusion of Asche's Orientalism in the long tradition of musical productions on the London stage. Nevertheless, they position themselves very clearly in opposition to Macqueen-Pope, whose work they castigate as "the fruits of reminiscence rather than objective historical research."[33]

A transformation in historical method after World War II coincided with a radical shift in the academy, following the social and political shifts in postwar British society. In consequence, a more meritocratic pathway to university teaching (as well as social status) opened up in Britain. (And a new generation of American, Canadian, and Australian scholars began to take up the study of British theatre history.) In the years following Macqueen-Pope—and in partial reaction to his sentimental narratives—scholarship on British theatre history revealed a new critical method. Unlike Manders and Mitchenson, these new historians were not theatre insiders. In most cases they were university teachers and scholars.

Signs of the professional shift in methodology appeared in British theatre history of the 1960s and 1970s with the pioneering endeavors of Michael Booth on Victorian theatre, such as *English Plays of the Nineteenth Century* (5 vols., Oxford: Clarendon Press, 1969–1976). Along with his subsequent work, including *Victorian Spectacular Theatre, 1850–1910* (London: Routledge, 1981) and *Theatre in the Victorian Age* (Cambridge: Cambridge

University Press, 1991), came equally important studies on Victorian and Edwardian theatre by historians such as Allardyce Nicholl, George Rowell, Richard Foulkes, Martin Meisel, David Mayer, Russell Jackson, Peter Bailey, Jacky Bratton, Joseph Donohue, Diana Howard, J. P. Wearing, Jim Davis, Victor Emeljanow, Tracy C. Davis, Maggie Gale, John Stokes, Paul Ranger, Viv Gardner, Ellen Donkin, Thomas Postlewait, Dennis Kennedy, Joel Kaplan, Cary Mazer, John McCormick, George Taylor, Jane Moody, Elaine Aston, Richard Schoch, W. Davies King, Edward Ziter, Dagmar Kift, and Sheila Stowell. The list could easily be expanded, especially with the contributions of theatre historians during the last couple of decades.

Besides their commitment to archival research and cultural analysis, a number of these scholars revised the narratives on British theatre history by assessing theatre in the time of empire from a sociopolitical perspective. The disciplines of sociology and cultural studies emerged in an ever-decolonizing world, further cementing the move from the political Right to the Left in the universities, especially in the humanities. Theatre was placed within social and cultural paradigms. For instance, J. S. Bratton's *Acts of Supremacy: British Empire and the Stage, 1790–1930* (Manchester: Manchester University Press, 1991) provided a radical reassessment of popular entertainment that was notable for its emphasis on race and class issues. Bratton's subsequent monograph *New Readings in Theatre History* (2003) traced the historiographical trajectory of the same period by using several case studies to further the sociopolitical investigation of the realms of entertainment, including the theatre. Popular entertainment of the nineteenth century moved front and center in historical studies.

Because of a widespread tendency of historians and critics of twentieth-century British theatre to focus their attention on modern, modernist, avant-garde, and alternative drama and theatre, however, the post-Edwardian period of British popular entertainment remains largely neglected. In most cases, for example, historians and critics of the modern era have produced a revisionist narrative that has required the erasure of Asche and his form of entertainment from the histories of London theatre. West End theatre is often ignored (as Susan Bennett also points out in her essay in this collection). Although the history of British musical theatre (with its songs and stars who crossed over from the halls) is featured in seminal works by historians such as Kurt Gänzl, Andrew Lamb, and Len Platt, the contribution of the musical genre to British theatre rarely achieves recognition in broader histories, as seen in the treatment of Asche's contribution. For instance, Simon Trussler's *The Cambridge Illustrated History of British Theatre* (1994) devotes just half a sentence to Asche, who is only slightly more visible a decade later in Baz Kershaw's *The Cambridge History of British Theatre*, vol. 3 (2004), where *Chu Chin Chow* receives one long sentence, which notes that such entertainment was replaced by the revue in the 1920s.[34]

To their credit, Maggie Gale and Clive Barker in *British Theatre between the Wars, 1918–1939* make a valiant attempt to reinsert Asche into a historical narrative. Alongside their reassessments of modern theatre, which they contextualize socially and culturally, they reclaim the popular theatre.[35] But Asche, it appears, has remained something of a conundrum for historians. He was a celebrated actor and producer of Shakespeare, yet he was also a commercial actor-manager who, after popular success in light entertainment, gave up the stage for his native Australia. A 1996 essay by Russell Jackson on Asche's Shakespeare productions is one of the few contemporary attempts at reinstating Asche into the national narrative of British theatre history,[36] and a 1993 essay by Veronica Kelly on Orientalism in Australian theatre assesses Asche appropriately as Australian and thus as a "subject" of empire.[37] Yet despite these efforts Asche and British theatre, it appears, are not fully conjoined by historians.

The premise for my own monograph *Oscar Asche, Orientalism and British Musical Comedy* (Westport, Conn.: Praeger, 2004) was to offer a wealth of historical evidence of Asche's one-time dominance of the London stage, thereby addressing his near-absence in historical studies of recent decades. I had started the historical search with a postcolonial understanding of modern Orientalism, principally dependent upon two seminal works, Edward Said's *Orientalism: Western Conceptions of the Orient* (1978) and Ziauddin Sardar's *Orientalism* (1999). Yet contrary to these postcolonial theoretical narratives of the colonial construction of the world, I found conflicting evidence that both supported and refuted the claims of the postcolonialists. On the one hand, the autobiographical writing by Asche clearly replicated much of the propaganda, jingoism, and sense of supremacy that was endemic in British national culture at the height of empire. Furthermore, the criticism and the scandals that Asche's productions invoked in the middle-class presses fed neatly into the stereotypical attitudes and assumptions of British Orientalism. But, on the other hand, the documentary evidence from the productions, accumulated and annotated by Asche's costumiers, reveals that careful, detailed research had been carried out in support of the historical costumes and set designs in the representation of the Orient onstage. This evidence refuted the postcolonialists' claims that the Orientalists were ignorant of the Orient.

Essentially, though, my historical narrative had its own limitations. This became evident when I attempted to maintain a postcolonial reading, despite some of the historical evidence. Although I referred to the legal factors that applied to the scandals that surrounded Asche's productions and to the critics' commentaries on those scandals that purported to offend religious sensibilities and moral codes, I was only interested in placing these events and the actions of the principal agents within the context of the critique of postcolonial Orientalism, as represented by Said and others. For example, in my determination to avoid treating the Muslim as the "Other" (a reduction I was quite sensitive to), I took up the cause of one of the agents in the historical action: Muslim cleric Mustapha Khan. His action, based on his perception of Orientalist insensitivity to Muslims, had remained historically invisible until now. By rendering him and his perspective visible, I marked a reversal of the dominance of Orientalist perspectives historically. But in this effort my own narrative unconsciously slighted the mediating role of the Lord Chamberlain's Office. My postcolonial understanding and political stance, while of benefit to my analysis of Khan's activities and importance, apparently closed off attention to (and any sympathy for) the agendas of the people in the censor's office. In sum, all historical narratives, including my own revisionist study, offer partial perspectives on historical agents and events. Each and every historical narrative, from nostalgia or moralist critique to positivism and postcolonialism, has an agenda and an ideology.

What, then, does this survey of historical narratives about Oscar Asche's musicals reveal to us? Based on the scant secondary material that is available on Asche and his popular entertainment (his autobiography, a mix of theatre reviews, personal reminiscences of theatre people), it would be easy to write a narrative of a commercially successful Orientalist entertainment, as did several of the memorialists of the 1940s and 1950s, including Macqueen-Pope. In turn, based on the subsequent narratives of theatre historians, Asche's activities in musicals typically have been either decried (for example, by various moralists and campaigners for a serious or alternative theatre) or ignored (for example, by historians writing theatre history as a succession of modernist achievements and uplifting revivals of the canon).

The campaign against Asche, popular theatre, and/or West End commercial management (by William Poel and others) has generated the narratives of self-interested practitioner-reformers of the stage who sought to rid it of excesses in moral terms and to wrest control either for the middle classes or, interestingly, for those who were opposed to middle-class values. These practitioners happily jumped on the bandwagon of religious protesters from both the Muslim and Christian communities for their own ends. Asche also has to be implicated in this battle, as he fueled the protests against his own work for commercial gain. Surprisingly, despite its own Orientalist and class-based obsessions, the Lord Chamberlain's Office stands out as a voice of reason and rapprochement between the competing factions that sought control of the stage. These battles were often played out within the social and political matrix of race, religion, and sex.

Instead of accepting either of these narratives, I sought in my own study to interpret the actions of the historical agents, using the thread not of censorship but of the interventions of censorious others who either sought to shape the representation of Orientalist theatrical culture before and during its production and reception or subsequently wished to determine its place in theatre history. The impact of those "Others" was such that they helped to fuel subsequent censorious narratives that managed effectively to "remove" Asche from British theatre history, a feat that not even the Lord Chamberlain's Office ever set out to achieve.

What I have been attempting to demonstrate here is that a theatre history based solely on the actions of the agents of theatre and how they played out in terms of representation (read retrospectively through postcolonial theories) can never be complete. Each of their narratives is based on and determined by certain agendas, assumptions, and attitudes; it is these factors, according to Ricoeur, "that escape a simple reconstruction of the calculations made by the agents of the action."[38] Among several lessons here, it is important to recognize that Orientalism for the postcolonial scholar is not the same as it was for Oscar Asche. He not only represented the Orient onstage (in a bizarre mixture of accurate and fanciful details) but also narrated versions of colonialist Orientalism in an autobiography. The Lord Chamberlain's Office supported his commercial endeavors wholeheartedly, as the extant correspondence clearly demonstrates, contrary to the accounts of self-interested reformers of the stage. Further, while memorialists lamented the demise of actor-manager Asche, his like, and his form of popular entertainment, many subsequent historians proved quite willing to dismiss or ignore Asche as an irrelevant figure in their narratives of British theatre history.

In conclusion, this case study of Asche provides a lens through which we can chart a series of competing narratives that provide partial, often distorted perspectives on the productions and their reception. As the agendas and imperatives of historians have altered over the decades, the narratives have multiplied. As for my own historical narrative, I insist upon its significant value, with its recovery of Asche's career and its interpretive focus on Orientalism, but I also acknowledge the value of this historiographical essay with its critique of all historical narratives, including my own. Ironically, the encyclopedic scholarship of Kurt Gänzl, tied to either a chronology (*The British Musical Theatre*, 2 vols. [New York: Oxford University Press, 1986]) or an alphabetical organization (*The Encyclopedia of the Musical Theatre*, 2 vols. [New York: Schirmer, 1994]), offers perhaps the most reliable and succinct documentary record of the basic facts on the two musicals, but these truncated descriptions stop at just the place where historical narratives must begin—facing the challenge of representing the past and offering an interpretive understanding of history (in cultural, social, psychological, political, economic, geographical, or ethical terms).

NOTES

Research for this essay was enabled by the financial assistance of Trinity College Dublin's Arts, Humanities and Social Sciences' Benefaction Fund and Trinity College's Long Room Hub.

1. Edward Ziter, *The Orient on the Victorian Stage* (Cambridge: Cambridge University Press, 2003).

2. Daniel O'Quinn, *Staging Governance: Theatrical Imperialism in London, 1770–1800* (Baltimore: Johns Hopkins University Press, 2005).

3. Edward Said's *Orientalism: Western Conceptions of the Orient* (Harmondsworth, UK: Penguin, 1978) uses European literature as a touchstone for European misrepresentation. Ziauddin Sardar pushes forward Said's debate with his idea of orientalization as a performance of power in *Orientalism* (Milton Keynes, UK: Open University Press, 1999). In theatre studies Rustom Bharucha adopts a similar postcolonial approach to the practices of representing otherness in *Theatre and the World: Performance and the Politics of Culture* (London/New York: Routledge, 1993) and *The Politics of Cultural Practice: Thinking through Theatre in an Age of Globalization* (London: Continuum, 2000). John M. Mackenzie in *Orientalism: History, Theory & the Arts* (Manchester: Manchester University Press, 1995), however, cautions against a postcolonial reading of colonial culture.

4. Samuel Hynes, *The Edwardian Turn of Mind* (Princeton: N.J.: Princeton University Press, 1968), p. 353.

5. Susan Stewart, *On Longing: Narratives of the Miniature, the Gigantic, the Souvenir, the Collection* (Durham, N.C./London: Duke University Press, 1993).

6. Paul Ricoeur, *Time and Narrative: Volume 1*, trans. Kathleen McLaughlin and David Pellauer (Chicago: University of Chicago Press, 1984), p. 31.

7. Jacky Bratton, *New Readings in Theatre History* (Cambridge: Cambridge University Press, 2003), p. 168.

8. Thomas Postlewait, "The London Stage, 1895–1918," in *The Cambridge History of British Theatre, Vol. 3: Since 1895*, ed. Baz Kershaw (Cambridge: Cambridge University Press, 2004), pp. 34–59 (quotation on p. 54).

9. Stewart, *On Longing*, p. 136.

10. Oscar Asche, *His Life, By Himself* (London: Hurst and Blackett, 1929), p. 172.

11. Licensing report on *Mecca*, licensed as *Ali Shar* by G. S. Street, Lord Chamberlain's Correspondence File, No. 3627, June 21, 1921 (first report written on April 30, 1921).

12. Second licensing report on *Mecca*, licensed as *Ali Shar* by G. S. Street, May 2, 1921.

13. Letter dated May 14, 1921.

14. Report on October 18, 1921, by G. S. Street, Lord Chamberlain's Correspondence File No. 3627.

15. Internal memorandum, September 19, 1921, Lord Chamberlain's Correspondence File No. 3627.

16. Trendell's report, October 20, 1921, Lord Chamberlain's Correspondence File No. 3627.

17. For Maugham, who served as a British spy in the Intelligence Department (mainly as a go-between for agents), the Oriental and imperial topics also found narrative form and voice in his spy stories (*Ashenden*), short stories (*The Trembling of a Leaf*), novels (*The Painted Veil*), and travel books (*On a Chinese Screen*). His short story "Rain," set in the South Pacific, became a very successful play and movie. On Maugham's travels and various "Oriental" activities, see Ted Morgan, *Maugham: A Biography* (New York: Simon and Schuster, 1980).

18. William Poel, *What Is Wrong with the Stage: Some Notes on the English Theatre from the Earliest Times to the Present Day* (London: George Allen and Unwin Ltd., 1920), p. 10.

19. St. John Ervine, *The Organised Theatre: A Plea in Civics* (London: George Allen and Unwin Ltd., 1924), p. 11.

20. Clive Barker and Maggie B. Gale, eds., *British Theatre between the Wars, 1918–1939* (Cambridge: Cambridge University Press, 2000), p. 25.

21. Ervine, *The Organised Theatre*, p. 54.

22. Ricoeur, *Time and Narrative: Volume 1*, p. 31.

23. Ibid., p. 54.

24. Ernest Short, *Theatrical Cavalcade* (London: Eyre and Spottiswoode, 1942), p. 137.

25. W. Macqueen-Pope, *Nights of Gladness* (London: Hutchinson and Co., 1956), p. 208.

26. Jim David and Victor Emeljanow, "'Wistful Rembrancer': The Historiographical Problem of Macqueen-Popery," *New Theatre Quarterly* 17, part 4 (NTQ 68) (November 2001): 299–309 (quotation on p. 300).

27. Stewart, *On Longing*, p. 23.

28. Esmé Wingfield-Stratford, *Before the Lamps Went Out* (London: Hodder and Stoughton, 1945), p. 222.

29. Stewart, *On Longing*, p. 24.

30. J. C. Trewin, *The Gay Twenties: A Decade of the Theatre* (London: Macdonald and Co., Ltd., 1958), p. 35.

31. Ibid., p. 50.

32. Raymond Mander and Joe Mitchenson, *Musical Comedy: A Story in Pictures* (London: Peter Davies, 1969), p. 28.

33. Ibid., p. 63.

34. Simon Trussler, ed., *The Cambridge Illustrated History of British Theatre* (Cambridge: Cambridge University Press, 1994), p. 277; Baz Kershaw, ed., *The Cambridge History of British Theatre*, vol. 3 (Cambridge: Cambridge University Press, 2004), p. 155. Earlier in the collection, Viv Gardner quotes from Asche's autobiography two of his complaints about the "erosion of the estate of 'proper' theatre itself" by the late 1920s (pp. 78–79).

35. Barker and Gale, *British Theatre between the Wars, 1918–1939*, pp. 12–13.

36. Russell Jackson, "Oscar Asche: An Edwardian in Transition," *New Theatre Quarterly* 12 (1996): 216–228.

37. Veronica Kelly, "Orientalism in Early Australian Theatre," *New Literatures Review* 26 (Winter 1993): 32–45.

38. Ricoeur, *Time and Narrative, Volume 1*, p. 229.

Reenacting Events to Narrate Theatre History

For centuries historians have been reenacting events in their minds to understand what happened in the past and why. When writing his history of the Peloponnesian War, Thucydides engaged in reenactment in order to explain and narrate the motives of the major Greek politicians and generals caught up in the struggle. Historians continue to rely on the method of imaginative reenactment, known more familiarly as empathy, often without acknowledging that they are doing so. These include theatre historians Joseph Roach, who climbed inside the minds of British actors performing in the shadow of Thomas Betterton, and William Mahar, who imagined American minstrel performers crafting satires of grand opera—both to explain the thoughts and intentions of the actors involved.[1] Like Thucydides, they understand that empathy can enhance and even guide their narrative choices and explanations. Since at least the fifth century BCE empathy and narrative have been closely intertwined in historical inquiry.

Several historiographers understand this connection and also endorse the reliability of empathy for charting possible narratives. In her *Historical Theory*, for example, Mary Fulbrook applauds empathy as "a neutral tool" that historians should use "to try to 'get inside' the mentalities of key protagonists in the historical situation."[2] She carefully distinguishes empathy—what Max Weber called "interpretative understanding"—from sympathy. "Feeling with" particular historical subjects and imagining their thoughts need not involve a sense of personal identification with their goals and beliefs. Rather, the method of imaginative reenactment is a good strategy "for understanding mentalities," says Fulbrook, "quite unrelated to that of the sympathy or otherwise of the historian with the motives and ideas of those whose views he or she is trying to understand."[3] She endorses empathy as one of her five "supra-paradigmatic guidelines or ground rules" that she believes should constrain the practices of all historians. When conceiving and writing their narratives, historians should recognize "the creativity of the human imagination [and] the importance of empathic understanding of other cultures, other viewpoints."[4] According to Fulbrook, narrative, imagination, and empathy should be a part of the same ethical orientation for all historians.

 Fulbrook's endorsement aside, how reliable is empathy? If solid evidence is lacking for historical assertions, should historians venture onto the seemingly thin ice of imagination to support their narratives? Or, if historians must engage in empathy to help them understand past mentalities in order to shape their narratives, what are the likely pitfalls of the process? Can historians really avoid sympathy in identifying with historical agents when they engage in reenactments? When applying empathy to understand the minds of others in history, is there a reliable method that will help to produce valid results? Finally, how might the deployment of empathy enable or constrain the kinds of narrative explanations possible? There are no easy answers to these questions.

Not surprisingly, historians continue to differ in important ways on the advisability of empathy and its possible links to historical narration. Fifty years ago a poll taken among practicing Anglo-American historians would likely have discovered rancorous divisions in their opinions about imaginative reenactment. In defense of an idealist historiographical philosophy indebted to Kant and Croce, R. G. Collingwood (1889–1943) had presented and defended empathy as a necessary strategy for writing good narrative history, a method that also enabled the historian to fulfill a higher calling as the creator of a kind of history that approached art. Collingwood was not against fact-based evidence, but he believed that a full picture of the past could never emerge and that historians could not narrate its changes over time without relying on imaginative reenactment. Positivists of all persuasions at mid-century, from Ranke conservatives to orthodox Marxists, denounced Collingwood's notion of empathy as an unnecessary and misleading incursion of subjective imagination into the objective processes of historical method and reliable narration. Other historians committed to versions of hermeneutical investigation, however, celebrated Collingwood's insight as an important strategy for historical interpretation and storytelling.[5]

Schools of historical thought have shifted radically since then, however, and it is unlikely that any historian today would fully endorse the idealism or positivism that motivated the historiographical fight over empathy from the 1940s through the 1960s. Nonetheless, tensions about the validity of imaginative reenactment and its impact on narrative continued for the rest of the century and remain today. Postcolonial concepts and identity politics often underlie recent concerns. To put it baldly, can a white, straight, Western male historian, for example, really adopt the point of view and imaginatively reenact the thoughts of a brown, previously colonized, lesbian female from the Third World? How, under what circumstances, and within which limitations? And what kinds of narratives would likely result? These and similar worries keep the problem of empathy alive for contemporary social scientists and historians.

Recent evidence and theories about empathy in cognitive science suggest that it is time to reexamine this historical strategy and its implications for narrative. In brief, with the discovery of a mirror neuron system in our brains, many scientists now understand empathy as a natural and ubiquitous process that humans regularly use to understand the emotions and intentions of others. Because our brains are equipped to mirror the actions of others, we process imaginative reenactments many times a day; it is not a specialized activity reserved for artists or idealist historians. Cognitive scientists recognize, however, that empathy, though commonplace, can be misleading; mirroring the actions of others directly or empathizing with historical figures in our minds does not always produce accurate insights about them. To puzzle through these and similar problems, several philosophers in the social sciences are taking a second look at R. G. Collingwood's assertions about reenactment as a method to craft a historical narrative.[6]

From my point of view, scholars interested in empathy and narrative might best begin with Collingwood's ideas. Not only was the eminent philosopher-historian the first to explain how his colleagues might deploy reenactment, but he also justified its use and tied it directly to his goals for historical narrative. After summarizing Collingwood's position on imaginative reenactment and its implications for narrative, I examine it in the context of Evan Thompson's contemporary synthesis of phenomenology and new scientific research into empathy—a position that develops an understanding of human consciousness and action very different from Collingwood's. Nonetheless, I demonstrate that much that Collingwood asserted about the validity of reenactment has been reinforced by cognitive science, though for different reasons than Collingwood alleged. From Thompson's contemporary perspective, however, Collingwood was both too individualistic and too rationalistic about how historians might deploy reenactment. Further, Thompson's position undercuts the tight integration of empathy and narrative that Collingwood advanced, leaving the historians who rely on reenactment with more choices about the kinds of stories they might tell.[7]

COLLINGWOOD IN CONTEXT

The secondary scholarship on Collingwood's ideas and influence is immense. A recent bibliography lists over two thousand books and essays on the historian, with perhaps half of those titles related in some way to Collingwood's notion of empathy, his most famous (and notorious) concept.[8] My overview for this essay has been guided primarily by the scholarship of William H. Dray, whose *History as Re-enactment: R. G. Collingwood's Idea of History* (1995) presents a modestly critical but generally sympathetic account of Collingwood's big idea.[9] Collingwood disciples Alan Donagan and Louis Mink also prove useful on specific aspects of the philosopher-historian's thought. As his title suggests, Dray focuses on Collingwood's *The Idea of History*, published posthumously in 1946, which contains his most cogent statements about reenactment. Unlike some other advocates of Collingwood's ideas, Dray does not deploy Collingwood to reinforce his own philosophy of history. Rather, he attempts to stay within Collingwood's thought, often citing other books and essays beyond *The Idea of History* to supplement or qualify his statements. Dray also proceeds methodically, laying out the elementary aspects of empathy (and answering most critics' objections to it) before moving to more complex matters involving epistemology and narrative construction.

Collingwood recognized that historians often faced situations in which clear evidence about the intentions of a historical agent whose actions were crucial to understanding a past event might be missing. For this common historiographical problem, Collingwood recommended that the historian reenact the probable thoughts of the agent, based on all of the biographical and contextual evidence that could be mustered. To do this, he said, the historian "makes a distinction between what may be called the outside and the inside of an event" (*IH*, 213). For Collingwood, "the outside" was the relevant context and physical behavior of those people in the event. By "inside," Collingwood meant the motivations and intentions of the major participants. The historian, he said, "is never concerned with either of these to the exclusion of the other. . . . His work may begin by discovering the outside of an event, but it can never end there; he must always remember that the event was an action, and that his main task is to think himself into this action, to discern the thought of the agent" (*IH*, 213). Collingwood gave Julius Caesar's crossing of the Rubicon as an example. It was not enough for the historian to know the outside of this event—that Caesar crossed a small river in northern Italy with an army of so many thousand men on a certain date during a period when the future of the Roman republic was uncertain. Until the historian successfully interpreted the event's inside—Caesar's apparent intention to defy republican law, in this instance—the historian's work was not finished.

How is the historian to understand the inner thoughts of significant historical figures? According to Collingwood, "There is only one way in which it can be done: by re-thinking them in his own mind" (*IH*, 215). To figure out Caesar's crossing of the Rubicon required the historian's "envisioning for himself the situation in which Caesar stood and thinking for himself what Caesar thought about the situation and the possible ways of dealing with it." Reenacting the past experience of another, said Collingwood, involved "no passive surrender to the spell of another mind; it is a labour of active and therefore critical thinking." To do it successfully, the philosopher-historian recommended bringing to bear all of his knowledge and "all the powers of his own mind" (*IH*, 215). In attempting to think the thoughts of a person from the past, said Collingwood, the historian had to work within the general beliefs and values of the past culture. Our present beliefs about infanticide, he noted, could be of no help in understanding what an ancient Greek or Roman might have thought and done when faced with the possibility of killing an infant. Collingwood was also aware that imaginative reenactment could involve the historian in some psychological detective work. Indeed, he asserted that the historian might come to a better interpretation of the motives and intentions of the historical agent than the agent's own self-understanding at the time. Consequently, the historian might discover intentions about a past action that "no one ever knew to have happened at all" (*IH*, 238).

While this method might work well enough to interpret and explain the actions of past individuals, what about social groups? Several critics of Collingwood have assumed that his notion of empathy is only applicable to individuals; E. H. Carr, for instance, upbraided Collingwood for restricting historical inquiry to "the thought of the individual actor."[10] While Dray acknowledges that the kinds of historical questions Collingwood tended to ask about military and political affairs drew him toward individual figures and their actions, he denies that Collingwood's approach is only relevant for investigating individual beliefs and motives. Dray points out that, in addition to his interest in "great men" in history, Collingwood also explored archaeological sites and wrote widely about social and economic life in Roman Britain, his primary area of scholarship. Nonetheless, Dray largely agrees with historian Alan Donagan that Collingwood may be accurately characterized as a "methodological individualist."[11] That is, Collingwood tended to reduce social relations to agglomerations of individual actions and reactions, rather than attempting to analyze the past through categories such as class or gender that depend upon the historian attributing relatively stable characteristics to a social-historical group.

Collingwood's methodological individualism, however, facilitated his strategy of imaginative reenactment. "If we are told that there was a strike at the factory or a run on the bank, we can reconstruct in our minds the purposes of the people whose collective action took those forms," he stated (*IH*, 310). Those "people" striking the factory may not have been a "working class" for Collingwood, but the philosopher-historian believed he could empathize with discrete individuals in that situation and reenact some of their thoughts to understand their actions. This applied to institutional history as well. Collingwood recognized that anonymous individuals, rather than dynamic leaders, could be more important in the workings of important institutions over time, such as governments and major businesses. For all of the minor players in history's actions, however, Collingwood believed that social forces, including beliefs, norms, and mass emotions, might shape their thoughts and actions but could not determine them.

Collingwood did not take the next step, though, of explaining historical events in fully social terms. Committed to the notion that past events had to be caused by humans with purposes, he was reluctant to attribute conscious action to social collectivities. From his idealist point of view, historiographical positivists and realists were wrong to reduce human events to a series of causes deriving fundamentally from environmental and social factors—the kinds of forces that often shaped collective response, he believed. Individual action, whether singly or together, caused historical change for Collingwood; individuals might be influenced by social conditions, but social groups defined by race, class, or gender and other factors could not take the place of individuals as actors on the stage of history if their beliefs and goals were predominately reactive instead of active.

Collingwood's investment in purposive individual action as the explanation for historical change has been criticized as overly rationalistic. The thoughts motivating Caesar's crossing of the Rubicon and an individual's getting money out of a bank that is about to fail clearly depend more upon rational calculation than upon emotional response. It is not too difficult for the historian to rethink these kinds of reasons and to come to some conclusions about the intentions behind them. Collingwood's critics point out, though, that much of history is messier than this. Emotions and beliefs often sway individuals and groups: even when people think they are behaving rationally, they may be proceeding in confused ways. Worse yet, people may have attempted one thing and actually accomplished something else. The historian who knows only what happened in the end and is trying to figure out initial intentions may attribute reasons for an action in the past that had little to do with those agents in that actual situation. Dray points out that emotions, confusions, and inadvertent results complicate Collingwood's argument that any human action in the past (whether individual or group) can be understood through reenactment.

Dray defends Collingwood's position on most of these matters but admits that the philosopher-historian "seems at times not quite to have made up his mind on the question of how far human rationality has to be assumed in claiming historical understanding."[12] Dray concedes that empathy may simply be unsuitable for handling the problem of inadvertent results: "Although there may always be something about an inadvertency which can be explained in the Collingwoodian way, what was done may have no Collingwoodian explanation [reenactment may be impossible] under the description which historians are most likely to apply to it."[13] As for confusing and illogical reasons as the basis of past actions, Dray points out that Collingwood never assumed complete rationality on the part of historical figures. "On his view, historical understanding is always to be sought from the agent's point of view, and entails only the subjective rationality of the agent," states Dray. He concludes that Collingwood insisted in *The Idea of History* on "the historian's envisioning the situation as the agent saw it."[14] Fair enough, but how can the historian be sure about the degree to which the historical agent may have departed from a relatively clear-eyed perception of the situation? Collingwood implicitly throws this problem back to the historian as a matter for interpretation but provides no clear guidelines.

Collingwood also exacerbates the problem of the agent's degree of rationality by refusing to consider unconscious emotions and appetites as a part of human actions. Although he recognized that people often acted within a context of strong feelings and deep-seated desires, Collingwood sought to exclude these aspects of behavior from the historian's mental work of reenactment unless the historical subject was able to bring these unconscious drives into consciousness. At various moments in *The Idea of History* Collingwood rules out "feeling, sensation, and emotion," "immediate experience," "animal nature," and the "blind forces" of human life as the proper arena for imaginative empathy (*IH*, 205, 216, 231, 306). From his point of view, people possessed different levels of consciousness and could use imagination, perception, and self-reflection to recognize their emotions, appetites, and desires. Even if one grants that people can gain conscious awareness of their unconscious desires, however, this does not mean that most agents in history actually achieved a sufficient level of self-knowledge to incorporate their appetites and emotions into their thoughts. Collingwood recognized that the historian, empathizing with the agent's thoughts in hindsight, was in a better position to integrate the subject's thoughts and feelings, but how was this to be done without relying on some general theory of psychology? Collingwood offered none, implicitly leaving it to historians to integrate past agents' beliefs and emotions as best they could.

Focused on the possibilities of reenactment and the importance of thinking, Collingwood also believed that those human appetites and emotions that did not make their way into the consciousness of an agent were too transient to matter for active thought. "We shall never know how the flowers smelt in the garden of Epicurus or how Nietzsche felt the wind in his hair as he walked on the mountains," Collingwood explained, "but the evidence of what these men thought is in our hands" (*IH*, 296). Dray's gloss on this passage probably comes close to Collingwood's meaning: "The reason that human experiences of the indicated kind are to be excluded, it seems, is that they are not re-thinkable. On Collingwood's view, when a past action is to be understood, the historian must literally think what the agent thought, since he must grasp and find valid the practical argument which his action expressed."[15] How Nietzsche experienced the wind in his hair was too fleeting to be memorable and, consequently, could not be rethought by the historian, according to Collingwood. Because thoughts lead to actions and actions lead to history, the historian must be able to reenact the thoughts of past agents to get at the essence of historical causation.

Collingwood's notion of purposive action as the springboard of causation led him to specific ideas about historical narrative. First, it limited what he regarded as the proper subject matter for narration. Because natural processes were not initiated by thinking human agents, Collingwood normally excluded matters such as human evolution and the formation of volcanoes from his idea of history. Although he certainly understood that nature had an impact on human life—that the Alps restricted the development of European trade, for example—Collingwood advised historians to include such natural facts only to the extent that human beings thought about them. From this perspective, the Alps could become a part of narrative history when European traders began to consider how to get over or around them. (Interestingly, Fernand Braudel and other historians in the Annales school of historiography reversed this interpretive priority; biology, climate, and geography were the key determinants of history for them.)

Collingwood's insistence on excluding most of nature from history has troubled some of his staunchest supporters, however. Alan Donagan, for example, did not accept Collingwood's refusal to "concede that historical explanations might incorporate some of the results of natural science."[16] Donagan noted that while many historical narratives could rest on their readers' elementary understanding of physics or geology, others could not. In the case of a history of farming that involves soil depletion through erosion and poor crop rotation, for example, the historian "must explain to his readers . . . certain advanced theories about the fertility of soils," he noted.[17] Without such a discussion, Donagan believed, a historian's narrative of the history of early farming may fail to convince readers of the links among matters such as poor harvests, recurrent famines, and political unrest in the countryside. To introduce into historical narrative the kind of science that Collingwood's historical agents could not have comprehended, however, works against his desire to build narrative explanations through reenactment. Knowing nothing about the chemistry of soil fertility, the early modern farmers in Donagan's example could not have considered such a factor and the historian, consequently, could not reenact the farmers' thinking about it. The Collingwoodian historian would run into the same problem when attempting to write a narrative about the history of astronomy.

Donagan's concern and the larger problem of incorporating nonhistoricized knowledge into historical narratives point up Collingwood's interest in separating scientific from historical understanding. For Collingwood, the major goal of writing history was to help people come to know the variety of the human mind: "All knowledge of mind is historical. . . . If I want to know whether I am as good a man as I hope or as bad as I fear, I must examine acts that I have done, and understand what they really were: or else go and do some fresh acts and then examine those. All these inquiries are historical. . . . The same historical method is the only one by which I can know the mind of another, or the corporate mind (whatever exactly that phrase means) of a community or an age" (*IH*, 219). Collingwood understood that this ambitious goal put him into direct competition with psychology and other sciences devoted to investigating human brains, emotions, and modes of consciousness. From his point of view, however, there were ontological differences between philosophy, within which he included the writing of history, and science. By the time he wrote *The Idea of History*, he had already spelled out these differences in his *Essay in Philosophical Method* (1933). Regarding the kinds of concepts that regulated the discourse of both fields, for instance, philosophical concepts, said Collingwood, allow for more flexibility than the formal definitions required by the sciences. For him, this meant that his brand of philosophical history was better able to gain insight into human minds than psychology ever could. Not surprisingly, the philosopher-historian rejected several of the premises of behaviorism and Freudianism, the two major fields in psychology that claimed scientific validity during the 1930s and 1940s.[18]

Collingwood's assumption about the primacy of history for revealing mental processes in all of their variety underlies his conception of the purpose of narrative and its necessary link to the method of imaginative reenactment. Given his aims, Collingwood rejected two modes of ordering events and advocated a third, which he believed to be the only possibility for a "convincing narrative" (*IH*, 278–279). He dismissed chronological "scissors and paste" history (a collection of past testimonies arranged in the order of their occurrence) and also discarded what the positivists termed "critical history" (a compilation of facts that had been checked and organized for historical accuracy) (*IH*, 202–204, 257–259). Collingwood appreciated the importance of validating reliable facts about the past but insisted that valid facts were not yet evidence. He complained that positivist historians who only did critical history confused the two. Because they believed that their chronicles somehow had to accommodate all of the facts that they had uncovered and validated, the positivists turned such facts into evidence and produced unwieldy books that lacked a coherent narrative.

Instead of beginning with "the facts," historians should begin with questions about past events involving human thought and allow their historical questions to prompt a search for the kinds of evidence that could reveal the relevant actions and, eventually, structure a narrative. This was Collingwood's third option, which he called "scientific history," a somewhat contradictory term, given the opposition he posed between positivistic science and philosophical history. Although Dray notes that the philosopher-historian was not consistent in his use of the terms "events" and "actions," Collingwood generally defined the first in terms of the second. "An action is the unity of the outside and inside of an event," he said at one point (*IH*, 213), which effectively reduced the significance of a whole event to human action. In addition, Collingwood's reliance on reenactment led him to collapse the interpretation of events into descriptions of them. When the historian "knows what happened," said Collingwood, "he already knows why it happened" (*IH*, 279). If all actual events contain thoughts and thoughts motivate actions, when the historian reenacts the thoughts of an agent, the description of that agent's actions necessarily also entails its interpretation. Collingwood's rigorous logic, derived from his philosophical idealism, gradually reduced all history to the history of people thinking.

Describing/interpreting related events should culminate in a narrative, Collingwood believed. Narrative was simply the historical way (as opposed to the scientific way) of knowing reality. Tentative answers about some early events in a probable sequence gradually open up questions about later events. "If this event occurred as it did, did some of the same thoughts motivate the next event related to it?" the Collingwoodian historian usually asks. For Collingwood, relations among events in a narrative had to be necessary as well as plausible. A historical narrative should involve "nothing that is not necessitated by the evidence," he insisted (*IH*, 241). Narratives, in other words, should unfold directly from the kinds of questions posed about human actions and the kinds of answers—the descriptions/interpretations—that the historian discovers through reenactment.

Louis Mink offers a convincing explanation of how Collingwood's notion of necessity underlies his idea of constructing a narrative, an explanation that also reveals Collingwood's epistemological expectations for history. Mink uses as an example the question of why Field Marshal Douglas Haig continued to send British troops to certain death during the battle of the Somme in World War I:

> What results from the historian's series of questions and answers is not a theoretical explanation but a *narrative*. . . . The narrative is not a story *supported* by evidence, but the statement of the evidence itself, organized in narrative form so that it jointly constitutes the unique answer to specific questions. That evidence might indifferently confirm several different *theories* (e.g., that Haig was mad, or sane) and could at best *confirm* (not prove) a theory even if the theory had no rivals. But the story is the uniquely necessary answer to the question about what Haig was doing because it *shows* him doing it. And in this respect it has a kind of incorrigibility or immunity to the threat of new evidence, which at best could serve to answer some other question or questions in conjunction with some or all of the evidence which answers this question.[19]

As Mink understood, Collingwood's idea of history as a mode of human understanding, as an epistemology, was both modest and ambitious. Unlike science, history could not "prove" anything, if proof is understood within the narrow boundaries allowed by positivism. Also unlike science, the narration of past events interpreted primarily through empathy could reveal a much wider and richer understanding of human thought and action than positivism could deliver. Further, by reenacting the thoughts of past figures, the historian could experience their actions vicariously and come to know past minds personally as well as professionally. Historical narratives might only be one version of a part of the past—Collingwood never claimed positivistic objectivity—but that was enough to gain insight into the human mind in action.

Few historians today share Collingwood's elevation of historical narrative over accepted science as a necessarily superior way of understanding human thought and action. While many deploy his strategy of imaginative empathy, few seek to limit the context of their historical explanations to the subjectivity of their historical agents. Nonetheless, Collingwood's method, if not his confidence that reenactment alone could primarily determine relevant context and narrative development, continues to be influential. In her award-winning *Molière: A Theatrical Life*, historian Virginia Scott relied extensively on the same kind of question-and-answer approach advocated by Collingwood and also deployed empathy to think through the motives and intentions of several historical agents who played significant roles in Molière's life.[20]

Scott used both to understand and narrate the *Tartuffe* controversy, Molière's attempts between 1664 and 1969 to overcome Catholic and court opposition to his comedy in order to gain the king's permission for public performances of the play (and the financial success that Molière believed the production would bring to his struggling troupe). In good Collingwoodian fashion, Scott begins her narration of the *Tartuffe* events with a question. The initial performance of Molière's incomplete script of *Tartuffe* in 1664, she states, "raises several questions, first among them being 'why'? Why would Molière perform an unfinished and potentially scandalous play on such an important occasion" (a celebration to honor the queen and queen mother of France?)[21] Answering this question leads Scott to several others, such as "why *Tartuffe* was the cause of such strife."[22] In working through the major events of the five-year conflict, Scott often puts herself into the minds of its major protagonists to understand their intentions. Why did Molière decide to introduce a new version of the comedy in August 1667? "[P]erhaps Molière believed that with *le tout Paris* out of town, the *dévots* [Catholic fundamentalists] would be less inclined to react. If that is what he hoped, he was wrong," she concludes.[23] In these and many other cases, Scott used her understanding of the context and her empathic skills to explore events for which solid documentary evidence was lacking and to build a plausible narrative about Molière's life. She did not pursue the thoughts of Molière and others, however, primarily to narrate modes of historical agents' thinking and acting. Empathy was less central for Scott's narrative than Collingwood would have wished.

In other ways, too, Scott departed from Collingwood's aims and methods. Although *Molière: A Theatrical Life* rejects positivism just as firmly as Collingwood did, she does not assume that Molière's purposive thoughts primarily shaped his actions and must consequently shape a narrative of his life. Scott shows the reader an emotional, ailing, vengeful, conniving, and occasionally rational Molière in the midst of the *Tartuffe* conflict. Instead of producing confident explanations of Molière's thoughts during the twists and turns of the struggle, as Collingwood might have done, Scott hedges nearly all of her forays into interpretation through reenactment with phrases such as "may have," "perhaps," and "probably." Where Collingwood predicted that a complete narrative should emerge nearly effortlessly from the descriptions/interpretations arising from his empathic method, Scott can track very few abiding traits of Molière's thought and action that might have provided her with narrative coherence, although the messiness of the conflict certainly lends her story credibility. Finally, Collingwood would likely have complained that Scott designed her narrative about *Tartuffe* to prove a thesis only partly related to the thoughts and actions of the major players. In brief, Scott states at the top of her story that Molière and the king were involved in a tug of war over what his troupe owed to the crown and that, appearances to the contrary, Louis XIV won more than the actor did in the battle over producing *Tartuffe*. While Collingwood understood that historians could use empathy as one means of demonstrating almost any historical thesis having to do with human intentions, this was not his preferred deployment of reenactment. Better to let empathetic interpretations drive the narrative and explore varieties of mind in action, according to the philosopher-historian, than to narrow the focus to a thesis that must draw on many kinds of methods and evidence. In short, Scott demonstrates the value of Collingwood's approach but uses it more tentatively and selectively, often to speculate about emotional matters that Collingwood would have avoided.

COLLINGWOOD AND COGNITIVE SCIENCE

Scott's decision to empathize as much with Molière's passions and appetites as with his conscious thoughts in the *Tartuffe* controversy led her to craft a narrative that moved beyond the Collingwoodian unfolding of a mind (or several minds) in action. Put another way, Scott refused to separate Molière's mental reasoning from his bodily responses, a Cartesian dichotomy upon which Collingwood built his idea of history.

Like many of his generation, Collingwood assumed that practical reasoning could be separated from human emotions. While he did not take this Cartesian dualism as far as some idealists do, Collingwood did presume that the conscious minds of historical agents could master their material bodies to create the driving forces of history. Historians, in turn, could master the emotions of their subjects to understand and narrate these same forces in the past. In his example about Nietzsche, for instance, Collingwood divided the philosopher's body from his mind, trivialized Nietzsche's experience of physicality, and then elevated his thought so that he could reconstruct the man's rational thinking. But why did Collingwood believe that historians could not empathize with the feelings that Nietzsche (or anybody else) may have experienced when he walked on a windy mountain side? Scott's success in *Molière: A Theatrical Life* implicitly demonstrates that historians can reenact the emotions as well as the thoughts of past agents in history. If Nietzsche told us that tramping through the mountains inspired him to think certain thoughts, this experience might be relevant to his intellectual biography, even to European thought in general at the turn of the last century. In other parts of her biography, Scott shows that Molière's passions had a significant effect on his thinking, especially in shaping the form and content of his plays. Further, what if Nietzsche's bodily experiences actually provided the foundation for all of his thought, as some cognitive scientists are now claiming about the general relation between embodiment and mental concepts? Scott does not explore this possibility in her work on Molière, but neither does her approach rule it out.

Collingwood's Nietzsche example also underlines the importance for him of individual rather than social thought and action. Although Dray explains that the historian did not entirely exclude social dynamics from consideration for imaginative reenactment, it is clear that Collingwood would have vetoed audience response in the theatre as a proper focus for historical inquiry and empathy. He would have viewed spectating as largely emotional and reactive, a feeble second cousin to thinking and action. If spectating is considered to be irrelevant to the real stuff of theatre history, however, its exclusion from narrative accounts will necessarily short-circuit the reality of theatrical communication. Actors and playwrights continually adjust their performances and, eventually, their new plays to the thoughts and emotions of their actual and anticipated audiences. Understanding Molière's life in the theatre, for example, must take his spectators into account, as Scott's narrative demonstrates throughout.

The related needs for theatre historians to understand both audience dynamics and the emotions of past theatre artists, plus new scientific insights into empathy, demand that the problem of reenactment be reexamined. Empathy means different things to different scientists and philosophers in cognitive studies. In the following discussion, I work within a general definition of empathy offered by those who point to empirical data and intermediate theories that support an embodied notion of cognition.[24] Specifically, I rely primarily on the ideas of Evan Thompson, whose *Mind in Life* (2007) posits empathy as a foundational element of identity and culture.[25] From Thompson's embodied perspective, it is clear that Collingwood's general notion of empathy, while narrowly correct, was too limiting. This new definition of empathy allows the historian to broaden Collingwood's method and to apply it to the emotional lives of artists and spectators in the past.

Nearly all scientists now agree that a human being is able to "read the mind" of another person by imaginatively putting himself or herself in the place of the other and seeing the world from that unique point of view. Most call this activity simulation or empathy, and many scientists use the terms synonymously. Citing several empirical studies, Thompson usefully distinguishes among three different levels of empathy, the first two of which are important for historical study. The first level, which is based on the recent discovery of the mirror neuron system in our minds, Thompson calls "sensorimotor coupling."[26] In brief, groups of neurons in the brain are equipped to "mirror" intentional motor activity produced by other humans. When one person watches another grasp a coffee cup, for instance, the same group of neurons is activated in the observer as if the observer had grabbed the cup. In this way, by mirroring the muscles of another, we can begin to know "intuitively" what that other person is experiencing. Although humans only simulate others' intentional actions, intentionality is much broader than Collingwood's understanding of conscious thought. People can grasp a cup of coffee for many reasons, including emotions and confusions that have little to do with conscious choice.

Through sensorimotor activation, simulation links our brains to the emotions and intentions of others. As Vittorio Gallese, one of the first to investigate mirror neuron systems in monkeys, notes, "When we observe actions performed by other individuals, our motor system 'resonates' along with that of the observed agent."[27] The classic example is two crying babies in the same room; when one starts to wail, the other one will too, in empathy with the first. In a good theatrical production, spectators "resonate" with actors for much of the performance; their stage movements alone prompt the activation of our mirror systems, putting us "in tune" with their basic emotions and intentions. For this reason, Gallese and his co-workers have identified the mirror system as "the basis of social cognition."[28] This makes sensorimotor coupling, the lowest level of empathy, the physiological basis for the other levels noted by Thompson.

"The second type of empathy is the imaginary transposition of oneself to the other's place," states Thompson.[29] This is much the same as the commonsense notion of empathy as "putting yourself in another person's shoes." On the basis of sensorimotor coupling, humans can recall what it is like to experience the thoughts of others and, through memory and imagination, can attempt to see the world through another's eyes, even when that other person is not present. Thompson emphasizes that this form of empathy can range from simple emotional agitation to a rich understanding of another's situation. Imaginary transposition, which develops in children at about nine to twelve months of age, requires more active cognition than sensorimotor coupling. Thompson draws on the scientific work of Michael Tomasello to explain how infants learn to gaze with a parent at an event in which neither is directly participating. Tomasello, says Thompson, "proposes that the infant uses her primal understanding of others as 'like me' and her newly emerging understanding of her own intentional agency, on the basis of which to judge analogically and categorically that others are intentional agents 'like me' as well."[30] The infant can put herself into the picture of an event outside of herself, a practice she soon learns to do in her mind when there is no actual event directly in front of her.

On the basis of Thompson's discussion of empathy, it is clear that Collingwood's assertion that a historian can undertake imaginative reenactment is scientifically sound. Thompson's second level of empathy, imaginative transposition, allows the historian (or anybody else) to construct a figure from the past in her or his "mind's eye," place that person in a historical situation, and attribute thoughts to that imaginary subject on the basis of a problem the person might have been trying to solve. From a cognitive perspective, people focus on the goal-directed behavior of an other when they empathize, which easily includes Collingwood's interest in the conscious thoughts of the imagined figure. Finally, Collingwood was right to claim that he could imaginatively reenact a past person's thoughts and remain neutral in his feelings about that figure. Without sliding into compassion for or antipathy against Julius Caesar, the historian could dispassionately think about what he believed to have been Caesar's options in northern Italy and imagine why he decided to cross the Rubicon. As far as the fundamental cognitive operation of empathy is concerned, Collingwood claimed no more for historians than what a five-year-old child can accomplish through imaginative transposition.

Thompson's perspective, however, opens up a much wider range for empathy than Collingwood imagined and practiced. As we have seen, Collingwood distinguished between the inside and the outside of an event and claimed that the inside—the conscious thoughts that motivated actions—produced real history. Thompson, however, along with others who embrace an embodied notion of human thought and action, denies that humans actually make this apparently straightforward distinction between an "inside" and an "outside" when they engage in events. Specifically, Thompson posits an approach that he, with others, has called "embodied dynamicism." In his summary of this position, Thompson distinguishes it from two earlier conceptions of cognition, both of which have ties to Collingwood's Cartesian idealism:

> Cognitivism and connectivism left untouched the relation between cognitive processes and the real world. As a result, their models of cognition were disembodied and abstract. . . . [E]mbodied dynamicism focuses on self-organizing dynamic systems rather than physical symbol systems . . . [and] maintains in addition that cognitive processes emerge from the non-linear and circular causality of continuous sensorimotor interactions involving the brain, body, and environment. The central metaphor for this approach is the mind as embodied dynamic system in the world, rather than the mind as neural network in the head.[31]

This quotation makes it clear (if it was not evident before) that "science" for Thompson entails procedures and possibilities very different from the positivism and behaviorism in 1940s "science" that Collingwood found so objectionable.

Aside from this massive difference, Thompson's embodied dynamicism is distinct from Collingwood's idealist historicism on several other significant grounds. If brain, body, and environment are in continuous interaction, as Thompson relates, there can be no foundational distinction between what the mind does on the "inside" of an event and what is happening to bodies within a physical and social environment on the "outside." Nor is it always necessary to divide thoughts from emotions and actions from reactions—two dichotomies that play central roles in Collingwood's thinking. Conscious thoughts are always mixed in with beliefs, responses, feelings, and desires in the ongoing interplay among brain, body, and environment that constitutes human experience. For Thompson, empathy is an important cognitive operation that distinguishes intentional actions from general motion in the environment and keeps humans attuned to other bodies that also have dynamic systems. Thompson's orientation to embodiment and context counters Collingwood's interest in marginalizing emotions and confusions from the historian's practice of empathy as a method of generating narrative.

While Thompson's merging of phenomenology and cognitive science opens new possibilities for historical narrative, it does little to guide historians in the practical matters of research and writing. Collingwood moved easily between vaulting ideas and mundane practices; any approach that hopes to replace his understanding of empathy and narrative must also provide a path for practice. In this regard, Thompson's orientation to experiential knowledge is generally consonant with what has been called "simulation theory" (ST), an approach to cognition and epistemology that carries with it several ideas for practical application. In brief, those who argue for simulation theory believe that Thompson's imaginative transposition provides the basis for most social knowledge. By mentally simulating the intentional actions of others, people come to know others' emotions and intentions and, on that foundation, gradually build their understanding of human experience.[32]

In their essay "Simulation and Epistemic Competence," David Henderson and Terence Horgan point out that ST has two significant "blind spots."[33] When attempting to determine the emotions and intentions of others through empathy, inadequate information in setting up the simulation and cognitive inflexibility in running it can limit and distort what is learned. For the first, simulators do not always know or do not take into account differences between themselves and the other person whose situation they are simulating. Historians, for example, may not factor in sufficient knowledge about the cultural context of the agent whose subjectivity they are attempting to understand. Second, the simulator may lack the imagination to enter fully into the situation of the other. Even historians with good sensitivity to cultural context may have difficulty imagining the subjectivity of an agent who is undergoing extreme grief or in great physical pain. (In this regard, Scott's narrative demonstrates a keen sensitivity to Molière's recurrent illness during the *Tartuffe* controversy.) These blind spots lead Henderson and Horgan to suggest that social scientists and historians who rely primarily on empathy should supplement it with other sources of knowledge, including empirically validated facts and general theories about human behavior.

How these other sources of knowledge might be coordinated with imaginative reenactment is suggested by philosopher Georg Vielmetter. In his essay "The Theory of Holistic Simulation: Beyond Interpretivism and Postempiricism," Vielmetter emphasizes that interpretation gained through simulation "is basically a *natural process* controlled by our hard wiring."[34] Evidence based on empathy, however, is "a necessary, though not sufficient, condition of understanding others,"[35] according to Vielmetter's program for holistic simulation. Like Henderson and Horgan, Vielmetter emphasizes the importance as well of "empirical and theoretical evidence,"[36] in order both to immerse the empathizer in the given circumstances of selected subjects and to connect the subjects to relevant events and causes in the cultural-historical world. Theories, documents, illustrations, and a range of other evidence can help social scientists and historians to ensure that one of the blind spots of simulation identified by Henderson and Horgan does not occlude their scholarly vision.

Although Vielmetter has little directly to say about moving from empathy to constructing historical narratives, some conclusions follow from his advice. As Collingwood would suggest, historians should begin with questions and then set up imaginative simulations to pursue their answers. From Vielmetter's perspective, however, historians may need to return several times to the same historical players on the same contextual stage, adding more relevant evidence each time to their reenactments, before they arrive at an adequate explanation of their intentions and emotions. This process of progressively enhanced simulations to weigh interpretive possibilities and gradually build conclusions will lead the historian to understand the subjective realities embedded in discrete events from the past. Vielmetter implies that such events will provide the building blocks of narrative for the historian, but he does not mandate a specific aim for narrative construction. Unlike Collingwood, Thompson and Vielmetter focus concretely on the science of empathy and its epistemological possibilities but draw no firm or necessary connections between this methodology and constructing historical narration.[37]

To flesh out the transition from empathetic method to narrative construction within the general orientation provided by Thompson and Vielmetter, it may be helpful to examine a narrative history that appears to be based on these premises and succeeds in its several tasks. As previously noted, when it came to empathy and narrative, Collingwood had difficulty including unconscious emotions and collective responses. It should be instructive, then, to examine a history that focuses on emotional spectators as the subjects of a historian's empathy and whose experience as a group becomes, in the historian's hands, a primary explanation for historical change. In *Tragedy Walks the Streets: The French Revolution in the Making of Modern Drama* (2006), historian Matthew Buckley empathizes with theatregoing Parisians who experienced the Revolution. He crafts a narrative that explains the gradual demise by the early 1800s of the major genres that dominated French theatre before 1789.[38] Because Buckley's admirable narrative does not reveal the writerly strategies that made possible its creation, however, I must play historiographical detective to sleuth out the methods and moves that led him from empathy to narrative.

Part of Buckley's storytelling traces the decline in popularity of neoclassic tragedy after the Revolution, which Buckley traces to Maximilien Robespierre's botched attempt at suicide following the period of the Terror (1793–1794). In brief, Buckley claims that many Parisians looked to Robespierre as a new Brutus or Cato at the start of the Terror; they cast him in the role of a neoclassic tragic hero. The failure of the Terror to cleanse the Revolution of villainy and Robespierre's untragic fall, however, undercut the believability of the neoclassic pattern of history and consequently of neoclassic dramatic tragedy for spectators in the theatre. To support his claim, Buckley discusses what literate Parisians usually expected from and experienced in performances of neoclassic tragedies before 1789. He demonstrates that neoclassic dramatic forms and the culture's construction of historical events often mirrored and reinforced each other before the Revolution. Buckley also notes the gradual decline in performances of neoclassic tragedies and the general refusal of emerging dramatists to write new ones in the wake of the Terror. In short, he presents a great deal of contextual evidence about plays, audiences, and theatrical and historical events.[39]

Although Buckley says nothing about his method, I can only assume that he used much of this evidence to set up what Collingwood would consider a reenactment and Vielmetter would regard as an imagined simulation. In his mind, Buckley placed a mid-1790s audience which expected to be moved by neoclassic situations and characters into a Parisian theatre of the period, opened a mental drop curtain on good actors performing a regular neoclassic tragedy with conventional line readings and stage business, and watched for actor-audience interaction in his imagination. Perhaps he ran this simulation several times, adding more details and subtracting others to get as close in his "mind's eye" to the probable historical situation as possible. What happened between the figures in the house and those on the stage in his simulation? Buckley's thesis suggests the results: spectators recently traumatized by the Terror and disappointed by Robespierre's foolish actions responded politely and the actors, sensing their tepid applause, gave them a professional but by no means inspired performance. If Buckley is a regular theatregoer, he probably used some of his own sense of possible audience-actor relationships to calibrate the likely interaction more precisely. (Although the social-theatrical dynamics of this relationship have changed immensely since the 1790s, the historian with theatrical experience can expect to understand and perceive some cognitive and emotional commonalities across the centuries.) Knowing the actual decline in the number of performances of neoclassic tragedy during the 1790s, Buckley may also have run a simulation among spectators and actors set two or three years after the first one. This probably led him to conclude that Parisian spectators who might have chosen to spend their theatregoing time and money on a neoclassic tragedy decided to attend other theatrical fare and that the actor-managers, aware of shrinking houses, gradually moved those plays out of their repertoire.

Some theatre historians, even those with no particular attachment to positivist rules of evidence, may object that Buckley's simulation of audiences and performers in productions of neoclassic tragedy was probably unnecessary. Indeed, Buckley might not have attempted this exercise in educated empathy if he had discovered conclusive documentation that linked altered audience tastes and desires directly to the traumas of the Terror. Had he discovered evidence that would directly have confirmed his thesis, however, we can assume that he would have used it. But Buckley cites no such evidence. The historian knew what had happened (the steep decline in the popularity of this theatrical genre) but not why. Buckley also knew about the emergence of other dramatic genres in the wake of the Revolution and presumably had already come to agree with those historians who attributed the rise of melodrama to spectators' experience of the Revolution, especially the Terror. This probably led him to ask a Collingwoodian kind of question: how did Parisian spectators experience performances of neoclassic tragedy after the fall of Robespierre? In pursuit of the answer, he collected all the relevant evidence that he could find and proceeded to run several simulations, as Vielmetter would have suggested.

Already, though, my own imagined simulation of Buckley's historiographical dilemma, his question, and his decision to employ empathy has moved far beyond Collingwood's strictures and goals. The historical agent in this reenactment was a group, audience members, and Buckley imagined them acting and reacting more or less together, as theatre audiences generally do. In this simulated scenario, the actors became minor players; because they must attempt to please their public but are fated to perform a genre declining in popularity, the spectators had more genuine agency over time than did the performers. Unconscious emotions and desires, along with the conscious expectation that neoclassic tragedy would thrill them as it had before, probably were motivating audience agency. As a historian who attempted to empathize with his imagined, anonymous figures, Buckley would have looked at their whole experience.[40] If we follow Thompson in characterizing their general mode of cognition as "embodied dynamicism," the Parisian spectators were intending agents, extending their minds into the auditorium, aware of and interacting with social others and their theatrical environment. On this basis, the historian may have concluded that audiences found that neoclassic tragedy no longer matched their knowledge of the past and their expectations for the future. In the simulation, some spectators were likely irritated, others merely bored. Given their generally negative response, they no longer patronized the genre.

Buckley relied on deep contextual awareness and his knowledge of the declining numbers of performances of neoclassic tragedies to make his move from simulation to narrative. *Tragedy Walks the Streets* partly charts the decline of the genre from its modest success before 1789 to its upswing in popularity after 1791 when theatrical monopolies were abolished, its crisis of credibility right after the Terror, its slow fade during the last half of the 1790s, and its replacement (more or less) by melodrama after 1800. While simulating audience engagement with a performance soon after Robespierre's fall helped Buckley to understand the turning point of his narrative, that simulation (or series of simulations, *à la* Vielmetter) did not determine the overall narrative itself. Like Scott, Buckley deployed reenactment strategically to understand significant events but did not use it to shape his general narrative. Buckley's book is not a Collingwoodian story about human thought in action. Rather, the narrative as a whole charts what Collingwood would have dismissed as a reaction—the response, first of spectators then of dramatists, to the realities and experiences of the French Revolution, an interaction that does not eventuate in good drama, from Buckley's point of view, until Georg Büchner's *Danton's Death*.

I do not know if Buckley actually undertook the series of simulations that I have imagined above to enable him to write the sections of *Tragedy Walks the Streets* that support his thesis about the Revolution and neoclassic tragedy. But in another sense it does not matter. Thompson's insights into empathy, supported by a wealth of new research in cognitive science plus advances in philosophical theories of mind, can support and justify this kind of an investigation (whether Buckley embarked on it or not). Collingwood set historical research on a path that tightly integrated his empathetic method with his construction of an idealist narrative. Although new insights into empathy and new demands for different kinds of narratives have pulled apart this Collingwoodian synthesis, it is clear that reenactment as a method and the requirements of narrative construction will continue to inform each other. Collingwood's historiographical legacy lives, now ironically legitimated by science.

NOTES

1. See Joseph Roach, *Cities of the Dead: Circum-Atlantic Performance* (New York: Columbia University Press, 1996), pp. 16–17, 73–118; and William Mahar, *Behind the Burnt Cork Mask: Early Blackface Minstrelsy and Antebellum American Popular Culture* (Urbana and Chicago: University of Illinois Press, 1999), pp. 101–156.

2. Mary Fulbrook, *Historical Theory* (London and New York: Routledge, 2002), p. 167.

3. Ibid.

4. Ibid., pp. 187–188.

5. See R. G. Collingwood, *The Idea of History* (1946), revised ed. (Oxford: Oxford University Press, 1993) (abbreviated as *IH* in subsequent citations in the text). Collingwood's advocates include Alan Donagan, *The Later Philosophy of R. G. Collingwood* (Oxford: Oxford University Press, 1962); Rex Martin, *Historical Explanation: Re-enactment and Practical Inference* (Ithaca, N.Y.: Cornell University Press, 1977); Louis O. Mink, *Mind, History, and Dialectic: The Philosophy of R. G. Collingwood* (Bloomington: Indiana University Press, 1969); Heikki Saari, *Re-enactment: A Study in R. G. Collingwood's Philosophy of History* (Abo, Finland: Abo Akademi, 1984); and W. J. van der Dussen, *History as a Science: The Philosophy of R. G. Collingwood* (The Hague: Nijhoff, 1981). Mostly opposing Collingwood's position are E. H. Carr, *What Is History* (New York: Knopf, 1962); G. R. Elton, *The Practice of History* (New York: Crowell, 1967); Patrick Gardiner, *The Nature of Historical Explanation* (Oxford: Oxford University Press, 1952); and A. R. Louch, *Explanation and Human Action* (Oxford: Oxford University Press, 1966).

6. See, for example, several of the essays in *Empathy and Agency: The Problem of Understanding in the Human Sciences*, ed. Hans Herbert Kogler and Karsten R. Stueber (Boulder, Colo.: Westview Press, 2000). While Simon Blackburn's essay in this anthology, "Re-enactment as Critique of Logical Analysis: Wittgensteinian Themes in Collingwood" (pp. 270–287), directly addresses Collingwood's ideas, several others include a mention of them. See also Karsten R. Stueber, *Rediscovering Empathy: Agency, Folk Psychology, and the Human Sciences* (Cambridge, Mass.: MIT Press, 2006). In their "Introduction" to *Empathy and Agency*, Kogler and Stueber point out that the new insights about empathy prompt a reexamination of the ongoing debate among historians and social scientists concerning

Verstehen (understanding) and *Erklaren* (explanation), two epistemological positions that date from the turn of the last century (pp. 7–46). Although my essay necessarily touches on aspects of this debate, I focus more narrowly on the problematics of reenactment as a reliable strategy for historical investigation and its relations to narrative construction.

7. I have addressed some of these problems in a previous essay, "Cognitive Studies and Epistemic Competence in Cultural History: Moving Beyond Freud and Lacan," in *Performance and Cognition: Theatre Studies and the Cognitive Turn*, ed. Bruce McConachie and F. Elizabeth Hart (London/New York: Routledge, 2006), pp. 52–75. I also recommend empathy for historical use in my *Engaging Audiences: A Cognitive Approach to Spectating in the Theatre* (New York: Palgrave, 2008), pp. 65–123, 223–225.

8. See http://www.questia.com/library/history/historians/r-g-collingwood.jsp (accessed June 24, 2008). This bibliography lists 2,134 books and 221 journal articles on Collingwood.

9. William H. Dray, *History as Re-enactment: R. G. Collingwood's Idea of History* (Oxford: Clarendon Press, 1995). Also helpful is Peter Johnson, *R. G. Collingwood: An Introduction* (Bristol: Thoemmes Press, 1998).

10. Carr, *What Is History*, p. 46.

11. Donagan, *The Later Philosophy of R. G. Collingwood*, p. 206. See Dray, *History as Re-enactment*, pp. 1–90.

12. Dray, *History as Re-enactment*, p. 115.

13. Ibid., p. 120.

14. Ibid., p. 116.

15. Ibid., p. 124.

16. Donagan, *The Later Philosophy of R. G. Collingwood*, p. 203.

17. Ibid.

18. Collingwood (correctly) understood behaviorism as a type of positivism, which he also disdained. His relation to Freudian thought was a little more complicated, however. Collingwood tried to incorporate the Freudian unconscious into this idea about reflective thought and action but, in Mink's view, could not get past "the root notion of psychoanalytic theory that there are unconsciously purposive acts in which there is no reflective thought" (Louis Mink, *Historical Understanding*, ed. Brian Fay, Eugene O. Golob, and Richard T. Vann [Ithaca: Cornell University Press, 1987], p. 262).

19. Ibid., pp. 283–284 (emphases in original).

20. Virginia Scott, *Molière: A Theatrical Life* (Cambridge: Cambridge University Press, 2000).

21. Ibid., p. 161.

22. Ibid., p. 162.

23. Ibid., p. 176.

24. A number of scientists and philosophers are committed to embodiment as a foundational principle in cognition and emotion, including Antonio Damasio, *The Feeling of What Happens: Body and Emotion in the Making of Consciousness* (New York: Harcourt, 1999); Merlin Donald, *A Mind So Rare: The Evolution of Human Consciousness* (New York: W. W. Norton, 2001); Gilles Fauconnier and Mark Turner, *The Way We Think: Conceptual*

Blending and the Mind's Hidden Complexities (New York: Basic Books, 2002); Raymond W. Gibbs, Jr., *Embodiment and Cognitive Science* (New York: Cambridge University Press, 2006); Mark Johnson, *The Meaning of the Body: The Bodily Basis of Meaning, Imagination, and Reason* (Chicago: University of Chicago Press, 1987); and George Lakoff and Mark Johnson, *Philosophy in the Flesh: The Embodied Mind and Its Challenge to Western Thought* (New York: Basic Books, 1999). The scientists and philosophers cited in the following pages also agree with the basics of embodiment as understood by these thinkers.

25. Evan Thompson, *Mind in Life: Biology, Phenomenology, and the Sciences of Mind* (Cambridge, Mass.: Belknap Press, 2007).

26. Ibid., pp. 393–395.

27. Vittorio Gallese, "The 'Shared Manifold' Hypothesis: From Mirror Neurons to Empathy," in *Between Ourselves: Second Person Issues in the Study of Consciousness*, ed. Evan Thompson (Thorverton, UK: Imprint Academic, 2001), p. 38.

28. Vittorio Gallese, Christian Keysers, and Giacomo Rizzolatti, "A Unifying View of the Basis of Social Cognition," *Trends in Cognitive Sciences* 20 (2004; rpt. http://www.sciencedirect.com): 1–8. Interestingly for theatre studies, the authors speak of empathy as an "as if" performance: "Side by side with the sensory description of the observed social stimuli, internal representations of the state associated with these actions or emotions are evoked in the observers, 'as if' they were performing a similar action or experiencing a similar emotion" (p. 5). Jean Decety and Philip L. Jackson also link research on empathy to Gallese's work on mirror neurons. See their "A Social-Neuroscience Perspective on Empathy," *Current Directions in Psychological Science* 15.2 (2006): 54–58.

29. Thompson, *Mind in Life*, p. 395.

30. Ibid., p. 397. See also Michael Tomasello, *The Cultural Origins of Human Cognition* (Cambridge, Mass.: Harvard University Press, 1999).

31. Ibid., pp. 10–11. Thompson notes that his 1991 book with E. J. Varela and E. Rosch, *The Embodied Mind: Cognitive Science and Human Experience* (Cambridge, Mass.: MIT Press), began this work and that his present 2007 book continues it.

32. Most commentators recognize three major positions within simulation theory, corresponding to the ideas of Alvin Goldman, Robert M. Gordon, and Jane Heal. For representative examples of their work, see Goldman, "In Defense of Simulation Theory," in *Folk Psychology*, ed Martin Davies and Tony Stone (Oxford: Blackwell, 1995), pp. 191–206; Gordon, "Simulation without Introspection from Me to You," in *Mental Simulation*, ed. Martin Davies and Tony Stone (Oxford: Blackwell, 1995), pp. 53–67; and Heal, "Simulation, Theory, and Content," in *Theories of Theories of Mind*, ed. Peter Carruthers and Peter Smith (Cambridge: Cambridge University Press, 1996), pp. 75–89.

33. David Henderson and Terence Horgan, "Simulation and Epistemic Competence," in *Empathy and Agency*, p. 130.

34. Georg Vielmetter, "The Theory of Holistic Simulation: Beyond Interpretivism and Postempiricism," in *Empathy and Agency*, ed. Kogler and Stueber, p. 92 (emphasis in original).

35. Ibid., p. 90. Similarly, Stueber, in *Rediscovering Empathy*, states that "we have to agree with critics of empathy in their insistence that empathy cannot be regarded as

the only method for interpreting other agents. . . . [W]e have to supplement the stategy of pure empathy with theoretical information within or outside of the folk-theoretical framework. I want to stress, however, that admitting limitations of the strategy of pure empathy does not at all diminish the central epistemic importance of empathy for our ability to understand other agents" (p. 216).

36. Ibid., p. 92.

37. Vielmetter holds that his method of "empathetic observation" avoids the pitfalls of the participant observation model used by many sociologists and anthropologists and also moves social scientific explanation "beyond postempiricism and interpretivism" ("The Theory of Holistic Simulation," p. 83).

38. Matthew S. Buckley, *Tragedy Walks the Streets: The French Revolution in the Making of Modern Drama* (Baltimore: Johns Hopkins University Press, 2006).

39. Ibid., pp. 34–68.

40. For commentary about consciousness and culture and how they relate to the experience of historical audiences, see my *Engaging Audiences*, pp. 23–42, 121–144.

Notes on Contributors

Christopher B. Balme holds the chair in theatre studies at the University of Munich. His most recent publications are *Decolonizing the Stage: Theatrical Syncretism and Post-colonial Drama*, *Einführung in die Theaterwissenschaft*, *Pacific Performances: Theatricality and Cross-Cultural Encounter in the South Seas*, and *The Cambridge Introduction to Theatre Studies*.

Susan Bennett is University Professor in the Department of English at the University of Calgary in Canada. She has published on a wide range of topics in theatre and performance studies, including *Theatre Audiences: A Theory of Production and Reception* and *Performing Nostalgia: Shifting Shakespeare and the Contemporary Past*. Her current work is focused on British women playwrights in the 1950s. She is also participating in a project on manuscript drama in the 1640s as part of a funded project by the Social Science and Humanities Research Council of Canada.

Charlotte M. Canning, Professor of Theatre, teaches in both the Department of Theatre and Dance and the Gender and Women's Studies program at University of Texas at Austin and heads the Performance as Public Practice program for M.A., M.F.A., and Ph.D. students. She is author of *Feminist Theatres in the USA: Staging Women's Experiences* and *The Most American Thing in America: Circuit Chautauqua as Performance*, which won the Barnard Hewitt Award for Theatre Excellence. She frequently serves as exhibit curator at the Harry Ransom Humanities Research Center, where she organized *Rehearsing the American Dream: Arthur Miller's Theatre*, an exhibit of Miller's papers. She served as President of the American Society for Theatre Research (2003–2006), and became Associate Editor of *Theatre Research International* in 2009. Her current book project is on United States theatre and internationalism.

Marvin Carlson, the Sidney E. Cohn Professor of Theatre and Comparative Literature, Graduate Center, City University of New York, is the author of fourteen books and over two hundred articles in the areas of theatre history, performance studies, and theatre theory and dramatic literature. He is founding editor of *Western European Stages*. His work has been translated into fifteen languages, and he has translated German, French, Spanish, and Arabic plays into English. In 2005 he was awarded an honorary doctorate from the University of Athens.

Xiaomei Chen is Professor of Chinese literature at the University of California, Davis. She received her Ph.D. degree in comparative literature from Indiana University (1989) and is author of *Occidentalism: A Theory of Counter-Discourse in Post-Mao China* and *Acting the Right Part: Political Theatre and Popular Drama in Contemporary China*. She is the editor of *Reading the Right Texts* and the *Columbia Anthology of Modern Chinese Drama*. With Claire Sponsler, she co-edited *East of West: Cross-Cultural Performances and the Staging of Difference*.

Catherine M. Cole is a Professor in the Department of Theatre, Dance, and Performance Studies at the University of California, Berkeley. She is the author of *Ghana's Concert Party Theatre* and *Performing South Africa's Truth Commission: Stages of Transition*. With Takyiwaa Manuh and Stephan Miescher, she co-edited *Africa After Gender?* She also served as editor of *Theatre Survey*. Her dance theatre piece *Five Foot Feat*, created in collaboration with Christopher Pilafian, toured North America in 2002–2005.

Tracy C. Davis is Barber Professor of Performing Arts at Northwestern University. She served as President of the American Society for Theatre Research (2006–2009). She edits the book series Cambridge Studies in Theatre and Performance Theory and is the author of *Actresses as Working Women*, *The Economics of the British Stage: 1800–1914*, *George Bernard Shaw and the Socialist Theatre*, and *Stages of Emergency: Cold War Nuclear Civil Defense*. She also co-edited *Women and Playwriting in Nineteenth-Century Britain* (with Ellen Donkin), *Theatricality* (with Thomas Postlewait), and *The Performing Century: Nineteenth-Century Theatre's History* (with Peter Holland). She is editor of the forthcoming *Broadview Anthology of Nineteenth-Century Performance*.

Aparna Dharwadker is Professor of Theatre and Drama and English at the University of Wisconsin–Madison. Her articles and essays on Indian and postcolonial theatre have appeared in various journals, including *PMLA*, *Modern Drama*, *Theatre Journal*, *New Theatre Quarterly*, and *Theatre Research International*. She won the 2006 Joe A. Callaway Prize for *Theatres of Independence: Drama, Theory, and Urban Performance in India since 1947*. She is currently completing an edited collection of primary sources in theatre theory entitled *A Poetics of Modernity: Indian Theatre Theory, 1860 to the Present*.

Harry J. Elam, Jr., is the Olive H. Palmer Professor in the Humanities at Stanford University. His books include *Taking It to the Streets: The Social Protest Theater of Luis Valdez and Amiri Baraka*, *The Past as Present in the Drama of August Wilson*, and *Black Cultural Traffic: Crossroads in Performance and Popular Culture*. His articles have appeared in *American Drama*, *Modern Drama*, *Theatre Journal*, *Text and Performance Quarterly*, several critical anthologies, and journals in Israel, Belgium, Poland, and Taiwan. With David Krasner he edited *African-American Performance and Theater History: A Critical Anthology*. He also edited an anthology of plays: *The Fire This Time: African-American Plays in the 21st Century*.

Susan Leigh Foster, choreographer and scholar, is Professor in the Department of World Arts and Cultures at the University of California, Los Angeles. She is the author of *Reading Dancing: Bodies and Subjects in Contemporary American Dance*, *Choreography and Narrative Ballet's Staging of Story and Desire*, and *Dances That Describe Themselves: The Improvised Choreography of Richard Bull* and editor of *Choreographing History*, *Corporealities: Dancing, Knowledge, Culture, and Power*, and *Worlding Dance*. She is currently working on a genealogy of the terms "choreography," "kinesthesia," and "empathy."

Shannon Jackson is Professor of Rhetoric and Professor and Chair of Theatre, Dance, and Performance Studies at the University of California, Berkeley. Her publications include *Lines of Activity* and *Professing Performance* and numerous essays in journals and collections of visual culture, theatre studies, cultural studies, and performance studies. She is currently completing a manuscript on socially engaged performance that integrates theatre and the visual arts. She is working with Marianne Weems to write a history and analysis of the Builders Association, the intermedia theatre company, from its founding to the present. Jackson is also on the executive boards of the Arts Research Center, the Berkeley Center for New Media, the Beatrice Bain Center for Research on Gender and Sexuality, Cal Performances, and the Berkeley Art Museum.

Bruce McConachie has written widely on U.S. theatre history, theatre historiography, and cognitive theory for theatre and performance, including *Melodramatic Formations: American Theatre and Society, 1820–1870*. His recent books include *American Theatre in the Culture of the Cold War* and *Engaging Audiences: A Cognitive Approach to Spectating in the Theatre*. A past President of the American Society for Theatre Research (2000–2003), he chairs the Theatre Arts department at the University of Pittsburgh.

Thomas Postlewait, an Affiliated Professor in the Ph.D. program, School of Drama, University of Washington, has published a half-dozen books, including *Prophet of the New Drama: William Archer and the Ibsen Campaign* and *The Cambridge Introduction to Theatre Historiography*. He co-edited *Interpreting the Theatrical Past* with Bruce McConachie and *Theatricality* with Tracy C. Davis. He served as President of the American Society for Theatre Research (1994–1997). Since 1991 he has edited Studies in Theatre History and Culture, a series at the University of Iowa Press that has published over forty books by scholars from over a dozen countries.

Willmar Sauter, Professor of Theatre Studies at Stockholm University, has carried out a series of studies on theatre audiences. He has also written on Swedish theatre history and developed theories of the theatrical event, documented in *The Theatrical Event: Dynamics of Performance and Perception* and *Eventness: A Concept of the Theatrical Event*. He is co-editor of *Theatrical Events: Borders, Dynamics, Frames*. He served as President of the International Federation for Theatre Research (1991–1995) and Dean of the Faculty of the Humanities (1996–2002) at his university. Since 2006 he has been head of the Research School of Aesthetics, Stockholm University.

Brian Singleton teaches in the School of Drama, Film, and Music at Trinity College, Dublin, and is also a Fellow of the Interweaving Performance Cultures Research Center at the Free University, Berlin. He served as President of the International Federation for Theatre Research (2007–2011). With Janelle Reinelt, he is co-editor of the book series Studies in International Performance, published by Palgrave Macmillan. Besides two books on the life and works of Antonin Artaud, he has published *Oscar Asche: Orientalism and British Musical Comedy* and *Masculinities and the Contemporary Irish Theatre*.

Claire Sponsler, Professor of English at the University of Iowa, specializes in medieval culture and performance history. Her books include *Drama and Resistance: Bodies, Goods, and Theatricality in Late Medieval England* and *Ritual Imports: Performing Medieval Drama in America*, winner of the Barnard Hewitt Award. With Xiaomei Chen, she edited *East of West: Cross-Cultural Performance and the Staging of Difference*. She is preparing a study and edition of the performance pieces of the fifteenth-century writer John Lydgate.

David Wiles is Professor of Theatre at Royal Holloway University of London. His publications include two books on Shakespearean theatre and four on Greek theatre plus *A Short History of Western Performance Space*. His 2007 study of the Greek tragic mask rested on an analysis of the iconography. He is currently working on a history of theatre in its relation to the idea of citizenship.

Index

STUDIES IN THEATRE HISTORY AND CULTURE

Actors and American Culture, 1880–1920
By Benjamin McArthur

The Age and Stage of George L. Fox, 1825–1877: An Expanded Edition
By Laurence Senelick

American Theater in the Culture of the Cold War: Producing and Contesting Containment
By Bruce McConachie

Classical Greek Theatre: New Views of an Old Subject
By Clifford Ashby

Czech Theatre Design in the Twentieth Century: Metaphor and Irony Revisited
Edited by Joseph Brandesky

Embodied Memory: The Theatre of George Tabori
By Anat Feinberg

Fangs of Malice: Hypocrisy, Sincerity, and Acting
By Matthew H. Wikander

Fantasies of Empire: The Empire Theatre of Varieties and the Licensing Controversy of 1894
By Joseph Donohue

Jews and the Making of Modern German Theatre
Edited by Jeanette R. Malkin and Freddie Rokem

The Making of Theatrical Reputations: Studies from the Modern London Theatre
By Yael Zarhy-Levo

Marginal Sights: Staging the Chinese in America
By James S. Moy

Melodramatic Formations: American Theatre and Society, 1820–1870
By Bruce A. McConachie

Meyerhold: A Revolution in Theatre
By Edward Braun

Modern Czech Theatre: Reflector and Conscience of a Nation
By Jarka M. Burian

Modern Hamlets and Their Soliloquies: An Expanded Edition
By Mary Z. Maher

Molière, the French Revolution, and the Theatrical Afterlife
By Mechele Leon

The Most American Thing in America: Circuit Chautauqua as Performance
By Charlotte M. Canning

Othello and Interpretive Traditions
By Edward Pechter

Our Moonlight Revels: *A Midsummer Night's Dream* in the Theatre
By Gary Jay Williams

The Performance of Power: Theatrical Discourse and Politics
Edited by Sue-Ellen Case and Janelle Reinelt

Performing History: Theatrical Representations of the Past in Contemporary Theatre
By Freddie Rokem

The Recurrence of Fate: Theatre and Memory in Twentieth-Century Russia
By Spencer Golub

Reflecting the Audience: London Theatregoing, 1840–1880
By Jim Davis and Victor Emeljanow

Representing the Past:
Essays in Performance Historiography
Edited by Charlotte M. Canning and Thomas Postlewait

The Roots of Theatre: Rethinking Ritual and Other Theories of Origin
By Eli Rozik

Shakespeare and Chekhov in Production: Theatrical Events and Their Audiences
By John Tulloch

Shakespeare on the American Yiddish Stage
By Joel Berkowitz

The Show and the Gaze of Theatre:
A European Perspective
By Erika Fischer-Lichte

Stagestruck Filmmaker:
D. W. Griffith and the American Theatre
By David Mayer

Strange Duets: Impresarios and Actresses in the American Theatre, 1865–1914
By Kim Marra

Textual and Theatrical Shakespeare:
Questions of Evidence
Edited by Edward Pechter

Theatre and Identity in Imperial Russia
By Catherine A. Schuler

Theatre Is More Beautiful Than War:
German Stage Directing in the Late Twentieth Century
By Marvin Carlson

Theatres of Independence:
Drama, Theory, and Urban Performance in India since 1947
By Aparna Bhargava Dharwadker

The Theatrical Event:
Dynamics of Performance and Perception
By Willmar Sauter

The Trick of Singularity:
Twelfth Night and the Performance Editions
By Laurie E. Osborne

The Victorian Marionette Theatre
By John McCormick

Wandering Stars:
Russian Emigré Theatre, 1905–1940
Edited by Laurence Senelick

Writing and Rewriting National Theatre Histories
Edited by S. E. Wilmer